Modern Christian Theology

Modern Christian Theology

Second edition

Christopher Ben Simpson

t&t clark

LONDON • NEW YORK • OXFORD • NEW DELHI • SYDNEY

T&T CLARK
Bloomsbury Publishing Plc
50 Bedford Square, London, WC1B 3DP, UK
1385 Broadway, New York, NY 10018, USA

BLOOMSBURY, T&T CLARK and the T&T Clark logo are trademarks
of Bloomsbury Publishing Plc

First published in Great Britain 2016
This edition published in Great Britain 2020

Cover design: Terry Woodley
Cover image © Brooklyn Morgan

A catalogue record for this book is available from the British Library.

A catalog record for this book is available from the Library of Congress.

ISBN: HB: 978-0-5676-8845-3
        PB: 978-0-5676-8844-6
        ePDF: 978-0-5676-8847-7
        ePUB: 978-0-5676-8846-0

Typeset by Integra Software Services Pvt. Ltd.
Printed and bound by CPI Group (UK) Ltd, Croydon CR0 4YY

To find out more about our authors and books visit www.bloomsbury.com
and sign up for our newsletters.

Contents

9   Early-Nineteenth-Century Catholic and Anglo-Catholic Theology 167

10   Ritschlianism 179

11   Late-Nineteenth-Century Catholic Theology 199

Part III Twentieth-Century Crisis and Modernity

20 Revisionist and Secular Theologies 357

21 Postliberal and Postsecular Theology 375

Acknowledgements

Charles Waterman provided the transcriptions that served as an early draft of this text. Kathryn Clayton provided invaluable assistance in the editing and preparation of the second edition. Marshall Nelson and Timothy Morgan compiled the index for the first and second editions respectively.

The author and publisher gratefully acknowledge the permission granted to reproduce the copyright material in this book.

Illustrations

Every effort has been made to trace copyright holders and to obtain their permission for the use of copyright material. The publisher apologizes for any errors or omissions in the below list and would be grateful if notified of any corrections that should be incorporated in future reprints or editions of this book.

Introduction

When we think about modern theology, we are thinking about two things: modernity and theology. In many ways this book is about two interrelated stories—the story of theology in the modern age, but also the story of modernity as something that came into being and developed over time. Our interest is not merely historical, but is also intended to inform the question of how we do theology today.

0.1 Our Theological Situation

We start from our present experience. What is our theological situation today? Our current situation is characterized by what Charles Taylor (in his book *A Secular Age*—more on that in a moment) calls **an immanent frame**. We in the West, in Europe, the UK and America especially, have an immanent perspective. What this means is that it is perfectly normal for people to pass through their lives with little thought for God or religion. In fact, in many university settings religion is seen as sort of backward, something the unenlightened and the naïve hold on to, something an educated person might be embarrassed about. Another way of putting this is to say that a religious perspective is no longer a privileged perspective in our society—it no longer has the taken-for-granted authority that was perhaps once the case.

In much of Western society a particularly Christian perspective is at best one perspective among many. This is not to say that people are no longer Christian, but that we (who are Christians) are now aware that we are Christians and other people are something else. Some are religious; many are not. So Christian belief, as well as that of other specific religions, is by and large not 'natural'—is not a given—in the broader culture. Rather, in many ways, the present age is, as Kierkegaard reflected, a 'reflective' age. By this, he means we are aware of different options.

For many people it is the norm for them to live out their lives in a purely secular mindset, or immanent frame, making use of the material goods of the world, without any reference to anything beyond humans and the material world. There are humans, there is the world and that's it. And then, humans decide what is or is not a good way to treat each other and to treat the world. Even though this is certainly not the way that everyone thinks, there is, in many areas, a presumption of unbelief—perhaps especially in academic circles. The presumption is that if you are a bright person you will not believe in this religious stuff. William Desmond describes this with the term

Figure 0.1 Taylor.

'Charles Taylor' by Makhanets: Own work. Previously published: http://makhanets.wordpress.com/2012/06/22/charles-taylor/. Licensed under CC BY–SA 3.0 via Wikimedia Commons.

postulatory finitism. This means that we live as if (the 'as if' is the 'postulatory' bit) the universe, and everything in it, is finite. There is no religious or ultimate horizon either beyond or within us.

And so, the situation today is that, within this immanent frame, religion—and Christianity in particular—often finds itself to be struggling for plausibility. Those readers who are involved in ministry and dealing with those outside of (or on the borders of) the Church likely experience this all of the time. It is often not natural for people outside (and often inside) the Church to think in terms of Christianity, and you have to help them think in terms of that story—as if it were a different world. This is the initial point I'd like to make: a strong component of our current situation has to do with the difficulty, the dissonance, the strangeness of believing in the present.

0.2 The History of Secular Modernity (a First Sketch)

The next point to make, however, is that this was not always the case. John Milbank opens his controversial work *Theology and Social Theory* with this statement: 'Once, there was no "secular".' Once, and by 'once' we're meaning as recently as the Middle Ages, humanity, the natural world and the divine held together, and were understood together as a community, as an inherently ordered and harmonious community. We see an image of this old world, within a theological frame, in Thomas Aquinas' *Summa Theologiae*. This extensive systematic theology relates God, humanity, the world and everything to each other, in a very intricate and orderly way. Or, you could look at something like Dante's *Divine Comedy*, for a similar kind of thing in a more poetic mode.

There is a difference in these understandings, and the modern universe is different than the pre-modern cosmos. Before, there was an understanding of the relation between the human and the divine, particularly the Christian God, which gave meaning to the whole of the world and to the whole of human experience. But that has changed. Charles Taylor in his magisterial work *A Secular Age* makes the point that in the year 1500 it was 'virtually impossible not to believe in God'. Very few people were atheists or even considered it as a possibility. This is not to say that everyone was some kind of saint, or that it was a better place to live, but it was nearly infeasible not to believe in God in some way.

However, in the year 2000 (or thereabouts), many of us have found that it is not only easy, but sometimes inescapable not to believe in God. Sometimes, it is very difficult indeed to believe in God in our present age. Even the staunchest believer will see religion sometimes as one human possibility among others. And so, at the very least, there has been a fundamental erosion of the immediate certainty of belief. There is no longer this naïve (in the sense that the individual was not aware of options) acceptance of transcendence or anything beyond the immanent world.

So between 1500 and 2000, a huge change happened in the Western world, and we have named this profound, epochal change 'modernity'. So, what happened? What was the change? This is a significant question, and the answer is not at all obvious. The way that that question is answered has a huge impact on the way that we understand our world and the way that we understand ourselves.

Now, as soon as we ask the question: 'What happened? How did we go from the Christian worldview being the natural thing for people, and it being odd for someone not to believe, in 1500, to it being perfectly normal for people not to think about religion that much at all?' There are some ready (and, to many, totally obvious) answers to this question waiting in the wings. Some of the most common are fairly simple (if not simplistic or even reductionistic) stories or narratives. For more traditional, religious people, those stories might look like a 'slippery slope', where people turned away from God, and everything went to pot. At some point in history, there was a golden age when people really believed in Christianity. Then they stopped, and now we have our secular, pluralistic, postmodern cats-and-dogs-living-together world.

However, that is not the dominant reductionistic narrative. For most people, there is an understanding of things that got underway in the Enlightenment that some people call the 'Whig history', which sees secularization as being synonymous with, or at least a corollary of, modern progress. As society progresses in modernity, one thing that naturally happens is that we stop being religious. As science, philosophy, technology and the Enlightenment get going, we naturally shed our superstitions. 'Now we believe in science, not that pre-modern hokum.' Taylor describes these stories as **subtraction stories**. Some people talk about this as being supercessionist. By a subtraction story, Taylor means that what you have in this secular modernity is the same kind of humanity and reality that you had in pre-modern society, just minus said religious hokum— free of the crusty barnacles of superstition. Modernity (to use another metaphor) gets rid of the chocolatey cover of illusion, getting right down to the wholesome nut of scientific reality.

In a subtraction story, what has changed is that this bad part has been sloughed off. As you grow older you no longer believe in Santa Claus, and this is just the kind of thing that happened in all of Western history. We used to be children, and believed in gods and fairies and stuff, then we grew up—and now we don't believe in that stuff anymore. This is a natural, progress-oriented and optimistic view that things are getting better, and, as things get better, we don't believe in such things anymore. It is kind of the opposite of a slippery slope.

This kind of story is also described as the **secularization thesis**: that as modernity progresses, people will become less and less religious. Secularization, in this sense, is often thought of in terms of liberation. This view has come to be seen as natural, the normal way that people seem to think: that we, in the present age, are more enlightened, and that people, in the past, believed silly, primitive things.

But this is a particular perspective. That secular modernity is not simply the way things really are, but it has to do with a new way of looking at things. It is not the way things are minus the religious lens, but it is a new, historical lens. The modern secular perspective is rather the result of history, of a particular historical development. In that sense it is 'positive'—meaning it came to be in a certain way. And one way of talking about the modern world, the secular world, is to say it has a genealogy. It came from somewhere. It is a new invention that we can trace in history. And so, what I would like to present is that in the modern world we have a real departure from what came before.

Modernity, as the product of historical development, is something that is **sedimented**. That is, our past is sedimented in our present. The particularities of our past significantly influence the way we see things in the present. To understand the present age, we need to understand where we have come from, because we are still being shaped by our past. This is more obvious when we think of our immediate past. Of course, we are shaped by the way we were raised and (more distantly) the way our parents were raised and so on. On a larger scale, we are still being shaped by our sedimented distant past. And again, this is not simply the way things are, but also the way things have come to be. This is a history, a story.

The final, and perhaps oddest piece of the story to be introduced here is that when we talk about this history, this genealogy of secular modernity, what we will find is **that modernity has a theological history**. What we think of as modernity came about for what were, at least in part, theological reasons—such that if there were not certain theological concerns, developments and controversies, there would be a fundamentally different modernity than the one that has come to characterize our world.

In this book, then, we will look at two interrelated stories: the narrative of modernity and the narrative of modern theology against the backdrop of modernity. Before beginning this story in the first chapter, we can pause to consider very generally some of our major terms like 'modern', 'secular' and 'theology'.

0.3 'Theology'

In the word 'theology', we have etymologically two Greek words: 'logos', which has to do with meaningful communication, and 'theos', which implies that the meaningful communication is related to God. Traditionally, Christian theology was structured something like this: *First*, there is the Word, a revelation; a meaningful communication regarding God. This is God's Word to us, *God's communication to us.* Then, there is also our talking, *our using words about God.* And then, finally, there is *our communicating with God*—our words to God in prayer. This brief depiction of theology is framed in terms of the *lectio divina*, an ancient Christian spiritual practice of relating to scriptural text. First, there is *lectio* (*see* table below), the reading and the hearing of God. Here, we are receiving God's word. Second, there is *meditatio*, the meditating—the mulling over of these words. Thus, we talk amongst ourselves and think within our own imagination, our own hermeneutical frame. Third, there is *oratio*, the prayer. Out of that meaningful meditation upon the Word, we then respond to God. (The fourth moment, *contemplatio*, is the allowing of our relation to God through these words to 'be with' us—for us to be open to God's living work and presence in our lives. While this moment is less 'word'-centred, one can see resonances between it and the manner in which our theologizing relates to the rest of our lives.)

Lectio divina	Theology
Lectio	God's communication to us
Meditatio	Our thinking and talking about God
Oratio	Our communication to God

Normally, when we think about theology, we think about the second sense: thinking and talking about God. However, it does us well to remember that for the believer, this second moment is always couched in the midst of the others. Our understanding of and thinking about God gets its meaning and purpose from words that did not originate from us and has an end beyond our own curiosity, our own immediate or mediated knowledge. In terms of the practice of theology, this is something to keep in mind. Thinking and talking about God was traditionally always couched within a spiritual practice.

When it comes to the scope of theology, it is quite broad. It has to do with God, but also God's relationship to all things, and their relationship to one another. The simplest way to discuss the topic of theology is to talk about the natures of and relations between God, the world and humanity.

0.4 The Secular and Three 'Secularities'

Next, we will talk about the two big frames of theology in the present age that not only have an impact on theology, but also have theological roots. The first is the *secular*. This term comes from an earlier Latin term, *saeculum*, which literally means a 'century', or an 'age', in a broad sense. Interestingly enough, there was a 'secular' before there was a 'Middle Ages', but it meant something different. The concepts of the 'secular' and 'Middle Ages', as we come to understand them, came into being around what is commonly considered to be the close of the Middle Ages.

Secularity 1	retreat of religion from public life	20th century	storey above the ground floor
Secularity 2	decline in belief and practice	19th century	ground floor
Secularity 3	change in conditions of belief	14th(?)–18th centuries	basement/foundation

To move beyond etymology, we can see with Charles Taylor, three different meanings of the secular, or secularity (*see* it above). **Secularity 1** is the retreat of religion from public life. This was what most people, especially in America, normally think of as secular. There is a separation of the religious as private from the secular as public. The public realm is the secular realm, while you can still be religious if you so choose in your private life. So, the public square is not tilted towards any one religious affiliation, but it is neutral. It is secular. (This is something that is probably a lot more obvious in Europe than in the United States.)

Secularity 2 is the decline in belief and practice. Here, people do not have religious beliefs or go to church as much (not that those are the same thing). This is where we see the modern ethos as one of a postulatory finitism. This is the way in which modern people are not often, or less often, thinking of things beyond an immanent frame. As Taylor describes these different 'secularities', he uses the metaphor of the different storeys of a house. Secularity 1, he sees as the storey above ground floor, what Americans would call the second storey. Secularity 2 would be the ground floor. It is on the basis of Secularity 2 (that people just do not believe religious things as much) that our public discourse is going to be largely free of religious reference (Secularity 1). If we are going to have the most universal perspective, it would be one free of religion because religion polarizes people.

The basement or the foundation is **Secularity 3**. This is, for Taylor, the most significant sense of secularity. He talks about it in terms of the 'change of the conditions of belief'. This, as we mentioned before, is the more fundamental move from a society, where belief in God is unchallenged and unproblematic, to one in which it is understood to be one option among others, and frequently is not the easiest to embrace.

As Taylor presents them, these different secularities happened, or came about historically in reverse order. The later ones, of course, are more fundamental. In Part I, we present the development of Secularity 3 from (roughly) the Late Middle Ages into the eighteenth century. In Part II, in the nineteenth century, we see Secularity 2 come on the stage. In Part III and Part IV we will see Secularity 1 as largely a twentieth-century reality.

So, when Taylor writes about modernity as 'a secular age', he primarily means the third sense—that which is concerned with the possibility and impossibility of certain kinds of experience in our age. Another way that he puts it is that with Secularity 3 something that he calls 'exclusive humanism' becomes an option. Part of what he means here is that for humans to flourish, they do not need to see any goals beyond that of flourishing in the present life. It was the elites in society that began to think this way. You could live a perfectly fulfilled life without thinking about anything traditionally seen as religious. How this became an option is the first thing we are going to look at—not how it became what everyone believes (they certainly don't now). The modern ethos that includes all of these different senses of secularity, beginning with the third, and going to the first, is (as William Desmond writes about it) one of **deracination**—of a kind of contracting or narrowing of perspective, or a loss of feeling for a fuller sense of being.

0.5 'Modern'

Generally, the *modo* is the 'now', the present age, in a very general sense. The modern age is something that wishes to distinguish itself from that which came before it, usually (but not always) in terms of the modern's superiority. We are moderns, as opposed to the ancients. We are, presumably, in the better position. And so, this way of talking comes about with a need to contrast the present with the past, to talk about the privileged position of the present.

So, modern, in that sense, is an adversarial stance, that you can really only understand in its opposition to the thing to which it is opposed. Etymologically, the term *modernus* shows up, for the first time that we can find it, in the fifth century, doing this same sort of thing: distinguishing the present age from a prior age. Here, *modernus* was used to distinguish the Christian era (the times of the Church Fathers) from the pagan past—about how 'now after Christ things are different', as opposed to the Roman pagans.

In the Late Middle Ages, this term becomes used quite a bit more, in terms of what is called the *via moderna* (which we will talk about in Chapter 1). The *via moderna* designates what many, today, would call *nominalism*, in terms of a particular philosophical way of looking at knowledge. There's also the *devotion moderna*, the modern way of devotion that has to do with the growth of lay religious life outside of monastic orders. And, when we get closer to the Renaissance, we come across the term *modernitas*, which starts being used around 1400. The early humanists would refer to their time as *modernitas* vs. *antiquitas* (the ancient). But one has a more complicated perspective with the Renaissance people, because the Renaissance itself was about a rebirth of ancient wisdom. People at the time had a tripartite view of history, seeing the modern, as opposed to the Middle Ages, as opposed to the ancient. The ancient period (for Renaissance humanists) was great, then things went downhill into the 'middle' ages. But the 'modern' age is when we begin to recover (a rebirth, renaissance) ancient wisdom.

Today, the way modern is used, in the general sense, begins in the Reformation, or the Renaissance, and is, generally, depicted as **what comes after the medieval**. The *Oxford English Dictionary* presents the 'modern' as the historical period that begins after the medieval. If we are going to speak very generally, this is a perfectly serviceable definition. This is why we are going to start our story of the modern by going back to the medieval.

Further reading

Desmond, William. *God and the Between*. Oxford: Blackwell, 2008.

Dupré, Louis. *Passage to Modernity*. New Haven, CT: Yale University Press, 1993.

Milbank, John. *Theology and Social Theory: Beyond Secular Reason*. 2nd edn. Oxford: Wiley-Blackwell, 2006.

Taylor, Charles. *A Secular Age*. Cambridge, MA: Belknap Press of Harvard University Press, 2007.

Part I

Emerging Modernity

The Middle Ages and the Lost World

1.1 The Modern and the Pre-Modern

In the title of this chapter, the 'Middle Ages' is plural—there is a distinction between what some people call the High Middle Ages, the Early Middle Ages and the Late Middle Ages. What we want to attend to is a shift that happens within the medieval period such that there is not necessarily a monolithic 'medieval' perspective. The title also speaks of the 'Lost World'. With this we are referring to a unity, a 'world'—a way that everything holds together and makes sense—which is passing away in the Middle Ages. We will talk about that in terms of the *classical synthesis*.

Looking at the distinction between the modern and the pre-modern, if we want to understand the present (the modern), we need to begin not just with the Enlightenment (what many see as the beginning of modernity), but also with a much earlier cultural layer—with the Late Middle Ages. Many thinkers even go so far as to write about modernity as if, in some sense, it is a modification of medieval thought. This might be a strange way of looking at things for some people—that modernity is not just a rejection of what came before it, but also a continuation, or a modification, or an appropriation of what came before it. Modernity came from somewhere, and it came from the Middle Ages—it takes up and follows in certain medieval trajectories.

While it is difficult, if not impossible, to locate precisely the shift towards modernity with any one particular thinker or any one particular event, many have pointed to a general constellation of changes and some thinkers who are associated with them. This constellation of shifts brings about the beginnings of Taylor's first stage of modernity as the emergence of exclusive humanism as a possibility. While nothing like exclusive humanism comes up in the Middle Ages, developments in the Late Middle Ages, Renaissance and the Reformation bring about something that makes the exclusive humanism of the eighteenth century possible.

1.2 The Lost World

1.2.1 Characteristics and Practices

In his book *The First Thousand Years*, church historian Robert Louis Wilken presents a global history of the first millennium of Christianity. One of Wilken's key insights is that Christianity in this era is transcultural. One cannot talk about Christianity as simply a modification within Palestinian—Jewish culture because it migrates into different continents, languages, cultures and thought-forms. And so, the question lies with not just trying to find a diverse Christianity, but also how one accounts for this diversity, being an identity called 'Christianity'. How is what's going on in Lyon, France, and in northern China, and in Ethiopia the same thing?

Common elements

---

1. Canon

2. Creed

3. Bishops

4. Eucharist and Baptism

5. Monasticism

Wilkens finds five common elements, or points of unity (see above) that describe the transcultural unity of Christianity in its first millennium. They had something like a common **canon of Scripture**. Christians had a sacred Scripture, and it was more or less the books in the Christian Bible today. They shared certain **creeds**, especially the Nicene Creed. They had **bishops** as a common structure of church leadership. There were variations but the same basic Episcopal structure. The **Lord's Supper/Eucharist and Baptism** were definitive practices in the lives of Christians. Finally, Christianity, in this period, is marked by the practice and institution of **monasticism**. It was not that all Christians were monks, but rather that in every place there was Christianity, there was also monasticism, those who had that kind of special role. Without these common, unifying, transcultural elements, Christianity would cease to be an observable unity, or reality. It would be multiple, different religions. And what we will see is that the unity of the first thousand years is going to begin to be redefined by the end of the fourteenth century, and by the time we get to the sixteenth century it is going to be radically challenged.

1.2.2 The Classical Synthesis

In addition to the unity of Christianity, as evident in these characteristics in the early centuries of the church, we can see in the Middle Ages an understanding of the world that has been called (by Dupré) **the Classical Synthesis**. The ancient view of the world is that it is a **cosmos**. A cosmos is not simply everything that is. It is an ordered whole. The difference perhaps between a 'cosmos' and a 'universe' is that while a 'universe' is everything, a 'cosmos' is also everything, but there is an order to it. There is something **normative** to the order of the world. In the ancient Greek view, of course, the divine was included in the cosmos: the divine, human and physical were all an ordered part of this world, and all had different parts to play. Here, the cosmos is a very reasonable, intelligible reality.

With the advent of Christianity, there is still a cosmos, but there is a significant change in the understanding of God. In the Christian understanding, God is not a part of the cosmos. He is not the highest, best and/or first part of the world. (Which God was with, for example, Aristotle. The Greek pantheon saw deity in this way as well. The Greek gods, of everything in the world, were the best of beings.) Because of this, in the Christian view of the world, God and the world will have a different relation. Paradoxically, God's relationship to the cosmos is more intimate. God is not a high, distant, especially awesome part of the cosmos. He can then be immediately present to everything in a different way.

The order of the cosmos in the Christian pre-modern view of things marks the presence of God. When you look at the world, the world declares the glory of the Lord. It does not declare its own glory alone, but makes one mindful of God. These marks, however, are less scientific than enigmatic/strange indicators.

The classical synthesis is usually organized around three terms: God (*theos*), humanity (*anthropos*) and nature (*kosmos*). The classical synthesis has to do with the deep interrelation between these three distinct and yet related domains. The human is not merely the natural, simply a part of the natural world, but it is related to the natural world. God is related to the world, but God is not the world. Humans are related to God, but God and humans are not the same thing.

In the classical synthesis there is a relationship between God and humanity. Humanity is specially created in the image of God, the *imago Dei* (**God → Humanity**). Humans are in some sense an image of God. Humans are also internally oriented towards God as our end, as the ultimate object of our desire. 'Our hearts are restless until they find their rest in Thee,' as Augustine wrote (**Humanity → God**). Humanity is also the height of God's creation. As God creates the natural world, the height of that natural world is the human (**God → Nature → Humanity**). So people will talk about humanity in this period as a **microcosmos**—in that in our humanity we somehow sum up the rest of reality, bringing together the divine and the natural (as the image of God and the height of Nature). Humanity can also come to know of God through nature because of the mark or signs of God in the world (**Humanity → Nature → God**).

When it comes to the relationship between God and nature, the latter is seen as being created by God, and, therefore, as being good (**God → Nature**). The material world is not evil or something that stands in opposition to the spiritual world in a Gnostic sense. The classical Christian perspective sees nature as created by God, and as, thus, reflecting the wisdom and goodness of God. It's not only that God created nature, but also that nature has signs of God's goodness and wisdom within it. So, the order of nature is significant. It can help tell us something about its origin (**Nature → God**).

Finally, the classical synthesis presents a relationship between humanity and nature. Nature in the ancient world is hospitable to humanity. We live and dwell within the natural world as something that sustains our lives, and not merely as something deathly to be escaped (**Nature → Humanity**). Nature is also intelligible; we can understand the world (**Humanity → Nature**). The order and wisdom that we have within us—that we received from God—matches up somehow with the way that world is structured, and therefore we can understand the way the world is (**God → Humanity → Nature**). In some of the earlier understandings of humanity, you have the entire natural world reaching towards God, that in human salvation you have the salvation of the entire created order summing up everything that came before it (**Nature → Humanity → God**).

1.2.3 Divine Transcendence and Creation

To understand the distinctively Christian understanding of this classical synthesis, we should think a bit about the relationship between divine transcendence and creation. As mentioned above, one of the particular differences of the Christian view of the world (as represented in such pre-modern thinkers such as Augustine, Anselm and Aquinas) over against the pagan view of the world is a different understanding of God. God has a different kind of transcendence, or maybe God is truly transcendent in the Christian view. William Desmond refers to this as an **asymmetry**. There is a fundamental asymmetry between God and the world—God is 'the unequal' itself. Because of this there is a common understanding that God is ultimately unimaginable, ultimately shrouded in mystery and ultimately incomprehensible. God is not one among many things in the world that we can understand, but God is distinct in such a way that we cannot get a position of mastery over Him. Nevertheless, this is not to say that God is utterly unthinkable. There is still some intelligible relation between God and God's creation—humanity and nature.

So, God in this perspective is not the highest and best and most powerful entity in the collection of all of the entities. It is not as if the universe is an aggregate of beings, and God is the biggest (or best) of those beings. God is, instead, radically distinct from the universe as a whole. God is not one more being, not one more thing. David Bentley Hart, in his book *The Experience of God*, says that this more traditional perspective is against the view that 'God is a very large object or agency within the universe, or perhaps alongside the universe. A being among other beings, He differs from all other beings in magnitude, power and duration. But not ontologically' (p. 32). This is to say that the traditional view of God is that He is of a different order of being than us. We, and everything we know in the world is created, and God is not—this difference is not quantitative but qualitative.

Figure 1.1 Augustine.

In order to name this difference that distinguishes God in the Judeo—Christian perspective from the pagan gods (who were the divine, best and even governing parts of nature), Robert Sokolowski and David Burrell (twentieth-century Catholic philosophers and theologians) use the term: 'the distinction'—the distinction between 'God and all things.' 'The distinction'—the difference—between God and everything else is unlike any other distinction that is made within the world. We cannot say that just as I distinguish between a human and a desk, so will I distinguish between God and the world. There is another order of distinction.

This distinction or difference is implied in the doctrine of creation. If we believe in creation, we have to believe that God is something fundamentally different, although not unrelated, to everything else. The beginning of all things cannot be contained within the set of all things. Interestingly, as we'll see, being fundamentally different can be more intimately related to everything else than just the biggest, baddest, most powerful part. This is what Kierkegaard means when he says that there is an 'infinite qualitative difference' between humans and God. It is not a quantitative difference. It is not that I can lift my writing table, Superman can lift planets, but God is even more powerful than Superman. 'How strong is God? He is stronger than anything!' That's a quantitative difference, that God can beat you in arm wrestling. God's power is not an amplified version of our own—it is something different. It is that which makes anything that is *be* as such.

Interestingly, one of the most consistent things that Thomas Aquinas (perhaps the pre-eminent representative of the classical synthesis) has to say about God is that we do not know *what* God is. Maybe we can know *that* God is (from God's creation), and maybe we can know *who* God is (from God's self-revelation), but we do not know *what* God is. (Hence when we think about what we mean by 'is' when we apply it to God, things get weird.) The 'what' question has to do with the genus and species of things in the universe. I can classify this as that kind of animal—this one has fur, this one has scales, etc. But God is not contained within our 'what'-answering capacity. The story goes that that was his question as a child: 'What is God?' You can never get beyond that sense of wonder. Some Christian thinkers, like Aquinas, will say that God is in some sense being itself: *esse*. There are things that exist in particular forms, but God is the very beingness of being. Others say that God is beyond being; that is, that God is otherwise than being. These are two very opposite ways of talking, yet both are ways of struggling with the mystery of a God who is the Creator—the origin of the universe who is other than the universe. Our categories, as we can see, start breaking down when we talk about God. Being is the most general category that we have in our language, and when we talk about God we struggle with this language. We obviously do not have conceptual mastery over God.

Figure 1.2 Aquinas.

'Andrea di Bonaiuto. Santa Maria Novella 1366–67 fresco 0001' by Andrea di Bonaiuto (fourteenth century) scan. Licensed under Public Domain via Wikimedia Commons.

This 'understanding' of divine transcendence is linked to the traditional view of creation as *creatio ex nihilo*. In this view, creation is an act of freedom. God does not create the universe out of necessity. Everything is created freely—more particularly, out of deliberate love—and so, creation is not a sort of necessary emanation, or bringing forth of things. When Christians start to talk about creation out of nothing, it is in contradistinction to the kind of Neo-Platonic thought that sees the material universe as a necessary emanation of the spiritual world. Instead of being a natural (and necessarily lesser, i.e. degraded) version of the divine, the world as it is has been given forth with a sense of gratuity, of freeness, of intentionality. The world is because God wants it to be, not because it has to be. The traditional understanding of creation, then, is that the universe is a gift. The universe is fundamentally dependent on God, on creation as a free gift.

The origination in creation is of a different kind than the kind of origination we know of in the world—which is always something made from something. (This is stated negatively by the ancient Greek philosopher Parmenides: *ex nihilo nihil fit*—'Out of nothing, nothing comes.') Philosopher William Desmond then talks about this kind of origination as a **hyperbolic origination**—that of all of the origins that we know of, of things being created artistically by humans or biological things being brought into being by other biological things, this is not the same kind of origination. This is a radical coming to be in which we are thrown (*ballein*) beyond (*hyper*) our normal understandings. This is looking at God as an answer to the question, 'Why does anything exist whatsoever?' The traditional answer is that this is a freely letting be, a giving of the world to be as itself. Such is not then a **pantheism**—seeing the world as a necessary expression or manifestation of God. With someone like Hegel, we will see the world as in some sense the divine as necessarily trying to work itself out, as if it had to create to come to completion. But instead of such an **erotic** view of creation (creation as self-fulfilment), the classical Christian view is that of an **agapeic** creation, or origination (creation as giving-forth as a gift).

A side effect of these understandings is a different understanding of **divine immanence**. The paradox here is that this more radical transcendence makes a more radical immanence possible. Here, immanence and transcendence are correlative and not set in an exclusionary opposition to one another. It is not that transcendence is really far away and immanence is really close, but, because God is other to the spatial world, there is no distance from God. There can be no separation from God because God is not in a different space within the world.

And so, ultimately there is a non-competitive togetherness of the God who is transcendent in such a manner that our language breaks down when we talk about Him—who is higher than our highest (*superior summa meo*)—and the God who is more intimate to me than I am to myself (*interior intimo meo*), as Augustine would say. This is the vision that we see in the mystics through the centuries—that they are seeing the very presence of God in their lives and to express this they have to use paradoxical language. The overriding sense, though, is that of **communion**—of otherness AND relation. That's the kind of master way of looking at things, that ultimately God, humanity and the created order are other to each other but they are in relation.

1.2.4 Paradoxical Harmonies

People talk about the quality of the civilization as having to do with complexity and harmony—the greater complexity, the greater difference, but also the greater harmony that exists, the higher the quality of a civilization. If that is the case, then the High Middle Ages is a high-quality civilization indeed. In its vision, which we are talking about here as the 'classical synthesis', there were different elements that were united within a coherent and harmonious vision. As mentioned before, this idea of **communion** or **community**, of otherness-and-relation, is not just about the way we can talk about God's relation to the world or perhaps the constituents of the classical synthesis, but can be seen to characterize the pre-modern understanding of Christianity as a whole. Classical Christianity is characterized by **paradoxical harmony**. There are points of real difference, of paradox, and yet they are held together in harmony. We see them as '**fitting**', even if we cannot understand precisely or determinately how that which is opposed **fits** together. These oppositions seem to be fundamentally other, but they are held together in harmony.

Trinity as …	Three	One
Incarnation as …	God	Human
Eucharist as …	Bread/Wine	Body/Blood
Faith as …	Beyond reason	Reasonable
	Uncertain	Certain
God as …	Transcendent	Immanent
	Knowable	Unknowable
	Eternal, unchanging	Loving, involved in time
World as …	Dependent upon God	Independent of God
Regarding humanity:	Providence	Freedom
	Grace	Nature
	Body	Soul
	Glorious/Free	Fallen/Enslaved
Christ as …	God	Man
	King	Servant
	Saviour	Model
The Christian life as …	Contemplative	Practical
	Solitary	Communal
	Joy	Suffering
	Becoming human	Becoming divine

The Trinity is three and one. In the incarnation, Christ is fully divine and fully human—two natures, one person. The Eucharist is bread and wine and body and blood. These have been singled out as the central mysteries of the faith, and what characterizes them as mysteries are these paradoxical harmonies. But we can also see it in many other areas.

There is a community between faith and reason—faith has to do with that which is beyond reason, and yet, it is related and in a harmonious relation to reason. Faith entails both certainty and uncertainty. God is knowable to us, but ultimately unknowable. God is transcendent, but also immanent at the same time.

God is a loving Father and cares for us, but is also changeless and eternal. The world is dependent on God, and yet, it is independent from Him in some sense. God is prudent and has a providential care over the world—God orders things in some sense—and yet, there is genuine freedom. There are an order of nature and an order of grace that do not destroy or negate each other.

The human being is both body and soul; it is not that one of these is the real human bit and the other a superfluous add-on. Humanity is glorious and free and good, but also fallen and enslaved and condemned. Christ is both God and man, both king and servant and both our saviour and our model. He is the one who does what we can't do for ourselves, but also shows us what we truly can do.

Finally, the Christian life is both contemplative and practical (though this will be emphasized and nuanced differently in different places). This is particularly a medieval distinction, the question of whether the Christian life is something you do in your prayer closet communing with God, or out there working in the world. It is both solitary and communal. It is characterized by both joy and suffering—joy in the midst of suffering. It is ordered at once towards our becoming truly human and our becoming divine.

With all of these things, if you wanted to double down or focus exclusively on one side as the master category this would exclude the other. Yet, in the above, both are held and held together. This is a non-exhaustive list of the paradoxical harmonies of the Christian faith that we can see up into the High Middle Ages. One of the things which happens in modernity is the collapsing of these paradoxical harmonies. So, when we think about the world that was lost, we are mindful of these harmonies that have been lost and are often sought again in various ways.

1.3 The Late Middle Ages

Dates for the Late Middle Ages	
1274	Death of Thomas Aquinas
1277	Parisian Condemnations
c. 1266–1308	John Duns Scotus
1280s–1347–50	William of Ockham
1337–1453	The Hundred Years War

Dates for the Late Middle Ages	
1348–50	The Black Death
1378–1417	The Great Schism/Avignon Papacy
1453	Fall of Constantinople

The High Middle Ages—with the growing influence of the papacy and the development of medieval scholastic 'cathedrals of thought' culminating in that of Thomas Aquinas—is commonly seen as extending up to 1300. The Late Middle Ages can be seen as lasting from roughly 1300 to 1500. There are different ways of looking at the Late Middle Ages—even just in terms of dating it. One significant date is 1274, the death of Thomas Aquinas, in that one can begin to locate late medieval thought relative to what comes after Aquinas.

Another way of looking at what characterized the Late Middle Ages is a significant sense of trauma in Europe. One can consider three big factors in this regard. The first is **the Hundred Years War** (1337–1453) that was fought off and on between France and England, almost entirely in France. This was a war between the first two nascent European nation—states. These two big and powerful states were engaged in very long, very bloody conflict that decimated central Europe.

The second traumatic factor is **The Black Death** (1348–50)—the bubonic plague that swept through, and killed perhaps a third of the population of Western Europe. It is said to have killed very quickly—sometimes within a day. Besides the deep psychological destabilization and insecurity of seemingly random mass death, the socio-economic situation was shaken by multiple peasant revolts, spurred on by labour shortages.

The final traumatic and destabilizing factor we will address is what is called **The Great Schism** or 'Western Schism' (1378–1417). The Papacy had moved from Italy to Avignon, a city in France. When this happened, the Italians were none too happy about this because they thought it made the Pope too much of a satellite of the king of France, which it probably did. When the papacy eventually returned to Rome after the election of an Italian pope, the cardinals who originally elected him changed their mind and decided to pick someone else to fill the role, who would rule from Avignon. So, there were two popes for a time. Eventually church leaders had a meeting (the Council of Pisa), and elected a third pope to be the real pope, but the other two did not step down. And so, for a time, there were three popes. Then, during the Council of Constance (1414–18) a fresh pope Martin V (who had been previously excommunicated by one of the papal claimants) was elected, and the Church went back to having one pope again. However, for many, serious damage had been done to the credibility of the Church hierarchy in the wake of such chaos.

We also have, during this period, the fall of Constantinople, to the Ottoman Turks, in 1453 (same year as the end of The Hundred Years War). This is a further threat: now there are not just wars between France and England, but also a Muslim conflict on the borders of Europe.

In the realm of theology and philosophy (which we will deal with in the remainder of this chapter), the changes have to do with providing a basis for what will eventually fracture the classical synthesis described above. This would have to do with the sundering of the relationships between faith and reason and between nature and grace. And this is related to ideas that would come to dominance in the Late Middle Ages on into what we think of as the Reformation. These two ideas are **nominalism** and **voluntarism**, and they are intimately related.

1.3.1 Nominalism and Voluntarism

Nominalism in its more specific meaning has to do with metaphysics or epistemology and has to do with the status of universals. Nominalism stands in opposition of what is called 'realism'—here meaning that universals are real. The nominalist would say that universals, like humanity, do not really exist but are merely names (hence nominalism). So, when we are talking about more general categories, this is just a convention or a way of speaking. All there are in reality are particular individual things, and we use names as a way of distinguishing between them. There is not a real thing that is 'the human being,' or 'humanity,' that matches up to all of you individual things out there reading these words. Things like humanity, goodness or beauty do not exist in themselves, but are just a way of talking about individual things.

Nominalism is usually associated with the figure of **William of Ockham**. He was born somewhere in the 1280s, and died between 1347 and 1350. For a time he was at the papal court at Avignon before leaving town somewhat hastily after proclaiming the pope to be a heretic. (But that, as they say, is another story.)

Nominalist theology, more broadly, is a theological perspective related to this metaphysical perspective. A significant aspect of nominalist theology is what's called **voluntarism**, which focuses on the will (*voluntas*) of God. It emphasizes God's will as primary. God's power or freedom is God's primary attribute. If we are to say anything about God, the most true thing we can say is that God can do whatever He wants: His power is unlimited. Previously, God was indeed thought of in terms of power or will, but God's power and will were thought of in relation to God's love, goodness and wisdom. Will was not the preeminent name for God. But in the Late Middle Ages there is a shift towards a focus on God's incomprehensible power—a power whose acts cannot be answerable to us or our reason, at all.

With voluntarism, creation will come to be seen as having less reference to anything beyond itself. The order of the world is not so much a reflection of the wisdom of God, but the world is the way it is simply because God chose to make it that way. Here, we begin to see a disconnection between God and nature. Nominalists still believe that God created the world, but it is going to be much more difficult for them to look at nature and then to reason to God in some sense.

With nominalism the link is severed between our human words, the divine Word and the order of the world. Our names are simply imposing an order on the things that exist. Previously there was a common Wisdom that both made human thinking and made the world as it is so that it was possible to understand the world and, though that, understand God through the world. But these things are being disconnected in nominalism.

Following voluntarism is a shift in emphasis when it comes to God from wisdom to absolute power. The main concern that theologians would have, as seen in the condemnations by Bishop Stephen Tempier of Paris of some 219 (or so) propositions in 1277, is that no one puts a limit on God's sovereign power. Many of the condemned propositions were those that questioned in some way God's omnipotence as His chief characteristic. The Condemnations of 1277, then, reflect this focus on the power of God.

One way to see the change is to see the change in the meaning of God's *potentia absoluta* and God's *potentia ordinata*. The first names God's sovereign power, or His omnipotence; the second is what God actually does—so, what God can do and what He actually does. This distinction came about in the eleventh century, but changed in nominalist theology. One of the things that happened was that the *potentia absoluta* was expanded beyond any rational or moral limitation. They wanted to say that it made no sense to talk about good and evil when talking about God, that somehow God was limited by goodness or evil, because whatever God does is good. He is totally free. Ultimately, the only thing that limits God's power is logical contradiction. Second, they made the *potentia absoluta* and the *potentia ordinate*, two independent moments of what God was doing temporally, instead of two aspects of looking at God's continually operative power. Nominalists would say that God first had this *potentia absolutia*, and then He created things in a certain order—in this order, that God establishes and practically abides by rules that he arbitrarily makes up (*potentia ordinata*). There is, then, ultimately, only one order of causality, and God has established this as the first (efficient causal) mover. Involved here is a shift in the way causality is considered. Efficient causality is going to be privileged, and God will begin to be seen a cause in the way that physical events cause other physical events.

One of the key contributions of **John Duns Scotus** (*c*. 1266–1308) is what is called the **univocity of being**. This is the doctrine that says that being is predicated of God and creatures in the same sense or univocally. When we say creatures are and that God is, we are saying the same thing of both things such that being is conceptually prior to both God and creatures. This obscures the earlier understanding of 'the distinction' between God and the world. Within this frame, what makes God supreme is that God is the most powerful of beings. Univocity of being, then, and voluntarism go hand-in-hand. God is the super-powerful being in the order of beings.

Such an understanding of univocity feeds into a focus on efficient causality—that God is a supremely powerful divine will who rules all things by causing them the way that other things cause each other. And, even in this period, the way that people start to talk about God is in terms of that which causes even Himself. He is the efficient cause of Himself, the *causa sui*. This was one of the names of God that Descartes will eventually use—the power so powerful that it causes itself.

When God is acting in relation to the world in this univocal frame of efficient causality, God is the highest being among beings. Therefore, God and other beings are in competition. It is a zero-sum game in that if God is doing something, then we cannot. Either God does it, or we do it. Either it is natural, or it is supernatural. Some theorists say that when this happened, it became almost fated that modern science would lead to God's disappearance. For, as theologians redefined God in terms of efficient causality, they made Him a particularly powerful being within the causal nexus of the world. However, if you find you do not need this masterfully powerful force to explain the phenomena of beings, then there really is no place for God.

1.3.2 Nature and Grace

In this univocal frame of understanding, the supernatural (God) is seen as in competition with the natural sphere. Part of what is happening is a constriction of the sense of 'nature', which comes to be defined in opposition to 'grace' in the Late Middle Ages: It is that which is not grace or the supernatural. Because of that, it ends up that the natural is that which you can talk about without reference to theology. The natural is that which is distinct from grace and super-nature. So it starts to get its own independent domain.

The focus on voluntarism among nominalist theologians diminishes the ability to think about the relationship between God and creatures not only in terms of creation but also in terms of in grace. As the creation of the world betrays no order or meaning beyond God's will that it be thus, so is there no reason why God chooses to save one person and not another. Grace is simply and solely due to God's inscrutable choice. It appears as if from that perspective that grace is given or withheld seemingly randomly, and there is then a rising of a need in this period to come to fruition in the Reformation for some kind of guarantee of grace—perhaps some kind of immediate experience.

1.3.3 Reform

Another significant development coming to the fore in the Late Middle Ages is the medieval impulse towards reform. Charles Taylor points out that there is a trajectory towards reform within medieval Catholicism, arising from dissatisfaction with an earlier view of **hierarchical complementarity**. Such hierarchical complementarity sees that there are different vocations within the Christian life. There were different intensities of the Christian life ranging from the layperson to the priest to the monk. The point was less that monks were the real Christians and the rest were just a 'buncha dirtbags', than that there was a complementarity—that there was a place for different intensities within the whole of the body of the Church.

As mentioned, in the Late Middle Ages there was a growing dissatisfaction with this thought of there somehow being multiple ideals, and that the masses were not living up to perfection. As early as the Hildebrandtine Reforms in the eleventh century, and on up through the Catholic and Protestant Reformations, we see an opposition to any kind of a hierarchical complementary, any hierarchy in Christian life. Such reform demanded that everyone should be a real, one hundred percent Christian. Everyone needed to live up to the highest demands of the Christian life. And so there was a new kind of stringent perspective on the Christian life, and on Christian perfection.

This became a dominant piety in the fifteenth century called *devotion moderna*. This was put forward by a group called The Brothers of the Common Life, founded by Thomas à Kempis, author of *The Imitation of Christ*. The idea was that the laity should aspire to the religious devotion of the clergy, that there should be no distinction. We can see how this very naturally fed into the Protestant reformation, but this kind of impulse was there well within the Middle Ages.

1.3.4 Disconnections

One way of looking at the Late Middle Ages is in terms of disconnections of things that were previously united. One kind of disconnection could be considered a 'moral' disconnection. Part of the impetus of reform was that lay people were perceiving a disconnect in that the clergy were not living up to the Church's ideals—it was a situation of botched moral execution and the hierarchy of the Church was seen by many as bending to the whims of temporal powers. And so, that which was supposed to be higher—the clerical orders—were perceived as being driven by base motives. But also that which was supposed to be lower—lay people—were aspiring to higher modes of Christian life through avenues (like *devotion moderna*) that were more or less disconnected from the Church hierarchy. This is a kind of the systemic sociological structure that is going to lead us towards the Protestant Reformation.

Of perhaps equal importance for the long story of modern theology are the disconnections that happen in the realm of ideas—particularly in the dissolution of the classical synthesis (see p. 13). **Nature and God** are increasingly disconnected. Nature is created by God, but that is all that can be said. It has nothing to tell us about God. Nature does not reflect the wisdom and goodness of God; there are no signs of God in nature; God could have created it in any way. In fact, some nominalists would go so far as to say that God could utterly recreate the created order at any given moment. God could do things like make us experience the world in a way that it is not. Why not? God can do anything. How do you know He's not doing that right now? How do you know you know anything? We can begin to see how something so supremely 'modern' as Cartesian doubt is perhaps uncomfortably close to a late medieval form of Christian theology.

Humanity and nature are disconnected from each other. Nature in itself is not intelligible to humanity. With nominalism, whatever intelligibility is found in nature is not really 'in' nature—it is something that we put there, a name we give it. This, too, opens the door to Scepticism. With voluntarism, as just intimated, that God could even change our perceptions and our relation to the world. Therefore, this different understanding of God makes it so that our connection with the natural world is seriously eroded.

The final disconnection is that of the relationship between **God and humanity**. Humanity could have been created in any particular kind of way, and so there is no real place for the image of God. Humanity, in this perspective, is no longer ordered towards God. Our hearts are not restless nor do they find their rest in God because that would imply that humans are intrinsically ordered towards God. But instead, the only connection we have with God is that He is operating external to nature and to us through grace in a mysterious way. He is saving us and doing things to us as kind of a competing power, as seen in hyper-Augustinianism and Calvinism. God's mysterious operative power is here perceived by some to be arbitrary—as there is no way for us to think about it or make sense of it other than simply saying that 'God did it'.

Taking a step back, and seeing how some of these things are going to echo into later modernity, we see the beginning of what William Desmond calls the **objectification of being and the subjectification of value**. Pre-modern perspectives such as we have in the classical synthesis saw the world as having value and meaning apart from human beings—that there was something in the order of nature itself that was good and meaningful. And so, objects were not just things out there, but they were charged with value. They had meaning; there was something more to them than mere material things. But with perspectives like nominalism humans are going to end up being the source for the meaning of the cosmos. The only meaning and value we are going to find in the universe is the meaning and value that we put there. This might sound quite postmodern, but it is also quite (late) medieval.

Being, then, is something objectified: It is made a neutral object 'out there', a valueless happening. The world apart from human purposes is just stuff, just matter. Value is something that is subjectified. There is no value, meaning, or goodness in the world. The only value that there is is human self-determination. So ultimately the supreme value is going to be the value of human freedom, that we can make whatever value we want—constrained by nothing—just like God … but not any God. In the end, the *imago Dei* sneaks back in and becomes the way that we think about ourselves—little erotic sovereigns, voluntarist deities in the material world, coming to terms with our own freedom.

Sources and Further Reading

Brague, Rémi. *The Wisdom of the World: The Human Experience of the Universe in Western Thought.* Translated by Teresa Lavender Fagan. Chicago, IL: University of Chicago Press, 2003.

Burrell, David B. *Knowing the Unknowable God: Ibn-Sina, Maimonides, Aquinas.* South Bend, IN: University of Notre Dame Press, 1986.

Desmond, William. *God and the Between.* Oxford: Blackwell, 2008.

Dupré, Louis. *Passage to Modernity.* New Haven, CT: Yale University Press, 1993.

Gillespie, Michael Allen. *The Theological Origins of Modernity.* Chicago, IL: University of Chicago Press, 2009.

Gregory, Brad S. *The Unintended Reformation: How a Religious Revolution Secularized Society.* Cambridge, MA: Belknap Press of Harvard University Press, 2012.

Hart, David Bentley. *The Experience of God: Being, Consciousness, Bliss.* New Haven, CT: Yale University Press, 2013.

Sokolowski, Robert. *The God of Faith and Reason.* South Bend, IN: University of Notre Dame Press, 1982.

Taylor, Charles. *A Secular Age.* Cambridge, MA: Belknap Press of Harvard University Press, 2007.

Wilken, Robert Louis. *The First Thousand Years: A Global History of Christianity.* New Haven, CT: Yale University Press, 2013.

2

Reformation and Humanism: 1400–1650

Chapter Outline

2.1 Reform and Reformation

The interrelated developments of the Protestant Reformation and the development of Renaissance Humanism have a key part to play in the story of the emergence of modernity. Though there are a variety of dates for these periods in Western history, the Renaissance is often placed in the fifteenth and sixteenth centuries, and the Reformation from *c.* 1500 up to *c.* 1650. We take as the end of this period the Peace of Westphalia, in 1648—which Louis Dupré names as the date of 'the conclusion of the formation of modernity'. As we will see, there is considerable overlap and interrelation with both the Late Middle Ages before, and the period of the Enlightenment and the Awakenings to come after.

Persons and events of the Reformation and Renaissance

1304–74	Francesco Petrarch
1453	Fall of Constantinople/End of Hundred Years War
1463–94	Pico della Mirandola

Persons and events of the Reformation and Renaissance

c. 1469–1536	Desiderius Erasmus
1483–1546	Martin Luther
1484–1531	Huldrych Zwingli
1509–64	John Calvin
1516	Erasmus' publication of the Greek New Testament
1517	Luther's 95 Theses
1521	Diet of Worms
1533–92	Michel de Montaigne
1536–59	Calvin's *Institutes of the Christian Religion*
1545–63	Council of Trent
1555	Peace of Augsburg
1618–48	Thirty Years War
1648	Peace of Westphalia

A certain continuity exists between the Middle Ages and the Reformation. Both were in a sense doing something that was characteristically medieval. They were both looking back for their model, for their standard. They are not necessarily progress-oriented; both would say that we should return to the origin, to the source, ***ad fontes***. Most medieval monastic movements—which were themselves reform movements—arose from saying: 'Things have kind of gone off the rails, so let's go back to the purity and simplicity of the Christian life of the early church, of the apostles.' The Renaissance advocated a return to the golden ages of pagan Greece and Rome, and their elegant literature.

The Protestant reformers were also driven by the same spirit of **reform** that we saw in the Middle Ages, perhaps cranked up to a greater severity. They did not want there to be any hierarchy when it came to vocations. There should be no differentiations between Christians, but everyone should be held to the same high standard of the Christian ideal. There is a modern levelling here in which everyone should be the same—but it was a 'leveling up'. Along with this 'leveling up', however, is a **heightened anxiety** because there is the feeling that everybody has fallen short of what they are supposed to do. Now if there is no differentiation or different modes of life and you fail to live up to the highest mode of life, there is something wrong with you. In this period, there was also a considerable focus on death. (The plague probably didn't help.) And when these concerns converge, people become fixated in a new way on the question of their salvation. It gets a new importance because people are aware that they are not living up to the ideal. Issues of judgement, damnation and salvation are becoming something that normal people are thinking about. This is part of why Luther's understanding of salvation by faith is so revolutionary. There is an anxiety about salvation being cranked up on one side, and then the release that comes with faith as an opposite positive.

Figure 2.1 Luther.

'Lucas Cranach (I) workshop—Martin Luther (Uffizi)' by Workshop of Lucas Cranach the Elder. Scan by Carol Gerten-Jackson. Licensed under Public Domain via Wikimedia Commons.

We also see during this period—especially in Calvinist areas—a focus on the reform of society. Reform is not only something that individuals do in their private life, but it has to do with reordering of society. So in places like Geneva, Puritan England or New England—where you have dominant Calvinist groups—they are restructuring society as a whole around certain ideals.

2.2 Discord

2.2.1 *Sola scriptura*

Along these lines of reform, the question in the Late Middle Ages and the Reformation is how to narrow the gap between Christianity's ideals, and what we're currently doing, or at least how to get a better understanding of what the ideal is or what it means to be a Christian. And the answer to this for the Reformers is—of course—you return to Scripture. Go to the Bible, that's how you get on the same page. However, in trying to get on the same page, unity didn't quite come about the way they wanted it to. The Reformers tried to answer the big questions of life through Scripture alone—*sola scriptura*. The problem is that they failed to reach meaningful unanimity. They failed to agree on what Scripture said. And so, from the early 1520s, all of the different protestant groups agreed on the central authority of Scripture and something like a *sola scriptura*, but the agreement often ended there. There was widespread disagreement about what Scripture said about such topics as the nature of salvation, the nature and extent of human sin, the nature and practice of the Lord's Supper and Baptism, and the understanding of the character of the Old Testament for Christians. Some of the things that had previously held Christianity together as a unity were now disputed in the midst of different understandings of Scripture.

One of the results of *sola scriptura* then is a 'fissiparous disagreement'. The disagreement over what the Scriptures said led to a constant splintering. *Sola scriptura* quickly became ensconced in the various ecclesial and political authorities that arose in and around a particular group of Protestant Christians. This process—called **confessionalization**—happens in a more acute form after 1570 when these different understandings start to crystalize into different distinct groups—usually along political and national lines.

So, relative to what Wilken observed in the first thousand years of Christianity as cohering around several common elements, we see these being stripped away in Protestantism: Monasticism is out the window; the bishop or any common governance structure is gone; Baptism and the Eucharist are contested among the different Protestant groups; the historic creeds are questioned by some and accepted by others. All you have left is the Bible—one remaining of the five unifying elements.

Without these more common unifying elements, Christianity begins to cease to be an observable unity. In the broader culture, there ceases to be any one thing called 'Christianity'. Instead, there is a plurality: what the Roman Catholics say, what the Calvinists say, what the Lutherans say, what the X, Y and Z Anabaptists say, what the Anglicans say and so on. This situation leads to an open-ended proliferation of contested and competing doctrines, and this leads to a crisis of authority. With these different understandings of Scripture—which were to be the final authority—Scripture starts to cease to have a unifying and foundational function. Instead, it often became the basis for our division—it became Scripture-as-read-by-party-X. 'Scripture', as such then starts to disappear, as it functions increasingly as a weapon against other Christians. Scripture is then overlaid with these confessional particularities. You do not have Scripture without an understanding of what it says, without an interpretation that comes along with it.

Such confessionalization divided the church in such a fundamental way that it is difficult for us today to understand. We have never known anything but a fundamentally divided Church—or 'Churches'—and this was unimaginable beforehand. As Michael Legaspi points out, the sad irony is that Scripture ultimately loses its place in culture at the hands of its defenders in the Reformation, when it ceases to function as a Catholic (in the sense of 'universal') Scripture—something that holds together as a unity. It ceases to be a cornerstone of European culture and becomes a force of division. The whole idea of *sola scriptura* was to get away from the Church's official interpretation and to return to Scripture, but there were different and often opposed 'returns' to Scripture. 'When you return to Scripture you find what my party says!' *Sola scriptura*—in generating multiple interpretations—becomes a divisive force.

2.2.2 Authority and Certainty

One of the things that really comes to the fore, along with *sola scriptura*, is a new focus on the individual during the Reformation. The piety—the kind of religiousness that is characteristic of the Reformation—is an interior piety. There is a certain opposition to outward religiousness, whether that is organized institutions or material things like sacraments, relics or artworks. In many places there was a large-scale destruction of church art because the real religiousness is something that's inward. The great northern Catholic Humanist Erasmus (1466–1536), in his immensely popular little book, the *Enchiridion*, focuses on the Christian life as centred on individual and inward activities: reading the Bible and praying. The broader emphasis on Scripture becomes coupled with the interpretation of Scripture as individual: inward, personal and often coupled with the inward work of the Holy Spirit.

One key to the Christian life and the understanding of Scripture in this period is the question of conscience, and this comes out of a broader milieu in which there is a greater anxiety about one's salvation in self-examination and contrition. And so, on the one side there's an anxiety about your not being right with God, and seeking an assurance of your salvation. A broader example of the importance of conscience is the scene of Martin Luther (1483–1546) before the Diet of Worms—a formal meeting in which he was put on trial for his publications. When Luther's views are challenged by the Catholic examiners, he defends himself on the basis of Scripture and plain reason as being authoritative saying: 'Here I stand. I can do no other.' This phrase (in Diarmaid MacCulloch's words, 'the most memorable thing Luther never said') instructively represents the coupling of individual interpretation of Scripture and an inner conviction willing to take a stand for such an interpretation.

When John Calvin (1509–64) reflects on the source of this conviction, certainty and authority, he will focus on Scripture of course but also on the Holy Spirit. He will give a new emphasis on illumination and inner persuasion. One's certainty then comes from the Holy Spirit's illumination such that there can be divine authority alongside of something that seems like it is the individual reader's own interpretive authority. There can be some kind of assurance that your reading of Scripture is more than simply your own idiosyncratic opinion—you are being persuaded by Someone other than yourself. This is underwritten in Calvin's understanding of grace insofar as those who are truly elect are the ones that are illumined; the ones who are chosen by God to be saved are also the ones who have the better reading of Scripture. Of course the people who are

Figure 2.2 Calvin.

'John Calvin 21' by Georg Osterwald (1803–84). *Bibliothèque publique et universitaire de Neuchâtel—BPUN*. Licensed under Public Domain via Wikimedia Commons.

not saved are not going to agree, they lack the gift of the Holy Spirit and so cannot read Scripture properly.

Part of what gets going here, however, is this is going to feed into what will become modern scepticism. Formally there is what is called the problem of the criterion—of what should be the criterion for what counts as knowledge for religious or theological knowledge. Part of what was so radical about Luther was that he denied the given authority—that the Church and the bishops had the authority to interpret Scripture. Luther strips it back to say that we have no obligations to believe the teaching of the Church apart from Scripture such that his new criterion is conscience as compelled by Scripture. Making subjective certainty a criterion is the beginning of a modern understanding of a subjective criterion for religious knowledge. And, herein, you have the problem of the criterion—how do you establish that this is the right criterion? Do you have another criterion to determine it? Calvin started to back this up by underwriting it with the Spirit's illumination, but how do you know that the Holy Spirit is at work? Ultimately, it is going to have to be some immediate sense that you are getting it right—some kind of spiritual clarity that is given to you. So, in many ways, Luther opened a Pandora's Box. On the surface he is looking for truth in Scripture, but when the judge is ultimately your own conscience there is going to be a lot of controversy. There are lots of different consciences and lots of different hermeneutical frames. The most extreme version of this is what came to be called the Radical Reformation, sometimes called the Anabaptists. Some of the followers of the Swiss reformer Huldrych Zwingli (1484–1531) radically focused on the belief that every individual has the right to interpret Scripture for themselves. There seems to have been a cycle with them of regularly saying that the group they were in at the moment were not real Christians because they failed to interpret Scripture properly so they started a new group and so on.

As the Reformation progresses, particular differences of interpretation are hardened into **institutionalized doctrinal disagreement**. Not only does there happen to be some controversies, but these get crystallized into formal positions defined in opposition to others. Brad Gregory considers this 'the most fundamental and consequential fact about Western Christianity since 1520' (pp. 45–46). Such 'literally interminable doctrinal controversy' proceeded to redefine Christianity in the West. Much of the apparent anxiety in this period has to do with these kinds of issues. When your background beliefs—the things that allow you to make judgements—are called into question, that is an anxious situation. It seems that what is being contested is Christianity itself.

2.3 Voluntarism in the Reformation

There is then a great deal of variety in what is called the 'Reformation', including the Catholic side. But I would like to look at how some common elements of influential strands of the Reformation come together, and one of those is the connection to voluntarism. Both Luther and Calvin were educated in environments heavily influenced by Scotus and Ockham, and which laid a heavy stress on the unfettered sovereignty of God. There was also an emphasis in these settings on an understanding of the Fall, such that in the Fall of Adam nature itself was damaged so that the nature had to be recreated by grace. For Calvin, this salvation comes about based on divine election—God's inscrutable decision to save someone by grace, and not having anything to do with their deserving or works.

For Luther, we see much more anxiety and uncertainty when it comes to his understanding of salvation. We really see the struggle he was going through. It seems that this issue is answered with him with the certainty that comes from Scripture that we are saved by faith. Calvin also needed this inward certainty—but he had more of a doctrinal framework to talk about it. Once you have an understanding of divine activity or grace that focuses on unrestricted divine power—where you really can't think about what God's doing except that He does whatever He wants—this diminishes the ability for us to think about the relationship between God and creatures. It seems like grace is given, or withheld randomly. So, how do you find your place in that kind of a framework? And the way that you can see that you are one of the ones that have grace is through some sort of immediate experience or inward guarantee that gives you the assurance you are looking for in the face of the voluntarist anxiety. In both Luther and Calvin, nature is so damaged by sin that even divine justification does not cure the nature. Nature is not 'fixed' by grace in the Calvinist or Lutheran perspectives. Justification is understood in a Nominalist fashion—it is not something that changes in the world or in us, but it is something that changes in the mind of God. God considers us to be righteous. He imputes righteousness to us. It is related to the way a Nominalist would say we do not see goodness in the world but instead impute goodness to the world. This, then, is what really matters—the way God regards us.

Part of the earlier understanding of what is going on in salvation (from the Church Fathers into the Middle Ages) is that there's a closer connection between justification and sanctification, we might say, than there is in later Protestantism. What God is up to in us and with us is not just creative accounting that just takes Jesus' merits and applies them to our demerits, but actually transforming us into the image of Christ so that we actually become like Christ in the age to come. We are partaking of the divine nature. We in our reality are becoming transformed—not just in the accounts.

2.4 Renaissance Humanism

In the Renaissance there are attempts to revive something like the classical synthesis. In the southern Renaissance, there is a revival of ancient philosophies—particularly Platonism. There is also a stronger view of the value of nature but one that is different from a medieval view. In the northern Renaissance, the emphasis is going to be more on a unified vision of culture. But the central and unifying aspect in the Renaissance is the understanding of creativity. Even nature in the Renaissance is largely a backdrop for creative human action. It is a hospitable backdrop that enables us to be creative and provides inspiration and material for artistic transformation. There is a shift, however, from a previous, more passive mode of relating to nature towards a more active mode.

Nominalism caught on largely in the North (as we saw relative to the Reformation). The Platonism of the southern Renaissance however would stand in stark contrast to Nominalism. Platonists would say, 'Not only are these universals real, they are the really real thing. Everything else is a shadow of them.' So they (these southern Renaissance Platonists) will see nature as still having a connection to and as still telling us something about the divine and that it still tells us something about the divine. They are now going to use the metaphor that nature is a divine work of art, that God is an artist who created the world. As a work of God's creation we can therefore learn about God from it. But, as with many things in the Renaissance, this is not just about admiring God's creativity, it is about looking at models for how we ourselves can create. The emphasis is on your creativity. We are to become like God (in a lesser degree of course) in creating, and nature is best imitated and we are most true to our divine image when we are in an artistic mode and create along with God and after the more perfect creations of nature.

In Pico della Mirandola's *Oration on the Dignity of Man*, part of the special significance of humanity is our mutability: we can become like beasts or worse than beasts, but we can also become something angelic or divine. The creativity here is not just an outward creation, but it is a **self-creation**. It is not *creatio ex nihilo*, but a self-creation within a hierarchy: As we seek to become more like God, we can indeed become more like God.

However, we are also moving towards exclusive **humanism** as a live possibility (Secularity 1) in the Renaissance as we move on when some people break with Platonism and move towards seeing the human subject as the sole giver of form. With this we are moving back in the direction of a Nominalist understanding. We are still focused on **creativity**, but now we are not creating after nature—we are not seeing the form that is in nature that God as divine Creator created in it and then imitating that orderly creativity. Now we are the sole source of meaning. But we are not quite there yet in the Renaissance. We are not yet at the point of seeing the subject as the sole source of meaning, but you can see when this early Humanist understanding of creativity gets coupled with a Nominalist understanding—that the only meaning is what we put there as we have no connection to any meaning that is in the world in and of itself—you get a more radical kind of emphasis on autonomy. This Renaissance emphasis on creativity is a mode of human value and meaning that is at odds with the understanding of sin and total depravity that comes up in some Reformed understandings of humanity as diseased, hobbled and crippled by sin in every part of their being. The humanist vision of humanism is very different than that; they want to celebrate the value and untapped potential and possibility of humanity.

Michael Gillespie's *The Theological Origins of Modernity* opens with a scene at the Papal court in Avignon, which has become the centre of culture in France. Two particular people were there—Ockham and Petrarch, who will really catch on in the South; Nominalism will catch on in the North. Here we not only see two of the main trajectories for the period, we can also see how part of what is going on here is a conflict of **Augustinianisms**. B. B. Warfield once said that the sixteenth century was a struggle in the mind of Augustine—the first thinker in the Middle Ages—because what you have coming to fruition is a renewed interest in Augustine in both the North and the South. In a famous story about Petrarch, he hikes up Mount Ventoux and observes the beauty of nature. Because he is the Father of a Renaissance Humanism, of course, he brought books with him on his hike, including a copy of Augustine's *Confessions*. He opens it randomly—like Augustine opens the Scriptures randomly in *Confessions* and finds the passage that converts him—and reads about how the man looks at all of the beautiful things in nature, but fails to recognize the greatness that is within himself. He is looking at nature, but it is the thing that is doing the looking (himself!) that is

Figure 2.3 Petrarch.

'Altichiero, ritratto di Francesco Petrarca' by Altichiero. Licensed under Public Domain via Wikimedia Commons.

the greatest thing in nature. This cuts him to the quick. Here, we have a Renaissance reception of an earlier, more optimistic Augustine. This is the Augustine that was lost and was not the Augustine that was focused on in the Late Middle Ages. The Reformation followed suit in focusing on the Augustine that was ascendant in the Late Middle Ages, which is the later Augustine of the anti-Pelagian writings which were much more pessimistic. These works were written in a polemical setting and mode, and that really colours the way he does things. Rhetorically, you want to make humanity especially awful to show how grace is especially amazing—and completely necessary. He presents a very strong view of original sin as was then taken up by the Reformers (as did Franciscan theologians like William of Ockham in previous centuries).

2.5 Nominalism and Scepticism

By 1500, Nominalism is one of the dominant intellectual movements in northern Europe—in Paris, and in Germany and England. Almost all of the universities in Germany were Nominalist. One of the things that goes along with Nominalism is a certain scepticism about human reasoning—especially regarding what human reason can tell us that is relevant to religion. There is a strong divide between what can be known by reason and what can be known by revelation. Luther studied at the University of Erfurt and there was a strong emphasis on Nominalist philosophy there. He is often described as being an Ockhamist in his youth.

With the southern Renaissance also came the rediscovery of ancient philosophies. One of the philosophers thus rediscovered is one Sextus Empiricus, a representative of ancient scepticism or Pyrrhonian scepticism—a philosophy centred on how best to live in the absence of stable knowledge. Ancient scepticism as revived in the Renaissance matches up well with the already regnant Nominalism. This is because in Ockham's understanding knowledge is on pretty shaky ground—God can, as he says, cause the mind to know intuitively that which is not. If this is so, how do you know that what you are experiencing is the way things are? The world as you experience it is not trustworthy because the central aspect of reality is God's arbitrary power. Descartes is struggling with precisely this issue—Ockham's God looks uncannily like Descartes' evil genius.

Figure 2.4 Montaigne.

'Michel de Montaigne, Portrait from Tietz edition (1753)'. Engraving by J. C. G. Fritzsch: Scan of frontispiece from *Michel de Montaigne: Michaels Herrn von Montagne Versuche, nebst des Verfassers Leben, nach der Ausgabe von Pierre Coste ins Deutsche übersetzt von Johann Daniel Tietz, Leipzig: Lankischens Erben* 1753. Licensed under Public Domain via Wikimedia Commons.

As a mediator between the Medieval Ockham and the Enlightenment Descartes, we have **Michel de Montaigne** (1533–92). For Montaigne, the Nominalist God, or Nominalism, was the justification for doubting even the most obvious truths. In his writings, we have a meditation on how to live a moral life without certainty—on the basis of a fundamental instability. Montaigne is coping with uncertainty that arises from the Nominalism of Ockham. Descartes, however, is going to find such uncertainty unacceptable and seek to find certain foundations for knowledge. We will return to his story in the next chapter.

2.6 The Wars of Religion and Changing Political Order

During the Reformation the division in Christianity becomes starkly apparent. There is very little sense that there is any one Church, but irrevocably there are a plurality of Churches—not individual congregations, but big-C Churches. This leads in no small part to what is called the **Thirty Years War** (1618–48), but also various wars that are going on in France and Germany and civil wars going on in England, Scotland and the Netherlands. These wars are ruinously destructive—devastating all of northern Europe—especially Germany and France. So, between 1450 and 1700 we do not just have Thirty Years War, but there is a general state of ongoing (common though not constant) warfare in Europe. Part of what is happening is that we are witnessing the rise of what will become modern nation-states, and the birth of a Leviathan is a bloody thing. These wars were often fought by mercenaries' armies who—while going about busily pillaging and 'burninating the countryside'—were often more concerned with (a) not dying and (b) looting and carrying off maidens than any particular religious ideals.

When we get to the eighteenth-century Enlightenment and Awakenings (see Chapter 3), people in Europe will look back with a profound sense that the way things have been is totally unacceptable—that this cannot go on. The wars had decimated central Europe, and things simply had to change. But we are getting ahead of ourselves …

In the background of the Thirty Years War is **the Peace of Augsburg** (1555), in which representatives of the different sides (Catholic and Lutheran) met and decided that the ruler of a given land gets to choose (more or less) whether their land is Catholic or Lutheran. (This is mostly in Germany, which is not a unified state but a bunch of smaller states ruled by princes.) Note that these are the only two options: Calvinist/Reformed or Anabaptist was not an option. The Peace of Augsburg—something that the secular rulers and not the leaders of the Churches came up with—gave Germany relative peace for about sixty years. When the Reformation gets up and going in the first half of the sixteenth century, there is an obvious conflict that needs to get resolved so that there is not war. The Peace of Augsburg functioned to keep relative peace in Germany for the latter part of the sixteenth century.

In 1562, the civil wars of religion break out in France between the Catholics and the Huguenots, who were French Calvinists. (Calvin was centred in Geneva—in Switzerland, between Germany and France—and was hugely influential in France, something not viewed kindly by the Catholics there.) The French civil wars of religion went on for more than thirty years until 1600.

What is commonly called the **Thirty Years War** (1618–48) ended up involving most European countries at one time or another. There were different Catholic and Protestant countries outside Germany fighting because they were allies with other parties who were fighting, etc. In the end, everyone lost. It is widely regarded as an unmitigated disaster of enormous proportions. It was a disaster on the scale of the Black Death that was seen as being brought about by the conflict between different Christian confessions. Even if the wars of religion were less about religion than about the forging of modern nation-states, religious zeal is particularly convenient if you are a prince who wants to consolidate power.

In many ways what was going on in the wars of religion was a proxy war between Imperial Germany—the Holy Roman Empire—and France. In 1648, the Thirty Years War ended in the Peace of Westphalia. This signal event marks the end of the era of the Reformation, and the beginning for the next era. With the Peace of Westphalia, something like the Peace of Augsburg was re-established, except that now there was a Reformed/Calvinist option on the table—land could be Catholic, Lutheran or Reformed. The Peace of Augsburg, in many ways, established the modern religious map of Europe. The result is a division that is evident even today—a Protestant North and a Catholic South. This was a division that the princes came up with as a way to stop the warfare when they realized there was nothing to be won from it—that it was just constant bloodshed.

In the aftermath of the Thirty Years War and other confessional conflicts, we see the establishment of state churches. Confessional warfare was contained by making the Church an arm of the government. Countries like Sweden, Norway and Denmark, and regions like north and central Germany were Lutheran. The Reformed Church was established in places like Scotland, the Netherlands and some of western Germany. The Catholic countries and regions were in the South—Italy, Spain, southern Germany, and also eastern Austria and Bavaria. There were some disputed places, like Ireland. And, we still have those problems today. In England, following a dispute about whether it should be Anglican or Reformed, there is a resulting splintering of religious groups which then gets exported to North America. France still has problems because of a remaining sizable Reformed Huguenot contingent within its official Catholic borders.

As a sign of the discord that happened, many of the religious labels from this period begin their lives as insults. The Calvinists didn't call themselves 'Calvinists', they were Reformed. Even 'Protestant' was not a word that the group came up with—they wanted to call themselves 'Evangelical'. 'Protestants' was a Catholic designation intended to demean. Similarly, no Anabaptist called him/herself Anabaptist … ditto, the Anglicans … or Methodists (at least, not initially). So, the main point, which we see going on from here, is that the Reformation leads to discord in the early seventeenth century, which, in turn, contributes towards exclusive humanism becoming a real option in the seventeenth century.

Sources and Further Reading

Chadwick, Owen. *The Reformation*. Rev. edn. New York: Penguin, 1990.
Dupré, Louis. *Passage to Modernity*. New Haven, CT: Yale University Press, 1993.

Gregory, Brad S. *The Unintended Reformation: How a Religious Revolution Secularized Society.* Cambridge, MA: Belknap Press of Harvard University Press, 2012.

Legaspi, Michael C. *The Death of Scripture and the Rise of Biblical Studies.* Oxford: Oxford University Press, 2010.

MacCulloch, Diarmaid. *The Reformation.* New York: Penguin, 2003.

Martines, Lauro. *Furies: War in Europe, 1450–1700.* New York: Bloomsbury, 2013.

Taylor, Charles. *A Secular Age.* Cambridge, MA: Belknap Press of Harvard University Press, 2007.

Wilken, Robert Louis. *The First Thousand Years: A Global History of Christianity.* New Haven, CT: Yale University Press, 2013.

3

Enlightenments and Awakenings: 1650–1800

Chapter Outline

3.1 The Second Wave of Modernity, Tension, Variety

While the general dates for this period are 1650–1800, a more precise accounting would be 1648–1789, with 1648 being the date of the Peace of Westphalia and 1789, the date of the French Revolution. Louis Dupré places everything that came before this period—from the Late Middle Ages up through the Renaissance and Reformation (see Chapters 1 and 2)—as the **first wave** of modernity. What we have here—in this chapter and Chapter 4—together with the Enlightenment and Awakenings (1650–1800) is the **second wave** of modernity. The **third wave** will come in the nineteenth century with Romanticism (*see* Part II, Chapters 5–11). This period is where modernity is beginning to crystallize—at least modern problems are going to start to assume a familiar form with which twentieth-century philosophy and theology will have to reckon.

First wave	Late Middle Ages, Reformation, Renaissance	1300–1650
Second wave	The Enlightenment	1650–1800
Third wave	Romanticism	1800–1900

In this chapter we will survey two broad movements. Especially significant when looking at the development of modern theology was a rising **dialectical tension** in this period between the elite culture of the Enlightenment and the more popular Evangelical Awakenings and revivals. This, then, was a period of tension, opposition and strife. This tension or **cross-pressure** (as Taylor calls it)—between enthusiasm on one side, and a more formal scientific thought on the other—served to generate much of nineteenth-century religious thought. Interestingly though, both sides defined themselves against the prior era—both the *Aufklärers* (*Aufklärung* being the German for 'enlightenment'), and the Pietists/Revivalists sought to be much more tolerant and avoid the confessional polemics and controversy of the sixteenth and early seventeenth centuries. Looking forward in time, 1800 and after was a period of a kind of mediation between these two impulses. In Immanuel Kant (see Chapter 4), we will see the first great mediation between the Enlightenment and the Awakenings—making him both the culmination of the second wave of modernity and the pioneer of the third.

In presenting these big movements and cultural forces in western Europe, we are using the plural as there were a variety of different movements happening in different places. Nevertheless, there are common enough characteristics between them that it is reasonable to talk of an international phenomenon called 'the Enlightenment' that manifested itself differently, and to various degrees, in Germany, France and England. Likewise, the various Awakenings were interrelated but happened in Germany, France and England in different ways.

To speak to the variety, there was (very generally) a different balance of sorts between the 'Awakening' and the 'Enlightenment' in different locales. Looking at France, Germany and England during this period, it would be something like in Figure below. There was more 'Enlightenment' going on in France than religious 'Awakening'. In Germany, both were present and vibrant (although the German Enlightenment begins later) and it is the location with the greatest religious tension. Perhaps one of the reasons that Germany became the central hub of modern theology in the nineteenth and twentieth centuries was the presence of this creative tension. England, while early on leading the way in the Enlightenment, was also the primary seat of the religious Awakenings via Evangelical revivals and the Methodists.

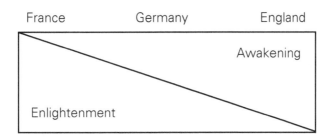

Key figures in the Enlightenment and Awakenings

Johann Arndt (1555–1621)	German	
René Descartes (1596–1650)	French	Enlightenment
Cornelius Jansen (d. 1638)	Dutch	
Baruch Spinoza (1632–77)	Dutch	Enlightenment
John Locke (1632–1704)	English	Enlightenment
Philipp Jakob Spener (1635–1705)	German	Awakening
Isaac Newton (1643–1727)	English	
Jeanne-Marie Guyon (1648–1717)	French	Awakening
Fénelon (1651–1715)	French	Awakening
Matthew Tindal (1655–1733)	English	Enlightenment

Key figures in the Enlightenment and Awakenings		
John Toland (1670–1722)	English	Enlightenment
Hermann Samuel Reimarus (1694–1768)	German	Enlightenment
Christian Wolff (1697–1754)	German	Enlightenment
Count Nicholas von Zinzendorf (1700–1760)	German	Awakening
John Wesley (1703–91)	English	Awakening
Charles Wesley (1707–88)	English	Awakening
David Hume (1711–76)	English	Enlightenment
Jean-Jacques Rousseau (1712–78)	French	
Denis Diderot (1713–84)	French	Enlightenment
George Whitefield (1714–70)	English	Awakening
Johann David Michaelis (1717–91)	German	Enlightenment
d'Holbach (1723–89)	French	Enlightenment
Johann Salomo Semler (1725–91)	German	Enlightenment
Gotthold Ephraim Lessing (1729–81)	German	Enlightenment

3.2 The Enlightenment and Its Contexts

We will begin with some preliminary observations. The Enlightenment marked the emergence of a new cultural synthesis after the collapse of the Classical Synthesis of the Middle Ages. There was a new, positive and particularly modern (as opposed to pre-modern) position that began coming forth. A significant breakthrough was in so-called **critical consciousness**. Along this critical posture, the philosophical discipline of **epistemology**—reflection upon knowledge—would become the key philosophical science.

It is also worth noting that until the late eighteenth century, the Enlightenment was primarily a movement that was happening among the cultural elites—among intellectuals such as philosophers and scientists. When one looks at specific years like 1776 or 1789, the Enlightenment ideas became the rallying cries for popular cultural events and revolutions. In the nineteenth century, the ideas of the Enlightenment were so widespread that there could have been a culture-wide dissonance in western Europe and America.

3.2.1 Enlightenments

The Enlightenment was largely English in origin. The English Enlightenment was a more gradual and intellectual movement focused on science and epistemology and led by men like John Locke and Isaac Newton. Deism originates in England as a more rational understanding of religion.

The French Enlightenment was much more influential, radical and controversial than that in England. This Enlightenment functioned in more of a critical and iconoclastic mode with regard to traditional authority. With Napoleon, the French Enlightenment went on the road all over Europe, and remade things in the light of ideas represented by the Enlightenment. The representatives of the French Enlightenment are called the *philosophes*—a generally cranky class of thinkers and scholars, associated with the intellectual salons in Paris, and who are characterized by their bitter opposition especially to religious authority. The central achievement of the French Enlightenment was a work entitled the *Encyclopédie*. Edited and coordinated by Denis Diderot, it is a collection of definitive articles on the most important issues of the time, from science to religion.

The German Enlightenment came later on, but in many ways it was the most developed and mature version of all the European Enlightenments, and ended up being the leading movement by the time we get to the nineteenth century. It became so, to no small degree, because the last main figure of the German Enlightenment is Immanuel Kant, and he ends up dominating the intellectual landscape of Europe. Some early German Enlightenment figures are people like Leibniz and Christian Wolff in the later seventeenth and early eighteenth centuries. Both of these men were not just rationalist philosophers, but also Christians (this is unlike the French Enlightenment which was largely anti-Christian) and would argue for a rationalized, respectable Christianity. They might still have believed in revelation, but they would reject lots of other doctrines—original sin, predestination, certain theories of atonement, Hell and other issues that were offensive to a reasonable mindset. Deism spread from England into Germany, and became very popular. German Deism, however, was more hostile to Christianity. There was an easier transition between the German Enlightenment and Romanticism (via Kant and German Idealism), and what was to become the main line of respectable thought in Europe. Thus, while the Germans came later to the Enlightenment, they came strong. We will discuss many of the details of these Enlightenments below.

3.2.2 The Wake of Confessional Anarchy

By marking the beginning of this period with 1648, the Peace of Westphalia, we start the Enlightenment and the Awakenings in the aftermath of the Reformation. This followed a period of considerable violence, but also one of serious decline in religious life among the common people in Europe. The previous period was seen as one of seemingly interminable controversy, such that Christianity was seen as failing to provide a common ground for a liveable peace. It could not enable a moral consensus. The different ways of understanding the Christian faith kept Christians from recognizing other Christian groups as having a right to exist. On a popular level, this led to an enormous amount of confusion. What began to arise in this period theologically was the development of **Protestant Scholasticism**, within Calvinism and Lutheranism particularly. This was where the Lutheran revolution and the Calvinist revolution became more formalized and rationalized intellectual systems. With this formal definition of doctrines, there was also a crystallization of division. The classical Christian doctrines were defined in such a way as to exclude the other groups' understanding of justification, or the work of Christ, the Eucharist and so on.

Ultimately, the various wars more or less associated with confessional strife came to an end. This, however, was not because of the churches, but rather the secular state. In this period, we see secular states and rulers becoming increasingly powerful. The beginning of this period was what is called **Absolutism** in politics—where the monarchy was more powerful than it had been in any period of Europe going back to ancient times. In the seventeenth century, we see an increasingly powerful state dealing with the mess of religion and its seemingly attendant disorder and violence.

In the Enlightenment, we witness a move towards what Charles Taylor calls the **Modern Moral Order** as a positive social ideal, as a way of thinking about the best way of ordering society. This was, more particularly, an **order of mutual benefit**. The highest goal in life should be human flourishing, and society should be structured such that we should benefit from one another. But this is set over and against an impulse to pursue an ideal beyond a generalized order of mutual benefit that would endanger this order. This was seen as 'enthusiasm' or 'fanaticism'. Now people who were striving to be the higher and better Christians were the ones you had to worry about because it was apparent that there was no common language between the religious groups. Instead, we needed to focus on a secular order, where everyone could get along, and from which everyone benefitted.

The Western conscience in this period had been scandalized by the warring Christian confessions. The fact that there were now 'churches' and not the Church provided a way for rejecting religious common ground. The impetus at this point was simply to end religious strife on the basis of division. There was a strong emphasis on tolerance such as we will find with the Deists. It was not that there was a general wish to do away with religion as such—this was still a very religious period, even during the Enlightenments—but there was a new understanding of religion so that what was necessary in religion was something that was available to everybody. It became important that genuine religiousness was not just something that any one special group had. The religious ideals were not Lutheran, Reformed or Catholic, but were somehow universal—that is, available to everybody.

Because the heirs of the Reformation failed to reach a meaningful unanimity in that the project of founding a way of life on Scripture and conscience alone led to generations of conflict and warfare, the Enlightenment would turn towards **reason** alone as a basis for society. Religious communities obviously could not get along on their own terms, so we needed to find a way for them to get along—and reason was going to determine that. Reason should govern the relations between religious communities. However, as it turns out, 'reason' was not going to do all that great a job either, but that story will have to wait until later in this book.

3.3 Enlightenment Thought

3.3.1 Descartes

René Descartes (1596–1650), the father of modern philosophy, was a soldier in the Thirty Years War. Note that he died just after the Peace of Westphalia; he lived his entire adult life in the midst of the wars of religion. Descartes comes at the beginning and represents many of the seminal ideas of the Enlightenment. One might argue that the Enlightenment was being kindled in Descartes' mind in the middle of the wars of religion.

Descartes provided a new synthesis, a new understanding of the self, the world and God; but this synthesis was grounded in the self rather than in God. In this characteristically 'modern' synthesis, the self becomes the new foundation. Descartes was significantly influenced by **Nominalism**, in which you have a strong dualism between thought and things that made their way into Descartes' ideas. What is ultimately real for the nominalists are individual things 'out there'. Ideas do not have the kind of reality that such things do. Our naming of things is of a different order than the reality that we are naming. This was the origin for Descartes' division between the realm of thought (*res cogitans*) and the realm of things (*res extensa*).

Scepticism—as represented by people like Montaigne (and also rooted in Nominalist thought)—was also in the background. Descartes was dealing with a problem with Nominalist theology. He was drawing very distinctly the conclusion that if you have the totally unpredictable voluntarist God of Nominalist theology, then you cannot have knowledge of the world in any meaningful sense (because there is no reason to think that such a deity is not deceiving you). One of his innovations was the modification of the definition of God. For Descartes, the primary attribute for God was not power, but rather perfection. Because God is perfect, He is not going to deceive us. Descartes needed a perfect God for knowledge to work. He, then, went about redefining all of the different attributes of God in terms of perfection, and this was key to his response to Scepticism.

Figure 3.1 Descartes.

Courtesy of the Library of Congress. (No known restrictions on publication.)

The world for Descartes was a mechanism governed by efficient causality. He took some of the ideas that were incipient in Nominalist thought (such as the univocity of being) and made them determine the whole grammar of modern science. With the Classical Synthesis, ultimately, everything was suspended and grounded in God—as that which is beyond the world. But for Descartes, the foundation for knowledge would be humanity. You start with thought, and from there you have an inborn idea of God as a perfect being, and you believe in God because of certain things going on in your own thought world. The existence of God as a perfect being is then a basis for believing in nature as a reliably understandable and knowable system of efficient causality. So, Descartes reconnected all of these things, but with a new foundation in the self.

He viewed nature as a mechanism. There were two kinds of things in the universe—thinking things (souls) and machines (made of physical matter). For Descartes, animals were machines; for example, a cat is basically a very complicated, if insouciant, rock. Humans were complicated machines, connected (somehow) to a soul. What then was God's relation to this giant mechanism of the world? God underwrote the stability of the machine—He is the master architect that makes everything work in the most regular of ways. This is a perfect machine, and God is the great clockmaker who made the universe in a manner that is so regular that we can produce certain science (say of feline biology) on the basis of it.

3.3.2 Autonomy

The Enlightenment stream of modernity that we are talking about here came out of a crisis of authority, and of an attempt to find a new source of authority apart from previous external authorities. Emancipation from external authorities would become a strong theme in the Enlightenment. This became amplified in some strains of the Enlightenment into what William Desmond describes as an **antinomy between autonomy and transcendence** such that if one is going to be free there cannot be anything above one. If you absolutize one, it relativizes the other. In modernity, transcendence may survive but as a relativized transcendence—one that serves the overriding purpose of human autonomy. When Kant began looking back at the age of the Enlightenment, he would see freedom and autonomy as the dominant ideas of the age. For Kant, the motto of the Enlightenment was *sapere aude!*—dare to think for yourself.

As opposed to the anarchy of too many authorities that were claiming mutually exclusive positions, the *Aufklärers* wanted to have freedom and reason. Freedom and reason (and not external authorities and tradition) were the road to better order—to the Modern Moral Order of mutual benefit. Part of what made this understanding of autonomy possible was that in the Enlightenment there was a changed understanding of the self. Charles Taylor describes this understanding of the self as **a buffered self**. The self was buffered as opposed to porous. As humanity became disconnected from the classical synthesis, the self was not as affected by things outside of it as it once was; it was somehow safe from fear of foreign powers whether they be supernatural agents, things of the world or the divine. There was a greater sense that one was in control of one's life. There was a space between you and other things so that your life was not being constantly affected by other things. There was more of a space for you to have control over yourself. With this, there was less of a sense of being vulnerable and more of a sense that you had power over your own life.

Yet, it is this kind of 'buffer' that would begin to open up certain problems when it came to epistemology—namely a disconnection between the inner and outer. The inner world as the world of freedom where you could think for yourself (the *res cogitans*) was now set against the outer world as the world of external influences (the *res extensa*). The buffer that allowed a new degree of independence would in turn serve to make our relation to the world questionable. How could this disconnected immaterial spirit have any interaction with something that is material?

There were echoes of **voluntarism** in this primary emphasis on freedom. The focus was not the content of the self but that the self was free, self-ruling. The **autonomous** self was a law (*nomos*) unto itself (*auto*). The modern self was centred around this primacy of will—a person could choose and have the power to do this and not that. Increasingly, the self would be seen as the only domain of meaning and purpose in the world. In fact, in Descartes when he talked about the image of God, what the image of God was for Descartes was the freedom of the will. Even though he was seeing the problems with having a voluntarist conception of God, his understanding of humanity was after the model of the voluntarist God. It was a holdover from the earlier version. It was an image of a primarily free being.

Finally, in modernity the self was more and more active. The self was taking the position of **mastery**, usually over and against nature. If there was value in nature it was what we made of it. Nature was valuable because of what we could do for it. This is often the 'natural' way for us to think about nature today. How is nature valuable? Well, what can you do with it that can make you money or that is useful for you? It may strike us as odd to think about value apart from its instrumental value (its usefulness for us). There was then arising in this period an **opposition between the mind and nature**—between the active free actor that was this immaterial mind and the inactive inert mechanism that was nature. The mind as the locus of meaning acts upon nature and transforms its neutral thereness into something meaningful. There is then an opposition between the meaning-giving mental subject and the physical object. This goes back to what was mentioned before as the objectification of being and the subjectification of value. This was becoming amplified and expressly put into place in the Enlightenment. As pre-modern arguments explicate assumed connections between the world and God and the human mind, the modern arguments sought but failed to reconnect things. There was in fact a more thorough redefining of the world and of God on the basis of this dualistic opposition. And it is from this basis that we can talk about the rise of modern science, or natural science.

3.3.3 Reason and Natural Science

The model for reason in the Enlightenment was that provided by **empirical science**. This kind of knowledge was something one could attain with one's own reason alone, at least in principle. One need not be dependent upon any external authority. This new empiricism, a new understanding of what knowledge is, is rightly described as an **ascetic** regime. There was a restricting to a very thin slice of what counts as knowledge. Things that used to be a part of the picture—like final and formal causes—got cut out of the picture of what something really was or how it fit in terms of purpose in a broader scheme of things. These are hard to examine empirically. How do you investigate what something really is—its true identity, or real purpose, in the broader scheme of things? How do you mathematically investigate those things? They do not fit within the model of a giant mechanism, and so these ways of talking fall by the wayside. Formal and final causes are two of Aristotle's four causes—the other two being efficient and material causes. With modern science all that is left are the efficient and material causes. There are things that are moved by other things. Within the great mechanism, the moving of one part by another is the efficient causality. All there is are moving parts. The moving is the efficient part; the parts are the material part.

Central to the scientific perspective was the view that all of this could be investigated and described mathematically. The quantifiable and increasingly quantified machine becomes the primary picture of nature. The words 'reasonable' and 'natural' come to mean the same thing. The natural world is a purely, mathematically, reasonably, functioning mechanism. Where things get distorted is where the ambiguities of human culture get involved. Interestingly, as you have more and more of a focus on the autonomous rational human, the rational ideal is increasingly placed in the inhuman.

This perspective comports with a **disengaged stance** reminiscent of the buffered self. There is a revival of Stoicism (described as neo-Stoicism) in this period such that the best stance that we should have towards reality is a disengaged one. You should control your passions or your interests. The way to truth is to be free—free from attachments or partiality to any part of the world. We disengage from the world and see it as a likewise passionless, spiritless mechanism of material bits moving other material bits as governed by mathematically precise and exceptionless laws.

In the Renaissance—in the Humanist picture of things—the main model for the way the world is and the way we relate to the world and perhaps God relates to the world was that of the artist. The world is a work of art, and our work is a work of creativity after the Great Artist. That metaphor changed in the Scientific Revolution to that of the Engineer—the One who knows how to build. You truly understand something when you can take it apart and put it back together again—not necessarily physically, but, at least, mentally. You can reconstruct, and thus explain why things do what they do mathematically. It is not coincidental that Descartes was the pioneer of coordinate geometry—which is a way to say that space can be described with math. We can describe anything spatial with numbers.

Nature is, in this perspective, basically inert or static matter plus efficient causality. The most basic stuff in the universe are material bits that are then all moving and moving in relation to each other. Physics, with Newton, is the result of this homogenization of the universe. There are universal mathematical laws that describe masses in motion. But, as a corollary to this understanding of nature, many thinkers would struggle with **determinism**. If the universe is a grand mechanism governed by exceptionless laws, then things cannot be other than as they are. Just as if you know the mass and velocity and direction of a moving object you can then extend in your mind out into the future and know in five minutes exactly where this object is going to be, so you can do that with everything in the universe if you knew enough.

If this is the case, are we just mechanisms? Is it because the universe started in a certain way and all of these material bits started moving out that I am necessarily where I am right now typing the things I am and this situation could not be otherwise? Human freedom does not fit in this picture. There would come to be a real tension that we shall see, and it would come to a head and find a certain kind of resolution in Kant.

3.3.4 Progress and Optimism

There were, however, minority positions when it came to this understanding of nature. There were some people who thought a mechanism was not the best way of looking at the whole of nature—perhaps nature should be better understood in terms of living force or organic life. Ultimately, there is nothing organic in a mechanistic picture; there is no distinction between something that is alive and something that is dead. Living things are just very complicated mechanisms. Some thinkers saw this view as a distortion. Spinoza is going to be a good example of this—in seeing the whole of nature as having a kind of directedness to it.

Even for those figures who still held to a mechanistic world picture, there was a strong sense in this era of progress and optimism—that human history is going somewhere. The Enlightenment was very forward-looking. Followers saw reason and science as the road forward that could lead us towards liberation and make things fundamentally better. There was a kind of substitute eschatology in the Enlightenment, what was seen as a dawning of a new age of light ('the Enlightenment'), a coming out of the previous 'dark' ages. Now, we are coming out of ignorance and a subservience to external authorities, and are awakened to our true human possibilities.

3.4 Enlightenment Religion

3.4.1 Dangerous Religion

What then is the place for religion in the Enlightenment? First off, to speak negatively, in the Enlightenment there were certain ideas as to what was to be considered 'dangerous religion', and so to be avoided. Most religious *Aufklärers* used these markers to distinguish their rational religion from the lesser religion of previous generations. First, many people wanted their religion to steer clear of the **superstitious**. Most of us do not want to believe in everything being operated upon and influenced by fairies, spirits and demons, and stuff like that. For some, this meant that they did not want any kind of belief in the supernatural, or any kind of enchanted sense of the world or any kind of rituals where people thought something invisible was going on—like in Catholicism. Not all Enlightenment thinkers rejected the supernatural, but this is a point of contention. Many argued over what the supernatural meant, and whether we needed it in order to be good Christian people. For example, there would be issues arising from the idea of miracles. What are they? Can you explain them scientifically? We especially see questions of miracles become significant when the authority of revelation became a problem. Miracles became a site for people either to prove revelation was a fact or to show the opposite.

The second kind of dangerous religions for the *Aufklärers* was **confessionalism**—sometimes called 'fanaticism'. This had to do with religious people who were overly certain that their particular brand of Christianity was the right one, and that any others were wrong. This went beyond the order of mutual benefit, and these people were often dangerous. The prime exhibit here is the confessional anarchy of recent memory. Acceptable versions of religion are to be tolerated—at least other versions of Christianity.

The third kind of dangerous religion was that characterized by **enthusiasm**—by which Enlightenment people meant overly emotional or overly subjective. Such religion was not in

Dangerous religion
Superstition
Confessionalism
Enthusiasm

line with the disengaged and Stoic tonality of the Enlightenment mind. When people get overly emotionally worked up and start saying that they are hearing God's voice, they need to take a few breaths, settle down and be rational.

Generally, what was desired was a religion that was **domesticated**. Proponents of the Enlightenment did not necessarily want to get rid of religion, but rather they tried to find a way to live with it. One of the ways that this happened was through **scholarship**, which became a way to overcome confessional divisions. One such story (as recounted by Michael Legaspi) has to do with the founding of the University of Göttingen, in 1737. This was established by the state with an eye towards avoiding the kind of religious conflicts of earlier ages. The state saw it as being in society's best interest to have a version of religion that would not lead to confessional conflict. A key scholar at Göttingen was **Johann David Michaelis** (1717–91), who ended up being of great importance

Figure 3.2 Michaelis.

'Voit 027 Johann David Michaelis' by Carl Arnold Friedrich Lafontaine. Voit Collection. Licensed under Public Domain via Wikimedia Commons.

to biblical studies. Also, in the early nineteenth century, the University of Berlin opened, an event considered by many people to be the beginning of the era of the modern research university. Berlin would become one of the model universities of Germany, and for the rest of the Western world. In these modern universities, theology was a discipline which lived in a particular department—quarantined, so to speak. In the modern university, the faculties of knowledge itself were divided up in these separable pockets—and theology was one among many of those. Other disciplines such as physics or biology could effectively ignore theology and operate independent of it.

3.4.2 Rational Religion

During the Enlightenment, the preferred option was rational religion. This is sometimes called 'rationalism'—not in the philosophical sense, but with regard to how religion is reasonable. Rational religion originated, for the most part, in England, in the eighteenth century, in the face of past controversies. It wanted to discuss how Christianity was something that was attractive to reasonable people.

Here are some attributes of rational religion:

Rational religion was **anti-dogmatic**. It wanted to steer clear from the kind of disputes and controversies that caused the religious wars. It was not going to get caught up in exactly what is going on in the Lord's Supper or in Baptism, because those fine points of dogma were what caused division.

Following closely upon this was a posture of **tolerance**, which advocated a religious perspective from where people who came from different traditions were able to live with each other. While they may have expected more homogeneity in other domains of culture, religion was increasingly exempted.

This type of rational religion is often described in terms of **natural theology**. The most important knowledge that we have of God comes from nature, from what we can know from reason. We shall see in this period the design argument becomes especially significant—the argument for the existence of God based on the intricate design of the world. If you look at the order of nature—this mechanism of efficient causality—it looks like a great, intricate clockwork. The order of the clock points to a clockmaker. Our best and most rational understanding of God is that starting with science—the orderly nature of the world. This was really the backbone for theological rationalism.

There was also a strong **moralism** in that the religious life was seen as having primarily to do with morality. Moral duties were seen as divine commands. One of the main functions that God serves in rational religion then is to provide divine sanction for morality. Thus, if you did not have a God then people (especially the non-elites) would not behave as well. The masses may not have a reason to be good without God.

Religion, then, for them also had the virtue of being **simple**. The *Aufklärers* did not want a whole complex tangle of different doctrines and practices because there were things about which people disagree. They would rather strip religion down to the essentials. In order to bring this about they wanted to keep the Churches or the clergy from playing too large a role. Religion was primarily something you could do on your own. You could try and live a moral life, and that was what was pleasing to God.

The rational religion of the Enlightenment was characterized by a certain **optimism**, inasmuch as it emphasized the inherent goodness of humanity. The moral laws that we have are not something we necessarily need special revelation or the Bible to know. As the order of the universe is given, so the moral laws are evident—written on the human heart. We know right from wrong inherently. Immanuel Kant famously wrote in his *Critique of Practical Reason*: 'Two things fill the mind with ever-increasing wonder and awe, the more often and the more intensely the mind of thought is drawn to them: the starry heavens above me and the moral law within me.' These were the two starting points for a natural theology—both the natural law evident in the 'starry heavens above' and the moral law within required a law-giver. The apparently inherent clarity of humanity's moral compass on this telling was on the far side of any kind of depraved human state due to sin.

Finally, rational religion made a distinction between natural religion and what is called 'positive' religion. This term is not meant in the sense of positive vs. negative, but rather particular vs. universal. Positive religion was the particular way something has come to be through the vagaries and contingencies of history. Rational religion wanted to see the **universal** core or kernel that was ultimately identical beneath the positive particularities of particular religious expressions. What was important was what was general and common beneath the particular and plural.

Rational religion

Anti-dogmatic

Tolerant

Knowable from nature

Moralistic

Simple

Optimistic

Universal

Looking at this rational or 'natural' religion in relation to the Christian faith, we can see different stages of development. The **first** stage—represented by **John Locke**—was that Christianity was seen in harmony with natural religion. We have the things we talked about in rational religion plus revelation. Christianity was a revelation that was beyond and in harmony with what we could know naturally. There was a place for revelation and the various distinctively Christian doctrines— but it was definitely not against what we could know from just using our reason and looking within ourselves and out into the world. Christianity was like a harmonious addition to natural religion.

Second was the development of seeing Christianity as an instance of natural religion. Rational religion was the essence of Christianity. The things that were particularly Christian—the positive elements of Christianity that had to do with Jesus and the Holy Spirit and Salvation—were more secondary. When you understood Christianity, it was really talking about moral living and believing in God. This perspective was something found in some of the more prominent **English Deists**. The core of Christianity—or any particular positive religion—was this essential natural religion. Initially, people like John Locke saw Christianity as something that was more than natural religion—as being supplemented in revelation. One, however, did not *need* special revelation to be a Deist. If there was revelation, it just helped one emphasize the things that they could know already without it.

Third, and finally, were the more **radical Deists** who were not just saying that revelation was something that you *could* do without, but rather it was something that you *should* do without. While the first stage required that you have revelation, and the second stage allowed you to go without revelation, the third stage avoided this revelation stuff entirely. The primary focus was on 'rational religion', and they were positively suspicious of positive (or particular) religion. A religion that saw itself as more than this stripped-down natural religion distracted people and kept them from a religion that was properly tolerant, simple, universal and so on.

3.4.2.1 Locke

Regarding different key representatives and contributors to Enlightenment rational religion, in general, the first to consider is **John Locke** (1632–1704). Raised a strict Calvinist, Locke came out of a confessionalist Reformation Protestant background. For close to a century, he was the most influential intellectual in Europe. When we talk about the Enlightenment getting started in England, we are talking about John Locke. Part of this is certainly due to the conjunction between his thought and that of his friend **Isaac Newton** (1643–1727). For many, Newton and Locke were closely associated: Newton *was* science, and Locke *was* the philosophy that was consonant with, and made sense of, this kind of science. If the natural world worked in the way Newton said, then human knowledge worked in the way that Locke said. Locke's *Essay Concerning Human Understanding* (1690), his main philosophical work, came out two years after Newton's *Principia*. In between, Newton and Locke became close friends.

Along with his general philosophical ideas, Locke also had certain understandings, opinions and thoughts about Christianity and these ideas were spread about widely as well. He believed that you could not bring about what Taylor called the Modern World Order—a social situation of moral (and, for Locke, religious) unity—by appealing to Scripture alone. He realized as a post-

Figure 3.3 Locke.

'John Locke' by Sir Godfrey Kneller: State Hermitage Museum, St. Petersburg, Russia. Licensed under Public Domain via Wikimedia Commons.

Reformation Christian that this had not worked. If there was going to be unity in a Christian society, you had to start not only from Scripture, but also from reason. He made a distinction between **faith** and **knowledge**. Faith had to do with revelation, while knowledge had to do with what we could know through reason and our senses. Faith then was not against reason or knowledge. Rather, knowledge allowed us to determine what should count as revelation. If there were difficulties that came from thinking about faith, reason was the court of appeals to help us resolve the difficulties of faith. He wrote about this in *The Reasonableness of Christianity* (1695). Ultimately, he would state that there was no serious contradiction between revelation and reason.

John Locke asserted that revelation was something we could know through reason. They were not in opposition. In fact, revelation needed to be verified. We can reasonably judge whether something is revelation or not. His two primary criteria that functioned as rational indications of revelation were **miracles** and **fulfilled prophecy**. This became a common theme for apologetics (efforts of rationally defending Christianity) in this era. However, he wanted to strip Christianity down to its more basic elements. Christianity for him was reduced to (1) the belief that Jesus is the Messiah—which was something you could know through fulfilled prophecies and miracles—and (2) the need to repent and live a righteous life. He gave a pretty standard 'rational religion' picture of the divine sanction for morality. So, there was still a place for revelation here with Jesus being the Messiah and for the supernatural with fulfilled prophecy and miracles. (See the first stage above in 3.4.2.) But he de-emphasized or rejected outright other aspects of Christianity, such as the idea of eternal punishment for the unsaved. Such an idea of eternal punishment, at least for Locke and many other Enlightenment thinkers, did not rationally make sense and left one with an unjust God. If one of God's functions was to underwrite morality, it did not work with an immoral God who did things like make finite beings who made finite decisions suffer infinite punishment for finite mistakes.

Key works for Enlightenment 'rational religion'

Spinoza's *Tractatus Theologico–Politicus* (1670)

Spinoza's *Ethics* (1677)

Locke's *An Essay Concerning Human Understanding* (1690)

Locke's *The Reasonableness of Christianity* (1695)

Lessing's *Nathan the Wise* (1779)

Lessing's *The Education of the Human Race* (1780)

3.4.2.2 Spinoza

The next figure to treat (all-too-briefly) here is **Baruch (or Benedict) Spinoza** (1632–77). A fascinating person, Spinoza has come to be what later people want him to be: whether that be a hero or villain. He has come to be described as the 'arch-atheist', so much so that when people talk about atheists, they sometimes call them 'Spinozists'. He is also described as supremely religious. The Romantic writer Novalis called him '*ein Gottrunkener Mensch*'—a 'God-drunk man'. Thus, he is so religious that he is drunk on God.

To many, Spinoza was the poster child for the critical edge of the Enlightenment. During the Enlightenment, Spinoza's influence was more of an undercurrent until the *Pantheismusstreit* controversy in the early nineteenth century (see Chapter 5). A descendent of Spanish Jews who migrated to the Netherlands, he initially identified himself as a Cartesian—working out the details of Descartes' philosophy. Eventually, he was excommunicated (in strong terms) from the Synagogue because of his perceived evident departure from the Jewish faith.

In *Ethics* (1677)—published posthumously—Spinoza presented a view of metaphysics that was focused on **substance** as that which exists of itself. He understood that if there was going to be such a substance that there could only be one of them, and that one substance was God. This sounded like **pantheism** (where God is identical with the universe) to many, and perhaps it was. The best view of God as he presented it in the *Ethics* was from a philosophical view. Such a view is that this one substance is an impersonal God. He would use the phrase *Deus sive Natura*—God or nature. He viewed thought and extension (things in space) as two different attributes of this same substance, and embraced a deterministic view such that there was no contingency in the universe. His view is described by many as an 'immanent pantheism'.

Perhaps the more interesting work—from a theological perspective—is an earlier one, published anonymously, while he was still alive called the *Tractatus Theologico-Politicus* (1670)—or the 'Theological Political Essay'. In this, he was reflecting on different religions. He was a Jew writing in the Netherlands, which was primarily Reformed. The reason that this tract was published anonymously and that *Ethics* was published posthumously was that he was writing in a place where the Reformed perspective was the legally correct perspective. In the *Tractatus Theologico-Politicus*, he talks about trying to find a proper way of thinking about the positive religions. He was thinking about how the truth of Scripture was not about the truth of the stories within, but

Figure 3.4 Spinoza.

'Baruch de Spinoza cover portrait' by Historical and Public Figures Archives—New York Public Library Archives. Licensed under Public Domain via Wikimedia Commons.

rather was intended to convey timeless truths. The point was not the truth of the story, but the moral truth that was displayed in the story. The main point was ethical. Ultimately, the main point of Scripture was that you should love God and love your neighbour. You should have a universal love for humanity and for God. Interestingly as an ex-Jew, he saw God as most clearly revealed through Christ. Christ had the purest insight into what the true religion was. True revelation then never contradicts reason, though he asserted that what should be sifted out of the Bible were the superstitious and miraculous elements.

Spinoza has come to be recognized as an early forerunner of later significant modern movements—someone ahead of his time. His *Tractatus* was one of the first books in modern biblical criticism (which we will address further below in Section 3.5), a half-century before that discipline really got going. In the nineteenth century, the Romantics fall back in love with Spinoza. They do not necessarily fall in love with the positions that I have outlined above, since they have their own picture of him kind of as a romantic hero or a genius. He was someone who suffered for his genius.

3.4.2.3 Lessing

Gotthold Ephraim Lessing (1729–81) was one of the great figures of the German Enlightenment. He did most of his work in the later part of the eighteenth century; he was also very influential in Romanticism. Lessing wrote a play entitled *Nathan the Wise* (1779), a fable of three rings. A father has three sons, and a ring that has the power to make the possessor beloved of God and humanity. But the father loves all three of his sons alike, so he makes two perfect imitations of this ring. When the father dies, the three rings are given to his sons and are indistinguishable from each other—just like true religion. True religions all look the same. The point of this play was that people of different religions should be tolerant of each other because ultimately you could not know which religion was true.

To be a bit more specific, we should be tolerant of each other for two reasons. First, God loves everyone alike. God is the father that loves all of His children alike—Jew, Muslim or Christian (Reformed, Lutheran or Catholic). Second, ultimately the truth of religion can only be known by its fruits. If you are concerned about true religions, the truest religion is the one that is the most virtuous. So, strive to outdo one another in being virtuous in your religion.

The other significant contribution that Lessing made when it came to thinking about religion was in his short treatise called *The Education of the Human Race* (1780). This was a work in which he was crossing from the Enlightenment into the Romantic period. In this work, Lessing considers religion as God's project to educate the human race over the course of history. Helping the human race move to a better state was progressive, happening over time (like education). In this work, Lessing had a place for the positive religions as always helping progress towards a more mature understanding of God and religion—so there was a development from a less developed and less mature to a more developed and more mature understanding of God and religion. Historical revelation for him was indispensable, but he still believed in a natural religion—ultimately, the religion we are heading towards is this rational religion. But the positive religions help push us in this direction. He would even see this in the Christian Scriptures—that you had a progression from a morality that was based on immediate rewards and punishments, and then a religion based on future rewards and punishments. He thought that was moving towards a trajectory towards a true morality or religion, which was something based on duty. You did not do it because of rewards or punishments; you did it because it was the right thing to do. This was what an adult did. His religion then was basically Deist in content, but he had a place for the historical religions.

3.4.2.4 Wolff

Christian Wolff (1697–1754) was a significant figure in the German Enlightenment. Very briefly: a professor at Halle, which was initially a Pietist university, his primary contribution was his advocacy of the work of the Enlightenment in Germany. Wolff was not a terribly original thinker by many accounts, but he was the first German philosopher to really found a school of thought— German Rationalism. Kant is going to cut his teeth in the midst of this Wolffian rationalism. When it came to rational religion, Wolff saw revelation as something that could go along with natural reason, so he believed that the Trinity and Incarnation were things that were not against reason but that were above reason. Like Locke, Wolff emphasized that reason functions to allow us to decide what counts as revelation.

3.5 Biblical Criticism

One of the significant developments in relation to modern theology that happened in the Enlightenment era was the development of biblical criticism. With the previous era—with the early Humanists and Reformers—there was a focus on a literal meaning of Scripture over and against a multi-layered sense of the different meanings of Scripture that you found in the Early Church or the Middle Ages. There was then much more of a focus on a literal level of meaning or an explicit single meaning in the text and figuring out what that was. This was usually described as seeking out what the authors meant or the authorial intent. Now, to be able properly to figure out what the authors meant you had to start asking and answering questions like, 'Who were the authors? When was this written? What kind of text is this? What was the situation in which it was written?' This involved locating the text historically.

The upshot was that by the eighteenth century, historical–critical examinations of the biblical text were fully underway—although it would develop quite a bit more in the nineteenth century. And with these historical examinations many things were called into question. With the dominance of a new scientific world picture, many scholars looking at the Bible would think that it—if it purports to be about the real world and things that actually happened—looks like a huge pile of exceptions to everything we were coming to know about the physical world and human history.

3.5.1 Spinoza

Let us look at some particular figures in the way they addressed some of these issues. To begin we return to Spinoza. In his *Tractatus Theologico–Politicus* (1670), one of the ways Spinoza approached the question of how to find a way to positively appropriate the Bible was that he made a distinction between the meaning of the text and its historical reliability. You could get to and appropriate the true meaning of the text without believing that it was necessarily providing accurate history. Like some of the people in the Reformation, he was focused on the intention of the author—what the author really had in mind. He thought that what the author really had in mind was not as much to convey certain narratives as historically accurate as to convey timeless, universal truths.

When Spinoza considered the trajectory of the Hebrew religion in the Jewish scriptures (or the Christian Old Testament), he saw that they were not merely meant to present religious institutions and miracles, but the essence of it was a religion of universal truth. Again, he saw Jesus as the best communicator of this religion of universal truth. When it came to the biblical accounts, he was looking for universal truths. In order to get to these, you had to weigh the text to see what was plausible and what was not believable. He ended up rejecting a lot of the historical accounts in the Old Testament because they were just not believable from a scientific standpoint. He published the *Tractatus* anonymously, and it ended up being quite scandalous. It raised a lot of people's hackles, because it was one of the first books to very seriously question the historical truth of the accounts of Scripture. However, it foreshadowed some of the ways of reading Scripture that would come to be dominant in the eighteenth century—we will talk about that in terms of the 'Academic Bible'.

3.5.2 The Academic Bible

Part of what was going on with Spinoza was that, whereas the Bible of the Reformation was brought to serve the purposes and promote the agendas of different confessional communities, Spinoza's primary agenda was to use Scripture to promote peace and tolerance. He would approach Scripture in such a way that less confessional strife would result. The immediate upshot of the *Tractatus* however was not so much peace as a phalanx of angry Reformed Dutchmen.

Nevertheless, Spinoza foreshadowed what we will see in the eighteenth century as the birth of what Michael Legaspi called the 'Academic Bible'. In his book, *The Death of Scripture and the Rise of Biblical Studies*, he described the re-appropriation of Scripture into a new community for different purposes. In the eighteenth century, we see the birth of the Academic Bible, or the Enlightenment Bible, or the Cultural Bible. Biblical scholarship here was not simply scholarship for its own sake—merely trying to find the truth—but it served a particular cultural purpose, and those involved in this project thought they were doing the Bible a service. On the heels of the religious conflicts and wars, many people—at least among the elite—came to have a lower view of Scripture. This was because it had been used as a battleground. Biblical scholars were interested in revivifying the Bible, in making it meaningful again if in a different way.

By the middle of the eighteenth century, some scholars were observing that the Bible was no longer able to function as Scripture—something that had its own authority that could provide a basis for society. The Academic Bible, then, was a new role for Scripture to play in society. While many Deists might have said you did not need the Bible at all, and that you should just stick to natural religion, these early biblical scholars wanted to have a positive appropriation of the Bible. This largely happened in the universities. Part of what they were doing was that they were capitalizing on the Bible's residual authority—that the Bible was seen as having an authority, even though in the forefront of people's minds there were problems with it. The project was to find a truly universal or 'catholic' Bible—not in the Roman Catholic sense, but rather a Bible that everyone could agree upon and approach. They were looking for a Bible that could foster unity as opposed to the way Scripture had been used before which had brought about division.

How then did you bring about a maximally inclusive take on Scripture? The answer for the *Aufklärers* was, of course, reason. Reason was the maximally inclusive tool, the new *organum* through which people of goodwill could come to a common agreement. Part of what was going on here behind the rise of a particular kind of biblical criticism was the intent to foster peace through the universities—the universities were founded by the governments and set up in such a way as to help encourage a more peaceful state. The universities also often were training clergy. They were trying to present a way that the Bible could function as a unifying ground in the midst of a deconfessionalized state. The state did not wish to support any particular confession or a particular perspective on Scripture, but it still wanted to have Scripture play a key role. Modern biblical criticism was a part of a broader cultural project: to put at a distance the various confessional communities, but still preserve religion (preferably rational), and some form of Christianity.

The rise of critical biblical studies was not secularist in the sense that it was against religion—it supported a particular kind of religion that served a particular kind of cultural purpose. It was not purely objective; there was an agenda. The Bible was in service of a cultural project. In a sense, just as the Lutheran, Reformed, Anabaptists, Catholics, etc. previously used the Bible to further their particular position, so the Academic Bible was simply another version, and a kind of successor to what came before. It was just intended to address a broader community than these particular confessions. Instead of being the Bible for this community or that community, it was the Bible for the broader community that people could all agree on, using the most minimal rational standards.

Scripture so appropriated to function as a ground for unity simply became a book for another interpretive community. It was not a book without a community, but the new community was that of the university within the increasingly secular state. The Bible was then redeployed with an eye towards revivifying it—giving it a living place where it could have a foundational role in modern life. As will become apparent, even though such a redeployment had an apologetic drive to it (i.e. it was intending to do Christianity and the Bible a favour), many Christians would look upon this favour with suspicion.

3.5.3 Reimarus

The German scholar **Hermann Samuel Reimarus** (1694–1768) was one of the more prominent of the German Deists. He represented a more radical version of Deism that was opposed to revelation. He advocated a rational, natural religion in opposition to Christianity. His main book—if you can call an unpublished 4,000-page manuscript a 'book'—was entitled *An Apology for the Rational Worshippers of God*. While it was not published during his lifetime due to its radical nature, Lessing did publish fragments of it as what came to be known as 'The Wolffenbüttel Fragments'. (Lessing was at this time a librarian at Wolffenbüttel.)

In this massive manuscript, Reimarus presented a naturalistic critique of the Bible in the sense that he used what he knew about science and proceeded to reject as false the biblical accounts that

Figure 3.5 Reimarus.

'H. S. Reimarus' by Unknown; file: James Steakley—*Alles begann mit Ansgar. Hamburgs Kirchen im Spiegel der Zeit* (Hamburg: Pressestelle des Senats der Freien und Hansestadt Hamburg, 2006), p. 65. Licensed under Public Domain via Wikimedia Commons.

did not fit. For example, he calculated the number of Israelites in the account of the crossing of the Red Sea, how long it would have taken people to walk and how big the Red Sea was, and then concluded that it would have taken them nine days to cross it, even if they were walking as fast as they could—so there was no way that the account could have been true. Regarding what was historically true in the New Testament, Jesus for him was an apocalyptic visionary. While Reimarus was one of the first in the modern era to put Jesus in a distinctly Jewish frame, his picture of Jesus was a tragic one: that he thought the world was about to end, and was executed and so failed in his purposes. Thus, the historical Jesus was wrong when it came to the main point of his teaching and failed. Therefore, Christianity for Reimarus was a fraud. He thought that the apostles made up all of the material about a suffering Messiah, and they stole Jesus' body from the tomb.

While Reimarus' extreme views did not have much influence on the biblical criticism of the eighteenth century (because his work was not published until later), he did end up influencing nineteenth-century biblical criticism. In that period, we will see many scholars writing historical lives of Jesus. Many would look back to Reimarus as a pioneer in this area.

3.5.4 Semler

One last figure of note in eighteenth-century biblical studies is **Johann Salomo Semler (1725–91)**. A professor of theology at the (once Pietist) University of Halle, Semler was raised in a Pietist home—and, as sometimes happens, this made him hostile towards Pietism. He ended up being influenced by some of the English Deists. He is often considered the father of the critical study of Scripture. Semler was quite critical of Reimarus—he thought that his methods were irresponsible and his scholarship shoddy. In fact, Semler sees Reimarus as less a scholar, than an angry crank with an axe to grind.

Semler's influential approach was that we should approach Scripture with an eye towards differentiating between the permanent truths in Scripture, and the elements that were simply due to the times in which the biblical books were written. The permanent truths were the **kernel**, while the latter were the historically bound **husks**. When the New Testament is merely using the thought forms of its day, it yields only historically located truths that are not valid for us today. What is to be sought after is the kernel—the essence of Christianity that is true for all time.

The essence of Christianity for Semler was the moral teaching of Jesus. This beneficial, humanitarian ideal fits well with the 'good', rational religion of the Enlightenment. (Interestingly, Semler was the first figure to embrace the name *liberalis theologia*, or 'liberal theology'—though it came to mean several different things later on.) Biblical revelation in Semler's understanding was ultimately going to be reasonable and moral. Like Spinoza, but less radical, Semler saw the point of Scripture as a moral one, not necessarily to provide absolutely accurate historical accounts—especially when it came to supposedly supernatural events.

3.6 Deism

Deism was the dominant form of rational religion, the main new synthesis, among the elite in the eighteenth century. It entailed an 'enlightened' self-understanding that saw the Middle Ages as a violent, dark period, and that since that time there had been steady progress towards a more refined, civil and sociable society. Deism was a religion for such a refined, civil and sociable society, and would provide for public order without (much) appeal to ecclesiastical authority. There was a definite buffer between the church and polite society, and the latter could have perfectly decent religion without the former.

One of the things Deism did was to **excise the heroic** (a hero-ectomy, if you will). It wanted to narrow religion to a kind of religiosity that fit well with the idea of the buffered self or a disengaged Neo-Stoicism. Deists wanted a religion that fit with the normal moral order of life. In a way, they were continuing Protestant reform by levelling the expectations and aspirations of religion to a common level—but lowering that level even further from where it was during the Reformation.

Charles Taylor describes the dominant view in the Enlightenment as **Providential Deism**. This was the intermediate form or stage between pre-modern, naïve religions' faith, and exclusive humanism. Providential Deism held that the world was designed by God, that He had a purpose in the world (that the world was providentially ordered), and that the purpose of that world was human well-being. It was to support an order of mutual benefit. God had created the universe towards the end of humans enjoying an immanent good of mutual benefit. As advocates of natural religion, deists thought that you could understand these things about God by simply observing the world around you. Providential Deism also cohered with a strong focus on morality—God had created the world for our good, and gave us divine commands towards that end. The religious life, thus, had to do with following these commands. Many deists believed in immortality as well—punishments and rewards after death as a way of underwriting morality. Some deists believed in revelation; others did not. But even for those who did believe in revelation, it was not crucial for them.

Ethics would end up having a central place in religion for deists. In essence, the whole content of religion for deists was ethical or in orbit around ethics. God had designed the world so that a certain ethical order—an order of mutual benefit—would be obtained. All divine commands—what God wants from us—fit into a certain kind of ethical way of being, and life after death had to do with rewarding or punishing your ethical life. God was around at the beginning (in creation) or at the end (with the afterlife) to sanction morality.

Deists thought of theirs as a **purified** religion. As a religion based on reason alone, it did not have the need for superstition, revelation or priestcraft. But they also did away with what before was more personal relations to God. Petitionary prayer then—or prayer at all—did not have much of a place in Deism. What God wants in you is moral behaviour, not your talking to him. Again, the primary purpose of God in the world was the human order of mutual benefit—the world is ordered towards the good of human beings or human flourishing. The providential part of Providential Deism was reminiscent of Adam Smith's Invisible Hand—that there is an ordering towards the best situation for the largest number of people. But it should be noticed here that the purpose was a human flourishing without God; this was not a God-centred human fulfilment. The fulfilment that is happening is an immanent fulfilment of the good of a good society where people's activity benefits one another.

Unitarianism was a movement that was especially influenced by Deism. Unitarianism—which came into being in this era in Europe—reflected some of the Deist anthropological shifts listed below. While Unitarians still had Jesus, they did not have traditional soteriology—Jesus is less a saviour than a teacher and an exemplar. There was a good deal of Deist thought that was taken over into Unitarianism—largely from the Presbyterians in England.

Now, we will look at a couple of the main figures named as influential Deists. The first is Englishman **John Toland (1670–1722)**. The book for which he is well known is *Christianity Not Mysterious* (1696). Toland believed that there were no truths above reason. There was then no need for mystery or anything beyond reason in Christianity. The revelation that was in Christianity was perfectly rational. In fact, everything that Christianity revealed could be discovered from reason alone. What was revealed in Christianity was nothing more than natural religion. Toland is significant because he helped spread Deism through Germany in part to his speaking tours there.

The other important early English Deist is **Matthew Tindal (1655–1733)**, and his principle work is called *Christianity as Old as the Creation* (1730). He believed that creation—the design of the world—reveals God perfectly. In fact, Tindal made the point—which became popular with other Deists—that additional revelation beyond creation would imply the imperfection of creation. He believed that God in creation reveals perfect religion equally to all. Christianity, for Tindal, was fully reducible to natural religion—the particularly Christian bits of it were not necessary. Christianity then, in its essence, is as old as the creation. The essence of Christianity has been there since there have been humans to observe it. For Tindal, the purpose of religion was basically moral and anything beyond the moral was suspicious and led to superstition.

3.6.1 Deist View of Humanity

Deism's fourfold eclipse of transcendence vis-à-vis the human
Of purpose beyond that of human flourishing
Of grace
Of mystery
Of life after death

In the developing story of modernity and modern Christian theology, the most significant aspect of Deism was less its understanding of the Deity than its understanding of humanity. Charles Taylor described four anthropological shifts at the heart of Providential Deism. These shifts could also be understood as a fourfold reduction of the place of transcendence. To generalize, what we see in all of these four shifts is a double movement having to do with the ends or goals of humanity and our capacities to attain those goals. In all of these we see a **lowering of the goals**—the ideals we are aspiring to—and a **heightening of our capacities**. These double movements can then be understood as a **fourfold eclipse** of the transcendent by immanent human capacities. In this sense, Providential Deism is accentuating the Protestant Reformation's accentuation of the general movement of Reform that we saw earlier on coming out the Middle Ages. In Deism, there is a definitely increased sense of human power—that humanity is increasingly less (and ultimately not) in need of rescue. This is a more immanent view of humanity. This provided for an easy transition towards an exclusive humanism—to saying that one did not need to think about God or religion at all to have a perfectly fulfilled life.

The **first shift** was an eclipse of any purpose beyond that of **human flourishing**. The goal of human life was not anything beyond human life. The purpose of life had been revised downward. The purpose of human life was the order of mutual benefit. Humans could find their proper fulfilment as something immanent to finite human life and ultimately without God.

The **second shift** was an eclipse of **grace**. In the view of Providential Deism, humans could achieve God's intended order—the order of mutual benefit—by reason and discipline alone. The end for humanity (to incorporate the first shift as well) was to achieve a finite order of mutual benefit apart from God—and this was something that we could do on our own. This was very much in opposition to the kind of strong Augustinian understanding of grace—especially in strains of Calvinism—that would focus on human impotence and perversion following from original sin. While the Deists believed that God created us and would judge us, there was at the same time a decline in traditional beliefs in eternal punishments. But when it came to our present life, to fulfil our human purpose we did not need grace to fulfil that goal; we could do that on intra-human powers alone. We had within our humanity the requisite reason, benevolence and universal concern to be good people; we did not need God to make us into better people.

The **third shift** was an eclipse of **mystery**. We can see this with Toland's book. When it comes to our intellectual aspirations, what was to be understood was something that was more accessible, while at the same time our capacity to know was elevated. We had a much higher view of what we could know and a lower view of what we should know, whereas in a previous way of looking at things the trajectory of human knowledge led beyond human knowledge towards God. The fulfilment of knowledge was—paradoxically—something that was beyond knowledge. But for the Deists, God's design for us is that we can know God's existence and God's purposes—everything we need to know about Him—by rationally observing the design of the world. There is nothing mysterious.

The **fourth shift** was an eclipse of **life after death**. While many still believed in life after death, this was no longer the central focus of life. The end of humanity was in this life. The life after death that they had was one of reward, peace or repose—a rest and reward for a good life. This was a downgrade from an earlier understanding of life after death in terms of the beatific vision or *theosis*—a God-centred life after death. The Deist understanding of the afterlife was not an ultimate fulfilment of our being as being in communion with God.

3.6.2 Deist View of God

In the Deist view, God is primarily presented as a supreme craftsman, an arch-architect. Deists tended to have a distaste for God acting in any way out-of-the-ordinary or specially in nature. This would mean that he did it wrong in the first place, he did not set up the world properly. Only a poor architect would have to intervene later on.

Deists also did not tend to view God as an agent in history. In fact, they took many of the presentations of the actions of God in Scripture and traditional theology to be at worst morally offensive. They believed that in the Old Testament God was portrayed as a capricious tyrant who ordered genocide: this was not moral. Or, if they were looking back to Augustine's picture of God as sending most of humanity to Hell (the *massa damnata*), it seems like a poor design on God's part, at least—that he could not bring a more optimal result out of life. They had a high view of God, and did not want God acting in inappropriate ways—such as ordering people to murder children.

Basically, in the world picture of the Deists, God retreats to the beginning—setting up the system—and to the end—giving people their benefits or demerits. God, then, is largely an impersonal Creator—a remote efficient cause. He is the force that gets everything started, setting the world up so that it will run in the best possible way. While God has an extrinsic relationship to the material world, he is still within the univocal picture—one being or cause among other beings and causes. Yet, God is a Supreme Being and the First (efficient) Cause. Ultimately, God is a part of this grand order, otherwise the design argument would not work. You have to have the first cause to account for the order of the universe—until you get to the place in science where you decide you do not need a designer to account for the order of the universe. Then, all of a sudden, God becomes redundant.

God, then, was a guarantor of order that provided and underpinning for natural philosophy. God not only functioned to underwrite morality, but also to underwrite the scientific order of the world. We should believe the universe is ultimately orderly because it was designed by God. He is the first efficient cause, but is removed from the nexus of physical causality thereafter, in order to ensure its universal regularity. Deists realize that when you started talking about God in terms of being an efficient cause—a cause like all the other causes in the universe—then eventually you would start to have conflict with science, which was talking about efficient causality. If God was doing something, something else could not be doing it as well. God cannot act through the creation—if God is going to act it is always going to be against the creation in a zero-sum game. Divine or supernatural events are defined in contradistinction to, and operate in competition with, natural events. One then ends up with the 'God of the gaps'—God can only function where we do not have another natural explanation. God's place had been set up as helping us explain things in the world, and as God ceased to serve that purpose He began to be redundant. A great (if possibly apocryphal) example of this was that when the scientist **Pierre-Simon Laplace**, the 'French Newton', presented to the Emperor Napoleon his grand scientific system, Napoleon asked, 'Where is God in this?' Laplace replies: 'I had no need of that hypothesis.' With Deism, God is not yet so dismissed, but he is relegated to a position that will show itself to be tenuous.

3.7 Exclusive Humanism

Secularity 1	retreat of religion from public life	20th century	storey above the ground floor
Secularity 2	decline in belief and practice	19th century	ground floor
Secularity 3	change in conditions of belief	14th(?)–18th centuries	basement/foundation

Exclusive humanism became a living option for Europeans during the eighteenth century. With it came the completion of the basement, or foundation level, of secularity: what Charles Taylor called **Secularity 3.** Here, exclusive humanism arose as a real cultural possibility. In fact, by the time we get into the twentieth century, unbelief will have become more and more common. Part of what we will see in moving out of the eighteenth century and into the nineteenth century is the advent of **Secularity 2**—not only the possibility of exclusive humanism, but the actual decline in practice and belief. Exclusive humanism arose in the story of modernity as a continuing of the self-alienation of religion—more distantly in the Late Middle Ages and the Reformation, but more proximally from Deism.

Starting with Deism, we went from having a picture of the world where God was at the origin of a universal mechanism of efficient causes to having either agnosticism about God—maybe the design of the world does not tell us much about God—or asking how important is this really distant, initial efficient cause? Cannot we just use science to explain the things that we experience throughout our lives? Or, why not just think about matter as itself eternal and dynamic with order somehow arising from matter itself immanently?

3.7.1 Hume

Considering significant figures related to exclusive humanism, we begin with **David Hume (1711–76)**. While raised as a strict Calvinist, Hume was an agnostic. (He was agnostic about all kinds of things.) While he had a vague belief in divine order, he did not really have any belief in immortality

Figure 3.6 Hume.

'David Hume, 1711–76. Historian and philosopher—Google Art Project' by Allan Ramsay—7QGP9S6m_l_-3g at Google Cultural Institute. Licensed under Public Domain via Wikimedia Commons.

or the afterlife. When it comes to Hume's philosophical significance, he severely limited the things we could know with rational certainty. He did not say that God does not exist; he said that we cannot know. Nor can we know if the soul exists. Ultimately, we cannot even know that causation exists. (While we see events followed by other events, we never actually observe a 'cause'.)

When it came to religion, Hume put forth a strong attack on the rational or natural religion of the Enlightenment. For eighteenth-century apologists arguing for the existence of God, the **argument from design** was very important. For those who wished to go further and argue for the trustworthiness of Scripture or Christian revelation in some form, the **argument from prophesy** or **miracles** was significant. Hume attacked both of these in his *An Inquiry Concerning Human Understanding* (1748).

Hume's attack on the design argument occurred in a more extended form in his *Dialogues Concerning Natural Religion* (published posthumously in 1779). Apparently he was working on this quite a bit in the later part of his life. Being a dialogue, it can be difficult to tell which of the speakers represents Hume's own thoughts. However, the basic critique seems to be that for those who thought that the cause of the universe must be wise and benevolent, they were going beyond the effects and warrants that could be given for such. He said that the design argument could give us enough of a God to serve the purpose that Deism wanted. It might push in the direction of some kind of divinity, but it could just as well point in the direction of bumbling polytheism as it could a perfect, rational architect. Ultimately, the nature of God was something that was inaccessible to reason for Hume.

Hume also attacked natural religion—especially in his *Natural History of Religion* (1757). He said that if there was a natural religion, it was not monotheistic—like the Deists and the rational religionists wanted to argue—but that it was actually more likely to be polytheistic. He also posits that, if you were looking at the history of natural religion, what you would mostly see was that religion was based on fear and often had a negative impact on humanity, or a balance. So, if you wanted to look at religion naturally, you would get a negligibly beneficial potential polytheism— which was not really what the Deists were looking for.

When it came to miracles, Hume had a critique that was based on the rule that, when it came to matters of fact, we should be guided by our experience and that our beliefs should always be proportioned to the evidence that we have. When we make a judgement about something, we should make a judgement based on the evidence. The more evidence we have, the more probable the judgement is. His argument was then that no testimony concerning miracles could be probable because the overwhelming majority of our experience was of a regularity of events that made any departure from this norm improbable. Therefore, miracles as improbable were not believable.

In all of these areas, Hume was not saying that people should stop being religious. He was simply removing religion from the domain of reason. In this regard, religion was far from alone; he removed quite a bit from the domain of reason, including most of what was usually regarded as science, and, indeed, most of what people thought was obvious knowledge of the world he relegated to the domain of habitual belief. He did not intend to remove any validity from such belief, just the claim that such 'knowledge' was fully and rationally justified. He thought that religion in particular was founded on faith and not reason, and that it should not claim that it was rational religion. He thought that the Deists were overstating what they could know about God, although he would also say that, at the end of the day, most people overstated what they could know about most anything.

3.7.2 Radical Enlightenment

There was a radical side of the Enlightenment, where it was positively atheist and materialist. The more radical French Enlightenment often presented reality as entirely explained through material forces. **Julien Offray de La Mettrie**—in *L'homme machine* (1748)—endeavoured to present a consistently **materialistic** and **mechanistic** perspective on the world, such that all there was was matter in motion. Everything was a machine, even human beings. Even thought itself was purely physiological.

Denis Diderot (1713–84), leader in the French Enlightenment and editor of the *Encyclopédie*, used more organic metaphors for the mechanism of the universe. He believed that matter itself had its own creative powers. But he, like these others, was a radical immanentist—whatever order there was in the universe was all there is, with no place for God whatsoever.

Baron d'Holbach (1723–89) was the author of a book (humbly) titled *Système de la nature* (1771)—'the system of nature'. The German nobleman believed in a stridently dogmatic and all-inclusive materialism—seeing the universe, and everything in it, as material. In his reductionistic picture of the world, everything that did not seem to be material was (or would ultimately be shown to be) material in the end. This world picture was strongly deterministic—everything was ultimately predetermined by prior causes.

Figure 3.7 Diderot.

'Portrait de Diderot' by Anna Dorothea Lisiewska-Therbusch. *Frontispice de l'édition Brière des oeuvres de Denis Diderot.* Licensed under Public Domain via Wikimedia Commons.

Such perspectives were shared by the *philosophes*—the worldly men of letters who held court in the salons of eighteenth-century Paris. While they often drew from and popularized the ideas of English Deists, they were considerably more hostile in their approach. Much of this could be accounted for by looking to their leading lights like Diderot and d'Holbach, and their French context in which the French Catholic Church was a stronger opponent that could persecute its opponents. There was a considerably more militant opposition to religion coming from French *philosophes* than that found in the rational religion of the Deists.

3.8 Awakenings

As was mentioned before, the period of 1650 to 1800 was a period of tension between the Enlightenment, on the one hand, and the Evangelical Awakenings, on the other. The nineteenth century would be characterized by various attempts to negotiate between the Enlightenment and the Awakenings. There seemed to be at work here an alternative between different understandings of religion. The alternative came down to whether religion was dependent on another domain of human life or was its own independent domain. So—for instance—the Enlightenment would see religion as dependent for its justification upon a broader rational discourse. It was a religion of reason; religion was valid inasmuch as it was reasonable. Its validity depended upon the broader Enlightenment discourse. With the various Awakenings, however, we have a more independent view of religion. Religion was something inward that did not need any external justification beyond itself. Religion had its own justification. So, in a sense, the Awakenings affected a withdrawal from any public discourse that demanded justification. Part of this was that, with the advent of the Enlightenment, religion that did not fit into the mould of rational religion was forced to the side.

Part of what was going on with the Awakenings was an orthodox resistance to Deism. In Germany and England especially, you had people who were rejecting the pre-shrunk religion of Deism as but a pale imitation of Christianity. In the rejection of Deism, and the religion of reason, the radical atheistic *Aufklärers* were united with Pietists—for the former they were not rational enough, for the latter they were not religious enough. As was previously mentioned, the Evangelical Awakenings were more popular, having more to do with the common people, while the Enlightenment was largely confined to the elite until 1776 and 1789 when you had these two rival visions that clashed within the broader culture in the West.

The various spiritual revival movements going on during the Enlightenment were a kind of revivalist counterculture that often **separated** from the broader culture. This was one point of commonality among them. Interestingly, there was, indeed, a curious uniformity among all these different Awakenings in these different places. 'Awakening' is one of the common terms used in different places, so we will use it as a general term. Another of the common elements of the Awakenings was a strong stress on **conversion**—that the event of conversion should be an important and emotional event in your life. This was usually understood to entail a change of life with an emphasis on **curbing one's vices**. Drinking alcohol and sexual promiscuity were common topics of sermons in this time. So having a get-saved experience and becoming a family man were what they were often pushing towards.

Common elements in the Awakening

Separation from broader culture

Stress on conversion

Curbing vices

3.8.1 French Devotion: Jansenism and Quietism

First, we will discuss different versions of French devotion. In France, there really was less of an equivalent counterpart to the widespread revivals that happened in other countries at this time. French movements were more discrete. **Jansenism** was probably the most powerful movement in the French Church during this time. It had its distant origin in the work of Dutch theologian **Cornelius Jansen (d. 1638)**, Bishop of Ypres. Jansen was basically a radical Augustinian. He focused on humanity's helplessness and absolute dependence upon God's grace against the Neo-Stoic self-sufficiency of nascent modernity. His (mammoth) work was entitled *Augustinus* (1640). What came to be called 'Jansenism' was associated with the French Arnauld family (Antoine Arnauld being foremost among them), and also with the convent at **Port Royal**. Jansenism became well known mostly through an ongoing public debate with the Jesuits. The Jesuits attacked the Jansenists' belief in hardcore predestinationism (that salvation was entirely preordained by God apart from any human activity), while the Jansenists attacked the Jesuits' moral 'casuistry' that they saw as tantamount to dishonesty. They would later be marked by a more emotional and 'enthusiastic' mode of expression entailing speaking in tongues and apocalyptic rhetoric. They were later strongly repressed and persecuted under Louis XIV and were eventually condemned in a papal bull from Clement XI.

Another significant development in French devotion was a group called **Quietism**. Again, this was a derogatory term that was imposed upon them rather than a name they chose for themselves. A movement in France that entailed a withdrawal from society—a self-ghettoization, what was characteristic of Quietism was its condemnation of human effort. **Jeanne–Marie Guyon (1648–1717)** was one of the well-known leaders in this movement, and she emphasized total passivity in spiritual life. There was nothing that a human could do to earn God's grace. She also taught that pure love cared more about God than even one's own well-being—that is, you were more concerned with loving God and excluding all selfish concerns, even to the point of being indifferent towards your own salvation. **Fénelon** (François de Salignac de La Mothe-Fénelon) **(1651–1715)**—one of the great French writers of the eighteenth century—raised this issue as well. Quietism was something of a mystic, contemplative movement that had a lot to do with extreme self-examination. Through Fénelon's writings, these ideas influenced the Awakenings in several other places.

3.8.2 German Pietism

German Pietism was more widespread and much more influential. After the Thirty Years War, there was a real religious and moral decline in Germany. The common people were weary and, indeed, wary of theological and confessional controversies. The way a lot of these Protestant confessional groups had developed was that they crystallized into a Lutheran or Reformed scholasticism, but this strict orthodoxy seemed overly intellectual and arid to the common people. Pietism arose primarily in a German Lutheran context—within Lutheran scholasticism's domain of influence. It arose as a challenge to a lifeless orthodoxy—a Christianity that over-emphasized intellectual debate on the fine points of doctrine. The Pietists would say that doctrine, indeed, was useless unless it is related to life. They were not as interested in theology or theological innovation as much as they were interested in living out the Christian life.

While the Pietists defined themselves against Lutheran scholasticism, they also stood opposed to Deism. Christian life for them was not just living morally—although it certainly was that—it also had a much more inward and passionate perspective. Pietism laid a definite emphasis on inward, religious experience—and not just for the spiritual athletes, but for the normal layperson. They were often subjective and emotional to the point of disparaging the use of reason when it came to Christian life. There was a real focus on heartfelt intensity—this was not a part of the Protestant scholastic perspective or of the Enlightenment Deist perspective. Pietists advocated introspection, examining one's inner life, even to the point of a morbid preoccupation with one's own thoughts. The reform they pursued was an inner, individual reform. But, on the other hand, they did place a high value on religious fellowship—that people who were doing this kind of inner reform should meet together and encourage one another.

'Pietism' was yet another derogatory term. An early forerunner for Pietism was **Johann Arndt (1555–1621)**, who wrote *True Christianity*. His intent here was to restore Lutheran piety, and to do that, he asserted that you had to restore the more mystical elements of the Christian faith. Arndt was a Lutheran who stated that we needed to revive some of the more mystical elements of medieval piety and incorporate them into Lutheran piety.

Philipp Jakob Spener (1635–1705) was a key figure in the founding of Pietism. A pastor at a few different churches, he invited people to meet at his home, read the Bible, pray, and discuss the Sunday sermon. These small groups multiplied, and different groups popped up, becoming known as the *collegia pietatis*—or 'pious congregations'. This was where the term 'pietism' came from.

Pietism became a broader movement when Spener republished Arndt's *True Christianity* with a long introduction written by himself. That introduction was later published on its own as the *Pia Desideria* (1675), and became one of the central texts in German Pietism. It was a revolt against the sterility of orthodox Lutheranism, and a call to return to a simpler and more fervent dedication to the Christian life. It encouraged preachers to make their preaching relevant and more devotional—that the purpose of preaching was not polemics with other Christians, but rather to draw Christians deeper into the spiritual life. In order to do this he encouraged the founding of schools for the proper training of preachers. They also believed that the laity should be responsible for promoting the religious life. This lay involvement was centred on the communal aspect of Pietism: small groups of Christians that met together regularly.

Spener's ideas spread and gained in influence in the latter part of the seventeenth and early eighteenth centuries. The **University of Halle** was founded in 1694, and this was initially the centre of the Pietist movement. **August Hermann Francke (1663–1727)** was a disciple of Spener and a faculty member at Halle. He helped to spread the ideas of Pietism all over Germany.

Probably the most significant figure that we will talk about here, however, in German Pietism was **Count Nicholas von Zinzendorf (1700–1760)**, a nobleman with an intense, child-like faith. Beginning in 1722, he opened his home as a place for Moravian refugees, fleeing from other German lands. The **Moravians** were Anabaptists—from the radical Reformation in Moravia, in what is now the eastern part of the Czech Republic. They commonly referred to themselves as the *Unitas Fratrum*—'the unity of the brothers'. One of the central figures in the early days of the Moravian Brothers was a figure called **Jacob Hutter (*c.* 1500–1536)**, and their organization was called the *Bruderhof*—the 'brother house'.

Zinzendorf took in refugees from Moravia who had this heritage in the radical Reformation, and his estate came to be known as the **Herrnhut**. This was a new phase of Pietism—that of combining the inward life with a corporate organization. Here, they had a way of communal living in which, for instance, children were often reared apart from their parents and marriages were arranged. They were trying to institute an ideal community, but a community that was separated from the world. This influential group came to be known as the Moravian Brotherhood, Moravians, the Brethren or Herrnhuters.

Though Pietism encouraged an expansion of missionary work, and spread throughout many parts of northern Europe, its time as a focused religious movement was brief—waning by the middle of the eighteenth century due to an excessive legalism, an exclusive posture towards outsiders and a perceived anti-intellectualism. Nevertheless, the legacy of Pietism would show itself to be a significant factor in the shape of the religious landscape in Germany in the nineteenth century.

Figure 3.8 Zinzendorf.

'Nikolaus L. v Zinzendorf' by Balthasar Denner. Scanned from *'Die großen Deutschen im Bilde'* (1936) by Michael Schönitzer. Licensed under Public Domain via Wikimedia Commons.

3.8.3 English Awakening

In Britain, the Awakening, which occurred, went by the name of the **Evangelical Revival**. It was associated initially with the figure of **George Whitefield (1714–70)** (pronounced 'Whit-field'). This revival expanded rapidly in England at the end of the eighteenth century. It remained within the Church of England, by and large, and did not form a separate group. Like the Awakenings elsewhere, there was a strong focus on individual salvation. But in England there was also a focus on good works, on making society better. Evangelical Revival in England was primarily Calvinist and often entailed a Puritan avoidance of different forms of amusement—like playing cards, going to the theatre or dancing. They were associated with various dissenting groups in England, such as the Congregationalists/Independents, Baptists, Presbyterians and Quakers (and eventually made their way over to North America).

Also associated with the Evangelical Revival was what came to be called **Methodism**. This had to do with many people within the Church of England seeing it as needing reform. Associated with Methodism are the brothers **John (1703–91)** and **Charles Wesley (1707–88)**. The Methodist revival began as something called 'the Holy Club' at Oxford, where the Wesleys met together with Whitefield and others. John Wesley travelled to Georgia, in the New World, and met some Moravian Pietists on the way and was greatly impressed by them. One significant event for the founding of Methodism was the so-called Aldersgate experience of 24 May 1738, when John Wesley was brought very unwillingly to a meeting on Aldersgate Street. Though he did not want to go, he heard there a reading of Luther's preface to Romans. Wesley reports:

Figure 3.9 John Wesley.

'John Wesley. Engraving by J. Thomson after J. Jackson. Wellcome V0006250' by http://wellcomeimages.org/indexplus/
obf_images/9a/65/f24e0f1e95ea40ffc0e65b439448.jpgGallery: http://wellcomeimages.org/indexplus/image/V0006250.
html. Licensed under CC BY 4.0 via Wikimedia Commons.

> About a quarter before nine, while he was describing the change that God works in the heart through faith in Christ, I felt my heart strangely warmed. I felt I did trust in Christ, Christ alone, for salvation, and an assurance was given me that He had taken away my sins, even mine, and saved me from the law of sin and death.

This experience of his heart being 'strangely warmed' and this assurance of salvation was a transformative experience for John Wesley. He ended up travelling to Germany to learn more about the Moravians, and met with Count Zinzendorf there. Wesley ended up preaching in England, but he got a very poor reception in the churches, and so his friend, George Whitefield, encouraged him to preach elsewhere—outside of the churches. So Wesley preached in the fields, in the streets, on the highways—wherever he could find people willing to listen. He ended up travelling all over England, speaking often to large gatherings, numbering in their thousands. Apparently, he had an uncanny personal magnetism. He attracted great numbers of people that had very strong emotional reactions to his preaching, thus bringing about a religious revival in England.

Theologically, Wesley was intent on restoring some of the elements that were minimized by the religious rationalists—like the Fall, the atonement, humanity's need for grace, the need for the Spirit's testimony in your heart and the need to strive to live a holy life. He also focused on the inward experience of Christianity. For Wesley, inward feeling—the heart strangely warmed—was an infallible testimony to the truth of Christianity in our lives.

John Wesley had a gift for organization, and so, as he preached, he also left people with a structure for close-knit community, government and discipline. His brother, Charles, is probably best known for writing many of the Wesleyan hymns. For a time, both John Wesley and George Whitefield were joint leaders of the revival in England. However, Wesley was an Arminian, and Whitefield a staunch Calvinist. Their followers ended up migrating apart. While the Wesleys—and their group that come to be called the Methodists—never originally intended to separate from the Church of England, they nevertheless operated outside of its official activities. As John Wesley preached and found new communities, they often developed into congregations that had no previous attachment to Anglicanism. So, the Methodists de facto developed into a separate group (and, as many of the groups from this period do, ended up dividing amongst themselves).

3.8.4 American Revivalism

George Whitefield was instrumental in North American revivals. In America—in a slightly different way than in Germany—the revivals happened in response to unbelief and indifference about religion, instead of a sterile orthodoxy. American Revivalism was intensely personal—again stressing emotion and immediate feeling. Revivalism appeared early in the eighteenth century in North America. The first half of the eighteenth century was a period called the Great Awakening— often called the **First Great Awakening**, and this was not a concentrated movement. It was drawn together by George Whitefield when he visited America. Many churches during this period had experienced enormous growth, particularly Presbyterians and Baptists because those were the groups with which Whitefield was more associated. Also at this time, Methodism experienced significant growth in North America. Through the Great Awakenings, the Reformed churches were revivified as well, spurred on by Calvinist leaders like Whitefield and Jonathan Edwards. Congregationalist churches were divided in their relation to the Great Awakening into the 'New Lights' who were more amenable to the Awakenings and the 'Old Lights' who were less so. Like the Awakenings in other places, there was a strong individualistic and emotional focus. However, in America there was also a strong emphasis on education.

The First Great Awakening	Early 18th century
War of Independence	Later 18th century
The Second Great Awakening	End of 18th and Early 19th centuries

The **Second Great Awakening**, spanning the end of the eighteenth century, and into the first half of the nineteenth century, came after a period of denominational rivalry and distraction around the American War of Independence. In the eastern part of the United States, the Second Great Awakening, to no small degree, was a reaction, or a countering, to the kind of moral rationalistic religion that was evident in Deism and Unitarianism. On the western frontier, it was more of an evangelistic movement. Largely because of the Second Great Awakening, a common ethos was instilled in the Christianity of the young United States. This Awakening was the bigger, and more influential of the two. While it might not be the case that America was founded as a 'Christian nation'—many of the founders are more Deist than anything—the nation quickly became a Christian nation in a meaningful sense during the Second Great Awakening. This became the broad ethos of America, and Deistic ideas were marginalized.

3.9 Rousseau

To close this chapter, we will briefly touch on the important and transitional figure of **Jean-Jacques Rousseau (1712–78)**. Swiss, and born into a Calvinist family, Rousseau was strongly influenced by French Quietism. He could perhaps best be described as an affective or sentimental Deist. His beliefs were largely Deist in terms of their content—God as first cause, the purpose of humanity, immortality and the focus on morality—but he wanted to ground this Deism less in reason than in the emotions. He called this emotional grounding of religion 'religious sentiment'. This was what was new and influential in Rousseau—particularly when we get to Romanticism. When he looked

Figure 3.10 Rousseau.

Courtesy of the Library of Congress. (No known restrictions on publication.)

for the justification of religion, he did not look to reason. He looked instead to an innate, intuitive sense—to conscience. We know what the divine law is through our feelings, and God is revealed primarily through the heart. That is how we know what truth is. For example, he advocated in his 'Creed of the Savoyard Vicar' (which was raised in a novel called *Émile* [1762]) discarding the distinctive elements of Christianity to focus on an essentially heartfelt Deism—a strange conglomeration of the Awakenings and the Enlightenment.

Rousseau was particularly important as a precursor to Romanticism in the early nineteenth century, although he died before Romanticism really got under way. He was opposed to the mechanistic picture of the world and had a much higher, even sacred, view of nature. He was also opposed to the rationalism of the Enlightenment, but shared the view that all you needed to know was what was naturally available to you through what you already had—not through reason, but through the emotions.

Sources and Further Reading

Axt-Piscalar, Christine. 'Liberal Theology in Germany'. In *The Blackwell Companion to Nineteenth-Century Theology*, edited by David Fergusson, 468–85. Chichester: Wiley-Blackwell, 2010.

Buckley, Michael. *At the Origins of Modern Atheism*. New Haven, CT: Yale University Press, 1987.

Cragg, Gerald R. *The Church in the Age of Reason: 1648–1789*. Rev. edn. New York: Penguin, 1988.

Dorrien, Gary. *Kantian Reason and Hegelian Spirit: The Idealistic Logic of Modern Theology*. Oxford: Wiley-Blackwell, 2012.

Dupré, Louis. *Passage to Modernity*. New Haven, CT: Yale University Press, 1993.

Dupré, Louis. *The Enlightenment and the Intellectual Foundations of Modern Culture*. New Haven, CT: Yale University Press, 2004.

Dupré, Louis. *The Quest of the Absolute: Birth and Decline of European Romanticism*. Notre Dame, IN: University of Notre Dame Press, 2013.

Legaspi, Michael C. *The Death of Scripture and the Rise of Biblical Studies*. Oxford: Oxford University Press, 2010.

Livingston, James C. *Modern Christian Thought: Volume 1, The Enlightenment and the Nineteenth Century*. 2nd edn. Minneapolis, MN: Fortress Press, 2006.

Popkin, Richard H. *The History of Scepticism from Erasmus to Descartes*. Rev. edn. Assen, The Netherlands: Koninklike Van Gorcum, 1960.

Stout, Jeffrey. *The Flight from Authority: Religion, Morality, and the Quest for Autonomy*. Notre Dame, IN: University of Notre Dame Press, 1981.

Taylor, Charles. *A Secular Age*. Cambridge, MA: Belknap Press of Harvard University Press, 2007.

Vidler, Alec R. *The Church in an Age of Revolution*. Rev. edn. New York: Penguin, 1990.

Welch, Claude. *Protestant Thought in the Nineteenth Century*. Vol. 1, *1799–1870*. New Haven, CT: Yale University Press, 1972.

4

Kant

Chapter Outline

Kant's principal works

Critique of Pure Reason (1781, rev. 2nd edn. 1787)

Groundwork of the Metaphysics of Morals (1785)

Critique of Practical Reason (1788)

Critique of Judgment (1790)

Religion within the Boundaries of Mere Reason (1793)

Foundations of the Metaphysics of Morals (1797)

With Kant, we see the beginning of the German domination of modern theology for at least a century. **Immanuel Kant (1724–1804)** is from Königsberg in Prussia. His life is often caricatured as being boring and obsessively orderly, but he was actually a brilliant and revolutionary thinker. He had a radical political streak to him; he was obsessed with the French Revolution. This passionate engagement was wrapped in an often-nervous personality and frequent poor health.

4.1 Pietism and Enlightenment

In the background to Kant are both Pietism and the Enlightenment. Kant's parents were devout Lutheran Pietists; he later remembers them as sincere Christians. As a child, he attended a strict Pietist school—the students were required to regularly write reports on the states of their souls. The school was trying to discipline the children into heartfelt devotion, and he believed that this was deeply hypocritical. It seems that Kant's Pietist upbringing left him sour about Pietism—especially its overly emotional side. Perhaps as a reaction to this, there would be little or no place for emotion and sentiment in Kant's understanding of religion at all. Kant would place a strong emphasis on morality in religion, echoing an Enlightened and Deist perspective, but also on the place of a person's moral conscience, which reflected his Pietist upbringing. He thought that good works were more important than intellectual achievements—certainly when it came to religion. So he also—like some of the Pietists of his day—stood against the orthodox Lutherans who believed that the proper thing for a Lutheran to do was have the right beliefs. Kant thought that good religion had much more to do with living in the right kind of way. As we will see, both Pietism and Enlightenment thought were reflected in Kant's mature thought.

To continue briefly with regard to the Enlightenment, Kant wrote, later in his life, an essay entitled 'Answering the Question: What Is Enlightenment?' (1784). In this little essay, he says that Enlightenment has to do with criticism—critiquing or examining established beliefs—not just accepting things as true because they have been accepted as true before. He is citing this all approvingly. The Enlightenment had to do with being a rational individual and not just following along with institutions and received wisdom. 'Enlightenment', he writes, 'is mankind's exit from its self-incurred immaturity'. We have been immature, but we have made ourselves immature by not thinking for ourselves. In view of this, he says that the motto of the Enlightenment is rather *Sapere aude!*—'Dare to think for yourself!' In other words, Kant is a strong believer in autonomy.

4.2 The Possibility of Knowledge

To dive in at the deep end, we begin with Kant's views on knowledge. One of his major contributions has to do with the possibility of knowledge, answering the big question of modern philosophy in the seventeenth and eighteenth centuries: 'What is knowledge and how do we know things?' His primary work in which he examines this is *Critique of Pure Reason*, published initially in 1781, but in a significantly revised second edition in 1787. It is, to use an understatement, a difficult work. Gary Dorrian writes: 'The age of bad writing in philosophy began with the first Critique—the greatest work of modern western philosophy.' It is called Kant's 'First Critique' as it is the first of three—the *Critique of Pure Reason* (1781/87), the *Critique of Practical Reason* (1788) and the *Critique of Judgment* (1790). The *Critique of Pure Reason* is his principal work on epistemology—on what we can know—and largely has to do with providing a metaphysical or philosophical foundation for natural science. He is trying to account (in the face of sceptical challenges) for how it is possible that the things science tells us can actually be true and can actually count as knowledge. In the end, he concludes that if we wish to have a responsible approach to knowledge, then reason needs to set its own limits—to say what we can and cannot know.

One way to understand Kant's epistemological project is to see him as trying to avoid two extremes: scepticism and dogmatism. The 'scepticism' that Kant has in mind is what he saw in David Hume, whose sceptical treatment of causality woke Kant from his 'dogmatic slumber'. Kant felt the need to find a way to answer Hume's critiques, because if they stood the consequences would be devastating. The 'dogmatism' that he is trying to escape from is a failure to properly take stock of human reason's limitations. So, Kant is attempting to steer a course between a scepticism that put too strict a limitation on knowledge, and a dogmatism that fails to recognize reason's serious limitations.

So, how is knowledge possible for Kant? There are two primary parts of the *Critique of Pure Reason*. The first is called the 'Transcendental Analytic'; the second is the 'Transcendental Dialectic'. 'Transcendental Analytic' is about what we can know and how we know things—about how objective knowledge of the world is possible. The key here—and the key in all of his works—is the way human beings are constituted. Human beings are constituted in a particular kind of way, and this is what makes Kant's philosophy work.

Part of what makes Kant so significant is that he solves the problem of knowledge by turning things on their head by what he calls his 'Copernican Revolution'. The historical Copernican Revolution was where there was a shift in the view of the universe (largely the solar system) from seeing the Earth as the centre to seeing the Sun as the centre. There was a change of what was seen as the centre—the primary starting place—and what was secondary or dependent. Kant's 'Copernican Revolution' has to do with a shift from seeing knowledge as being focused on things out there in the world ('objects', to put it simply) to knowledge as being focused on the structure of experience itself ('subjects', to put it again simply). Instead of the mind being focused on objects in the world and trying to match up with objects out there, the mind is rather seen to be actively ordering our experience. His 'Copernican Revolution' is a movement from knowledge that is centred on the world, to knowledge that is centred on the self. There is a shift from the self as being in a passive position (where we receive data and simply 'see' what is there) to the self as being actively involved in constituting or constructing the world.

Kant describes three different faculties involved in human thinking: Sensibility, Understanding and Reason. (There are more than three, but these are the ones that we will focus on for this simplified picture.) **Sensibility** is our capacity to be affected by sensations, by our five senses. This is the more empirical side of knowledge. Then, there is the **Understanding**—the German term is *Verstand*—which is the ability to identify and categorize different sensations. Understanding has certain concepts or categories to which it then applies experience. **Reason**—or *Vernunft*—is the ability to entertain concepts apart from experience—or to apply concepts to concepts. Sensibility is our capacity for experience; Understanding is the applying of concepts to experience; and Reason is the manipulation of concepts apart from experience. But where is knowledge?

The key here is that the **Understanding** applies concepts to sensory perceptions to produce knowledge. So knowledge has to do with the **Sensibility** and the **Understanding**—to have knowledge, you have to have empirical experience and you have to organize it through your categories of understanding. **Reason** is applying concepts to other concepts; this deals with things that we can think of, but we have no experience of them. Given that you can have knowledge only through applying concepts to sensible experience, Reason cannot give us knowledge and often overextends itself. If you are just using Reason and are not being bound to what you actually experience, you run into paradoxes. An example of this is that by using Reason alone you can make equally valid arguments for the existence and the non-existence of the soul, or of God, or of the universe having a beginning or not. With reason you can think about these things, but you cannot know them. Because reason is not bound by experience, it can yield contradictions.

This knowledge—the hard data of experience that is processed by the categories of our understanding—is trustworthy because the faculties of the Sensibility and the Understanding in Kant's argument have a necessary and universal structure. These faculties are structured in a certain way, and that structure is the same in everyone. Ultimately, Kant says, you can truly know things because you know how you know. You can have a trustworthy way of judging because the structure of your experience can be shown to be universal in everyone.

Kant makes a distinction between what he calls **phenomena** and **noumena**—between what we can know and what we cannot know. The **phenomena**, what we can know, are objects as they appear to us through our Sensibility and our Understanding. But we can see them as objective—true for someone beyond ourselves—because we are all applying the same categories to our experience. Therefore, objectivity resides in a universal trans-subjectivity. All of our experiences are subjective, but all of our subjectivities are structured the same.

When it comes to **noumena**, things that we can think of but cannot know—and for Kant it is a long list—one of those is objects as they are. We cannot know reality as it is in itself beyond our experience—our perception—of it. How do we know that our perception matches up with reality? If you were to jump outside of yourself and compare the perception and the reality, that would simply be another perception. What he is trying to do is say that this is a silly problem. You cannot know the thing-in-itself—*Ding an sich*. All you know is your perception of the thing-in-itself, but all of our perceptions have a common structure. Therefore, we can act as if there is a common reality out there that has common features that can be described precisely, even mathematically.

Noumena

Ding an sich (the thing-in-itself)

The universe

God

The soul

Freedom

Immortality

So practically knowledge works, but only certain kinds of knowledge of certain kinds of things work—primarily things we can experience. And we cannot have knowledge of that which is beyond the appearances—the object as it is (the 'thing-in-itself', *Ding an sich*) beyond the object as it appears to one. These are noumena—the thing-in-itself, but also the self or the soul. They are things you can think about, but you cannot experience them with your senses. You also do not know about the universe—the totality of things in time and space. You can talk about it—such as whether or not it had a beginning—but you cannot experience those things. Also, the existence of God is something we can think about, but we cannot have knowledge of. Freedom—the ability to choose your own actions—is not something you can experience either. In fact, everything that you experience of the world, when it comes to applying these categories to your experience, will make you expect that everything is determined. You can think that you have moral freedom, but you do not experience it. Finally, when it comes to your soul you do not know about your immortality.

So what you have in the First Critique is a pretty serious trade-off. Kant secures knowledge of the normal things of our experience. However, the most important things are the things that we cannot know anything about. The most central questions of religion and philosophy are placed beyond the pale of knowledge. So, where does this leave us?

4.3 Theoretical Knowledge of God?

Kant deals with the theoretical knowledge of God in the part of the *Critique of Pure Reason* called the **Transcendental Dialectic**. His basic conclusion is the impossibility of natural theology—that you cannot know that God exists. He attacks three of the main traditional arguments for the existence of God. The first argument he attacks is the **ontological proof**, which is the proof of God by definition. If you understand what we mean by the word 'God'—that it is something that necessarily exists—then God must, therefore, exist. Kant's critique of the ontological proof is that existence is not a predicate. More technically, being or existence is not a real predicate—it cannot be a part of something's definition. Being or existence is a logical predicate, but it is not a real predicate. So when you say something existing is part of its definition you are confusing categories.

He also critiques **the cosmological proof** for the existence of God. The cosmological proof is arguing from contingent being—from being that could be otherwise or could not exist—to there needing to be a necessary being. If everything that we experience cannot have come to be, then why does anything exist at all? At some point, there has to be something in the chain of beings that had to exist necessarily—otherwise nothing else would exist. Kant says that this is taking causality beyond its proper domain. Causality is one of the categories of understanding, and it only makes sense when you are applying it to the sensible world. When you start applying it to that which is beyond the sensible world—to something that is a necessary being that we have no experience of—you are going beyond the proper bounds of knowledge.

Finally, he critiques **the teleological argument**—the argument from design. He says that in the design of the universe there is an order and it might point to an 'order-er', but that does not necessarily get you to a divine creator. It falls short of its goal if taken as a proof. When it comes to knowledge, all you can talk about is the phenomenon of order in the world, but you cannot take that beyond experience.

This all sounds quite negative; it would seem as though Kant is against God and the soul and does not believe in this religious stuff. But that is not the case—certainly not in Kant's view. He is just making good fences, in a sense. He has another place for these things to go. In fact, even in the theoretical domain, he thinks that the idea of God has a regulative or heuristic use—in that it is best if science proceeds *as if* the world is the product of an intelligent mind. Even though you cannot know whether God exists, the idea of God as a designing creator is a very fruitful one that helps us in doing science by imagining the world as an intelligible unity, as a systematical whole. Such is the ideal of science—to see the world as a systematically ordered whole, as if one mind put it all together. Science—then as well as now—is not a unified whole, but we have this ideal that it all would fit together as if it is a singular creation. The idea of God helps us to think about that.

Kant writes famously in the preface of the second edition of the *Critique of Pure Reason*, 'I have found it necessary to deny knowledge in order to make room for faith.' The *Critique of Pure Reason* is about knowledge, and by knowledge here he means Newtonian science. So when it comes to God, we do not have that kind of *knowledge*—but what he wants to make room for is *faith*. He wanted the religious domain to have its proper place. So when it seems that Kant is throwing all religion and Christianity out the window, he is not at all. In fact, he will come to see the religious domain in the human to be the most important element of what we are.

4.4 Practical Reason

Though he is perhaps more well known for his theoretical philosophy or epistemology, Kant placed a great—likely greater—value on practical reason. His practical philosophy is laid out in three of his books: *Groundwork of the Metaphysics of Morals* (1785), *Critique of Practical Reason* (1788) and *Foundations of the Metaphysics of Morals* (1797). The *Critique of Practical Reason* is often called Kant's Second Critique.

From the perspective of Kant's theoretical philosophy—when it comes to the things that we can know—it seems that there is no such thing as human freedom. If you are only using the categories of the understanding and applying those to what is manifest in the world, this can give you a knowledge of natural science (the grand mechanism of efficient causality in the world), but this also yields a universal determinism (that everything is determined by causal, Newtonian laws). Determinism is at odds with freedom in the sense of being able to determine yourself. Kant sees this as a problem, because if there is no freedom there can be no morality—and morality is incredibly significant for Kant. To him, there obviously is such a thing as morality, therefore, we have to think of ourselves as free. So, we will talk about freedom as—if not something that we can know theoretically—something that is practically necessary.

What we can know of the phenomenal world is that it is a determined mechanism following natural laws with no place for human freedom. But these are not the only laws that we encounter. Kant writes in the *Critique of Practical Reason*: 'Two things fill the mind with ever new and increasing admiration and awe, the oftener and the more steadily we reflect on them: the starry heavens above and the moral law within.' The starry heavens above follow natural and deterministic laws, but there is also the moral law within—and this is another fundamental experience with which we have to reckon. The experience of the moral law necessitates the existence of freedom. So, Kant is going to have, on one hand, determinism, and, on the other, moral freedom.

How do we have knowledge of this moral law? Kant sees such knowledge as being of a different order than that of the empirical science. He even would say it is of a *higher* order when it comes to certainty and when it comes to significance (it has to do with the way you live your life). Morality for Kant usually has to do with certain *a priori* propositions. When he thinks of morality he is not thinking of engrained habits or virtues, he is thinking of what he will call **maxims**—which are more or less explicit rules that we follow. Kant's ethics is an ethics of duty. There are things that we should do, and we should do them simply because it is our duty to do them—not for any reward. We do not do what is right because it will bring about a good in society or in ourselves, but simply because it is the right thing to do—regardless of the consequences. So, it is not a consequentialism in terms of ethics.

To act morally is to act in conformity with the moral law, and he calls the moral law a **fact of reason**. It is something that is simply a fact, but is not an empirical fact—it is a fact of reason. It is something that is known *a priori*—apart from experience and simply by reason alone. While Kant formulates the moral law in different ways over time, an important formulation is in terms of what he calls the **categorical imperative**. One of his presentations of the categorical imperative (in his *Groundwork of the Metaphysics of Morals*) is: 'Act only according to that maxim whereby you can at the same time will that it should become a universal law.' A maxim is a rule for acting. So, his ethics are about following rules that are more or less explicitly thought out. The categorical imperative is about choosing the right maxims; it is a rule for choosing moral rules. It is a guide to tell you if the maxim you have for acting is in line with the moral law—and the criterion here is universalizability. So, only act in such a way that you would want everyone to act if they were to act in the way that you are acting. That is one way of thinking of the moral law.

Another way Kant approaches the moral law is regarding human persons as ends in themselves and not means. This approach to the essence of the moral law has to do with human dignity. You should not treat people as means to any purpose beyond themselves—they are the purpose that should be served. Where does he ground that human dignity? Why are humans so special? It is ultimately grounded in their capacity for freedom. What is significant about humans here is their autonomy.

It is important to notice that in Kant's explication of practical reason—his ethics—there are no extrinsic rules being imposed upon you. You are not submitting yourself to any kind of external authority. The rules are coming from yourself—these are your rules coming from your reason. The moral law is something within you, so this is a self-legislating morality. When we come to theology, we will see that morality is not based on theology—you do not need revelation (say, the Ten Commandments) to know what is right and wrong. However, theology and morality are closely linked for Kant.

4.5 Moral Faith

Again, Kant writes: 'I have found it necessary to deny knowledge in order to make room for faith.' The 'knowledge' that he is talking about here is that of theoretical reason—that which he denies the Transcendental Dialectic. But what he means by 'faith' is not a particularly religious domain so much as practical reason. Practical reason is the domain of freedom; for one to have morality one must believe in freedom. So when he says faith, he means **moral faith** or 'rational faith'. Kant is not here opposing faith and reason. His point is that faith—moral, rational faith—is in an order that is separate from that of empirical knowledge. So they are not in opposition, they are just in different domains. Kant is all about making fences and proper limits.

As mentioned previously, morality was not based on theology or religion—you did not need divine commands. However, for Kant religion is based in morality. We see this laid out especially in his work entitled *Religion within the Boundaries of Mere Reason* (1793). We do not need God to let us know what is right and wrong; reason is the moral legislator. Religion comes into the equation through what Kant calls **the postulates of practical reason**.

In place of the kinds of proofs and arguments that metaphysics and rational theology had given previously—for such things as human freedom, immortality of the soul and the existence of God—Kant puts forward these postulates. A postulate is not a demonstration, and it is not properly knowledge in the sense of proper empirical knowledge. They are postulates—things taken to be true—about subjects that transcend experience, about noumena. However, he gives a case for why we have to believe in these things, even if we do not have knowledge proper of them. So what are the postulates of practical reason and why should you believe in them?

The first postulate of practical reason is **freedom**. Freedom is a necessary presupposition for morality. In order to have morality, we have to believe that we are free. So, given that we have this moral law—which is just a self-evident fact within our reason—and we postulate that we have to be free, what does that tell us about what kind of world must therefore exist? Kant supposes that there must be a highest or perfect good. He calls it the *summum bonum*. This is the purpose and end of our moral aspirations—an ideal of moral perfection. You can see his Pietist background here in that it is a very stringent demand that he is striving after. But this is not just moral perfection.

Figure 4.1 Kant.

'Immanuel Kant 2'. Licensed under Public Domain via Wikimedia Commons.

The *summum bonum* also includes not just virtue, but also the conjoining of virtue and happiness. So, the highest good would be a world in which moral perfection is conjoined with happiness in proportion to it. The best world would be the one in which those that are good are also happy—but, he observes, this is not the case in this life.

In order to have this highest good, it is a moral necessity that we have an endless approach towards perfect virtue that death would cut short. Therefore, you need the **immortality** of the soul if the ideal is to be achievable—and there is no reason to have an unachievable goal for your moral life. Kant's version of life after death entails continually approaching perfect virtue (a kind of moralistic *epektasis*).

As we need the immortality of the soul so we also need a Supreme Being that justly rewards moral good with what Kant calls natural good. You need **God** as the one who guarantees that virtue is rewarded with happiness, that there is a unity of virtue and happiness. God functions to sanction morality by balancing virtue with happiness in the afterlife. Thus, God, for Kant, brings about the highest good, the *summum bonum*.

In the end, these three postulates of practical reason are very similar to Deism. The difference is that while Kant does not need God to be Creator at the beginning of the universe, he still needs God 'at the end'—after death—to give rewards for a moral life. Kant had very little use for anything religious that was not related to morality; he does not really see the point of any kind of ritual, prayer or worship and thinks it is a lower form of thinking. For Kant, then, religion is in a **dependent** position. It is dependent upon practical reason. Like Deists, he would say that ethics constitutes the important content of religion and that God largely functions to sanction morality. Like Rousseau, Kant is going to find the way to God in **moral conscience**. Indeed, moral conscience in the form of practical reason is the most significant guide for human life. Kant is quite a fan of Rousseau, which is odd because of Rousseau's emphasis on feeling.

One of the reasons Kant is such a watershed in the history of Western thought and theology is that he shifted the ground of theology from the world to humanity. With Deism and with 'rational religion', the reason you believed in God was because of the order of the world. Much hinged on the design argument. But Kant, in the 'Transcendental Dialectic' of the *Critique of Pure Reason*, shows to the satisfaction of many that those kinds of arguments do not work. However, what Kant gave away with his right hand, he brought back with his left. He gave away theoretical knowledge of God, but brought back the practical necessity of believing in God. When God returns, he does so not due to the order of the world but from the necessity of human freedom. It is because of some aspect of humanity that theology has validity. This is going to lay the groundwork for much of the theology of the nineteenth century: often when nineteenth-century thinkers look for the validity or the reality of religion or theology, they are going to look within the human person as the starting place.

4.6 Christianity

In his *Religion within the Boundaries of Mere Reason* (1793), Kant does not just present a quasi-Deism. He also presents his particular take on Christianity. However, starting from his understanding of moral faith, Kant ends up having a very different understanding of Christianity than that which is traditionally held.

Kant thought that the historical religions, the positive religions, were vehicles for rational faith. Ultimately he would say that the validity of religion is this rational or universal core. There is a degree to which the positivity of religion needs to be overcome. There is something almost Platonic to Kant's view of religion—that pure religion is imperfectly embodied in historical religions and that we need to get through that imperfect embodiment in order to see the real essence that is there. Influenced by Lessing's 'The Education of the Human Race', Kant thought that the positive religions were especially helpful for the uneducated to become aware of the most important parts of religion—the moral parts—in a way that they could understand.

In *Religion within the Boundaries of Mere Reason*, Kant uses Christian doctrine to make philosophical reflections on morality. While Kant writes about Christian doctrine, what he is really getting at are some philosophical ideas about morality.

4.6.1 Jesus

For Kant, Jesus is primarily a moral teacher and an ideal of moral perfection. He is a moral exemplar. This again echoes Lessing's view of Jesus in 'The Education of the Human Race'. Jesus is significant because he is someone who perfectly fulfilled his moral duties. The most important parts of the New Testament in Kant's view are Jesus' moral teachings. This was the source of the Church's moral teaching—and that is what should be focused on. As Kant thinks that moral faith is something that we could have apart from any external tradition or authority, we do not ultimately need revelation or Jesus' teaching to live morally. What he taught is something that we can know on our own. We do not need Jesus' example to know what the moral law perfectly embodied is—that is something that we can figure out from simply having the moral law within us. However, Jesus' teaching helped spread true religion earlier and faster.

Kant sometimes takes a symbolic approach to Jesus. When Jesus is spoken of as the Son of God, Kant takes this as a kind of archetype of practical reason. For him, Scripture is using symbolic language, but you have to get past the symbols to get to the true content—which is the moral content. Ultimately, what Jesus as the Son of God is symbolizing is something that we have in our selves, the moral ideal. Jesus, here, represents humanity in its moral perfection. Kant would say that when we say Jesus is divine, what we should understand is that this is what a humanity that is pleasing to God looks like, and a humanity that is pleasing to God is one that fulfils the moral law. So, the divinity of Jesus is the God-pleasing aspect of Him. Jesus is a moral exemplar because we, too, are to become 'Sons of God' in this sense. We are to become well pleasing to God by following the moral law and, thus, to be rewarded with happiness. However, the moral exemplar is not necessary. This is something that we can know as being required by us by reason, but it helped. It was an expedient. The true object of faith ends up being the moral ideal, which we had within us all along.

4.6.2 Radical Evil

One of Kant's interesting contributions is what he says about radical evil. Here, Kant is between the Enlightenment and the Pietists. He is between the Enlightenment optimism about humanity and the Pietist emphasis on human sinfulness—the Pietist thought that there is something basically messed up in the human condition that probably had something to do with the Fall. Kant says that we have a **moral disposition** that grounds our choice of maxims. When we are choosing principles to guide our behaviour, there is a prior disposition that makes us more apt to choose better or worse maxims. Kant then observes that it seems like we are predisposed to choose bad maxims. There is something 'off' that is in the root of us—'radical' in the sense of a *radix* or root, and in-the-ground-ness. We keep choosing fundamentally selfish maxims—things that we would not want to be universalizable. We continually want to treat people as means and not as ends.

He is observing our fundamental self-love as a fact—that there is something in us that keeps us from this moral ideal. There is something in the root of us that is opposed to our fulfilling our proper moral autonomy. Radical evil for Kant is not something out in the world lurking about or smouldering in the microwave at the end of *Time Bandits*. It is something that is within us. Radical evil sounds like original sin. Kant ends up taking many of the traditional Christian doctrines and reinterpreting them in terms of his moral philosophy. However, one of the things he simply cannot deny is the presence of evil in the human heart. This again sounds a lot like original sin, but he does not regard radical evil as an inheritance—it is not something that has been given to us. He would say that we are responsible for our own dispositions. It is not Adam's sin but our sinfulness that we are responsible for. Yet, he would say that our propensity for evil is ultimately inscrutable—we do not understand it. Ultimately, we do not know the reason for our deep corruption. He would say it is something beyond memory. This is a much more mysterious side of Kant: It is him being very honest, saying there is this thing that does not really fit in his system, but it is undeniable and we do not know where it came from. Ultimately, he would have to say it is grounded in a noumenal reality. So what can one do about radical evil?

4.6.3 Justification

For Kant, justification has to do with the possibility of reorienting our disposition. Evil can be overcome. For this to happen, there needs to be a revolution in one's habits—in one's disposition towards selfishness. Christians usually talk about this kind of revolution in terms of grace. Grace for Kant, however, seems to be understood as earning God's cooperative aid. God compliments our righteousness with grace. But ultimately there is no real practical consequence to this. You cannot rely on grace; you rely on yourself. Ben Franklin's phrase, 'God helps those who helps themselves', is not in Scripture … nor is it in Kant, but it could have been.

Justification in Kant has to do with choosing to have the right disposition. Our problem is that we have a bad disposition, but we can choose to have the right disposition. When one chooses to have the right disposition this atones for past misdeeds. This is what your justification is: you are making your life right by making your life have the right disposition. Atonement then is a symbol for a renewed moral ideal. When you come to choose to have a new disposition in life, it is like you are a new person taking the place of the old person. So that is what justification is on our side, which is almost entirely what we are doing for ourselves.

So, where does God fit into this? For Kant, God sees all space and time, and so justification is where God sees our future completed moral progress. The immortality of the soul gives us a continual progress into the future beyond death approaching the moral ideal. God sees us as that perfected version of us in the future, even if we are not perfect yet at any given point in time. So if justification is considered in terms of what God thinks about us, what that doctrine can mean for Kant is that God is not seeing you as anything other than you are—he is just seeing a future version of you. He is not giving you a gift of anything, he is simply seeing you at the end of your moral progress. (Kant's afterlife sounds a lot more like Purgatory—continual moral progress with hope of perfection—instead of Heaven as a kind of repose.)

4.7 'Liberal Theology'

After Kant published *Religion within the Boundaries of Mere Reason*, he was censored by Friedrich Wilhelm II—the Prussian king—for spreading ideas that distorted Christianity, and was ordered to stop writing about religion. (Friedrich Wilhelm could not do much more than that because Kant was quickly becoming an intellectual superstar.) Kant complied—for three years, until the king dropped dead. Kant then resumed his work.

Kant's ideas went on to have considerable influence on theology and theologians in the nineteenth century and beyond. In fact, it was through Kant and the theologians influenced by him that the term 'Liberal Theology' became popular. In the early nineteenth century, 'Liberal Theology' particularly meant Kantian theologians who were not Deists, but also who were not supernaturally oriented orthodox theologians. This nomenclature became popular in the early nineteenth century, but there was also an enormous revival of Kantian thought in the latter part of the nineteenth century. So Kant was not just of historical interest, but became a significant influence again due to the Ritschlians.

But even for those who did not explicitly identify with Kant or with a Kantian programme, Kant significantly redefined the playing field for theology. This was what happened with significant thinkers—even if you disagreed with them you still had to deal with them. In the nineteenth century, you could not just simply ignore Kant or Hegel or Schleiermacher. Part of what Kant did was to divide religion off as a separate domain—religion was something that was distinct from scientific knowledge. Religion, if regarded in its proper domain, was then insulated from the critiques of science—science was not a threat to religion. They were not in competition because they were in different domains. Religion had to do with practical reason, while science had to do with theoretical reason. Thus, Kant denied knowledge in order to make room for faith.

Another significant influence that Kant had on theology was his intent to define religion—and to a lesser degree Christianity—as something that was universally accessible. The kind of faith he was trying to make room for was a **universal faith**. Kant also moved to identify religion **with a particular domain of the human**, as a dimension of anthropology. Some might have considered this to be a Procrustean bed—religion and/or Christianity is reduced to fit the tidy domain of the human reality allotted to it. So Kant, for instance, would say that what was significant or worthwhile about religion was really just morality. (There was a lot of talk about the 'essence' of religion or Christianity in this period.) He then reinterpreted all of Christianity in terms of morality and what did not fit was the husk and non-essential stuff. So, the doctrine of the Trinity, the Eucharist, and other doctrines that certainly seemed to be quite important to Christians through the ages were not part of the essence of Christianity. A certain anthropological site was the essence of religion, and this gave you a way of distinguishing between the essential kernel and the ephemeral husk of Christianity. While many, if not most, theologians in the nineteenth century agreed with Kant in identifying morality as the essence of Christianity, many, if not most, performed a similar procedure relative to such an anthropological site. The question also remained for many: 'Is Kant doing Christianity a favour by buying it intellectual credibility and giving it its own proper space? Or is he fundamentally distorting it such that Kant's version is no longer recognizable as Christianity?'

Sources and Further Reading

Adams, Nicholas. 'Kant'. In *The Blackwell Companion to Nineteenth-Century Theology*, edited by David Fergusson, 3–30. Chichester: Wiley-Blackwell, 2010.

Axt-Piscalar, Christine. 'Liberal Theology in Germany'. In *The Blackwell Companion to Nineteenth-Century Theology*, edited by David Fergusson, 468–85. Chichester: Wiley-Blackwell, 2010.

Buckley, Michael. *At the Origins of Modern Atheism*. New Haven, CT: Yale University Press, 1987.

Cragg, Gerald R. *The Church in the Age of Reason: 1648–1789*. Rev. edn. New York: Penguin, 1988.

Dorrien, Gary. *Kantian Reason and Hegelian Spirit: The Idealistic Logic of Modern Theology*. Oxford: Wiley-Blackwell, 2012.

Dupré, Louis. *The Enlightenment and the Intellectual Foundations of Modern Culture*. New Haven, CT: Yale University Press, 2004.

Livingston, James C. *Modern Christian Thought: Volume 1, The Enlightenment and the Nineteenth Century*. 2nd edn. Minneapolis, MN: Fortress Press, 2006.

Welch, Claude. *Protestant Thought in the Nineteenth Century*. Vol. 1, *1799–1870*. New Haven, CT: Yale University Press, 1972.

Part II

The Long Nineteenth Century

5

Romanticism: 1800–1850

Chapter Outline

The term 'Romantic' arose in seventeenth-century English to refer to writers in southern France. They wrote in a certain dialect—the Romance dialect—although this does not have a lot to do with what we are talking about in this chapter. It eventually came to describe a particular kind of popular literary style. The 'romantic', as we see it in the nineteenth century, however, was a cultural and intellectual movement of Romanticism, primarily brought into play by the thinker/poet/writer Friedrich Schlegel.

Romanticism is significant because it was in many ways the last unified movement in Western culture. It was, in a way, a return to the classical synthesis, but it was a different return. Romanticism presented itself as a corrective to the one-sidedness of the Enlightenment. Where the Enlightenment had become very subject dominated—where humanity was the ruling element—Romanticism was reconnecting the classical synthesis. However, its reconnecting of God, the world and humanity came after God, humanity and the world had undergone some modification. For instance, the self, in this new version of the synthesis, had greater freedom. It was more of a creative, active self as opposed to a passively receiving self of the classical synthesis. There was also a greater respect for the integrity of the world. A significant return to the classical synthesis, however, was in the Romantic understanding of transcendence. The distinctness of transcendence was perceived as wholly encompassing the finite realm while sustaining its autonomy. Transcendence was less apt to be seen in an oppositional relationship, it was present in and sustained the world.

5.1 The French Revolution

The dividing line that marked the beginning of Romanticism was the French Revolution. During the French Revolution and the Terror, a widespread de-Christianization occurred in parts of France. The Goddess of Reason was enthroned in Notre Dame Cathedral to signify a new Cult of Reason. This was an extreme of Enlightenment secularization—the anti-clericalism of the French Revolution. Many people would look on such 'Enlightened' extremes as the French Revolution and the Cult of Reason as a sign of unbalance or unreality in the Enlightenment ideals. It seemed like the Enlightenment was becoming quite a bloody ordeal—and that was precisely what many Europeans tried to get away from.

Romanticism was a reaction across the board to the French Revolution as an excess of the Enlightenment. But also, with the French Revolution, the Romantics were at the beginning of a new epoch. The French Revolution was an historical turn. A new page was being turned in history on the continent of Europe, although this was not as much the case in England.

5.2 Ideal and Desire

One of the broad aspects or ideas representative of Romanticism was the quest for the **absolute/un conditioned/infinite**. These were different ways that they would name divine transcendence: God was the Absolute, the Unconditioned or the Infinite. Here there was more than an echo of Spinoza.

While the divine was often understood in these terms, the relation to the divine was one of **desire**. A consistent theme in the Romantic ethos was a desiring or longing for something that you could never ultimately obtain. The 'forbidden fruitiness' made it all the more desirable. While for a lot of the Romantic artists of various stripes that often had to do with married women, it also applied to God. (The Romantics could be some randy characters, but we do not need to go into that here.) This vulnerability to desire for an unreachable ideal was very different from the buffered self and Neo-Stoicism of the Enlightenment.

The Romantic *eros*, or desire, was fundamentally **dynamic** and oriented on a trajectory. You were constantly on the move towards something—that often you realized you could never fully achieve. On the positive side, this entailed a continual progress. On the negative side, this desirous approach was tragic in that the desire was never fulfilled. You were always seeking and never coming to rest.

There was also an awareness in the Romantics of the **brokenness** of the world. The world as it is now is not perfect. It is not the ideal. For many of the Romantics, they thought about this in terms that have been lost. Many looked back to prior eras in history—to the ancient Greeks or the Middle Ages—relative to which something had been lost with the intervening advent of modernity. Romantics tended to have a more ambivalent attitude towards the modern world. Much of Romanticism was an artistic and poetic movement, and much of what drove the poetry and the art was trying to connect this lost-yet-desired-yet-unachievable ideal to their current broken situation—striving from the present broken age towards the unachieved, if not unachievable, fulfilment.

One of the key tropes that recurred in Romanticism was that of the **fragment**. Fragments are pieces of a whole, not just singular bits. Implicit in the broken part is the ideal of the whole. There was a lot of unrest and storminess to the Romantics. They were never at ease with where they were, never where they wanted to be.

The Romantic ideal, often put forward, was frequently connected with **creativity** as that which held or brought together the real and the ideal in the work of art. The works of the imagination as bringing together the real and the ideal could provide us with new symbols and new ways of being directed towards transcendence. They were trying to connect our present broken reality with our desire for a divine transcendence of some sort.

5.3 God, Nature and the Whole

5.3.1 The Divine and the Sublime

When the Romantics thought about God, they tended to steer clear of the kind of 'rational religion' that we saw in the Enlightenment. When they looked at nature—and they had a definite place for nature—they were not just going to see an intricate clockwork that needed a wise architect, but they were going to encounter the **sublime**. What struck them in the world was its beauty and maybe something even beyond the beauty. Several thinkers—like Kant in his *Critique of Judgment* (1790)—made a distinction between the beautiful and the sublime. The latter was another order of the aesthetic that was beyond mere beauty and moved into a more transcendent—almost terrifying—realm. And so, the way in which nature makes us mindful of God came in the site of **wonder**—that we look at the world and are struck with wonder and astonishment. As William Desmond says, the world is **hyperbolic**: the world makes us think of something beyond the world. There is in immanence that which 'throws us beyond' (*hyper-ballein*) the immanent world. It seems to be more than itself. It does not account for itself. It makes us think of something more.

The Romantics also had a feeling of **kinship with the whole of nature. Wholeness** will be another trope that is going to be evident in Romanticism. They also had a different cosmic imaginary over and against that of Enlightenment science. Instead of seeing the universe as something that we had a scientific mastery over, they saw a depth to the universe such that the universe was something **strange**. The way Charles Taylor described this was that they saw the world in terms of the 'dark abyss of time'. Some of this indeed had to do with scientific advancement in that the more you understood the cosmos the stranger it got. The universe was vast beyond our imagination, and as the science was being developed we found that it was old beyond our imagination. It retreated in space and time from our grasp and mastery into darkness and mystery. We realized that the further we got away from ourselves, the less we were really able to imagine things. The world was unfathomable; it was beyond human presumptions. (This will get amplified when we see the theory of evolution come on the scene.) The **wildness** of the universe was not something that was only outside of us, but for some of the Romantics they were going to see the wildness of humanness as something within us as well. We see a growing awareness of our inhuman animality or the operation of an unconscious beneath the ground of our conscious mind—that within ourselves there is this dark foundation that we cannot quite reach and are only barely aware of. That which was fundamental and divine was often seen by the Romantics as beyond the pale of the all-too-human lamps of the Enlightenment.

5.3.2 Overcoming Dualism

A central aspect of Romanticism was its project of overcoming the dualisms which had arisen in emerging modernity. One of the modern dualisms was that between **mind and body**—that there is a fundamental division between the mental world and the physical world, and that we experience most intimately within our own persons. Against this, the Romantics had different understandings of nature and the physical world. Instead of seeing the physical world as dead matter pushed around by force with Newtonian regularity—seeing it as the mechanism—they saw nature as itself being directed towards spirit. **Nature and spirit** were connected in some way for the Romantics. If they were distinct, then they were oriented towards each other such that nature was inhabited or directed by the spiritual or oriented towards the spiritual. Instead of nature as a dead mechanism, nature was a living thing that had an orientation, desires and direction. This resonated with pre-modern ideas of teleology—of there being a direction to the world and to nature.

One of the Romantic insights that would come back again and again was the **coincidence of opposites**. This was a pre-modern idea, but it gets revivified. The union or coincidence of opposites was not about negating difference. It was the creative tension in the relation of opposites. Even if they were different—be they mind and body, spirit and nature, God and the world—they were in relation. Romanticism was not primarily about collapsing differences into 'the one', but rather about seeking to see how these things were related to each other. It sought to understand how the infinite and the finite were in relation together or the ideal and the broken present. It was not that God was being identified with the world or that the ideal was being identified with the broken present. They wanted to talk about the relation, about how they were connected, were in communion. There was otherness but otherness in relation.

5.3.3 Spinoza, the Living God and Romantic Religion

There was a significant revival of interest in Spinoza in the Romantic period. This was largely an aesthetic reading of Spinoza that did not necessarily match up with the kinds of philosophical positions that one might read about in his *Ethics*. The Romantic Spinoza was not as much a rationalist and a determinist as a heroic and individual genius. Spinoza broke again into the popular conscience through something called the 'Pantheism Controversy' or *Pantheismusstreit*. As things happen oddly in history, the Pantheism Controversy was mostly someone trying to paint someone as having a bad position by calling it 'Spinozist'. Ironically, it brought Spinoza back into vogue and made him more respectable instead of demonizing the name. Sometimes even demonizing fails to go as planned.

The Spinozism of this era is described as Neo-Spinozism. Much of this involved a fascination with Spinoza as a person or a hero—as someone who suffered for his genius. There was a celebration of the end of the artistic, brilliant individual in Romanticism. So, Spinoza was placed alongside people like Plato, Dante, Shakespeare and Goethe—great geniuses of Western culture.

This is not to say that there were Spinozist ideas that inspired many Romantic thinkers. One of the aspects of Spinoza's thought that inspired the Romantics was the way in which his philosophy was an attempt to **overcome** the **dualism** between thought and things as rather being two attributes of the same substance. They also gravitated towards Spinoza's seeing **humanity as part of nature**. Probably most significantly, however, was the emphasis on the **immanence of God**—that God was not a distant cause or master architect, but rather somehow intimately present and alive. The Romantics wanted to see God as in the living present of the most significant things we experienced here and now.

It was in the context of the overcoming of dualism and the emphasis on immanence that the word '**Pantheism**' starts to get thrown about. The term itself (meaning something like the identification of the world, the 'all', with God) was created around this period, and was used almost entirely by detractors—by people who were trying to find a word to say why other people were wrong. It was very rarely used in any kind of positive sense by any of the Romantics. Indeed, most of the Romantics maintained some kind of distinction between God and the world. But what we really see in Romanticism is a third way between what they would consider a 'Theist' position and a 'Pantheist' position. By 'Theist', they meant seeing God in an anthropomorphic way. God was a person that thought and acted like us. They believed that this was idolatrous—because God was the absolute and thus master-able and understandable on the model of our psyches. They asserted that such an anthropomorphic theism was an overly simplistic way of thinking about God—that that was not much of a God. The kind of God that got jealous and threw fits was not a God worthy of our worship. So, it was between this and Pantheism, on the other side—that by God we meant the whole of nature. They did not utterly reject either of the ideas, but they saw them as two extremes to be avoided. So, it is not accurate to call the Romantics as a group Pantheists. They were trying to find something between a simplistic anthropomorphism and Pantheism.

Romantic religion was framed by seeking after an ideal, by the desire for that which was not fully present. The Romantics were seeking the presence of God; they wanted to be in communion with God. They were not just looking for the idea of this, but were somehow bridging that connection—sometimes through art. Creative art was one of the ways of connecting our present, broken, incomplete, finite experience and God. And the Romantics often drew on the Protestant Awakenings which were also desiring that sort of lived experience. Similarly, they also drew on medieval Catholic mysticism.

Important figures for Romantic theology

Immanuel Kant (1724–1804)

Johann Georg Hamann (1730–1788)

Friedrich Heinrich Jacobi (1743–1819)

Johann Gottfried Herder (1744–1803)

Johann Wolfgang von Goethe (1749–1832)

Johann Gottlieb Fichte (1762–1814)

Friedrich Daniel Ernst Schleiermacher (1768–1834)

Georg Wilhelm Friedrich Hegel (1770–1831)

Samuel Taylor Coleridge (1772–1834)

Friedrich Wilhelm Joseph Schelling (1775–1854)

5.4 German Counter-Enlightenment

In Germany, Romanticism began the *Sturm und Drang* ('Storm and Stress') artistic and cultural movement, also heavily influenced by German Pietism. It was a reaction against the Enlightenment's enthronement of autonomous reason, and the portrayal of the universe in mechanistic terms. One particular flashpoint was the Romantic movement's oppositional stance to Kant and his mode of engagement in philosophy.

5.4.1 Jacobi

Friedrich Heinrich Jacobi (1743–1819) was a central figure in the German Enlightenment. The German Enlightenment was the latest and most mature Enlightenment to come about. As such, it was more complex of an Enlightenment and Counter-Enlightenment. In this, the German Enlightenment transitioned more or less smoothly into Romanticism. Along with Kant—the culmination of the Enlightenment—there were contemporaries in Germany who rejected both him and the Enlightenment. Jacobi was central to this kind of dialectical Enlightenment (pro- and contra-) that morphed into Romanticism, and he was critical of Kant. He believed that Kant was destroying metaphysics and confining everything to the phenomenal world. He also thought that Kant was lifting reason above faith and common sense and, thus, was demeaning faith and the way in which normal people thought. He was also one of the initiators of the *Sturm und Drang* movement opening up Romanticism in Germany.

5.4.1.1 Jacobi and the *Pantheismusstreit*

The *Pantheismusstreit* (the 'Pantheism dispute'), as it has come to be known, was centred on a book that Jacobi wrote entitled the *Letters on the Doctrine of Spinoza* (1785). In this book, Jacobi recounts a conversation that he had with Lessing shortly before his death. While discussing a poem by Goethe, Lessing declares something along the lines of 'the orthodox concepts of the divinity are no longer for me. I cannot stomach them. *Hen kai pan*—one and all. I know of nothing else'. Lessing, on his deathbed, is presented as confessing that he does not care for the orthodox concepts of divinity and prefers a kind of pantheism. And so, when Jacobi asks Lessing if he agreed with Spinoza, Lessing responds: 'If I have to name myself after anyone, I know of nobody else.' Jacobi then goes on to argue (after this account of Lessing's statements) that this kind of Spinozistic Pantheism is the only consistent form of Enlightenment Rationalism. Such 'Spinozism', for Jacobi, amounted to atheism—because if the world was God then God did not exist (as something distinguishable from the world). This, Jacobi argued, was the only kind of theology that was left if you abandoned revelation—which was what he saw the Enlightenment as doing. Jacobi marshalled these arguments in a case against the prevalent Enlightenment Deism. He charged the Deists with being inconsistent. If they thought through their rationalism, they would be pantheists or atheists—like Spinoza and like Lessing. Jacobi was, in fact, honouring Lessing because at least Lessing had thought through his convictions to their logical atheistic conclusions. Jacobi's primary interest was to defend a conception of God as transcendent and personal. He believed that rationalism led to pantheism or atheism (thus abandoning God's transcendence) and also led to determinism or fatalism (thus abandoning God's personal relations with humans).

Conversely, Spinoza never used the phrase '*hen kai pan*' ('one and all'), and Lessing probably got that from his interest in pre-Socratic philosophers. There was also something kind of creepy about Jacobi using an intimate deathbed confession to go after people who supposedly thought like Lessing. Other thinkers sprung up to defend Lessing—figures like **Moses Mendelssohn (1729–86)** and Herder. (We will discuss Herder's response at length below.) They defended Lessing as well as Spinoza.

Ironically, the *Pantheismusstreit* ended up reviving interest in Spinoza, who had been largely ignored until Jacobi presented Lessing as claiming to be a Spinozist. After that, people began to think about him as having something to offer. Again, it was a version of Spinoza that actually was not terribly close to what you would find in Spinoza's *Ethics*; nevertheless 'Spinoza' was revived as an intellectual force in the nineteenth century.

5.4.1.2 Jacobi on Faith

Beyond the *Pantheismusstreit*, Jacobi also made some influential contributions regarding the understanding of the nature of faith. Faith for Jacobi was a certain acceptance for truth that was not achieved through rational argumentation. He got this idea of faith from—of all people—David Hume. Jacobi writes in his book, *David Hume on Belief* (1787), that faith is something that is closer to the certainty you have from immediate experience rather than something you get from a reasoning process. So, to talk about the certainty of God's presence in feelings was a Romantic thing. Now, there were some unintended consequences to what Jacobi tried to do—as there always are.

Figure 5.1 Jacobi.

'Jacobi (Eich)' by Johann Friedrich Eich (1748–1807)—*Das Jahrhundert der Freundschaft. Johann Wilhelm Ludwig Gleim und seine Zeitgenossen*, ed. Ute Pott (Göttingen: Wallstein, 2004), p. 57. Scan by James Steakley. Licensed under Public Domain via Wikimedia Commons.

Later in Jacobi's life, he presented what would become an influential understanding. For him, faith or intuitive feeling had to do with God—it was like a spiritual faculty. Just as Kant had the different faculties of Sensibility, Understanding and Reason, Jacobi said that faith was an immediate spiritual faculty—like sense perception. And he—confusingly—named this spiritual faculty by making a distinction between **reason** and **understanding**. He used the same German words as Kant did for reason (*Vernunft*) and understanding (*Verstand*). For Jacobi, however, reason (*Vernunft*) was the domain of immediate knowledge, faith or intuition. This was intuitive knowledge and knowledge of what was beyond the sensible; it is our immediate knowledge of spiritual things. Understanding (*Verstand*) was the domain of scientific empirical reason as it was with Kant. However, Kant would say that reason (*Vernunft*) was not knowledge; it was that which you could think about but it leads into contradictions and paradoxes. For Jacobi, reason (*Vernunft*) was a special kind of faculty that led to a truth that was other to the scientific and empirical knowledge of the world. So, in a way, he was doing something very Kantian. He was saying that religion had its own faculty that could not be challenged by that which belonged to another faculty. Religion had its own insulated category. We should not expect the empirical world to verify our faith; if we are doing so, we are looking in the wrong place. We should be looking at the immediate awareness and intuition, because that is the domain of faith.

5.4.2 Hamann

Johann Georg Hamann (1730–88) is a difficult-to-classify figure, who was not so much anti-Enlightenment, as simply bypassing the Enlightenment. Originally from Königsberg, the same town as Kant, he was not an academic, but rather a minor civil servant in a tax office. And yet, he came to be known as 'the Magus of the North'. Hamann was very critical of Kant, his fellow-Königsberger. After Kant wrote his epochal *Critique of Pure Reason*, Hamann wrote a *Metacritique*—a critique of the *Critique*. The *Metacritique* took him two years to write, although it was only ten pages long. But in them, Hamann ends up prefiguring much post-Kantian German thought, seeing what would become German Idealism. Hamann is a challenging read: literary, poetic, indirect and comical. He rarely comes out and says exactly what he is talking about.

A central focus of Hamann's philosophy was defending the particular and the individual over and against the general and the universal. Especially with religion, what was essential was not the universal but its particularity. The particular symbols were not dispensable husks but were necessary. If you dispensed with the so-called 'husk', you were dispensing with the 'kernel' as well. His thought was deeply influenced by Pietism. Hamann can be seen as presenting an odd, aesthetic, Pietist critique of the Enlightenment. Normally, the Enlightenment and the Awakening did not have a lot to do with each other, but in some people they came together. He was a deeply paradoxical thinker. He was fascinated by *kenotic* (self-emptying), Christological imagery in Scripture—such

Figure 5.2 Hamann.

'Johann Georg Hamann 2' by Unknown—Johann Caspar Lavater: *Physiognomische Fragmente*. 1775–78. Licensed under Public Domain via Wikimedia Commons.

as the Christ Hymn in Philippians 2. God's power was here most manifest in God's powerlessness. He saw Christianity as being at odds with many aspects of Enlightenment rationality. In fact, he argued that a lot of Enlightenment rationality was in fact a modern idolatry.

Hamann, like Jacobi, was also very sympathetic to Hume—particularly inasmuch as he attacked the pretensions of reason and brought back the proper place of belief. If it was the case (Hamann following Hume's thought) that reason alone could yield very little true knowledge—and less and less the more you looked at it—then to make this kind of reason the ultimate judge over faith did not make much sense. Ultimately, much about ourselves and the world had to be believed in, and could not be demonstrated (this actually resonated with Kant as well). Hamann emphasized the value of humility to human reason and human thinking.

With his focus on the particular and the concrete as opposed to the universal, he would end up focusing particularly on **language**. One of the distinctive aspects of Romanticism for Hamann was its emphasis on language. Instead of the Enlightenment ideal of mathematics as the master language, that is a pure, non-particular, universal way of communicating, Hamann and the Romantics gave particular and historical languages a foundational place relative to human thought. He reflected on this theologically as being rooted in the **Incarnation**. The greatest revelation of the divine was not an escape from particularity, but was incredibly particular. Indeed, many Enlightenment and Deistic thinkers were scandalized by the particularity of the Incarnation. They wanted a universal access to the revelation of God in nature through reason. But that there was a particularized access through this one point in time was not a very Enlightenment idea, and yet Hamann saw it as being particularly and definitively significant.

5.4.3 Herder

Johann Gottfried Herder (1744–1803) was from eastern Prussia and was heavily influenced by Pietism. He also went to school in Kant's Königsberg, where he studied theology and heard Kant lecture. Kant had a very high respect for Herder, considering him one of his more faithful students, even though Herder later came to interact with Kant critically during his life. Herder was also a

Figure 5.3 Herder.

'Herder by Kügelgen' by Gerhard von Kügelgen, http://hdl.handle.net/10062/3588. Licensed under Public Domain via Wikimedia Commons.

regular guest in the Hamann home—they became lifelong friends. Herder travelled all around Europe, meeting d'Alembert and Diderot in Paris and Lessing in Hamburg. He also became lifelong friends with **Johann Wolfgang von Goethe (1749–1832)**, and he emerged as one of the leading figures in the *Sturm und Drang* movement. However, he was also a Lutheran pastor, in addition to being a scholar and a writer. He was not a professional theologian, nor a professor.

5.4.3.1 Language, History and Holism

Herder presented a Romantic way between **the Enlightenment** and **the Awakening**. Herder negotiated between these two impulses in a manner that was otherwise than Kant's. Instead of giving each their own place—the Enlightenment as being about knowledge and the Awakening as being about morality and practical reasoning—Herder rejected dualism and, along with it, the extremes of a disengaged intellectualism and anti-intellectual emotionalism. Keeping emotion and intellect distinct was part of the problem.

Like Hamann—and probably more influential than Hamann—Herder played a significant part in championing **language** as the ground of human thought. Language for Herder was not a divine invention, but was a human invention and should be thought of in those terms. Humans for him were essentially linguistic—there was no non-linguistic humanity. There was no human consciousness without the formation of language; they were coterminous.

Along with this, Herder emphasized that humans were fundamentally **historical**. Things changed over time, and we, too, existed in a process of becoming. Humans as historical beings always took up what came before, reinterpreting and appropriating it. So, when you appropriated something, it became different—it was a non-identical repetition. When something was taken up, it changed relative to its new context. Herder, however, rejected the Enlightenment view of history as a rather shallow notion of progress—that later cultures were always superior to earlier cultures such that superstition was necessarily surpassed by Enlightenment. He also rejected a purely sceptical view, like Voltaire put forward—that there was no meaning or unity in history. In place of these, he placed a strong emphasis on **particularity**—on how perspectives were always embedded in a particular culture. It is significant that Herder was writing mostly in the 1700s, and this sounds like twentieth-century hermeneutics. He said that there was always advance, development and transformation within cultures, but that you should pay attention to the individuality and particularity of different cultures because they all had their own languages and ways of being. Cultures had their own criteria, and you should not rank cultures or ages relative to each other: There were no universal criteria.

Herder privileged metaphors of organic growth and development. Reality was more fundamentally a living thing that grew and developed organically, and a living thing that was not growing, developing and changing was dead. Yet, there was a continuity in the midst of change—living things were not just becoming utterly different all of the time. If your cat did that, you would come back into the room and it would be a jar of Cheez Whiz or a multiplication table. In organic development and growth, there was both constant change over time and continuity within the change.

When this organic model is applied to cultures, one sees that any given individual culture is dependent upon other cultures. Cultures were less isolated units than moments in a greater **holism**.

Cultures always think of themselves in relation to other cultures, be they in the present or in the past. Herder, ultimately, reflected on the particularities of the developments of history and culture in terms of providence. Herder looked at history as it was the way that God wanted it to be. God made the world alive—growing over time—and in the human domain that was manifest in the growth, development and creativity of culture. The development of culture was a part of God's plan for the world.

5.4.3.2 *Bildung* and Religion

Given the individuality of cultural movements, and that they are yet always related to each other, the past is always going to be related to the present, but the past is always in the present as reinterpreted. One of Herder's key ideas—as with the nineteenth century as a whole through the influence of German Romanticism—was that of **Bildung**, a term sometimes translated as 'culture', although there is more to it than that. It is etymologically like 'building', having to do with education and formation, building up the human. It has to do with what we would come to think of as the Humanities as having the purpose of such edifying education. *Bildung* as culture was then the 'cultivating' of the human (with a vague etymological relation to 'humus' or earth). It was not just what happened to express what people were thinking at a certain time, but as a part of an ongoing progress of a helping or building of humanity.

Elements of *Bildung* in Herder	
Tradition	dependence
Organic powers	appropriation
Humanity	teleology

There are three elements (highlighted by Marcia Bunge) that can help us see where Herder was coming from in his concept of *Bildung*. First is that of **tradition**—we are always shaped by our history. We are shaped by what has come before; we are heirs to what others have done. That we are, thus, fundamentally social and dependent (shaped by what came before us) goes against the grain of the Enlightenment impulse towards individualism and autonomy.

Second, there were what he called our **organic powers**. What each person does in a cultural way (as does, formally, any living thing) is receive something and take it up differently; we appropriate. This is seen very basically in the organic process of metabolism—an organism taking in something else (some other living thing) and transforming it in order that the organism can live and thrive. Humans do this not only when they have lunch, but also when they interact with, and cooperate in, the creation (continual recreation) of culture—we are continually appropriating (making our own and so transforming) that which we received. The vast majority of what makes up our thought-life we did not create from whole cloth on our own, but we also did not simply take it up and leave it the way it was received. In bringing it into ourselves, as it were, it has been transformed and becomes different. This is part of what makes us each singular individuals. There was again a non-identical repetition—a sameness and difference—when it came to what had come before.

The third element of *Bildung* for Herder was **humanity** (*Humanität*). In the midst of the various traditions and continual transformations of human culture, Herder held that all human beings ultimately shared a common purpose or direction. In a theological register, he directly related this to humanity as the *imago dei*—the image of God. In the chain of *Bildung*, the links are different from each other, but are all related. We are always taking what came before us, and transforming it in relation to a different situation, and people in the future will do the same thing—receiving, transforming and passing on. In this, Herder, ultimately, came around to see an over-arching teleology or directedness to history—though not traceable in through the particularities of specific cultures.

It was from the perspective of his understanding of *Bildung* that Herder argued for the appreciation of the individuality of religions. As opposed to some Enlightenment figures, he was not as interested in ranking religions, instead he wanted to try to learn what he could from other religions and appreciate their singularity. He did, however, come to see some general characteristics of religion by observing many different ones. The first was that he saw the religious impulse as **inherent and central to humanity**. He also saw in religion more broadly an **orientation towards the whole of reality**. It was a way of thinking about where you were relative to the cosmos beyond yourself, putting yourself in an ordered relation to the rest of the world. It was not just an inward or private domain, but was rather a view on the world. And, finally, he believed that all religion arose from a feeling of **wonder**—an astonishment that arises from the world around us that awakens the thought of God in us. The religious for Herder connected the inner and the outer, and tapped into the affective beyond the merely rational orientation of Enlightenment religion.

5.4.3.3 God and Revelation

Herder described God as, 'the source of all existence and the dynamic power that orders and unites it'. This was different from God as the distant moral legislator as presented by the Deists or Kant. But it was also not a pantheistic understanding of God. He was not collapsing the difference between God and world. God is an active and life-giving power. His goodness and wisdom are manifest in nature to the degree that Herder said that the order of nature is a symbol of God. Herder also contended that, though one cannot give a certain demonstration for the existence of God (such as could be found in the rational proofs that were in vogue in the eighteenth century), you could be intuitively certain of God's existence through the observation of nature. Herder's picture of God was such that his understanding of divine transcendence entailed God being the active source of all existence, the constantly evident source of life. God was present in the world, and was thus immanent as well.

Regarding the *Pantheismusstreit*, Herder responded by criticizing Jacobi's anthropomorphic God and defending Spinoza. (Jacobi and Herder were friends; this was not a mean-spirited disagreement.) Herder's response to the controversy is a small book entitled *God, Some Conversations* (1787). Herder was largely critical of the practice of seeing God as a person who was simply another being in the universe that acted the way we do. With his defence of Spinoza, Herder was influential in inspiring the revival of interest in Spinoza in Germany.

When it came to Scripture, Herder viewed the Bible as revelation, but for Herder this did not mean that it, thus, ceased to be a human document. While the Bible was a human document, this in no way detracted from its nobility. The Bible was nevertheless revelation—it taught us of God's plan in history. When it came to the particularities of different books of the Bible, we should appreciate the different cultures in which Scripture was written; Herder recognized that Scripture was written in Ancient Near Eastern, Hellenistic and Roman cultures. In other ways, Herder ends up anticipating much of what would be considered modern biblical criticism. For instance, he argued for Mark being the earliest Gospel and that there were oral traditions behind the Gospels— something that would become commonplace later on.

At the centre of Herder's understanding of Scripture and Christianity was the concept that humans were created in the image of God, and this image of God was most clearly seen in Jesus. In Jesus, true humanity was made manifest. So Jesus—while being truly God—was also truly human. Herder also focused on how revelation was given in the Bible in a way that humans understood it. So, if it was more than human, it was certainly nothing less than human. It was fully human, and you should expect what you should expect from human documents. Otherwise, it would not be understandable to human beings. Revelation for Herder primarily had the purpose of the education of the human race—you can see this idea going back to Lessing. He would say that revelation was not limited to Scripture. In some sense revelation was given to all—that all humans had a sense of God from the world and an inward desire for God.

Herder was a Lutheran pastor; in fact he eventually became a superintendent in charge of the education of clergy. When he looked at the work of Christ—Christ as the Saviour—he saw in Christ's life and death a revelation of true humanity. He saw the true image of God, true humanity presented as a model for us. Herder, ultimately, saw Christianity as the true religion of humanity, because in Christianity you saw what humanity was as truly revealed in Christ.

5.5 German Idealism

German Idealism was a return of sorts to Kant after the Counter-Enlightenment. Kant's philosophy could be seen to have formulated the questions and problems that the Romantics were trying to answer and German Idealism was going to take up these same Kantian problems and try to fix them. The German Idealists all began with the Kantian 'Copernican Revolution' of centring knowledge around the active thinking self, but they all had different understandings of the nature of that self. Many also started with the primacy of freedom—which was where Kant's moral philosophy focused—and used this for the basis for a new metaphysics. German Idealism also had a marked religious component and ends up influencing theology afterwards to a considerable degree. For the German Idealists whom we are going to talk about, the idea of God was indispensable. It was often key to the philosophical synthesis that they came up with.

German Idealism was something of a synthesis of the Enlightenment and Romanticism. From the Enlightenment it gets the idea that **active reason** is central to our understanding of reality—so German Idealism was going to focus likewise on reason. But the Idealists took this even further and said that not only was reason central to our understanding of reality, but reason was central to reality itself. The 'idealism' part of German Idealism had to do with the primacy of the mental whether in philosophy or in reality itself. Like the Romantics, the German Idealist would look to **history** as dynamic and progressing through different stages. They also had a Romantic emphasis on **holism**—using metaphors of organic wholes over a mechanism. (Here was where Spinoza's influence could be seen in German Idealism.) As with both Romanticism and the Enlightenment, there was an emphasis on the place of **self**—maybe even a more radical emphasis on the centrality of the self.

5.5.1 Fichte

Johann Gottlieb Fichte (1762–1814) provided an influential idealistic interpretation of Kant. Fichte basically turned Kant's epistemology into a monistic metaphysics—an understanding of there being ultimately only one reality as manifest in perceived plurality. So with Kant, you had the idea that the mind was the active source of knowledge. What Fichte did was to start with Kant's understanding of the freedom of the ego as being the key to surpassing the barrier between the *phenomena* and the *noumena*. The way to overcome this division was through the spontaneous activity of thinking itself. For Kant, this activity gave unity to our knowledge of the world, but for Fichte thinking activity united the world in a more ontological sense.

Fichte's most well-known philosophical work is the *Wissenschaftslehre* (usually translated as *The Foundation of the Science of Knowledge*, 1794). In it, he presents his own work as following through and drawing conclusions from Kant's philosophy. He progresses from Kant's transcendental ego, or self, to a larger understanding of a Self that is constructing reality, as such. As Kant sees the object of experience as constituted by the thinking subject, so Fichte thinks of the generation of the non-self from a single self-positing Self. Fichte's idea though had definite religious echoes—often suggesting a unity between religious and philosophical ideas. Fichte's later thought took a more religious turn: he eventually equated the absolute with this transcendental ego that was somehow generating the world. The absolute or divine, so understood, was more of a broader, impersonal, moral order in the universe. 'Being', for the later Fichte, was the metaphysical name of God, and, conversely, religion 'is the philosophy of the non-philosopher'. Fichte eventually lost his position as a teacher after being charged of atheism as a result of his pantheistic teachings.

5.5.2 Schelling

Friedrich Wilhelm Joseph Schelling (1775–1854) is often regarded as the Romantic philosopher par excellence. Schelling—instead of focusing on the ego, or the self, or the subject, and producing unity out of that—focused on nature instead. (There are many phases and periods of Schelling's thought; we are drawing attention to some of his significant ideas throughout his career.)

He thought that nature, like consciousness, was an independent manifestation of the absolute. The absolute for Schelling was the ground of the world, and was the ground of the unity between nature and consciousness. Many of the German Idealists were troubled by what seemed to be a problem that Kant left—that we can only know the way things appear but we cannot know reality in and of itself. But Schelling would say that both our consciousness and nature were manifestations

Figure 5.4 Schelling.

'Friedrich Wilhelm Schelling'. Licensed under Public Domain via Wikimedia Commons.

of—or were grounded on—what he called the absolute. There was then going to be a harmony between nature and consciousness as both of them were grounded on/in the absolute. Schelling would champion something called **intellectual intuition**, which was an immediate perception of the unity of the active self and the object in this ground. There was a sense that your thinking was lined up with reality as being based in the ground of the absolute.

Schelling also had an understanding of the **absolute** that it was **in the process of making itself**. In the free play of independent agents in the world, the absolute was coming to be itself. Ultimately, the absolute will only truly exist at the end of history. It was working itself out over time, and the human was where nature had become self-conscious and where spirit was starting to be the most self-aware. So spirit was a final product. If this sounds Hegelian, it is because Hegel ripped him off—and Schelling was cranky about it for a very long time, even after Hegel's death.

Schelling is also interesting inasmuch as he produced a **philosophy of nature**. He had a view of nature that was a dynamic one in that it presented the universe as developing towards the self-awareness of the absolute. He saw nature itself as whole as a great organism that was growing over time.

In Schelling's later thought, he gave considerable attention to **mythology and revelation**, as in his later lectures at the University of Berlin. In fact, he became much more orthodox in his understanding and his teaching. His later teaching can be characterized as Christocentric even. He came to think about faith as independent of science—as more personal—in a Pietist kind of experience or perception of the reality of Christ through Scripture and the testimony of the Holy Spirit. On a more philosophical level, he saw Christ as a fulfilment of the natural world of creation and also as being prefigured in pre-Christian mythology. So he had a kind of *logos* Christology, which was kind of similar to some of the Church Fathers—such that there has been a progressive revelation of the *logos* leading up to Christ, and Christ is the final revelation.

5.6 Coleridge

Samuel Taylor Coleridge (1772–1834) was the great representative of English Romantic thought. Coleridge was a very significant figure in philosophy and theology when it comes to England and America—largely because he was the one who brought Romanticism and German Idealism to England. This led to a certain rebirth of creative theology in Britain. He was as important for British and American thought as either Schleiermacher or Hegel. (Interestingly, Coleridge dies in the same year as Schleiermacher.)

That said, Coleridge does not have a big systematic philosophy or theology. The two theological/philosophical works which are mostly referred to are *Aids to Reflection* (1825) and *Confessions of an Inquiring Spirit* (1840, published posthumously). Coleridge broadly followed the Romantic trajectory as a revolt against Enlightenment rationalism. However, in the course of challenging the Enlightenment, he was not interested in any simplistic rejection of reason. Coleridge rather wished to present a better understanding of what reason was, of 'true reason'. This 'true reason' would occupy a ground abandoned by both the rational religion of the Enlightenment and the anti-intellectual fideism flaring up here and there in the Evangelical Awakenings. (He, ultimately, charges Schleiermacher with not being 'rational' enough either.)

The central idea for Coleridge was that the visible world was dependent upon an invisible one. The visible world was a manifestation of, or was continually dependent upon, an invisible one.

Figure 5.5 Coleridge.

Courtesy of the Library of Congress. (No known restrictions on publication.)

So, he would—and he got this from Jacobi's influence—make the distinction between **reason** and **understanding**. Reason had to do with this spiritual reality—that it was a kind of higher knowledge. It was that through which he would say that we had universal and necessary convictions. It was a place where you could have a kind of certainty. It was what had to do with ends—the ultimate purposes of things. He also said that reason had to do with the infinite and was known through an interior sense.

This all, of course, was in opposition to what we have in **understanding**—which had to do with the visible world. Understanding for Coleridge was the domain of scientific knowledge, as opposed to higher spiritual knowledge. It had to do with the objects of sense instead of universal and necessary truths and realities. (You can see a Platonism in the background here.) Understanding had to do with means as opposed to ends, finite objects as opposed to infinite and exterior things as opposed to interior.

So, he would say that the spiritual—religious things—was not against reason. It was rather true **reason**. That with which the scientific, Newtonian empiricists were most engaged was **understanding**. Reason was the domain in which one properly spoke about God and talked about religion. One of the key elements, here, that made Coleridge a Romantic was that you could not know spiritual reality through the understanding, and that one of the key elements of reason was the **imagination**. Reason had to do with creativity—the creative activity of the self. In fact, Coleridge locates the *Imago Dei* in imagination and the active mind. Our being able to create spiritual unities or wholes—seeing things as holding together—was part of what he meant by imagination.

With reason then, our access is not to finite realities but is most centrally to our knowledge of **ourselves, other selves**, and ultimately of **God**. All of this involved imagination, and so art and creativity were ingredients to reason—not in opposition to it. It was not reason versus art, but art as expressive of true reason. Reason for Coleridge also had to do with the **moral**. Just as in Kant's picture of things, this was the more stable side—it had to do with unchanging realities—and so morality, reason and conscience all went together.

'Reason'	'Understanding'
re: spiritual reality	re: visible, sensible reality
higher knowledge	scientific knowledge
re: universal and necessary	re: objects of sense
re: ends	re: means
re: infinite	re: finite
interior	exterior

When it comes to the **Bible**, Coleridge is going to be reading German critical scholarship on the Bible before it makes its way into the broader scholarly consciousness of England. For Coleridge, the experience of reading Scripture was key. It is in this experience that you could know its authority and what made it distinctive. The experience of the encounter with Scripture was its own evidence.

He thought that if you were just looking on the infallibility of the letter of Scripture, you would not be able to properly discern the nature of Scripture for Scripture truly exists in its living power to evoke faith and transformation. This was the spirit of Scripture as opposed to focusing on the letter of Scripture. So, Coleridge would argue that Scripture was true in spirit, but not infallible in the letter.

Coleridge saw his view as opposed to something that he called '**Bibliolatry**'. With such Bibliolatry, the Bible was made into its own object of devotion, instead of being in its rightful place as influencing us as the Word of God, and building us up as the people of God. People were more interested in giving the Bible divine characteristics than encountering it and allowing it to influence them—as was its true purpose. Coleridge also would say, as someone reading biblical criticism in Germany among people in England who believed in the inerrancy of Scripture: 'You all are playing right into the hands of Sceptics. You are making claims that, as soon as you see what the Germans have found, cannot be substantiated.' For Coleridge then, Scripture was truly human— it had to do with real human beings—but that was part of the divine activity. There was not a competitive agency where the more 'God' there was the less there was of 'us'. Coleridge's position was that Scripture became the living Word of God in our encounter with it. The Word of God was not an object that sat around, but it was God speaking to you—and that was not happening unless you were all ears. That was the transformative event that happened through Scripture—it became the Word of God.

Sources and Further Reading

Bunge, Marcia. 'Introduction'. In *Against Pure Reason: Writings on Religion, Language, and History*, edited by Johann Gottfried Herder, 1–37. Eugene, OR: Wipf & Stock, 2005.

Cragg, Gerald R. *The Church in the Age of Reason: 1648–1789*. Rev. edn. New York: Penguin, 1988.

Dorrien, Gary. *Kantian Reason and Hegelian Spirit: The Idealistic Logic of Modern Theology*. Oxford: Wiley-Blackwell, 2012.

Dupré, Louis. *The Enlightenment and the Intellectual Foundations of Modern Culture*. New Haven, CT: Yale University Press, 2004.

Dupré, Louis. *The Quest of the Absolute: Birth and Decline of European Romanticism*. Notre Dame, IN: University of Notre Dame Press, 2013.

Lamm, Julia A. 'Romanticism and Pantheism'. In *The Blackwell Companion to Nineteenth-Century Theology*, edited by David Fergusson, 165–86. Chichester: Wiley-Blackwell, 2010.

Livingston, James C. *Modern Christian Thought: Volume 1, The Enlightenment and the Nineteenth Century*. 2nd edn. Minneapolis, MN: Fortress Press, 2006.

Taylor, Charles. *A Secular Age*. Cambridge, MA: Belknap Press of Harvard University Press, 2007.

Vidler, Alec R. *The Church in an Age of Revolution*. Rev. edn. New York: Penguin, 1990.

6

Schleiermacher

Prussian-born **Friedrich Daniel Ernst Schleiermacher (1763–1834)** is widely considered to be the father of modern theology. Schleiermacher was a polymath. He invented modern hermeneutics—the science of interpretation. He was a philosopher and a cultural critic. He was a pastor and an administrator. He helped to found (with Wilhelm von Humboldt) the University of Berlin, in 1809. Perhaps his most lasting impact (though it is difficult to judge with such a titan) was his writing and teaching as a professor of theology at the University of Berlin.

While Schleiermacher was a professor at the University of Berlin, he also preached to the large congregation at Trinity Church. Trinity Church in Berlin was an example of a relatively new movement in Germany in the nineteenth century: the unity church movement, an attempt to overcome the division between Lutherans and the Reformed. (In 1817, Frederick William III would formally unite the Lutheran and Reformed Churches into the Evangelical Church of the Prussian Union.) Trinity Church was a mixed Lutheran and Reformed congregation, and Schleiermacher was a strong advocate of a united Evangelical Protestant Church.

6.1 Pietism, Enlightenment, Romanticism

In Schleiermacher, we have a confluence of Moravian Pietism, the Enlightenment and Romanticism—all of the big movements from the eighteenth and early nineteenth centuries come together in Schleiermacher. When it comes to **Pietism**, Schleiermacher's father was deeply involved in Moravian communities, and young Friedrich was educated by Moravian Pietists. Schleiermacher's piety was, thus, distinctively Moravian—focused on a personal and intense experience of Jesus. Religion is not merely something intellectual that you teach but is rather a personal relationship with Jesus Christ to be awakened in another. He later describes himself in a letter as a '*Herrnhuter* [a Moravian Pietist] of a higher order'. Schleiermacher went on to study at a Moravian seminary, though he did not care for it. He found the forced orthodoxy stifling. He ended up going to the University of Halle—which was Pietist in origin, but was one of the leading Enlightenment universities at the time he was there. He then begins his career as a professor at Halle.

Schleiermacher was also particularly influenced by the **Enlightenment**—specifically by Kant and Spinoza. He met Kant and studied Kant's work as a student. The focus on subjectivity in Schleiermacher can be seen as reminiscent of parts of Kant. Schleiermacher finally was deeply influenced by **Romanticism**. He was influenced by Jacobi and Schelling—in fact, in many ways he is trying to mediate between Jacobi's fideism and Schelling's idealism. He was also very inspired by Herder and his historicist understanding of religion—specifically that the historical particularity of religion is something that is not to be set aside.

Figure 6.1 Schleiermacher.

'Friedrich Daniel Ernst Schleiermacher 2'. Licensed under Public Domain via Wikimedia Commons.

6.2 The *Speeches*

Schleiermacher moved to Berlin in 1796 and fell in with some of the new literary types like Friedrich Schlegel. Schlegel (who coined the term 'Romanticism') was an older chum of Schleiermacher and encouraged Schleiermacher to start writing. His first book, *On Religion: Speeches to Its Cultured Despisers* (often referred to as the *Speeches*), is published in 1799 and becomes rather famous. Schleiermacher wrote this in his mid-thirties, in just over a few months while he was working as a hospital chaplain.

In the *Speeches*, Schleiermacher presents something of a new understanding of religion. He wants to talk about what 'religion' is beneath its various historic forms. As the title states, these speeches are addressed to religion's 'cultured despisers'—that is, his Enlightened and Romantic friends who think that Christianity is no longer relevant. Schleiermacher is observing how religion was losing its place in the broader culture—especially in the elite culture—and so he writes this book to try to regain its place. So this work presents a theology that is addressed very specifically to his particular culture. It is significant to have this in mind—they are speeches not to Christians or people who think of themselves as religious, but to people outside of the Church who would think of themselves as cultured and despisers of religion.

One of the points that Schleiermacher makes is that what Romantics dislike in religion is not religion itself but only certain external, dispensable aspects. What they do not like about religion is not religion itself, he argues, and so, he wants to let them know what religion is. He believes that his Romantic friends are missing something when it comes to religion—and that is piety or living religion. They were only looking at religion from the outside, but the inside of religion is *feeling* (*Gefühl*)—and that is what they were missing. This feeling is also what the Romantics were all about. So, the case that he makes in the *Speeches* is that religion is not outmoded and dispensable, but it is indeed part of the essence of human nature—a profound feeling that is at the root of human consciousness. (More on this below in Section 6.3.) In the *Speeches*, Schleiermacher ends up presenting an understanding of God that is often mistaken for pantheism. Indeed, after having to repeatedly defend himself against charges of pantheism, he significantly revises the *Speeches* several times to make himself more clear. Part of the issue is that his target audience (largely Romantic despisers) are not allergic to pantheism in the way his orthodox critics are, so he is not as careful initially with his often-poetic formulations as he perhaps could have been.

6.3 The *Glaubenslehre*

The *Speeches* is Schleiermacher's earlier work, addressing those outside the Church. His later work—which is equally if not more influential—is Schleiermacher's great work of systematic theology originally published in two volumes in 1821 and 1822. (He then revises the whole thing, and publishes it again in 1830). It is called *Glaubenslehre*—which is not translated because it literally means 'doctrine of faith', which makes you think that it has to do with, well, the doctrine of faith (what faith is), but that is actually misleading. It is a 'teaching' (a doctrine) that comes from and is rooted in 'faith'; it is an explication of faith. You start from faith and then unpack and unfold it. It is an understanding of the teachings that are inherent in your faith. And so what is key here

Figure 6.2 Schleiermacher.

'Friedrich Daniel Ernst Schleiermacher'. Licensed under Public Domain via Wikimedia Commons.

in his systematic theology from the outset is that it is rooted in the Church's living faith, her living experience of the work of Christ.

The *Glaubenslehre* proves very popular (especially for its size: a hearty 770 pages in its English translation). It becomes the standard for Protestant theology in the nineteenth century. It also becomes the classic of liberal Protestantism, something like the Thomas's *Summa* for Thomism or Calvin's *Institutes* for the Reformed. He explicitly intends it as a systematic theology or exploration of faith for the unified Evangelical Church in Germany. Throughout the work, he draws consistently on the official confessions of both the Lutherans and the Reformed. He is trying to lay out how Protestants share in the same living experience of the Church.

6.4 Religious Consciousness

One of the key insights for Schleiermacher is that experience is the starting point of theology. Theology begins from a particular kind of religious consciousness. In this, he is both like and unlike Kant. Whereas Kant makes a distinction between the theoretical and the practical—with religion being the practical—Schleiermacher does not agree with Kant's locating of the religious in the domain of moral consciousness. And yet, while Schleiermacher does not locate the religious within the distinct domain of the practical, he does something similar. He concedes that the theoretical and the moral were indeed distinct domains, but neither of these is the domain of religion. Religious consciousness for Schleiermacher has its own distinct and proper domain over against both the theoretical and the practical. Schleiermacher is like Kant in that he agrees that religion has an area separated and/or insulated from theoretical reason, but he is making it an even more distinct area than Kant did.

When Schleiermacher thinks about the essence of religion, one can see Pietism and the Awakenings in the background. Religious consciousness has to do with a particular kind of personal experience. Speaking negatively, religious consciousness is distinct from the theoretical—metaphysics or knowing. The Enlightenment rationalists would often emphasize this—specifically in their more apologetic mode. Hegel is going to emphasize this as a particularly religious domain as well. Religious consciousness for Schleiermacher is also distinct from morality, or practical reason, or doing.

He would say that the religious domain—rather than knowing or doing—has to do (generally speaking) with '**feeling**'. His understanding of religion is a religion of the 'heart'—very close to Pietism. What more particularly is meant by 'feeling' here? It is not just any experience—it is not even necessarily a particular or discrete experience. Schleiermacher would say rather that religious consciousness has to do with our deepest level of awareness. He uses the term *Gefühl*, and what he means by this is what he calls '**immediate self-consciousness**' that is a '**feeling of absolute dependence**'. This, for Schleiermacher, is our most basic level of awareness. This is something otherwise than Enlightenment autonomy. Dependence—our utter dependence—is our most basic or fundamental experience. Our very being or existence is dependent upon something other than ourselves, and we experience this in the depths of our consciousness.

For Schleiermacher, this *Gefühl* is a pre-objective sense. It is not about something out there in the world, but it is our intimate feeling that we ourselves are absolutely dependent. It is in this 'ownness' that one can see why he describes it as 'immediate self-consciousness': we are immediately aware that we are dependent. For Schleiermacher then, this most basic human awareness is an awareness of our relation to (our dependence upon) God. God is the 'Whence' of our feeling of absolute dependence. One's feeling of absolute dependence is then one's **God-consciousness**. God for Schleiermacher is that which I am ultimately dependent upon. Our God-consciousness is not knowledge, but is an order of feeling. In the *Glaubenslehre* he usually uses his more mature formulation for this feeling: the 'feeling of absolute dependence'. In the *Speeches* he just uses the term *Gefühl* or feeling. More specifically, in the *Speeches*, he describes this feeling as our consciousness of finite and temporal things that are existing in and through the infinite and the eternal. It is a feeling of dependence where finite things are dependent upon something else. They exist in and through the infinite and eternal— the 'in and through' being the dependence. And so religious consciousness is the intuitive sense that one's life and being—and everything else—is not independent but dependent, 'in and through' God.

Religious language expresses the reality of this concrete religious experience. In Christianity, this has to do with the particularity or the positivity of religion. Christianity arises out of a **Christian God-consciousness**—Schleiermacher even calls it a 'Christian consciousness'. The particularity of the Christian consciousness stems from the feeling or experience of redemption in Christ. He is here against a kernel and husk idea of religion and its particularities that is common in the Enlightenment understanding of natural religion. He says rather that religion is always particular; it is always positive. You only have religion that is manifest in certain definite, concrete, real forms. While he speaks about how the many positive religions entail the common essence of a feeling of absolute dependence, he goes on to consider Christianity to be the deepest and most sublime and universal religion because of the person of Christ. Only in Christianity do you have Christ who is a Mediator between God and humanity. So, Christianity is a religion like other religions, but it has something fundamentally different and fundamentally higher about it. Christianity can be called the fulfilment of other religions in that it is the fullness of what the other religions are striving for.

In this, Schleiermacher is very similar to Herder in the idea that religion is not abstract and universal, but is always particular and historical. Thus, you cannot do theology by ignoring history or by ignoring the Church. For Schleiermacher—the preacher and the theologian—theology is always done in and for the Church. That is the context in which it begins and that is the public that it serves. It is within this understanding that the *Glaubenslehre* is framed.

6.5 Christian Doctrine

In the *Glaubenslehre*, Schleiermacher sees **Christian doctrines** as accounts of Christian religious affections. Doctrine is not something that is abstract, rather it is a way of talking about religious experience. It is this grounding in religious consciousness that makes theological statements legitimate—not that they are theoretically or morally true, but that they reflect on religious self-consciousness. Christian doctrine is rooted in the Church's actual faith. It is rooted in the piety of the people that it is addressing. So, the *Glaubenslehre* is not an apologetic work; it is not addressing those who do not have faith but rather those who are within the Church. It is addressing those who have this experience of redemption in Christ.

Figure 6.3 Schleiermacher.

'Friedrich Schleiermacher'. Licensed under Public Domain via Wikimedia Commons.

When Schleiermacher considers the place of **Scripture** in theology, he views it as the first in a series of reflections after Christ. As such, as the first, it is the norm for all subsequent presentations of the Christian faith. It is the closest representation of the most immediate experiences of the historical person of Christ, and so as such it is normative for those who come after—hence the centrality of (at least) the New Testament in the Christian's life.

6.6 God

God is the Whence of our feeling of absolute dependence. When Schleiermacher talks about God, he is talking about God from the standpoint of our fundamental relation to Him. We do not start with an abstract language but with a relation, for God is always 'God for us'. This is a Lutheran formulation. And the proper language about God in Christianity is intrinsically related to an experience, feeling or awareness.

There are for Schleiermacher three loci in our experience that fund a Christian understanding of God. First is—as previously mentioned—**the feeling of absolute dependence**. This is our most fundamental God-consciousness. But there are also the related experiences of **sin** and of **grace**—and these are the experiences out of which Christian theology arises. From our awareness of our utter dependence Schleiermacher can find the language to talk about God as eternal, omnipresent, omnipotent or omniscient. Our experience of sin is the ground for talking about God as holy and just. Our consciousness of grace is the ground for talking about God as loving and wise.

Schleiermacher also talks about God in a Romantic milieu as **the unconditioned**. He bizarrely resurrects the classical understanding of God, almost despite himself. In his understanding, God is not a particular being among other beings. God is also beyond all speculative concepts—and while we cannot know God in Himself one of the theological tasks is to attempt to find the best way to talk about Him. When we speak of God we do so from our experience of our finitude, in our absolute dependence and in God's being for us. These are the best things we have to say and the best grounding we have for talking about God.

Schleiermacher is also **against a strict dualism** between the world and God as one would find in Deism. (If you have God as an efficient causality and want to have science, you have to keep God out of it.) God for Schleiermacher is not identical with the world but rather something like the picture the Romantics had of Spinoza's Living God—a God that is not merely anthropomorphic but is also not just an impersonal force like nature or fate.

6.7 Christ and Redemption

Schleiermacher's theology is deeply **Christocentric**. When he refers to himself as a *Herrnhuter*, that has to do with the central focus on the experience of Christ—not just beliefs about Christ, but one's personal experience of grace and redemption in Christ.

One of the ways Schleiermacher talks about Christ is in terms of **Christ's perfect God-consciousness**. Schleiermacher often uses this as a way to talk about the divine in Christ. Christ's perfect God-consciousness is 'a veritable being of God in Him'. Schleiermacher in the *Glaubenslehre*—because he does not want theology to be theoretical—is going to part ways with philosophical language that is used in the earlier Church confessions (like Nicaea or Chalcedon) that concerns Christ's 'natures'. For Schleiermacher, that is too close to speculative philosophy. As much as is possible, Schleiermacher wants to use language arising from the particularities of religious consciousness. So, he does not like using 'nature' language, because that is speculative— we are not even sure what that means when you apply it to God as the Creator of 'natures'. So, he talks about Christ being perfect, sinless and a miraculous manifestation of God-consciousness.

Redemption in Christ

Redeemer	Ideality (*Urbildlichkeit*)	Redemption
Exemplar	Exemplarity (*Vorbildlichkeit*)	Communication of redemption

---

In Christ's perfect God-consciousness, Christ is that which humanity is to be in its ideality. Christ in his God-consciousness is the Second Adam or the True Adam or the True Humanity. This kind of Christology echoes back to Irenaeus. In Christ, humanity is truly manifest in that He is the completion of the creation of man. In Christ, humanity is as humanity should be. Humanity as humanity should be is a state in which our souls are constantly at one with God—'praying without ceasing'—being constantly aware of our being in communion with God. In this, Christ is the norm for humanity and the full historical realization of this norm. This is not just a nice way of talking, but he truly had this perfect God-consciousness. Christ is not just an example—the experience that we have of Christ is that of **redemption**. So, Schleiermacher will talk about Christ as Redeemer and as Exemplar; these are the two sides to what Christ is to us. Christ has both **ideality**—*Urbildlichkeit*—and **exemplarity**—*Vorbildlichkeit*. In Christ's ideality, he is the Redeemer—the one who brings about a change in us. In his exemplarity, he is the One that is communicating His redemption to us. So for Schleiermacher, the essence of Christianity is redemption by Christ. Jesus is present to his disciples—whether in the past or in the present—and Christ is the Redeemer because he imparts God-consciousness to us. He communicates His perfect communion with the Father to us. It is through him that we have the kind of perfect communion with the Father that he has. And redemption has to do with the implanting or imparting of this God-consciousness as a new orientation or dominant principle within us. This is the core of redemption—that Christ communicates to us and gives us this new orientation of the soul. And it is a seed; we do not immediately have full God-consciousness.

Ultimately, Schleiermacher says that only this belief in Christ—that he communicates this God-consciousness to us—is what is necessary for faith. That is the key to Christian faith. The belief in miracles is not central to the work of Christ, and metaphysical categories about natures are not central to our faith in Christ either. Schleiermacher is pretty vague about the resurrection. He says that it does not necessarily matter what happened, what really matters is to know that Christ is your Redeemer. Redemption has to do with being made a new person. He is focusing on what is going on in us—the experience of redemption in Christ in us now.

The redemption that Schleiermacher presents is not an atoning blood sacrifice. Christ's redemption does not pay for our sins with his suffering. This is not an understanding of salvation where Christ's suffering satisfies God's honour or wrath. Schleiermacher did not think that this was a great view of God and did not see how the accounting (exactly what was paying for what) worked out. In fact, this was a long-standing beef of Schleiermacher. He had a lot of trouble with a view of redemption as blood sacrifice as a young man, and this ultimately brought about a break with his father, who disowned him for a time because of his rejection of such an understanding of redemption. For Schleiermacher, rather, Christ's work has to do with his coming so close to us that we are identified with Him. In this He gives us what He has, being the mind of Christ—which is this loving relation with the Father.

The communication of redemption happens when one experiences Christ—and one's redemption through the person of Christ—through the preaching of the Church. Preaching is central for Schleiermacher. One encounters Christ through preaching. He does not make a hard and fast distinction between your inward, spiritual experience of Jesus and your outward experience in the Church. The communication of the work of Christ and one's encounter with Jesus happens through the community and preaching of the Church. The disciples—in his terms—share Christ's ideality. It is as if his God-consciousness is extended through the Christian community, and he is present in the midst of that community—in the Body of Christ.

Jesus Christ is the historical Whence of the Christian common life. Christianity is a communal phenomena rooted in the person of Jesus. In him a new way of being came into existence; his personality—his person, his presence—is communicated through the Church and not apart from it. It is from this that he gets his doctrine of the Holy Spirit. The Holy Spirit is the common spirit of the Church—the presence of God in the Church. He does not have a whole lot to say explicitly about the Holy Spirit.

Schleiermacher, by and large, bypasses historical criticism when it comes to the question of the historical Jesus. He does not have the kind of historical–critical issues with the Gospel portraits of Jesus that later figures have. For instance, he thinks that the Gospel of John is probably the earliest and most accurate Gospel (contrary to the opinion that becomes more established that John is the latest and most heavily interpretive of the Gospels).

6.8 Sin

For Schleiermacher, one becomes conscious of one's sin only through redemption. Sin and grace come as a matched set. It is in the experience of redemption and conversion that sin is ultimately truly recognized. In describing the Christian consciousness, sin is present but as forgiven. Christian consciousness is of Christ's redemptive work in the face of one's sin. So sin is always set in opposition, in an antithesis, with grace.

Sin, for Schleiermacher, is a privation of the blessedness of God-consciousness. In an Augustinian mode, even our power to recognize our sin comes from Christ. Our sin-consciousness is a part of our redemption—it is a part of grace. Apart from the work of Christ in us, we are not even aware of our sin. So he will talk about sin as incomplete God-consciousness, or as denying one's dependence upon God. This denial of dependence is a selfishness. It is a disordering of one's loves—loving oneself more than loving God. It is valuing the temporal instead of the eternal. Sin, then, entails a discontentment or instability—a lack of a grounding or a connecting to that which truly grounds and establishes us (to smuggle in a bit of Kierkegaard's verbage).

We cannot overcome our own sin. Sin, for Schleiermacher, is not primarily moral, but is our disconnection from God. He will also call it our 'God-forgetfulness'. As redemption is social, something that is passed on, so is sin. Schleiermacher does not consider original sin as a past event. Rather, original sin has meaning for us in the present in our realization of our own incapacity. We have this universal condition in which all humans seem to lack this full God-consciousness. We seem to have an estranged relation to that upon which we should be fully dependent—God.

6.9 The Structure of the *Glaubenslehre*

Interestingly, Schleiermacher's *Glaubenslehre* is structured around three elements: the human, God and the world—just like the elements of the classical synthesis. To put it simply, the structure of the *Glaubenslehre* is a three-by-three grid. On one side you have the human, God and the world. Then, you have three aspects of Christian consciousness: our religious self-consciousness (which is our feeling of absolute dependence), the experience of redemption and then the experience of sin. These are the experiences from which our understandings of humanity, the world and God come in Schleiermacher's theology.

Below is a map of the *Glaubenslehre* along these lines. Schleiermacher is focusing on the unique character of the Christian faith in which everything has to do with our consciousness—with our God-consciousness and our consciousness of redemption in Christ. Part I of the *Glaubenslehre*—on the left—has to do just with our religious self-consciousness presupposed by and contained in the Christian affections (mainly the feeling of absolute dependence). From this religious self-consciousness, Schleiermacher draws forth the proper understanding of humanity, God's attributes and the world that it entails. Part II proceeds from our consciousness of sin and consciousness of grace and what those have to do with our understanding of humanity, the world and God's attributes. (We have inverted the last two points for ease of viewing in the chart below.)

In **Part I**, our state as humans is where we can think of the doctrines of **creation** and **preservation**. That is the closest to where we are—God has created us and is preserving us—we are a part of the created world. When we think of God from the perspective of the feeling of dependence, we can think of God's attributes as being **eternal** and **omnipresent**—and those as primary. Secondarily, we also see God as **omnipotent** and **omniscient**. Finally, our beliefs about the world from the standpoint of our feeling of absolute dependence have to do with the **original perfection of the world and of man**—the goodness and inherent ordering of the world of man towards God.

Part II proceeds from what Schleiermacher calls the 'antithesis of sin and grace'. Again, he starts with a certain site of experience or consciousness. So, when it comes to our **consciousness of sin**, what we can learn about our state as humans has to do with the doctrines of **original sin** and **actual sin**. When it comes to the world, it has to do with the doctrine of **evil**. The consciousness of sin is also the foundation for talking about God as **holy** and **just**. Our **consciousness of grace**,

The structure of Schleiermacher's *Glaubenslehre*

	Part I: Regarding the Religious Self-Consciousness Presupposed by and Contained in the Christian Affections (The Feeling of Absolute Dependence)	Part II: Regarding the Christian Experience of the Antithesis of Sin and Grace	
		Regarding the Consciousness of Sin	Regarding the Consciousness of Grace
Human States	Creation Preservation	Original Sin Actual Sin	The Person of Christ The Work of Christ Regeneration Sanctification
Divine Attributes	Eternity Omnipresence Omnipotence Omniscience	Holiness Justice	Love Wisdom
The Constitution of the World	Original perfection of the world Original perfection of man	Evil	The Church

however, is where Schleiermacher treats the **person and work of Christ** in terms of **regeneration** and **sanctification**. With regard to the world, this is where Schleiermacher treats the doctrine of **the Church**. With regard to God, this is where he talks about God as **love and wisdom**.

It is evident from this cursory glance at the outline of the *Glaubenslehre* that in it Schleiermacher is reinterpreting and representing most of the classic doctrines of Christian theology within the matrix of his understanding of God-consciousness or Christian experience. It should be noted that the doctrine of the Trinity only finds its way into the work in its conclusion. This is construed by many afterward to signify the lack of the significance of the doctrine of the Trinity for Schleiermacher (and indeed for much of the 'Liberal' tradition of theology that would look back to Schleiermacher as pioneer).

6.10 'Mediating' and 'Liberal' Theology

As a theologian, Schleiermacher was without peer until late in the nineteenth century. While he and Hegel dominated the field, Schleiermacher was *the* theologian of the two. His particular legacy—the work of the theologians who would follow after Schleiermacher, more immediately in Germany in the 1830s and 1840s—is a form of theology that is called 'Mediating Theology' or *Vermittlungstheologie*. Around the same time, there was a parallel stream of Hegelian theology in Germany.

For a long time, Schleiermacher was seen as the leading light in theology in Germany—especially for those who were interested in presenting Christianity in a way that was attentive to modern understandings. More generally, he is going to be very influential for what we today—or at least in the earlier part of the twentieth century—will look back on as 'Liberal Theology'.

As a professor and a well-known theologian and preacher, he was responsible for training many men who then went on to be church leaders, and he came to be seen as the eminent progressive–constructive theologian. As a constructive theologian, Schleiermacher was not interested in tearing down Christianity, but rather he presented a way that traditional Christian understandings could be believed and understood by people in the nineteenth century. The key to his influence was his emphasis on experience as the starting point for theological reflection, but it should be noted that for Schleiermacher it was never just experience—it was always experience as mediated through tradition. It is always our experience in the midst of the Church. Theology should be a *Glaubenslehre*—it should be a reflection on an experienced and communal faith.

Sources and Further Reading

Axt-Piscalar, Christine. 'Liberal Theology in Germany'. In *The Blackwell Companion to Nineteenth-Century Theology*, edited by David Fergusson, 468–85. Chichester: Wiley-Blackwell, 2010.

Dorrien, Gary. *Kantian Reason and Hegelian Spirit: The Idealistic Logic of Modern Theology*. Oxford: Wiley-Blackwell, 2012.

Helmer, Christine. 'Schleiermacher'. In *The Blackwell Companion to Nineteenth-Century Theology*, edited by David Fergusson, 31–57. Chichester: Wiley-Blackwell, 2010.

Lamm, Julia A. 'Romanticism and Pantheism'. In *The Blackwell Companion to Nineteenth-Century Theology*, edited by David Fergusson, 165–86. Chichester: Wiley-Blackwell, 2010.

Lamm, Julia A. *The Living God: Schleiermacher's Theological Appropriation of Spinoza*. University Park: Penn State University Press, 1996.

Livingston, James C. *Modern Christian Thought: Volume 1, The Enlightenment and the Nineteenth Century*. 2nd edn. Minneapolis, MN: Fortress Press, 2006.

Vidler, Alec R. *The Church in an Age of Revolution*. Rev. edn. New York: Penguin, 1990.

Welch, Claude. *Protestant Thought in the Nineteenth Century. Vol. 1, 1799–1870*. New Haven, CT: Yale University Press, 1972.

7

Hegel and Hegelians

Chapter Outline

7.1 Hegel

Hegel was the dominant philosopher in the nineteenth century and a significant influence on theology well into the twentieth. He did not really think of himself as a theologian. With Hegel in this chapter we have the three intellectual players that, to a significant degree, set the course for nineteenth-century theology: Kant, Schleiermacher and Hegel. These were the big three forces or strategies for defending, if not reconceiving, Christianity in the nineteenth century.

7.1.1 Life and Works

Georg Wilhelm Friedrich Hegel (1770–1831) was educated in a seminary in Tübingen. However, he soon lost interest in traditional theology and started studying the Greek classics. He also read some more recent philosophers, such as Spinoza, Jacobi, Herder and Rousseau. He ended up becoming roommates with Hölderlin and Schelling, and he also spent time with Schlegel and Novalis. So, Hegel was part of the inner circle of the Romantic artistic and philosophical scene. He was something of a hanger-on, however—a slow starter, as some might say. His roommate Schelling was a boy-genius—and he was the philosopher of the group then making a big splash. Hegel, however, in contrast, struggled well into middle age just to make a decent living. He taught at Jena for a brief time after he finished his education—until the university was closed when Napoleon took Jena. Here, Hegel writes his first major work, *Phenomenology of Spirit* (1807). After that, he ran a newspaper for a time (which beggars the imagination if you have ever read Hegel). Then for a period, he was a rector at a gymnasium—similar to a high school or grammar school—in Nuremburg. While teaching there, he writes *The Science of Logic* (1812–16)—precisely as exciting as it sounds—a large, intricate, hard-to-read work.

Figure 7.1 Hegel.

Courtesy of the Library of Congress. (No known restrictions on publication.)

During his time at Nuremburg, the *Phenomenology of Spirit* becomes more popular in intellectual circles. He was being read, even though he was stuck in a job that he certainly did not feel matched his talents. Eventually in 1818 he became a professor in Berlin, largely on the strength of his reputation based on *Phenomenology of Spirit* (written twelve years earlier). Schleiermacher taught at the University of Berlin as well, and is a big mover and shaker in Berlin at this time. Whatever popularity Hegel had, he always shared it with Schleiermacher. Nevertheless, Hegel quickly became a leading intellectual figure in Berlin; he is sometimes called the 'German Aristotle'.

Schleiermacher and Hegel had a strained relationship at best. Hegel did not care for Schleiermacher at all. He would say that if Schleiermacher is right about religion—that it is a feeling of absolute dependence—then 'a dog would be the best Christian since a dog is most strongly characterized by and lives primarily in this feeling'. He dismisses Schleiermacher's approach to religion as not serious intellectual work: you are just talking about your feelings, and my dog has feelings. Part of what you can hear here is the disdain of the professor for the preacher—the disdain of Hegel, the rational *Auflkärer*, for the Pietist Schleiermacher. Schleiermacher was, however, in a more powerful position—as one of the founders of the university—and he prevents Hegel from being admitted to the Berlin Academy of Sciences—the pre-eminent position for intellectuals to which Schleiermacher belongs—because Schleiermacher believes that speculative philosophy is not a proper discipline. He viewed what Hegel was doing as not even being philosophy. There is little love lost between these two intellectual giants.

In the years 1794 to 1796, Hegel writes what people describe as his early theological writings. He is inspired by Kant's *Religion within the Bounds of Reason Alone* and a basically Kantian picture of Christianity. His early theological writings are focused on the teachings of Jesus (where the content of these teachings are basically Kantian ethics). We also see, as he develops and becomes more interested in the Greeks, that he sees the social solidarity of the Greek *polis* as being replaced by Christianity. He sees this as a bad thing. He thinks that the Greeks had a better, more authentically social folk-religion, and that something went wrong with Christianity.

Main published works of Hegel

Phenomenology of Spirit (1807)

Science of Logic (1812–16)

Encyclopedia of the Philosophical Sciences (1817)

Philosophy of Right (1820)

Hegel's *Phenomenology of Spirit* was published in 1807. His *Science of Logic* was published in 1812 and 1816 in multiple volumes. His *Encyclopedia of the Philosophical Sciences* was published in 1817, and this in many ways came out of his teaching at the gymnasium. One of his jobs as a teacher was to simplify things. The *Encyclopedia of the Philosophical Sciences* is his summarization of his philosophical system. In 1820, he published his last proper book—although we have a lot of material produced by him—the *Philosophy of Right*. In general terms, this is Hegel's work on political theory.

Significantly, for our purposes—beyond the few books that he published—are Hegel's lectures. He was a professor, so he lectured on many different topics. He wrote lectures on the history of philosophy and on the philosophy of history. He had lectures on art and science, but he also had lectures on religion—in fact, that was the subject that he taught the most. He lectured on the philosophy of religion four times—in 1821, 1824, 1827 and 1831. So this was a repeated, developed interest in him. Thus, when it comes to Hegel's thought about religion we have a lot of material (multiple volumes) of his most mature, developed thought. Hegel died suddenly during a cholera outbreak in Berlin. This was a considerable shock at the time in Berlin, since Hegel was considered an historic figure, even in his own time.

7.1.2 Hegel's Philosophy

Hegel's philosophy shows the influence of Romanticism, the Romantic idea of the **unity** or the **reconciling of opposites**. But this unity, for Hegel, is always going to be a rational unity. He is not going to let go of the Enlightenment on rationality. Central to Hegel's thought is the idea that **reason** or consciousness develops or unfolds over time. That is part of what reason or consciousness does—it develops. Reason is a **process**. Our consciousness is a process through which thought develops in a particular direction: from a less satisfactory or true position to a more satisfactory or true position. What makes something more or less true or satisfactory has to do with its **wholeness**. A less satisfactory or true position is a more limited perspective, whereas a more satisfactory or true perspective is more all-encompassing. If this is taken to its logical extension you get a famous phrase of Hegel's (from the preface to the *Phenomenology of Spirit* and also from the *Philosophy of Right*): '**The true is the whole**.' The truest perspective is the perspective that is the most holistic; that takes the most into account.

Thought itself, for Hegel, has its own exigency or propulsion towards this more holistic perspective. It is not that we change the way we think, but this is what thought itself does. It changes, develops and unfolds over time—primarily through overcoming limitations. Thought overcomes previous limitations and more restrictive perspectives—expanding its own perspective.

When Hegel thinks about **logic**, he means the process of thought unfolding. Logic is thought's process as progressing through conflict. This process typically has a triadic (Hegel is three-crazy) structure that has traditionally been summarized as thesis, antithesis and synthesis—although those are not the terms Hegel uses. He refers to the **immediate**, the **dialectical** and the **speculative**. So, in any given process of thought, you begin with a simpler position. A simple identity. That then will move to see itself in opposition to its opposing position. It will move to a position of contradiction. Then, the third step is mediating between these two seemingly contradictory or opposed positions.

His idea is that the more you investigate a particular idea, the more it shows itself to be implicated or dependent upon its opposite. The more that you investigate one thing that seems to be simple and have an identity in and of itself, the more you realize that it only exists in opposition to something else. These two can then be seen as resting on a broader idea that includes and reconciles both within it—a broader identity that includes the other limited perspectives that seem to contradict each other. The third includes and describes the relation between the two, reconciling them within itself and into a new unity. That then becomes a new one that generates its own opposite, only to be subsumed into a new unity. This is the logic of how—when you are thinking—your perspective expands. In this, you move towards a truer and more holistic perspective.

Thesis	The immediate	Simple identity
Antithesis	The dialectical	Contradiction/opposition
Synthesis	The speculative	Reconciliation in new unity

One of the ways in which Hegel names this progression of thought is with the term *Aufhebung*. (*Aufheben* is the verb; *aufgehoben* the participle form.) This term is commonly left un-translated because of its richness and concomitant difficulty to translate. *Aufhebung* means two different—and perhaps opposite—things: It means to overcome or to **negate** something, but it also means to **preserve** something. Very literally, it means to lift. When something is taken up, it is preserved, but is also cancelled (it is 'taken'). The idea is that as things are moving on—as you move to a higher perspective—a higher, broader perspective includes the lower perspective. The higher perspective preserves the lower; but it also negates the lower perspective as being true in and of itself. The taking up also identifies the original perspective as being a partial perspective. In its own terms, the lower is wrong—however, in the broader terms of the higher, the truth of the lower can be preserved. So the highest truth of something always is in its future—things become truer in the future as we have a broader perspective. Looking back we always understand better than we could in the midst. Hence, the Hegelian saying: 'The owl of Minerva always flies at dusk.' Minerva is the goddess of wisdom (often accompanied or represented by an owl), and owls only fly at night: so it is only at the end of the day that wisdom comes. It is only after you have gained perspective do you understand the whole truth of the day. So there is a progression towards a truer position, and the truer position is always going to be the last one.

There is more at stake in Hegel's thought than what reason does and how we understand things. He thinks that this progressive structure is not just the way our thinking unfolds, but rather the way reality itself unfolds. Key here is Hegel's understanding of **Spirit** or *Geist*. In Hegel, there is a Romantic idea of there being a universal life that manifests itself in all things. (Hegel is following Schelling here.) This universal life manifests itself in the particularities of everything in history. This process of progress through opposition in history is an evolving of Spirit coming to realize itself. So, this is not just us coming to realize the truth about things. There is rather, a broader dynamic process that includes everything that is developing.

History is significant for Hegel because he thinks that history is the unfolding of *Geist* just as an individual's life is the unfolding of one's own spirit or consciousness. Through all of history, *Geist* is coming to a developed self-awareness and self-understanding through the world. Now, there is certainly some ambiguity as to what exactly *Geist* is. Scholars have interpreted Hegel in different ways—both in his day and since. Some people think that *Geist* sounds an awful like God, such that Hegel is presenting God as coming to self-awareness through the world. Others think of *Geist* as the whole of humanity. This deflationary and perhaps more believable reading is likely the less

Figure 7.2 Hegel.

'Georg Wilhelm Friedrich Hegel' by Unknown—Transferred from de.wikipedia to Commons by James Steakley using Commons Helper. (Original text: Hans Wahl, Anton Kippenberg: *'Goethe und seine Welt'*, Insel-Verlag, Leipzig 1932 S.161.) Licensed under Public Domain via Wikimedia Commons.

accurate of the two. If we are interested in figuring out what Hegel actually said, there is something much more than just human society going on here.

Hegel has some pretty grand metaphysical ambitions. There is a grand narrative of a **Spirit** that creates the **world**—generates that which is not its self—in order to come to self-consciousness. This **self-consciousness of Spirit** happens in humanity. Humanity is the synthesis of God and the world ultimately. More specifically this self-consciousness of Spirit occurs best in philosophy—and supremely in Hegelian philosophy, of course. So, Hegel here is looking at the big picture. He is not really interested in the individual, but he is looking at the grand sweep of history—and that sweep is about Spirit coming to self-consciousness.

7.1.3 Absolute Spirit and Religion

Spirit ultimately comes to self-consciousness in human self-consciousness, and this self-conscious Spirit is fully manifest not just in human consciousness, but what he calls Absolute Spirit. So when it comes to the human manifestation of Spirit, there are three levels. Again, we are always going to be moving from the least perfect to the most perfect—the later is always going to be better. These are the three kinds of Spirit that manifest as humanity. First is **Subjective Spirit**. This is simply individual consciousness. This is the domain of epistemology. The second is **Objective Spirit**. These are the social forms of thought—the forms, patterns and structures of society (such as he will describe in the *Philosophy of Right*). The third (and highest) kind of Spirit is what he calls **Absolute Spirit**. Absolute Spirit entails the highest forms of Spirit's unfolding, and Absolute Spirit itself has three levels. (Hegel loves him some threes.) All three forms of Absolute Spirit are identical in content but differ in form.

The first, and thus the lowest, manifestation of Absolute Spirit is **art**. So, you can see the Romantic influence on Hegel, in that art is part of Absolute Spirit. The fulfilment of human history is indeed happening in art (but not art alone). Art presents Spirit to consciousness but only in a sensual way—only as present to the senses.

The second aspect of Absolute Spirit is **religion**. Religion reveals the highest truth—in particular, he would say, Christianity does. Religion presents Absolute Truth, but it is bound to the form of 'representation'—a *Vorstellung* as he calls it. Religion uses picture-thinking. It is communicating Absolute Truth to people who do not have philosophical categories. So religious consciousness has to do with using stories and symbols to communicate the Absolute Truth about reality. Ultimately, in its highest form you find this in Christianity. But Hegel argues, one has to go beyond religion and Christianity to get to the highest form of Absolute Spirit.

The imaginative representations of the Absolute in religion have to be raised to their proper philosophical form. **Philosophy** is the highest form of Absolute Spirit. Philosophy has the same content as religion, except it has its proper conceptual form—the form of *Begriff* or the concept. In philosophy, we then understand reality as it is. In philosophy Spirit is coming to its most explicit and full self-understanding.

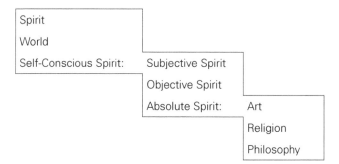

7.1.4 Hegel on Christianity

7.1.4.1 Christianity in Hegel's Philosophy of Religion

Hegel sees himself as a Christian philosopher. He believes that he is doing a great service to Protestant Christianity by bringing out the full philosophical truth of the Christian faith. In fact, he thinks that the theologies of his day—like Schleiermacher's—fall way short of helping people know anything intelligible about their religion. Kant and Schleiermacher are the most prominent of a bunch of poor options—and Hegel thinks that this is a tragedy. Hegel is a Christian and believed that people needed to think seriously about Christianity. He thinks it is a disaster for Christianity to retreat into a non-public, non-rational domain. As Claude Welch writes, 'If Christian theologians were unwilling to defend the rationality of Christian belief, somebody had to do it' (p. 87). If the theologians are not going to step up and help out Christianity, Hegel is going to take it upon himself.

Hegel sees the putting aside of Christianity as an intellectual option in the Enlightenment as a huge blow. Rather, he wants to say that Christianity is true—indeed, he wants to say that it is necessarily true. It, in a sense, cannot be false; it has an inherent truth to it.

Interestingly, Hegel gives certain names to Christianity in his *Lectures on the Philosophy of Religion*. He refers to Christianity as 'The Consummate Religion' or 'The Revealed Religion'. The Consummate Religion for him is the culmination of the progress of religion in history—thus yielding the highest religion. Christianity is then the truest religion. Now, religion is lower than philosophy—but Christianity is the top religion. Christianity is still a figurative expression of the truth that is revealed more clearly in philosophy. So why does he like Christianity so much? Part of his interest is in the manner in which Christianity presents itself as God reveals Himself—as a religion of **revelation**. In this Christianity coheres with Hegel's broader understanding of the Spirit's coming to self-understanding in the domain of Absolute Spirit. Part of Hegel's interest is that Christianity reveals the essential truth of **the identity of the divine and the human**. At the heart of Christianity is the incarnation—Christ being fully God and fully man—and for Hegel this is a symbolic revelation of the unity between the divine and the human and of how the two are brought back into unity. This again is a picture of the entire stretch of history—Spirit coming to union with that which is other than itself.

7.1.4.2 Creation and Fall

Creation for Hegel is a depiction of the initial expression of Spirit that is moving from an infinite to a finite, determined position. The Spirit goes forth and generates something that is other than itself. For Hegel, Spirit needs to become embodied in order to realize itself. Creation then for Hegel is necessary. If Spirit is going to come to self-manifestation, it has to create something beyond itself through which it comes to self-recognition. And this is a definite departure from Christian orthodoxy. The 'other' to *Geist* is the world—the world is part of the necessary unfolding of the life of God.

Interestingly, for Hegel creation is closely related to the **Fall**. Creation is a part of a necessary movement of the Spirit towards maturity and self-possession—but the first step in moving beyond its innocence is a move into self-opposition and estrangement. Then it will come to self-knowledge. Creation is like the Fall of God, except it is the creation of the world and the estrangement of the world from God in its creation. So, there is never a non-estranged world as the second, negative moment in the three-part dialectic. The world as other-to-God is always already estranged—though this is not a static relationship. When Hegel speaks of the Fall in relation to humanity, the Fall is not something that happens in history but is rather a Fall into history. It is not about the first humans, but a truth about humanity in general—and the truth is that humanity (along with all finite being) is implicitly incomplete. There is disharmony and separation that is always already there, and it is from that that we are trying to overcome our incompleteness and move towards a unity.

Hegel represents what in the history of theology is called **a fortunate fall**, saying that the Fall is not that bad of a thing. It is a part of a broader positive movement. Humanity's alienation is a part of humanity's coming to maturity.

7.1.4.3 The Incarnation and the Community of the Spirit

While there is an implicit unity between God and humanity, this unity becomes explicit in the person of Christ. It is only in Christ that God and man are united in a self-conscious way. While we might see Hegel here as taking Jesus to be a figurative way of depicting the truth of the unity of God and man, the way Hegel talks suggests he sees Jesus—the historical person—as unique. In Hegel's reasoning, God had to have an actual self-consciousness in a historical human being for the process of salvation and the Spirit coming to self-realization to happen. In Jesus this unity is realized—at least in part—in an event in history.

However, Hegel is primarily interested in the symbolic truth of the incarnation. He is interested in the meaning of the *Vorstellung* of Christ, the *Begriff*—the unity of the divine and human nature— and a self-consciousness of the divine within human nature.

The **reconciliation** effected in Christ is focused on Christ's death and resurrection. In the Passion the divine or Spirit is united with the finite most radically. The infinite truly becomes finite: it dies. In Hegel's understanding, death is an expression of Christ's finitude—his 'worldliness' as opposed to 'Godhood'. Death is the extremity of estrangement. He will then talk about the resurrection and ascension as a return from finitude—God's returning to God's self from estrangement. There are always the three movements: starting off in a given assembled unity, going out of yourself and then returning home with an awareness of the journey.

Figure 7.3 Hegel.

'Friedrich Hegel mit Studenten Lithographie F Kugler' by F. Kugler—Das Wissen des 20. Jahrhunderts, Bildungslexikon, Rheda, 1931. Licensed under Public Domain via Wikimedia Commons.

When it comes to the **community of the Spirit**, he sees the Spirit working on the ambiguity between Spirit—in his sense—and the Holy Spirit. The Spirit is incarnate in the Christian community, and in that community the implicitly divine Spirit is incarnated in humanity in a way that it is not just a singular person but can at least theoretically include all of humanity in the Church. So this is a transition towards God's full presence in the human community and in human awareness. For him, that is what the Holy Spirit means: when this awareness of the presence of God is within us. This spiritual community is the Kingdom, and this is the goal of history—for God to be present in the Kingdom of the Spirit, which is the Church. And so God, ultimately, is not being presented as a person—certainly the Spirit is not a person in our limited sense of the term.

7.1.4.4 Trinity

While in the Enlightenment the doctrine of the Trinity takes a very definite backseat, Hegel places it at the very centre of Christianity. To talk about the divine Persons of the Trinity for Hegel is representational. When we talk about the Person of the Father generating the Son, this is picture-thinking. This is not the most accurate understanding of the Trinity. For Hegel, rather, the whole of philosophy provides or proves the inner truth of the doctrine of the Trinity. So, the Trinity is basically fundamentally true. But what the Trinity is for Hegel is this essential movement of Spirit out of itself and returning to itself. The Trinity is a representation of the dialectical movement and nature of Geist—and only in Christianity does one see the fullest presentation of the process of the Spirit.

the Idea	going forth	and returning to itself
'in itself'	'for itself'	'in and for itself'
Father	Son	Spirit of love

Thus, first, you have the concept, or the idea—the 'in itself', as Hegel calls it. This is the initial starting point. Something is what it is in itself. He says this is the Father. But the Father then goes out from itself, becoming something other—generating the Son—in order to return to itself. It is both in and for itself. It is itself and knows itself. And this is the Spirit—which is itself as a relation, which is love. The Spirit is love between the Father and the Son—which is a traditional Augustinian understanding of the Trinity.

One of the things you can take from this is that the Spirit is the final form of God. The Spirit is the truest form of God that ultimately supersedes either the Father or the Son. The Spirit is the togetherness of the Father and the Son—the in and for itself. So, God is not a person in our limited sense, but the Spirit is actualized in a community.

7.1.5 Christianity and Philosophy

Christianity for Hegel is ultimately *aufgehoben* in philosophy—it is both negated and preserved. It is 'suspended', to use an English term (to prefigure Kierkegaard a bit). In religion—Christianity in particular—you have a more external, imaginative, pictorial mode of representation. But the core of religion is preserved in philosophy in the mode of a pure thought form. And so Christianity is maintained, except not in the same form. The form is negated as being penultimate, but the content is preserved—and the content is brought into its truth and made more explicit in Christianity. Hegel thought he was helping Christianity by translating it into the universal form of philosophy, thereby justifying it and showing that it is true—however there is some ambiguity in his position. It could be that he is indeed showing the content of Christianity in such a way that it is fully rational, and some of his followers will read him this way—they are going to be called the **Right Hegelians**, or the Old Hegelians. Or, you could say that Christianity is nothing more than a distorted, immature picture of the truth. Once you have the true truth—philosophy—you can then discard this superstitious religious nonsense. In this view religion is dissolved because you do not need it anymore. So the religious and the Christian is something that should be surpassed—this is the perspective of those who are called the **Left Hegelians**, or the Young Hegelians.

Both groups take Hegel as saying that religion has no independent domain—it does not have a separate area that belongs to it (and so is insulated from threat). On the positive side, Hegel says that religion is rational and that Christianity has really good reasons for being believed over and against what he sees Schleiermacher doing. However, religion can also then be dissolved into its more secular bases. So in the same move he seems to be supporting Christianity but also setting it up so that it can disappear into the most radical philosophical atheism the world has yet to see.

7.2 Hegelians

By the time of Hegel's death in 1831, Hegelianism was not only a major school of thought, but was dividing into different streams: Right and Left, 'old' and 'young', respectively. We will mostly talk about the Left Hegelians because they were frankly more influential. The division of Left and Right comes from David Friedrich Strauss, himself a Left Hegelian, in his influential and controversial work, *The Life of Christ Critically Examined*. He is the first to make the distinction presumably based on the division of French Parliament at the time between conservatives and non-conservatives.

7.2.1 Right Hegelians

The Right Hegelians (or 'Old Hegelians') were Hegel's most immediate theological disciples—dominant in the period of the 1820s, the last decade of Hegel's life. **Karl Daub (1765–1836)**, in Heidelberg, and **Philipp Marheineke (1780–1846)**, in Berlin, are two prime representatives of this approach. They tend to see Hegel as a champion of orthodoxy. Hegel does not just present an Enlightened and stripped-down version of Christianity but rather has meditated extensively upon the central mysteries of the Christian faith: the incarnation and the Trinity. These are the historical centres of Christian affirmation and are at the heart of Hegel's thought. The Right Hegelians saw Hegel's philosophy of religion as distinctively Christian and doing the Christian faith the service of showing it to be rational and believable to modern people. These more orthodox theologians saw the possibility of a happy marriage between Hegel and Christian theology.

For these Hegelians, Christianity is not superseded, replaced or made superfluous by Hegel's philosophy. His philosophy is used to reconstruct or translate Christianity into the modern world. It is a useful philosophical grammar for talking about Christian theology. Christianity has used various philosophical grammars in different eras of the Church—be it Aristotle or Neo-Platonism in the West. Hegel simply provides an especially advantageous way to talk about the Christian faith, in the Modern world.

7.2.2 Left Hegelians

The Left Hegelians are also called the Radical Hegelians or the Young Hegelians. This ends up being, in the long run, the more influential branch of Hegelianism—especially when we get to the 1830s. After Kant, Schleiermacher and Hegel are dead, there arises a more critical (if not downright suspicious) streak in European thought in the nineteenth century. Indeed, it is with them that we get two of the most significant modern masters of the hermeneutics of suspicion—Feuerbach and Marx. There is a definite iconoclastic and anti-Christian tendency that came to the fore with the Left Hegelians. They will present explicitly atheistic versions of Hegelianism.

One of the things that is evident is that the Left Hegelians do not shy away from modifying Hegel's philosophy for their particular purposes. Some will modify it quite radically to the point of inverting it—turning it upside down—in the sense of making Hegel's dialectical idealism into a dialectical materialism. (Dialectical materialism is one of the names for Marxism.)

With regard to Christianity, it is safe to say that the Left Hegelians believe that Hegel's philosophy *Aufhebung* of Christianity does considerably more negating than preserving. They hold that we do not ultimately really need Christianity or anything like it anymore once we have the philosophical content. They think that Hegel overcame Christianity, and that his *Geist* is only interesting as the Spirit of humanity. In their own time, almost all of these figures were outcasts. They had a rough go of it in trying to exist in the traditional academic circles, largely because they were outspoken critics of Christianity.

7.2.2.1 D. F. Strauss

The first figure to consider here is **David Friedrich Strauss (1808–74)**. As a student, Strauss went to Berlin to study with Hegel. Upon his arrival in Berlin, he visited Schleiermacher's home, where he learned that Hegel had just died. He supposedly said, 'It was to hear him that I came to Berlin!' While this likely did not score any points with Schleiermacher (or win Strauss any awards for tact), it is indicative of his dedication to Hegel.

A Hegelian, Strauss is likely the most 'orthodox' (in the sense of not radically modifying Hegel's doctrines) of the Left Hegelians. He viewed Christianity as an expression of higher philosophical truths generally. He saw Christ, more particularly, as standing for the idea of the perfection of humanity. He, like Hegel, wanted to reinterpret Christianity for modern people.

However, it is not for his Hegelianism that Strauss is most known. He is famous or infamous for the book he writes when he is twenty-six years old, *Das Leben Jesu* or *The Life of Christ Critically Examined* (1835). Its publication created an immediate controversy in Germany. This book and Strauss himself came to be seen as a symbol of the destructiveness of biblical criticism. The controversy also kept him from ever having an academic career, and he ended up living the rest of his life off of his inheritance.

In *The Life of Christ Critically Examined*, Strauss examines the Gospels through the lens of his understanding of **myth**. A myth is not a lie but a largely unconscious product of communal imagination. The mythical elements in the Gospels are the products of the imaginations of the early followers of Jesus. Such mythical elements for Strauss include the birth stories, miracles, resurrection, ascension—accounts that are blatantly supernatural. He would say that these are not historical facts, but they do express fundamental truths. They are symbolically true. These mythical stories are Jesus's early followers' ways of talking about the significance of Jesus. One could then, in Strauss's mind, let go of the historical reality of what the Gospels seem to be talking about but hold on to the truths that they express.

The truth that the Gospels express is the Hegelian idea of the unity of humanity and the divine—but not in a single person. Strauss asserts that the Gospel writers like other ancient people did not think like modern, scientific people. They did not think in terms of history or science, but in terms of myth. This is the natural way that religious consciousness operates. In Hegelian terms, religion or myth is truth in a representative form—as *Vorstellung*—and is not to be taken as an explicit expression of the truth. It is meant to be the truth put in a picture or story form.

Strauss thinks that the more mythical aspects of the Gospel stories were reconstructed out of Old Testament sayings about the Messiah. They were fulfilled prophecy; the prophesies were the

Figure 7.4 D. F. Strauss.

source of the imagination that generated these pictorial stories. Strauss thought that one generation after the life of Christ was long enough for such mythical elaboration to occur—which would entail (oddly) that people would forget or recreate what actually happened in their own lifetimes. (He would talk about the resurrection in terms of a sort of group hallucination.) While Strauss might represent an extreme of biblical criticism, it is the beginning of an influential way of looking at things. The Gospels were not fraud—which is what Reimarus says. But they contain the kind of unintentional fabrication that was entailed in the understanding of peoples at a more primitive stage of cultural development. Ancient people had a mythical way of looking at things.

Strauss believed that in the Gospels we have a mixture of history and myth. And in trying to get them away from each other—in trying to figure out what reliable, actual historical information we have about Jesus—he found that there was very little historical information there. Much of the Gospels were mythical or legendary. He had a much more negative view of the historicity of the Gospels than the vast majority of the critical Gospel scholars today. What he thought about the historical Jesus was something like this: He comes to believe Himself to be the Messiah, and his followers then take this and run with it with their myth-making imagination. They see him as the Messiah, and so they take material from the Old Testament that was associated with the Messiah—different prophecies and miracles—and then these make their way back into the stories of the Gospels as the mythical content. So, Jesus, for Strauss, sees his messianic vocation as eschatological. Eschatology is at the core of what the historical Jesus was all about for Strauss. This reflects what we see in Reimarus—that Jesus is a failed eschatological prophet—but also in Albert Schweitzer. Strauss was, in many ways, a firebrand who had a strong influence on intellectuals outside of the Church, especially in Germany and in England.

7.2.2.2 Feuerbach

Ludwig Feuerbach (1804–72) initially began his education by studying theology—as did Hegel— and studies under Hegel for a few years at Berlin in the 1820s. Through that experience, Feuerbach ends up gravitating towards philosophy as a vocation. For most of his adult life, he was a private author; he did not hold a teaching position.

Feuerbach is easily understood as Hegel turned upside-down. Instead of seeing the human as God or Spirit coming to self-recognition, he turns that around and says that God is the human coming to know itself. God is human nature objectified. Instead of seeing world history as the story of the divine becoming alienated from itself then returning to itself, he would say that it is really a story of humanity in religion becoming alienated from itself. Religion is the self-alienation of humanity. This estrangement— humanity's estrangements from itself—is largely unconscious. It is a zero-sum game, where the greater God is the less humanity is. So it is projecting onto God all of the valuable attributes of humanity, and then saying that humanity does not have any of these. God is the human alienated from itself.

Feuerbach's goal was a humanity that is post-religious—a humanity at one with itself and not alienated. What he is ultimately proposing is a humanism, though there is a strong religious tinge to his humanism. Feuerbach was not opposed to religion; he just wanted it to be a religion of humanity. In places, he presents himself as the second Luther. The real Reformation needs to be continued, and now instead of doing away with the Church we are doing away with God. Religion at its best should reveal humanity's uniqueness and what is infinitely valuable in humanity. A famous phrase

Figure 7.5 Feuerbach.

'Ludwig Feuerbach' by http://www.ludwig-feuerbach.de/Anselm_Brief.htm. Licensed under Public Domain via Wikimedia Commons.

of his is that 'theology is anthropology'. If you understand what is being expressed in religious language, you see it is talking about what is positive about humanity and projecting it into God.

What Feuerbach was advocating was a new humanism. He wanted to celebrate humanity, and he would say that religion—even though it entailed self-alienation—was a covert celebration of humanity. It was a celebration of the goodness, holiness and creativity of humanity; humanity just did not know it. As an inversion of Hegel's itinerary of *Geist*, religion that begins with the human manifesting itself in the divine then should return to itself realizing that the divine attributes (that it values and sees as praiseworthy) are actually its own and return to itself those attributes.

Feuerbach's most influential work is *The Essence of Christianity* (1841). In it are his ideas about religion explicit to Christianity, in which God in Christ becomes human thus manifesting the divine qualities in a human being. Like Hegel, Feuerbach saw Christianity as the Consummate Religion, and asserted that it was closest to turning into the religion of humanity because it indeed took all of these great divine qualities and gave them to a human being: Jesus. Feuerbach viewed Christian beliefs as revealing human self-consciousness. So what Feuerbach was striving for— he even presents it in terms of a 'realized Christianity'—was a Christianity that did not have a transcendent God, but was rather centred on the love of the neighbour. He was rejecting the transcendent and wanted to make the sacred to be something that was immanent. He wanted people to love their fellow human beings as intrinsically valuable. *The Essence of Christianity* had a significant effect on the other Left Hegelians—especially the next figure we will consider.

7.2.2.3 Marx

Karl Marx (1818–83) viewed both D. F. Strauss and Feuerbach as forerunners of his own philosophy, though he self-consciously pushed beyond them. Marx travels to Berlin, where he falls in with the other Young Hegelians there. Looking back on Strauss and Feuerbach, Marx writes that 'for Germany, the criticism of religion is in essence complete'. Strauss and Feuerbach convince

Figure 7.6 Marx.

Courtesy of the Library of Congress. (No known restrictions on publication.)

Marx that he does not need to bother with theology (even if that might not have been their original intent). He ended up moving to Jena and became a journalist involved in organizing workers. Like the other Left Hegelians, he did not work in an academic setting.

Marx believes that Hegel overlooked what was truly important in life. Like Feuerbach, Marx presents a sort of upside-down Hegelianism. He thought that while Hegel focused on abstractions like art, religion and philosophy as the highest expressions of Spirit, what he missed was concrete social reality. He missed where the masses of people in industrialized societies lived.

Marx's philosophy is described as a dialectical materialism as opposed to Hegel's dialectical idealism. He takes over Hegel's idea of a dialectic—of there being a necessary unfolding and progression and that this unfolding happens through the resolution of conflict. But he inverts the dialectic in a manner like Feuerbach. The world is not the product of Spirit; rather, Spirit—all the spheres of human culture—is the product of material forces. For Marx, ideas are the product of material—by this he normally means economic realities.

When it comes to **religion**, Marx, though appreciative of Feuerbach, moves beyond Feuerbach's abstract description of humanity's self-alienation to consider more concrete historical factors. He thinks that Feuerbach was too abstract talking about the divine being simply humanity in general self-alienation. Marx is more interested in what actually happened— what are the concrete, economic, historical factors that are going on here? Religion for him is an **inverted consciousness**, but he wants to answer the question of why humanity would do this. Religion's inverted consciousness for Marx is based on an inverted world, on a disordered economic situation. He is here addressing in his own suspicious genealogy of religion an issue that Feuerbach does not—the issue of why people project the best parts of themselves onto an imaginary divine. Marx says it is because of certain socio-economic realities that can be explained in a materialist frame. Marx does not think religion is pure illusion; it is rather a real symptom of a real sickness. This spiritual disturbance reflects a deeper material suffering. One of his ways of looking at religion is that it is just a way of escaping our present, troublesome reality. (This was his understanding of Pietism.) Marx saw religion as a secondary superstructure that was built over the primary reality of humanity in its socio-economic material conditions. In his 'Contributions to the Critique of Hegel's Philosophy of Right', he says that 'man makes religion, religion does not make man'. He states further, famously: 'Religious suffering is at once the *expression* of real suffering and the *protest* against real suffering. Religion is the sigh of the oppressed creature, the heart of a heartless world, just as it is the spirit of spiritless conditions. It is the *opium* of the people.' Normally if you hear religion as being the opium of the people you think that it is purely an illusion. However, Marx saw it in a context that it was expressing a deep reality; it was a way of trying to cope with a messed up sociopolitical situation. It is not a false suffering; it arises from real suffering. Religion is a way of trying to deal with such suffering when there does not seem to be any other way.

So religion, Marx says, is an expression of real suffering—but, he would further argue that it offers a false solution. The solution is to look to another world, to escape into a false reality—this is why it is an opium. Often religion is reinforced as ideology and as the interest of the ruling parties. The ruling parties, in Marx's accounting, are relieved when the oppressed get religion and anesthetize themselves of their present suffering.

It has to be said that there are other views of what religion does in the face of sociopolitical oppression. If one reads the Hebrew prophets and looks at the history of the Church, one can see more revolutionary aspects along with the more suspicion-worthy co-opting of religion by the powers that be. In fact, much of Marx's critique of religion (as brilliantly presented by Merold Westphal) echoes in many ways Jesus's and the Hebrew prophets' own critiques of corrupted religion. Devout believers in God should certainly agree (if for no other reason, on the basis of Scriptural authority) with Marx's critique of religion as having been used to abuse and manipulate people in their sociopolitical situations.

Sources and Further Reading

Dorrien, Gary. *Kantian Reason and Hegelian Spirit: The Idealistic Logic of Modern Theology*. Oxford: Wiley-Blackwell, 2012.

Fergusson, David. 'Hegel'. In *The Blackwell Companion to Nineteenth-Century Theology*, edited by David Fergusson, 58–75. Chichester: Wiley-Blackwell, 2010.

Livingston, James C. *Modern Christian Thought: Volume 1, The Enlightenment and the Nineteenth Century*. 2nd edn. Minneapolis, MN: Fortress Press, 2006.

Stout, Jeffrey. *The Flight from Authority: Religion, Morality, and the Quest for Autonomy*. Notre Dame, IN: University of Notre Dame Press, 1981.

Welch, Claude. *Protestant Thought in the Nineteenth Century. Vol. 1, 1799–1870*. New Haven, CT: Yale University Press, 1972.

Westphal, Merold. *Suspicion and Faith: The Religious Uses of Modern Atheism*. New York: Fordham University Press, 1998.

Vidler, Alec R. *The Church in an Age of Revolution*. Rev. edn. New York: Penguin, 1990.

8

Coping with the Nova

Chapter Outline

8.1 The Nineteenth-Century Nova

The background of nineteenth-century theology	
Defining movements	The Enlightenment
	The Evangelical Awakenings
	Romanticism
Defining thinkers	Kant
	Schleiermacher
	Hegel

Now that we have covered the Enlightenment, the Awakening and Romanticism—and Kant, Schleiermacher and Hegel—the playing field has been set for nineteenth-century European theology. In the **eighteenth century**, in trying to deal with the problem of the splintering of the Christianity identity left over from the Reformation and the Wars of Religion there were two opposed approaches: **confessionalism** and **anti-confessionalism**. One can circle the wagons and defend your particular group, or reject that altogether in more of an Enlightened direction. Some of the Awakenings as well reject confessionalism to focus on religious experience over creedal distinctives.

In the **nineteenth century**, there would be three options to deal with the splintering of Christian identity—which is still ongoing. (Neither the Enlightenments nor the Awakenings could stem the tide of post-Reformation ecclesial division.) First, you still had **confessionalism**. There were strong contingents of Lutherans that viewed this as the way forward, or at least the right way of doing things. There was also what could be called an **ecumenical confessionalism** trying to find broader confessional unity. We saw this in Germany with what is called the Unity Church—with Schleiermacher who explicitly wrote his systematic theology as something that would be valid for Reformed and Lutheran groups. Something like this can be seen with Hegel as seeking to provide for a broader Protestant unity. The Oxford Movement (as we will see in the next chapter) looked at such a broader Christian unity as well. Beyond stricter and broader confessionalism, straight-up **atheism** was now on the table as well. This became much more widespread in the nineteenth century than in the eighteenth, with it becoming increasingly a live option for normal people.

In the nineteenth century, the strength of the various confessional churches largely had to do with their relations to the state. This period is also described as an age of revolution. Things were changing at an increasing rate, and the Church often found itself in a position of resisting such societal change. Because of this the Church was often seen as out of touch with society—it was not taking part in the broader dynamism of the culture.

Charles Taylor describes nineteenth-century European culture in terms of a **Nova Effect**. He says that out of the eighteenth century—out of the Enlightenment and the Awakenings—there was a cross-pressure or tension that generated the Nova Effect of the nineteenth century. There was a tension between orthodoxy and unbelief, and neither of these two positions was able to be gotten rid of. Nor could be considered outside of the culture. So instead of having a unified culture, there were two positions that just did not fit together. Negotiating this cross-pressure ended up generating different expressions and perspectives, and it became more acute after the eighteenth century when the Enlightenment was not just an elite movement but was becoming a more influential perspective in broader popular culture.

Alasdair MacIntyre—in his brilliant book *After Virtue*—describes some of this effect. What you have once you get to the nineteenth century was a state of what he calls **interminable moral disagreement**. We were in a situation of, when it comes to a question of how people were going to live their lives, an 'un-end-able' disagreement because there was no longer a common language which people could appeal to in order to answer this question.

8.2 The Challenge of Biblical Criticism

Coming out of the Enlightenment, there was a developing discipline of biblical criticism that wanted to read the Bible like any other book. In many ways, this came out of the Reformation project of reading the Bible literally, and seeking to find the one meaning of the text. This is the way one reads any other book. To do this one must put the Bible in its historical context; one needs to know where it came from. But when this is done, certain traditional assumptions about Scripture (such as traditional ascriptions of authorship) end up being put into question. For example, whether certain books thought to be written by certain people—like the Pentateuch being written by Moses—actually were. Often the texts under consideration did not seem to come from the period of history in which the supposed author was alive. Beyond questions of authorship there arose the question of the degree to which the reports of events in Scripture should be taken to be historically accurate. This, again, was judged in the same manner that a scholar would evaluate the historical validity of any other document from the ancient world.

8.2.1 The Old Testament: De Wette and Wellhausen

Regarding the Old Testament (or the Hebrew Bible), there were several foci of biblical criticism in the nineteenth century. One of the points of consideration is the seeming **similarities** between the first couple chapters of the book of Genesis (the creation narrative or narratives) and other mythological origin accounts from the Ancient Near East.

There was also considerable attention given to how certain documents in the Old Testament— the Pentateuch and Isaiah in particular—seem to have **multiple layers of construction**. They seem to be composites of documents written by multiple authors at different times. This is when scholars began to talk about First, Second and Third Isaiah and the different authors or traditions that constitute the Pentateuch.

So, what was going on in the background of these considerations was the attempt to reconstruct the Israelite history and religion out of which Scripture came. Scholars saw the Old Testament as a product of a history and a religious practice that lay behind it; it was an expression of something that was going on in history. We will see this especially with de Wette. De Wette and Wellhausen are the founders of what becomes known as modern Old Testament biblical criticism.

The work of **Wilhelm Martin Leberecht de Wette (1780–1849)**, at the beginning of the nineteenth century, had a very significant impact on Old Testament biblical criticism. He worked in Jena and his contribution has to do with the Pentateuch and how it is, in his language, 'mythical'. By this, he does not mean that it is a lie, but that it is a literary way of expressing profound religious ideas in the form of a story. Such stories are not history, but a kind of storied creed. For de Wette and many other Old Testament historical–critical scholars, what you see in the Pentateuch—or perhaps in 1 and 2 Samuel—does not tell us as much about the events in the text as the period in which it was written. As with Reimarus and D. F. Strauss, de Wette's approach to Scripture was more radical than many of the scholars who came after him.

Julius Wellhausen (1844–1918), who came later on in the nineteenth century, takes up and develops de Wette's ideas. In the 1880s, he develops what has come to be called the **Documentary Hypothesis**, which has to do with how the Pentateuch is a composition with different layers of material. In the Pentateuch, there are multiple kinds of source material each of which was written at different times for different purposes, and this is usually summarized with four letters: **JEDP.** J is for the Yahwist source; **E** is for the Elohist source; **D** is for the Deuteronomist source and **P** is for the Priestly source. The Documentary Hypothesis basically sees these as different layers that are intermixed in the Pentateuch. They are generally seen to be written in the order listed (J, then E, then D, then P). The **Yahwist** and the **Elohist** are from the earliest period; they are believed to have been written before centralized worship in Israel. They get their names from the dominant names for God used in each source: generally the Yahwist will speak of God as 'YHWH', and the Elohist will speak of God using the name 'Elohim'—but that is not a hard and fast rule. The **Deuteronomist** layer comes after Josiah's reforms in 622. When 2 Kings 22 and 2 Chronicles 34 present King Josiah as recovering the 'Book of the Law', that is where scholars think a lot of the more explicitly written out bits of Deuteronomy came to be. The **Priestly** material comes after there is a more developed religious and priestly system in Jerusalem; this material is often seen as being written during or after the Babylonian exile, while it projects these religious practices back into the time of Moses. The liturgical material in Leviticus did not become formalized until much later, but is then projected back into the mouth of Moses as the authoritative teaching.

The broad picture of the development of the Old Testament is, from de Wette and Wellhausen's perspective, generally one of decline. They see pre-Exilic religion as primarily prophetic. The prophets had a significant impact in the fundamental formation of Israelite religion, and this religion is seen as more genuine. After the exile, Israelite religion becomes more legalistic and ritualistic. This is viewed as a decline.

8.2.2 The New Testament: F. C. Baur

The central figure in New Testament biblical criticism is **Ferdinand Christian Baur (1792–1860)**. Baur is significant in the history of modern theology for many different reasons. He was an important Church historian: the five-volume *The History of the Christian Church* (1853–63) was a standard

Figure 8.1 F. C. Baur.

'Ferdinand Christian Baur' by Emil Kornbeck—eingescant aus: Reinhold Scholl: Die Bildnissammlung der Universität Tübingen, 1477 bis 1927, Schriften des Vereins für Württembergische Familienkunde, Heft 2, Verlag von K. Ad. Emil Müller, Stuttgart 1927. Licensed under Public Domain via Wikimedia Commons.

church history for a long time—until the Ritschlians. Baur's primary focus is on how Christian theology, as an historical entity, changes and develops over time. Baur was significantly influenced by Hegel's understanding of a dialectical development operative in history. When it comes to the New Testament, Baur saw a dynamism at work not just in the development of Christianity after the New Testament, but in the development of Christianity during and prior to the New Testament. Through his delving into the development of the Church prior to the New Testament documents, Baur would end up laying the groundwork for much future historical–critical study of the New Testament. In approaching the history behind the New Testament, he utilizes a kind of Hegelian dialectic: just as all history progresses through conflict and resolution, this process can likewise be seen in the production of the New Testament documents.

The New Testament for Baur was the product of the working out of conflicts between different parties: the **Judaists** and **Universalists**. The Judaists were Jewish Christians led by Peter, who held that in order to be a true Christian you have to be a good Jew as well. On the other side is Paul, the Universalist, Gentile Christian, saying that you do not have to be a Jew to be a Christian. These are two opposing, mutually exclusive views of Christianity. Baur sees this tension between these two antitheses as evident in the documents that Baur saw to be Paul's genuine epistles: Galatians, Romans, and 1 and 2 Corinthians. In these texts, you see the conflict between these two perspectives. Ultimately, Baur sees that after about AD 150, a reconciliation comes about between the two in what he calls **Early Catholicism**. This is a Christianity that is universal, but has a new version of the Law, the priesthood and rituals. This is a peaceful reconciliation that incorporates elements of both parties. Baur presents what he considers to be the later documents in the New Testament as reflecting this peaceful reconciliation. These are books like Acts and John, which he dates after AD 150. He holds that Acts was a more fictional depiction of a more harmonious compromise between the Jewish and Hellenistic Christians. In Baur's view, such unity does not come about until long after the events depicted.

D. F. Strauss studied under Baur. Strauss published his infamous *Life of Jesus* when he was in his twenties. Thus, the student made a huge mark on scholarship before the teacher did, and Baur really did not care for Strauss's approach. He believes that Strauss goes way too far with his myth-making thesis. He thinks that it does not make sense that people within living memory would have such an unconscious myth-making imagination. Baur rather asserts that if there were fabrications, like the Book of Acts, then they were very conscious and purposeful. They had to come much later than the events—after the time of living memory.

8.2.3 *Essays and Reviews*

In February 1860, in England, a volume was published with the unassuming (very English) title: *Essays and Reviews*. A collection of seven essays by English clergymen and distinguished professors, it ended up creating controversy over the next decade or so. D. F. Strauss's book is an influential and sensational book, which brought to the popular consciousness critical New Testament scholarship in Germany. The *Essays and Reviews* collection has the same kind of effect with various critical issues relative to the Bible in England. Authored by professors and influential Churchmen, they were responding to the fact that students were hearing about these critical issues from Germany in the universities and were losing their faith. They saw that what was being presented was a strong opposition between historical criticism and science, on the one hand, and Christian superstition, on the other. *Essays and Reviews* is about addressing this situation, instead of just leaving the acids of criticism to go unanswered. (There is a bit of a time lag between Germany and England—Strauss's *Life of Christ* was stirring things up in the 1830s, while *Essays and Reviews* was in the 1860s.)

While there are many figures who could be discussed, the likely most significant figure contributing to *Essays and Reviews* is **Benjamin Jowett (1817–93)**. The Regius (appointed by the Crown) Professor of Greek at Oxford, Jowett is well known as one of the major translators of Plato's *Dialogues* into English. With figures like Jowett, and the other authors, who were almost all clergy, the book is hard to ignore.

As mentioned, much of what is going on in *Essays and Reviews* is presenting German historical–critical scholarship to an English audience. In it, many questions were brought out of the shadows and into the open. Questions about the doctrine of **substitutionary atonement** were aired. Many saw this doctrine—talking about God in terms of needing a blood sacrifice to satisfy His wrath—as morally problematic. They also questioned how essential **miracles** were to Christianity. There was the question of **unending punishment** for the lost. Similarly, the authors asked how we are to take the **Creation** story in Genesis.

Figure 8.2 Jowett.

'Photo of Benjamin Jowett' by Julia Margaret Cameron—The Chautauquan: http://babel.hathitrust.org/cgi/pt?id=uc1.
b3064914;view=1up;seq=144. Licensed under Public Domain via Wikimedia Commons.

One of the ideas that recurs in the *Essays and Reviews* is the question of progressive revelation—of how God could be revealing Himself in a progressive way over time and through Scripture, and addressing different contexts in different ways. What is being explored is how Scripture can be seen as, indeed, revelation, but also an historical and truly human document like other ancient human documents. They want to free theology from what they saw to be a crude biblicism and anti-intellectualism that would equate critical thought with denying the faith. The authors of *Essays and Reviews* think that you can believe in the inspiration of Scripture without having a simplistic belief in inerrancy. They make provision for inspiration through the doctrine of progressive revelation, which is tied to a Romantic idea about revelation being the education of humanity progressing over time. God addresses where humanity is at a given time, moving it forward, and again, addressing humanity at a different time and situation, in a different way. The earlier presentations are more primitive, while the later ones are more developed and more 'true'.

Essays and Reviews sold quite well, yet also came under vociferous attack. As such, it lies at the centre of one of the major religious controversies of Victorian England. **Samuel Wilberforce (1805–73)** is one of the figures at the forefront of the attack on the work. He put himself forward as the champion of orthodoxy.

Denouncing *Essays and Reviews* publicly (although he admitted that he had never read it), he says that it is at best a momentary stop on the road towards full-on atheism and scepticism. Wilberforce was primarily addressing church parishioners. Since *Essays and Reviews* caused considerable alarm among the Anglican laity, many other church leaders ended up following Wilberforce's lead.

Figure 8.3 Wilberforce.

8.3 The Challenge of Natural Science

The first perceived challenge to traditional Christian belief coming from natural science in the nineteenth century came from the direction of **geology**. In the 1830s, Charles Lyell and Dean Buckland found what would become the modern science of geology—looking at how the earth has developed through layers and strata of sedimentation. They conclude that the world is somewhat older than 6,000 years. Indeed, one of the essays in the controversial *Essays and Reviews* volume is on geology, asserting that the earth has existed for millions of years. Within the strata of the planet, we find the remains of species of animals that are nothing like what we have around today, so there is more of a sense that the world is a much older place than perhaps was previously thought—and the science of geology reinforced that.

In the first half of the nineteenth century, there was a growing sense—and part of this has to do with Romanticism—that the natural world was in a dynamic situation, where things were not always as they are now. Also, instead of looking at things in more static terms of a mechanism and current laws as they are as eternal, there was a growing tendency towards seeing life as developing dynamically over time as any living organism: life as life changes.

In 1844, a book is published anonymously in England, entitled *The Vestiges of the Natural History of Creation*. Its author was most probably Robert Chambers. This book sees natural history as a providential evolutionary unfolding. It is how God designed the world: unfolding over time, developing from more primitive orders to more complex orders including the human. So, one of the more popular presentations of what we later think of as evolution is presented explicitly as a religious perspective. This perspective is not that God set things up in a certain optimal way at the beginning, but that God ordered the progression of things. The way things unfold is part of God's care and wise design. Thus, it shows that the design is not just in a static, initial set, but is also in the unfolding. Even the doctrine of providence itself implies a kind of dynamic unfolding. This popular book's advocacy of providence helps evolutionary ideas to be accepted.

However, many people came to realize that the providence side of things—especially if you are going to think about providence as another efficient cause—suggests that God is an additional force beyond the forces of physics. The more explanation you get in terms of the other forces, the less you need God. Providence then started to disappear. Again, this was all a function of the univocity of being and seeing God as a particularly powerful efficient cause among other efficient causes. It had to do with the eclipse of what Thomas Aquinas called God's primary causality as opposed to secondary causality. For Aquinas, primary causality works through secondary causalities—including human freedom.

People in the nineteenth century increasingly realize that the utility of providence (as efficient causality) wanes the more you can provide a mechanistic explanation of the world. In the development of living things, such a mechanistic explanation is going to be what Darwinian evolution is seen as providing. **Charles Darwin (1809–82)** provides an explanation of the development of living organisms over time in terms of natural selection.

While the idea of evolution had been in the air before he comes on to the scene, Darwin brings forth a mass of data that helps to substantiate evolution. His most notable works are *On the Origin of Species by Means of Natural Selection, or the Preservation of Favored Races in the Struggle for Life* (1859) and *The Descent of Man* (1871).

The idea that humanity arose through a process of evolution from lower life forms is religiously problematic to some people. First, it challenges a literal understanding of Genesis. It is seen as particularly troublesome for the Christian doctrine of the Fall—especially for Calvinists, who hang an enormous amount of their theology on the Fall of Adam. Without the Fall (in their view), the work of Christ is meaningless. It is from this kind of perspective that Samuel Wilberforce (again) is going to come forth to spearhead a campaign against Darwin's ideas.

While Darwin's ideas are troubling, even for Evangelical Christians today, many thoughtful Christians at the time were not troubled by evolution. Prior to Darwin, a Christian (Chambers) popularized these ideas. English theologian **Aubrey Moore (1848–90)** also wrote about how evolution was, in fact, a more fitting way to look at the natural world for Christian faith. Thus, he looked at the Fall to see something that had to do with the inherent disorder from the beginning of human nature as it appeared in the natural world. Human nature always had a fundamental flaw in it. For Moore, evolution is only a problem for Christianity if one assumes that God's creative activity must be the exertion of an efficient causal influence on the development of life. If you do not need God as another efficient causality to bring about the creation of humanity, this negates the idea of providence.

Figure 8.4 Darwin.

Courtesy of the Library of Congress. (No known restrictions on publication.)

8.4 Conservative Response

Regarding biological evolution and other perceived challenges to Christian faith, the conservative reaction was usually to hold more rigidly to literal, biblical details—with evolution, to double-down that the particulars of Genesis 1–2 are literally, historically true. What was left out of this was an older understanding of biblical commentary as many levelled and using analogies and types. The reactionary response focused on there being one meaning to these accounts, and that one meaning was the most literal historical reading.

Often the conservative theology can be seen as arising as a dialectical generation of opposition. The more this biblical criticism and the challenges of evolution are there, the more there is a stronger popular conservative response—often reinforced by revivals. The threat to the faith generates the need to defend and revive faith. Often the extremes feed off of and reinforce one another. One example is the conservative response to the various 'modernist' challenges (as they were called), as reinforced by revivals in the United States in someone like **Charles Finney (1792–1875)** in the 1920s and 1930s. In the mid-nineteenth century we see a reaction to what people start to call 'Liberalism'. As a reminder, the names of things in history are usually put forward by critics as slurs. While certain Kantian theologians would claim the term 'liberal', it is largely due to self-designated conservatives that 'liberalism' comes to be used as a blanket term for what has gone wrong in theology. In opposition to this, there was a reassertion of biblical authority and the various confessions—usually the various Protestant creeds—whether they be the Westminster Confession or the various Calvinist or Lutheran confessions. (Note: they do not go back to the ancient creeds, but the creeds that define your particular Protestant group as having the proper interpretation of Scripture, as the one true source of truth and authority.)

8.4.1 Confessionalism and Princeton Theology

There was a revived interest in confessionalism in the face of challenges and greater pluralization. Whereas those involved in the earlier Awakenings wanted to get away from the dissention of confessionalism arising out of the Reformation, many Protestant groups in the nineteenth century wanted to return to the bulwarks of classical Calvinist or Lutheran theology. In Germany, we see a resurgence of Lutheran confessionalism, particularly in opposition to the historical–critical scholarship.

In the United States, a significant response is the so-called **Princeton Theology** based out of Princeton Theological Seminary. Princeton Theology is characterized by its emphasis on the

Figure 8.5 Hodge.

'Charles Hodge by Rembrandt Peale (1778–1860)' by Rembrandt Peale—Sotheby's. Licensed under Public Domain via Wikimedia Commons.

inerrancy of the Bible, and on Calvinist theology. The central figure in Princeton Theology is **Charles Hodge (1797–1878)**, who taught at Princeton for fifty-eight years.

Hodge is the author of a systematic theology that is still in print and in circulation today. His perspective is the dominant one. It is through his influence, and that of Princeton, that Presbyterianism in the United States becomes a bastion of Calvinism. The Presbyterians came largely out of English Puritan and Scotch Irish immigrants. However, this kind of Presbyterian theology became very influential in the twentieth century through Fundamentalism and Evangelicalism (see Chapter 16.) Another significant figure is **B. B. Warfield (1851–1921)**, a student of Hodge's, who taught at Princeton as well.

There was a strong emphasis—especially in America amidst the **Second Great Awakening (c. 1790–1840)**—on Calvinist orthodoxy. Hodge is not just defending against things like modern biblical criticism and evolution, but he also is—maybe even more so—responding to what he detected as the Pelagian leanings in some of the revivalist teachings. People were not being properly Calvinist, so Hodge really defends the doctrines of total depravity and irresistible grace. This wedding of orthodox Christianity with Calvinism continues up into recent decades, when organizations like the Evangelical Theological Society debated whether their statement of faith should be revised to exclude non-Calvinists (see Chapter 16.)

8.4.2 Inerrancy and Objectivity

If we are looking back on the Enlightenment and Awakenings, Princeton Theology is in a sense a reaction to both. It is a reaction to what it sees as the Enlightenment's intellectual apostasy, but also to overly emotional revivalism. This is an intellectual perspective, and they thought enthusiasm was dangerous as well. One's Christian faith needed to be grounded in something objective. It should be grounded in official Calvinist theology and an inerrant, objectively true Bible—not your living experience of redemption in Christ. That experience, of course, has its place, but it should not be the foundation of your existential Christian life.

In nineteenth-century theology, there is a definite emphasis on a more subjective starting place for theological reflection. This can be seen in some of the Romantics, Kant in some sense, and certainly Schleiermacher. On the conservative side, however, they wanted to reassert an **objective** starting place for theology. They would argue that the Bible and the particular Protestant confessions are objectively true—and you get your theology from that. They called themselves 'believing pastors', saying that they had a 'believing theology'.

The response to European criticism of Scripture was to emphasize all the more the uniqueness of Scripture—how it is not a merely human document, but is inspired, uniquely authoritative and infallible. In the Princeton theologians' definition of Scripture, they see the notion of inspiration as necessarily entailing that it is without error. They hold to Scripture's '**plenary**' inspiration. This means that the 'whole' of Scripture—all of it—is fully inspired, and that what theology should do is simply present what the Bible teaches in an orderly way. One has everything one needs in the form one needs it in the Bible. It is all right there, so theology should just re-present what the Bible teaches without error.

For this kind of theology, faith in Christ is intimately tied up with faith in the Bible as the Word of God. You cannot have faith in Christ without having faith in the Bible as the Word of God, and you do not properly have faith in the Bible as the Word of God unless you have a particular understanding of inspiration—that the Bible is the Word of God as the product of verbal, plenary inspiration. The very words throughout the whole Bible are inspired. This becomes the foundation to being a Christian. You cannot be a Christian without this particular understanding of Scripture. And so, the truth of Scripture is going to be understood as presenting true facts and true propositions. In a sense, there is a bit of an ahistoricism here. The truth is not to be seen as relative to a given situation—against a progressive view of revelation.

One of the elements that came up here as a way of trying to defend Scripture against the critical assaults was to focus on the inerrancy of what they called the 'original autographs'. This is still a part of the definitions of inerrancy today. What this means is that the inerrancy of Scripture has to do with the Scripture, as it was originally written by the biblical authors; that is what is safeguarded from error. Errors may have crept in afterward. If you look in your Greek New Testament, there are textual differences—inerrancy is not claimed for these. The claim of inerrancy is for the original autographs. This ends up being a convenient last defence—being unfalsifiable.

B. B. Warfield criticizes what he called Liberal or Modernist theologies as having a wrong understanding of the nature of Scripture. They are guilty of subjectivism. He sees the more recent theologies—such as Coleridge, who holds that revelation in the Word of God happens in our reading of Scripture—as being too subjective. The Bible itself and its very words are the revelation.

8.4.3 Scripture and Science

A sizable amount of the conservative response adopted the framework of **Scottish Common Sense Philosophy**. Part of what this teaches is that both physical science and theology use the same methods and are talking about the same kinds of truths. Just as science collects facts from the natural world, theology collects facts from Scripture. So, from this perspective, the Bible comes to be seen as, in Hodge's words, a '**store-house of facts**' and true propositions. So, theology, like science, uses an inductive method, starting with the facts as they are presented to us and seeing how they systematically fit together. Again, this is a basically static view of the world and of Scripture— that neither of these things develops over time.

When the perspective is adopted that theology and natural science are talking about the same things and using the same methods, this sets the stage for fundamental conflict. When you say that they are playing on the same field, then there is going to be a fight between the two; the conflict cannot be accounted for otherwise than by saying that one side is right and the other is wrong. This is the opposite of taking a Kantian view, where science is talking about one domain that largely has nothing to do with the religious domain. In the later part of the nineteenth century, the Ritschlians return to such a strategy of the insulating of faith from science, and largely with these major challenges from biblical criticism and historical and natural science in view.

In this view—that theology and science are talking about the same things in the same way—a **God of the gaps** scheme is usually entailed. If God is seen to be influencing things in the world the

Figure 8.6 B. B. Warfield.

'Benjamin Breckinridge Warfield' by Peter Somers Heslam. Licensed under Public Domain via Wikimedia Commons.

way that natural processes do, then God can only be seen as operative in domains in which another (scientific) explanation is presently lacking. The increasingly obvious problem with such a God of the gaps scheme is that science changes and develops—yesterday's mysteries are tomorrow's settled theories (and vice versa, but that is another story).

8.5 Mediating Theologies

There was a broad group of theologians in this period that go under the name 'mediating theologies'. Initially, scholars that went under this name primarily follow Schleiermacher. But generally they are between a perspective that says in order to hold on to Christianity you have to reject modernity, and one in which, in order to hold on to modernity, you have to reject Christianity. They sought a mediating position.

Mediating theologies were attempting to reconcile historical Christianity with modern culture. They were not a definite school of thought. While they were influenced by Schleiermacher, they also drew on Hegel. They wanted to understand Christianity in a way that was meaningful in the current times. Many of the mediating theologians in Germany were Lutheran advocates of the United Church. So there was also a social/political/ecclesiastical element to mediating theologies, following after Schleiermacher—seeking to find theological formulations that might bring together the Lutheran and Reformed traditions in Germany under the United Church. Often in the programme they put forward, there was a recognized need to adjust certain traditional or more recent confessional understandings of Christian doctrines.

8.5.1 Tholuck

Friedrich August Tholuck (1799–1877) began teaching at the University of Halle in 1826. Coming from a Pietist background, Tholuck is a Lutheran supporter of the United Church, in opposition to the more strident Lutheran confessionalist theologians of the time. There is a tension here between being a Lutheran theologian and supporting the United Church. Tholuck wanted to understand the possible positive and constructive interrelation between traditional faith and understandings of his time—be they philosophy or historical criticism. He was one of the earlier and more influential mediating theologians. One of his students was Martin Kähler.

Coming out of the Pietist Awakening, Tholuck strongly emphasized one's personal conversion and acceptance of Christ. You can see this as rooted in Schleiermacher as well, with personal experience being the key. He would tend to side more with Schleiermacher than Hegel. Indeed, he questions Hegel's credentials as a theologian from an Awakening perspective. He does not seem to have the proper pious feeling. Tholuck was not impressed with speculative doctrines. Following after Schleiermacher (and this will make its way into the Ritschlian perspective as well), he sees doctrines like the Trinity as having a dubious air to them because of all of the Greek philosophical baggage they entail.

8.5.2 Rothe

A professor at Heidelberg and a friend of Tholuck, **Richard Rothe (1799–1867)** made his principal contribution distinguishing between **manifestation** and **inspiration**. Manifestations are God's miraculous external acts in history whereas inspiration is the internal testimony of the Holy Spirit. Internal inspiration gives one the proper understandings and interpretations of external manifestations. These are always paired together for him. Like Schleiermacher, he believed that Christian consciousness comes from Christ, as mediated through the Church as the bearer of the accounts of the manifestations (leading up to Christ), and the locus of inspiration (through the Spirit of Christ).

Rothe has a somewhat positive view of historical criticism. He thinks that historical criticism could help us sift through and find the essential and non-essential (maybe even mistaken) elements in Scripture. He thinks that, rightly understood, Christianity cannot conflict with natural or historical science. Christianity is true, and there is only one truth. If one understands Christianity properly, then it cannot be opposed to science. He believes that in Scripture some things should be understood poetically. However, part of the problem is people are taking poetic statements as literal, historical descriptions. Rothe was influenced by D. F. Strauss, and his understanding of myth: that some of the things that seem like historical descriptions are actually pictorial or poetic presentations of ideas.

Another of Rothe's contributions was his distinction between two histories of humanity: the **normal** history of humanity and the **abnormal** history of humanity. The normal history of humanity, he sees as being consonant with something like evolution, where you have an ascent from the animal to perfect communion with God. The abnormal history has to do with our falling into sin, and our need for redemption through Christ. Regarding this abnormal history (after our falling into sin), the perfect communion with God could only come about through Christ. As you can see, with this talk about the normal history of progress, Rothe has a generally optimistic view of things with all things progressing towards the Kingdom of God.

8.5.3 Dorner

Isaak August Dorner (1809–84) was made professor of Theology at Berlin in 1862. A former pupil of F. C. Baur, he is probably the most significant of the mediating theologians in Germany because of his substantial systematic theology, *System of the Christian Doctrine of Faith* (1879). This is a system of the doctrines of faith in the tradition of Schleiermacher—starting with Christian faith, with the experience of Christ, and systematically unfolding it subsequently. He draws obviously on Schleiermacher, but also from Schelling and Hegel.

Dorner ends up being influential primarily because he was one of the more orthodox of the mediating theologians. His theology is a lot closer to historic Christianity than other mediating theologians when it comes to traditional doctrines. Largely this is because he was starting from Christian faith. Christology and the Trinity take a central place for Dorner. He has a strong sense for negative theology—that we are always going to have, at best, incomplete knowledge of God.

8.5.4 Bushnell

Horace Bushnell (1802–76) was an American Congregationalist who drew significantly on the work of Coleridge. One of Bushnell's key ideas was that of **Christian comprehensiveness**. He wanted theology to help to recognize and reconcile the truths in the various Christian sects. There was never anything like a United Church in America. There were a plurality of differentiated Christian denominations from the beginning. In order to bring about Christian unity, Bushnell believed one had to look for aspects of truth in the groups that were not your own—not just say your group has true Christianity and that everyone else is welcome to drop their deficient version and join. He wanted to try to recognize the truths in other Christian groups and try to work towards reconciliation.

Bushnell also had—rooted in Coleridge—a focus on the significance of **language**. Coming out of Romanticism, he believed that you had to separate out the real truth of feeling from the drapery of language. So, unlike some of the Romantics, he saw language itself as primarily distorting the underlying reality. One of the reasons that Christians are so opposed to each other is that language always seems to create oppositions. We need to realize that and get beyond some of the particularities of language. He would say that all language is either literal—dealing with physical objects or appearances—or figurative—that is, having to do with thought and spirit. Religious language, for Bushnell, is figurative language. It is expressing feeling and subjectivity, and so it is always going to be ambiguous. We should not then over-emphasize precise formulations of language when it comes to religious things (like those in confessional statements), because that is going to lead to distortions and divisiveness. Doctrine cannot, then, be precise. There is an irreducibly poetic side to Christian belief and doctrine. The fullest view of truth is not going to be the most crystal clear one, but is going to involve paradoxes. So he, like many theologians, is going to focus on experience as the locus of genuine Christianity.

8.5.5 F. D. Maurice

Frederick Denison Maurice (1805–72) is a significant influence in nineteenth-century English theology. He drew heavily upon Coleridge's *Aids to Reflection*. In England, Coleridge was a significant theological voice in the earlier part of the nineteenth century, while Maurice and Newman were the two big influential theologians around the middle of the century.

Maurice was seeking what he called a **critical orthodoxy**. While he had a strong belief in revelation and his theology is deeply Christocentric, he also sought to incorporate some of the insights of biblical criticism. He writes that the Bible shines with the light of divine revelation. Revelation happens through the Bible, but the Bible itself—those words as objects—is not necessarily divine revelation.

Like many other mediating theologians, he was trying to find a ground for unity for various Christian groups. So, he was intentionally ecumenical in this theology. Part of what happens with Maurice is that he is trying to find a unity between many different positions, so he did not have a hard-and-fast theological system that he himself was putting forward. He thought that as soon as you did that, it was going to be exclusionary and you could no longer bring people together. The ground of unity, Maurice explains, is not necessarily the ideas and opinions themselves but ultimately the reality to which they refer. Christian unity is a unity in relation to Christ. We should not strive primarily to be unified in our notions about Christ, but in Christ Himself.

From Maurice's view, every theological view is partial or one-sided. You can never have a comprehensive theological perspective, so you should seek what is of worth in another's perspective and not confuse one's own views with the whole of truth. He emphasizes humility as a theological virtue. Maurice believed that if Christians unified in their orientation to and love for Christ that this would be the greatest witness to the truth of the Christian faith, and more than any kind of intellectual apologetics or defensiveness.

The **Trinity** plays a central role for Maurice, specifically the Trinity as eternal communion of love. As Maurice grounds ecclesial unity upon the social nature of humanity, he then grounds

Figure 8.7 F. D. Maurice.

'Frederick Denison Maurice. Portrait c. 1865' by Acabashi—Own work. Licensed under CC BY 3.0 via Wikimedia Commons.

humanity's social being in God's Triune and social nature. God *is* in love and communion. The Trinity then is the ground of the unity and reconciliation in the Church and in humanity.

In his understanding of the doctrine of **Christ**, Maurice presents Christ as the head of humanity. In Christ we see humanity coming together. Like many people, he will reject the understanding of the atonement as appeasing the anger of God—as God is not primarily wrathful but is primarily love and communion—and come to reject the notion of everlasting punishment as well. He had an understanding of a limited punishment after death, but not an endless duration. This belief got him fired from his teaching position.

Maurice's abiding focus was on the **Church** and her unity. He presents the Church as a witness to true humanity and as a site of God's reconciliation in the world. He does not focus a message of appeasing the anger of God, but instead is ringing out the love and communion that is rooted in God and should be expressed in the Church.

8.6 The Beginnings of Modern Eastern Orthodox Theology

8.6.1 *Philokalia*

Modern Eastern Orthodox theology can (as Andrew Louth suggests) be seen as having its roots in the publication of the *Philokalia*. The *Philokalia* was published in Venice in 1782. This Greek work was published in Venice and not Greece because Greece, at the time, was under Ottoman rule, and its publication was not permitted. The *Philokalia* was compiled by two monks of the Holy Mountain of Athos: St Makarios (also bishop of Corinth) and St Nikodimos. (Athos was and is a preeminent Greek centre for Eastern Orthodox Monasticism.) 'Philokalia' roughly means an 'anthology', and the *Philokalia* is a collection of ascetic texts from the fourth through the fourteenth centuries. The tradition that is recovered and represented extends from the Church Fathers to Gregory Palamas (1296–1359) and the fall of Constantinople (1453). After this there is a 'dark age' extending up to the modern recoveries (beginning more or less with the *Philokalia*). This selection solidified a modern Orthodox understanding of Orthodox history. Its Slavonic parallel, the *Dobrotulubiye* (1793) was very popular in Russia.

The publication of this work served as a definitive event because it enabled Eastern Orthodoxy to talk about itself in the modern world relative to its own distinctive sources and not in terms of Western Catholicism or Protestantism. The *Philokalia* was an Orthodox *ressourcement*—a recovery of its tradition generally and of sources often not available otherwise in particular. Yet the selection of sources was informed by a particular vision. Influenced by Counter-Reformation spirituality and devotional writing, the *Philokalia* re-presents a tradition in which theology is primarily focused on the experience of God in prayer—on knowing God through ascetic practice. The editors on Mount Athos presented texts of Eastern Christian spirituality with an eye towards filling out a picture of the ideals of Byzantine monasticism. This was followed in Russia by a massive project undertaken by the Spiritual Academy of Moscow in the middle of the nineteenth century to translate the works of the Greek Fathers from the fourth to the seventh century. By the end of the nineteenth century, the Russians had the most extensive translation of the Church Fathers; it would not be surpassed until the *Sources Chrétiennes* series in the early twentieth century.

8.6.2 Russia: Westernizers and Slavophils

The revival of Orthodox thought after the post-1453 'dark age' happened largely in Russia—a Russia developing an ambivalent attitude towards Western modernity. **Tsar Peter I 'the Great'** (r. 1682–1725) brought about an opening-up of Russia towards the West so as to be a major European power—perhaps best symbolized by moving the capital from Moscow west to St. Petersburg. Peter's becoming a Western-style absolutist monarch (not altogether unlike his contemporary the French 'Sun King', Louis XIV) and seeking to incorporate Western Enlightenment ideals into Russia inspired a conservative, critical backlash.

The **Slavophils**, especially as represented in philosophers such as Alexi Khomiakov and Ivan Kireevsky, were concerned about corrosive influence of the West—in particular the bad effects of individualism, urbanization, industrialization. Western individualism—of seeing the individual as isolated and cut off from community—was seen by the Slavophils as one of the root causes of the problems for the West. In the face of such isolated individualism the Slavophils saw themselves as maintaining a **personalism**—seeing persons in the midst of relation and community—and preserving the Orthodox tradition. In their setting forth of the corrosive effects of individualism, urbanization, industrialization of the 'West,' the Slavophils drew on and were deeply consonant with Western sources like Romanticism and German Idealism (especially Schelling).

One figure worthy of special mention here is Aleksei **Khomiakov** (1804–60). Khomiakov introduced to the broader world the Eastern concept of *sobornost*—something like a particularly Eastern understanding of 'catholic'. Sobornost views the Church as free unity-in-diversity. Echoing romantic and idealist interests in uniting the one and the many in a manner that preserves freedom, sobornost represents a unity based on freedom and love as opposed to one based on external authority. This primary focus on unity and freedom is seen in opposition to both Roman Catholic unity without freedom and Protestantism's freedom without unity. Slavophil philosophers such as Khomiakov would later inspire thinkers like Solovyov.

8.6.3 Solovyov

Vladimir Solovyov (Solov'ev) (1853–1900) came from an academic family (his father was a noted historian) in Moscow. As a boy, Vladimir had a vision in church of the figure of Sophia as a young girl in a radiance of 'golden azure' holding a flower. This would be the first of three visions of Sophia in his life. As a young man, Solovyov studied history, philosophy (from Plato to Schelling and German Idealism), the Church Fathers and more exotic figures like Jacob Boehme. After his education at the University of Moscow, he went to England in 1875. While studying in the British Museum he had a second vision in which Sophia—in the same light of 'golden azure'—told him to go to Egypt. After going to Egypt, Solovyov has a third vision of Sophia—a vision of feminine beauty and encompassing unity. In 1876, he returned to Russia where he resumed teaching and writing. In 1878 delivered his Lectures on Divine Humanity which were attended by many influential figures including his friend Fyodor Dostoevsky (Solovyov was apparently an inspiration for both Alyosha *and* Ivan Karamazov). He would go on to teach at St. Petersburg University.

One of Solovyov's key contributions to modern Eastern Orthodox theology—for good or ill—is his understanding of **Sophia**. Partially emerging from (and yet likely also funding) Solovyov's three personal visions, the notion of Sophia has its roots in the personification of Wisdom in the Old Testament (Proverbs 8–9; Ps 103, 135) and in intertestamental Wisdom literature in the Apocrypha (Wisdom of Solomon and Sirach/Ecclesiasticus). In the Fathers, Sophia is largely identified with the Logos, with Christ. In Byzantine and Russian Christianity, Sophia came to be associated liturgically with the Mother of God. Solovyov's reception should also be seen against the background of a kind of unified whole sought after in the esoteric, mystical and speculative traditions in vogue in the nineteenth century especially in Romantic circles and certain strains of German

Idealism. Solovyov was interested in the more mystical side of things be that Jakob Boehme (early-seventeenth-century mystical theologian), Kabbala (Jewish mysticism), spiritualism (he attended seances) or 'Gnosticism'—here meaning less the ancient heresy as early modern mystical and esoteric tradition (not so much Valentinus as, again, Boehme).

For Solovyov, Sophia has to do with the interrelation between God and creation. God's Sophia (divine Sophia) means that God is eternally oriented towards—somehow in relation to—creation. God is the one who creates, and this truly part of God's character. What is implied here—controversially—is that creation is not purely extrinsic to God. Divine Sophia is the eternal creation-ward-ness of God. Solovyov goes on to see a 'created Sophia'—a Sophianic aspect of the created world—insofar as creation is intrinsically oriented towards its fulfilment in God. In trying to think about the relation between God and creation, Sophia is perhaps best seen as the 'between'—reminiscent of Platonic *eros, metaxu* or world soul. (Solovyov was in the process of translating and publishing a number of Plato's dialogues in Russian when he died.) Sophia so understood moves towards Solovyov's notion of 'divine humanity' or 'Godmanhood' (*bogochelovechestvo*). As a metaphysical principle, Godmanhood or 'divine humanity' can be seen as Chalcedonian Christology expanded to German Idealist (think Schelling and Hegel) proportions. It is an all-embracing view of the world that is a reconciliation of a totality of opposites ('all') into a unity ('one')—the 'all-one.'

Sources and Further Reading

Bebbington, David W. 'Evangelicalism'. In *The Blackwell Companion to Nineteenth-Century Theology*, edited by David Fergusson, 235–50. Chichester: Wiley-Blackwell, 2010.

Cragg, Gerald R. *The Church in the Age of Reason: 1648–1789*. Rev. edn. New York: Penguin, 1988.

Dorrien, Gary. *Kantian Reason and Hegelian Spirit: The Idealistic Logic of Modern Theology*. Oxford: Wiley-Blackwell, 2012.

Gockel, Matthias. 'Mediating Theology in Germany'. In *The Blackwell Companion to Nineteenth-Century Theology*, edited by David Fergusson, 301–18. Chichester: Wiley-Blackwell, 2010.

Livingston, James C. *Modern Christian Thought: Volume 1, The Enlightenment and the Nineteenth Century*. 2nd edn. Minneapolis, MN: Fortress Press, 2006.

Morris, Jeremy. *F. D. Maurice and the Crisis of Christian Authority*. Oxford: Oxford University Press, 2005.

Rogerson, John W. 'The Bible and Theology'. In *The Blackwell Companion to Nineteenth-Century Theology*, edited by David Fergusson, 455–67. Chichester: Wiley-Blackwell, 2010.

Taylor, Charles. *A Secular Age*. Cambridge, MA: Belknap Press of Harvard University Press, 2007.

Vidler, Alec R. *The Church in an Age of Revolution*. Rev. edn. New York: Penguin, 1990.

Welch, Claude. *Protestant Thought in the Nineteenth Century. Volume 1, 1799–1870*. New Haven, CT: Yale University Press, 1972.

9

Early-Nineteenth-Century Catholic and Anglo-Catholic Theology

Chapter Outline

9.1 Romantic Return to Tradition

The mediating theologians were primarily Protestant theologians in Germany, England and the United States. In this chapter we turn to Catholic and Anglo-Catholic theologians. In the beginning of the nineteenth century, Herder would talk about the Church of Rome being an ancient ruin—by which he meant dead. The Romantics, however, had an affection for ruins and fragments. With Romanticism there was a renewal of interest in Roman Catholicism, especially in Germany. A number of Romantics converted to Roman Catholicism in Germany.

Romanticism is looking back into history and tradition, but we are going to see that there are going to be two ways of doing this. There was a more **static** view—we will see this with the French Roman Catholic conservatives. When you look back to the tradition of the Church, you are looking to return to the authority of the Roman Church (as with the French Conservatives), or to an earlier stage in the tradition, like the Early Church as authoritative (as with the Tractarian or Oxford Movement). There was also, however, a more **dynamic** view of tradition, and we will see this especially with the Tübingen School. We have Catholic theologians who will look back to the earlier parts of the tradition in order to be true to the tradition as a part of its continual development—which means it is going to be different than what came before.

The questions that were being addressed are: 'What links us in the present to the tradition?' How do we be traditional? There would end up being very different answers to this. Those who had a more dynamic view of tradition (the Tübingen School) would eventually become influential again in the twentieth century in Catholic circles—after the intervening period of the conservative resurgence around the end of the nineteenth century with Neo-Thomism and the First Vatican Council.

9.2 French Traditionalism and Restoration

In early nineteenth-century France, defenders of traditional Roman Catholicism emerged. They served to defend traditional Roman Catholicism against the radical rationalism that was rampant in the eighteenth century. Remember, the Enlightenment was more stridently and explicitly anti-Christian and anti-clerical (anti-Catholic) in France. The French traditionalists were defending Roman Catholicism in such a context. After the horrors of the French Revolution, there was now more of a nostalgia for what came before—and they were looking back to the pre-modern era and the Middle Ages.

One of the dominant metaphors in France in this period is that of **restoration**. There was a restoration of the Bourbon Dynasty after Napoleon. Many traditionalists sought to restore not only the political structure post-revolution, but also to restore traditional Catholicism post-Enlightenment. This Roman Catholic renaissance in France is not centred on universities. It was closely tied to politics. Chateaubriand, Bonald and Maistre are the significant theologians of this movement. It is notable that none of them are (1) academics or (2) clergy. The main interest of the French traditionalists was not theology, but rather society and politics—primarily defending the authority of the pope against the national (French) authorities and/or the monarchy. But most of the interesting theological work in this period was going on elsewhere.

9.3 The Oxford Movement

In England, figures largely inspired by Coleridge were looking to tradition as having a spiritual authority for guiding people. Anglicans want to see the Church of England as a part of a broader, universal Catholic Church. The Church of England—because of its origins—is a bit different in its relation to Catholicism than Lutheranism and the Reformed Church. The Anglican Church claims Apostolic Succession for their bishops. Their parting company with Catholicism in the time of Henry VIII was largely political and not primarily due to doctrinal differences. They do not define themselves in opposition to Catholics in the same manner that other Protestant groups do. So it is slightly easier for them to see themselves as being part of this broader stream—although not as being Roman Catholic.

The **Oxford Movement** is an Anglo-Catholic revival that occurs largely during the 1830s and 1840s. It is centred on several figures. Probably the best known is **John Henry Newman**. (We will examine him in his own section below.) Otherwise, **Edward Pusey (1800–1882), John Keble (1792–1866)** and **Richard Fourde (1803–36)** are probably the most well known. Initially an academic movement centred on Oxford University, it started to expand beyond this academic circle and Oxford post-1845. It is also known as the **Tractarian Movement**, and its followers the 'Tractarians'. They were called that because one of the central organs of the movement was a series of tracts—*Tracts for the Times*—published between 1833 and 1841. There were ninety in total, all of varying lengths. Some were what you would expect from a tract; some of them were as long as short books. They were printed and made available cheaply for a wide distribution. This was a vehicle for dissemination of their ideas to help them to catch on in broader English Christendom. Tracts were written on many different topics: apostolic succession, the Anglican Church's relation to earlier Catholic tradition, advocacy of different elements of the liturgy, different aspects of the Church calendar, the classical spiritual disciplines, the Eucharist, baptism, the hierarchy of the Church, etc. What they were trying to do was to reawaken Christians to the significance of the Church's rites and institutions. They wanted to reconnect with such elements as they felt had gone by the wayside.

The Oxford Movement was in many ways a **Romantic** movement. There was an emphasis on the past, on mystery and on nature. There was a granted admiration for the more ancient ways—a looking back to the Middle Ages as a more unified Christendom and as something that they want to aspire to. There was also a mystical element to what they were presenting with the spiritual disciplines, the sacraments and the like.

As opposed to the Evangelical Awakenings of the previous century—which was more of a low church revival—the Oxford Movement was a high church revival. It is different than, say, Methodism. It was more of a reviving of the things that the other revivals did not like. The low church Awakenings often eschewed the outward trappings of religion such as rites and offices, but the Oxford Movement advocated the deep significance of such so-called outward trappings. The Oxford Movement also emphasized the danger of private opinion, in face of the various low Church revivals and their tendency to bring about the splitting into various disparate groups. They sought a ballast of tradition to go back and refer to in order to provide unity.

The Tractarians were also responding to the scientific positivism and reductionistic naturalism that was incipient in nineteenth-century English society. They wished to revive a feeling for the reality of the supernatural, and seek to reconnect to deeper, invisible realities that were manifest in the wonders of nature. One can see some Romantic aspects here. They wanted, more particularly, to recover supernatural elements in the Christian life. This is evident in their focus on the sacraments. In the sacraments—specifically in Baptism and the Lord's Supper—something is happening to you. Something is changing. They are not purely symbolic or mental events; they are supernatural events of some kind.

Again like the Romantics, the Tractarians were a protest movement within modernity. They saw the decay in Protestantism towards subjectivism (as evident in the Awakenings) as a key symptom to the problem with modernity as a whole: an obsession with humanity's Promethean autonomy. In the face of modern autonomy, they wanted to return to authority and tradition. Such autonomy did not seem to be taking society in a good direction. But to not be a purely autonomous individual as a Christian means that you needed to associate yourself in the broader tradition of the Church. So they located the authority of the Church in its tradition. This is very Romantic—looking backward into the past, trying to retrieve what English Christianity hitherto has discarded. Basically, they believed that they lost too much that was of value in the broader Christian tradition through the Protestant Reformation, and they wanted to bring some of that back.

One of the things they emphasized was **apostolic succession**. Part of this was a political point over and against what is called **Erastianism**—the State being in control of the Church offices. But apostolic succession showed that in order for the Church to be in continuity with the traditional and historical Church—going back to the Apostles—the bishops needed to be the ones who were appointing their successors and not some external agency—like the British government.

In practice, the Oxford Movement focused on the teachings of the Early Church Fathers (not so much the Middle Ages) as a guide for interpreting Scripture. When they talk about the tradition there is more of a **static** or even primitivist understanding. They wanted to go back to the earliest tradition: Scripture as read by the Church Fathers. They wanted to revive that instead of seeing an unfolding trajectory.

The Oxford Movement was not simply a theological or doctrinal movement, but it was also **pastoral** and **devotional**. They conceive of themselves as a renewal movement, as reviving religious devotion. The central virtues that they focused upon are humility and obedience—virtues that were seen as standing against the autonomous and individualistic sensibilities of modernity. In this they joined the concern for holiness that often accompanies the Awakenings.

Thus, they are suspicious of the Protestant doctrine of justification by faith alone because they think that it could easily become too intellectual. It could keep one from a properly Christian emphasis on a sanctified life, on a transformed existence. Again, they see obedience as central to the Christian life. They view sanctification as connected to justification—that the process of God's grace is at work changing a person and helping them become righteous. So they are retrieving a pre-Reformation understanding of grace as a transformative influence instead of strictly legal/accounting manoeuvre. Members of the Oxford Movement did not see salvation as something that was distinct from a life of holiness. They saw the separation of salvation from holy living as problematic.

The Tractarians emphasized the importance of the **sacraments**. Just as in the Christian life generally—where grace is a transforming influence within us—so in the sacraments grace is an objective reality that is mediated through the sacraments and infused into us. They are not mere memorials, but are channels of divine gifts. The Tractarians took up some earlier Patristic understandings of the Eucharist as 'spiritual food' that nourishes one and keeps one alive spiritually. While they would obviously reject the Eucharist being just a token, they also rejected the doctrine of transubstantiation because it was too metaphysically precise; it overly rationalized a mystery.

For the sacraments to be effective, the **Church** had to be seen as the channel of grace. So this is going to connect again to apostolic succession as a way of tracing back to the Incarnation. As with the Incarnation, so are the sacraments a manifestation of the real presence of Jesus in the life of believers now. Again, the Tractarians follow a strong Patristic connection between the Incarnation and Eucharist.

Not surprisingly, they are accused by their fellow Anglicans of '**Romanism**'—of being Roman Catholic, though they would often distinguish themselves from Roman Catholics. What many thinkers in the Oxford Movement were interested in was the Church Fathers—not the current Roman Catholic Church, but the early Church Fathers. However, when John Henry Newman is received into the Roman Catholic Church, this is seen as a big blow to the Anglo-Catholicism of the Oxford Movement: one of the leaders of a movement that vocally defends itself of the charge of 'Romanism' becoming Roman Catholic.

In close association with the Oxford Movement was the project of the translation and publication of the works of the Church Fathers (such as Athanasius, Augustine and John Chrysostom) into English. This project—edited by Pusey, Keble and Newman—bore the title *A Library of Fathers of the Holy Catholic Church: Anterior to the Division of the East and West*. It was published in forty-eight volumes (give or take) between 1838 and 1885. (A competing [less Catholic-y] alternative English translation of the Church Fathers would later come out published by the Presbyterian T&T Clark firm in Edinburg under the titles *Ante-Nicene Christian Library* [1867–73] and *A Select Library of the Nicene and Post-Nicene Fathers of the Christian Church* [1886–1900].)

9.4 John Henry Newman

John Henry Newman (1801–90), after having a significant influence in the Oxford Movement, was received into the Roman Catholic Church in 1845. Each of the central ideas that we will cover here is addressed in a particular book.

The first work that we will mention is his *Essay on the Development of Christian Doctrine* (1878). This is probably his greatest contribution to theology. In it, Newman considers how Christian doctrine develops through history. He has a more dynamic understanding of tradition than the Tractarians, though not as dynamic as some others. His understanding of the development of Christian doctrine is that though supernatural truths are given/revealed once and for all, they are expressed and explicated in developing forms throughout history. This is based on his study of the Church Fathers—of how they started to use different cultural forms to express the Gospel and to explore its meaning in a way that was not possible before these cultural forms were around.

One of the reasons Newman—unlike some of the other Oxford Movement figures—moves towards Roman Catholicism is that he comes to see a connection between modern Roman Catholicism and the Early Church. He focuses on how there needs to be an historical identity to the Church. The Church is not just an idea, and if there is to be a meaningful understanding of the Church it has to be a very real, concrete reality that can be identified somehow in some kind of continuity over time.

When Newman talks about the development of doctrine, he primarily uses organic metaphors—how ideas grow over time like living things. They change and develop in order to stay alive and the same. The true test of doctrine for him then is not that which has not changed

Figure 9.1 Newman.

'John Henry Newman 001' by Anonymous—American Annual Cyclopaedia and Register of Important Events, Vol. 15 (1891), Appleton and Co., New York. Licensed under Public Domain via Wikimedia Commons.

or that which is the oldest, but has to do with life and growth. He would say that the greatest truths of Christianity that are revealed were not and are not understood all at once. They require a long time and much thought in order to unpack, so we should not be surprised that developed understandings of the Incarnation or the Trinity were not present in the New Testament but are a couple centuries later—it takes time to unpack the significance of the revelation. But, everything that would eventually become a given plant is there at the seed, so is the seed of revelation going to become a particular thing. Part of being true to its identity is to develop—not staying the same or staying a seed. So this is one of Newman's ideas that became influential. In order to stay the same, to stay true to its identity in a changing and developing situation, the doctrine has to change. There is a quote of his where he says, 'Here below, to live is to change, and to be perfect is to change often.' Change then is not a deficit when it comes to tradition, but it is part of the life of a tradition.

The notion that ideas have to change in order to stay the same sounds odd—but if the context is always changing and you stay the same, you are not going to mean the same thing in the future. Your meaning is going to be distorted. So the idea has to change to continually remain true to the source. That is part of the thoughtful work of theology—reinterpreting and reappropriating the living truths of the Gospel in the ever-changing present. Newman is not advocating something like continual revelation. He thinks that the revelation was given to the apostles once and for all. We have in Scripture the revelation, but the full implicit meaning of that has to unfold and become explicit over time and in relation to different cultural contexts.

Newman is writing this as a Roman Catholic. It is quite likely that he received a lot more leeway from the Catholic authorities because he was a high-profile convert (he is eventually made a cardinal)—but his notions of the fluidity of doctrine make many in the Roman Catholic Church nervous. Many scholars today regard him one of the most significant Catholic thinkers of the nineteenth century, if not the greatest. (As we will see, a lot can change in a century.)

Newman's other significant idea is that which is presented in *An Essay in Aid of a Grammar of Assent* (1870), sometimes just called his *Grammar of Assent*. Here, Newman is representing the Romantic Coleridgian tradition of there being an intuitive access to truth, as opposed to a purely empiricist mode of knowing. Newman likewise distinguishes between different modes of knowing. There is a more implicit mode of knowing and a more explicit one. The explicit mode of knowing is the scientific way of knowing—the rational, empirical knowledge that would have been recognized in his era. But there is also another way of knowing that is more personal or existential, and faith and belief have to do with this other mode.

Newman would say that when it comes to matters of fact—as opposed to matters of logical deduction—there is a distinction between what he calls **assent** and **inference**. This is one of the philosophical contributions that he is attempting to make here. John Locke would say that assent—our affirmation of a state of affairs—is proportioned to inference. One should only believe as much as one can prove. If one has much evidence then one should believe in a state of affairs to a high degree, and if one has little evidence one should only believe it a little. But Newman says that inference never gets beyond probability. You will never get a 'yes'—an actual assent—from simply looking at the evidence. There will never have been enough evidence for you to fully affirm anything. Assent, then, is commonly in excess of probable inference. We are always believing things for which we would not seem to have enough evidence. So for Newman assent is something that is distinct from inference. Our affirmations go beyond the evidence all the time—this is a common thing in our life. We believe things are the case when our evidence should only add up to, 'it is probably the case'.

He also talks about a special power or faculty of judgement that helps to bring us to a personal certitude. Basically, if we just lived by the light of probable inference, all would be in a perpetual sea of sceptical uncertainty—because none of the evidence we have adds up to any actual kind of knowledge. But we do often have practical certitude—that does not mean that those things do not get questioned, but we assume that things are a given way. He calls this the **illative sense**. It has to do with that kind of a leap between inference and assent. Our best judgement is never going to add up to there being no risk involved. We are always going beyond the evidence and making judgements and conclusions.

Religious assent or faith as well is rooted in this more common understanding of faith. In seeing that faith is a part of our normal life—that we are always going beyond the evidence and making judgements—that makes religious faith less strange. The fact is that almost everything we call knowledge is saturated with faith.

Newman would also make a distinction between **notional** and **real assent** when it came to religious faith. He does not want people to think that religious faith is nothing more than making an ordinary intellectual judgement. Religious faith is not just a **notional assent**—which is what he would call an intellectual judgement about a given state of affairs—but he would say that it is a **real assent**. This is more holistic and existential. The real assent of faith involves our emotion, imagination and will as well. Our faith is a fully personal investment.

9.5 The Tübingen School

With the Tübingen School of Catholic theology, we see Romanticism making its way into Roman Catholicism in a robust way. Romanticism came to be deeply ingrained in nineteenth-century Germany and stimulated a revival in Catholic theology in Germany in Tübingen. The central idea at the Tübingen School was a renewed sense of **history**. The University of Tübingen—as was common in Germany at the time—had separate theology faculties for Catholics and Protestants. In 1817, an existing Catholic seminary at Ellwangen was reorganized and incorporated into the University of Tübingen, becoming the Catholic faculty of theology. Though the two theology faculties were distinct departments, an emphasis on history distinguishes theology at Tübingen as a whole—especially with F. C. Baur, the great Church historian and historical–critical New Testament scholar in the Protestant faculty.

Both of the figures we cover below—Drey and Möhler—seek to perform for Catholic theology the same kind of service that Schleiermacher had done for Protestant theology: namely to bring it into the present age, and show that faith should not feel threatened by the developments in modern thought—be they philosophy or historical criticism. In their understanding, the Christian faith is dynamic and lively enough to encounter and appropriate the best insights of modern thought. Key to the Tübingen perspective is a view of dogma as being **dynamic** and as part of an **organic** whole. The primary thing is the life of the Church, and dogma is the life of the Church being translated into intellectual terms. (The echoes of Schleiermacher are strong.) The primary thing is the living experience of Christ in and through the Church, and dogma is a *Glaubenslehre*—a reflection upon that faith. The continuity of dogma is not in an identical repetition of the living faith of the Church.

As a living cultural organism that is constantly developing in relation to different times and different conceptual cultural forms, dogma constantly needs to be rethought. With the Romantic emphasis, we see a focus on unity, universality and holism—on trying to have a most all-encompassing perspective. This is what they see as being distinctive with Catholicism—being forced to take into account a greater degree of variety. Theology must take ownership of the tradition of the Church going all the way back and not just fixating on one particular slice of it. It is with this regard that the Tübingen theologians view Protestants as being overly one-sided and territorial. Thus, they wanted to have an understanding of dogma or doctrine that could account for the greatest breadth of the tradition of the Church. In order to do this, they have to find a way of accounting for continuity in the midst of change.

While these ideas caught on at Tübingen, Rome was not as enthusiastic. Many of the scholars at Tübingen end up being critical of particular Catholic practices and beliefs, such as relics, pilgrimages or notions of Papal infallibility. They argue against these things, or at least their present validity. This did not lead to the popularity of these German theologians in the hierarchy of the Church and spurred on a response to solidify the Church's position against such perceived threats.

9.5.1 Drey

The first of the Tübingen theologians is **Johann Sebastian von Drey (1777–1853)**. He is the founder of this school of thought. He is, for a time, a very well-read parish priest—familiar with Kant, Fichte and Schelling. He eventually teaches theology at Ellwangen, and then at Tübingen, under the new Catholic faculty. He is hugely influential in making historical study a part of the Catholic theological training there. He believes that Catholic theological training at Tübingen should not merely be studying the current teachings of the Church, but should also entail studying the development of Christianity historically—engaging in historical theology. Part of his understanding of what has happened, however, is that there had been a decline in theology since the High Middle Ages and through the eighteenth century. He believes that theology has been degenerating into subjectivism and individualism—that things have taken a sour turn of late. This was because in this recent period, theology is failing to be true to its identity, which has always been rooted in history, and theology was now approached as if it were a static and abstract entity, somehow apart from the flow of the broader tradition of the Church.

Drey focuses on the concrete **positivity** of Catholicism. He does not merely point out the positivity of the Catholic tradition as a whole, but the particular differences and changes within the Catholic tradition as it developed over time. He looks at these changes as an historian. But he also considers God to be at work in that positivity. This is against the Enlightenment perspective where that which is from God is only what is universally true.

Drey stands against what he considers to be a particularly prevalent **dualism**: the separating of reason and revelation, of seeing the world as an independent domain over and against God. He wants to see the world as grounded in and intimately related to God, and that God's revelation happens through the events in the world. If revelation is only that which has nothing to do with the vagaries of history, we as historical beings would not notice it. (This difficulty is structured something like the mind-body problem: if the mind is purely immaterial, by definition it is never going to have influence on anything that is material or vice versa.) If the supernatural is set in opposition to the natural, then by definition it is never going to show up—how could it, unless we were supernatural ourselves?

Drey then wants to talk about religion as natural—that all human beings have an innate feeling for God. This is a very Romantic, Schleiermachian sort of thing. There is this natural human sense that is the basis for all religion—a natural desire for God. He argues that Christianity best fits these natural yearnings. He also, like many other figures, such as Lessing and Herder, talks about revelation over time in history in terms of the education of the human race. Throughout history, God inspires particular individuals as his instruments—the prophets, the apostles and supremely Christ—to bring humanity forward in the way that they need to be brought forward at a given point in time. He meets us where we are.

Drey also discusses the **development of doctrine**. Unlike Newman, however, he believes that revelation continues in the tradition. He does not believe that revelation happens at one time and then we are just later unpacking it. Rather God, the Holy Spirit, is continually at work in the life of the Church and in the organic unfolding of her tradition. Drey sought to understand the persistence of Christianity in the midst of change—that Christianity maintains some kind of identity over time is a testimony to its truth. In the midst of all of these very different cultural forms, the plasticity of the Church and so the Church's doctrines show it and their truth.

9.5.2 Möhler

Johann Adam Möhler (1796–1838) was once a student of Drey—although Drey survives him. His career was only twelve years long. Although he largely built on Drey's work, Möhler has become the better-known thinker. As a student, he visited Berlin, attending lectures by Schleiermacher and Marheineke, a Right Hegelian. His best-known work is *Symbolism: Exposition of the Doctrinal Differences between Catholics and Protestants as Evidenced by Their Symbolical Writings* (1832). Nineteenth-century books tended to have long titles. This is considered by many Catholic theologians to be one of the most important theological books of the century. In Möhler's approach to the development of doctrine, he positions himself as having a different position than both the Protestant understanding of *sola scriptura*, and the official Catholic teaching as presented in the Council of Trent. Both of these saw Scripture and tradition as distinct from one another. Möhler, however, sees all tradition as simply the living passing on of the Gospel, and Scripture is the earliest part of that tradition. The New Testament is the earliest written and preserved reflection of the tradition. With this Möhler was revivifying a high Medieval (pre-late Medieval) understanding of tradition. It was in the Late Middle Ages that the notion that Scripture and tradition were two different things became solidified. For Möhler Scripture and tradition, properly understood, always function together. Scripture is traditional and tradition is Scriptural. He would say that even in Scripture you can see how tradition changes to meet changing situations—at least changing cultural forms. You have Ancient Near Eastern, Egyptian, Syrian and Canaanite cultural forms in the Old Testament—Hellenistic and Roman forms in the New Testament.

As a Catholic, Möhler would say that the Church is gifted with a certain **infallibility**—but he understands this broadly. This has to do with the Church as a whole. No individual can be infallible—whether that individual is the pope or your run-of-the-mill Protestant who focuses on his own reading of Scripture, no individual is infallible. Möhler will then be critical of the notion of Papal infallibility. This is not yet a formal teaching of the Catholic Church, but it is definitely in the air at the time.

When it comes to his understanding of the **Church**, Möhler is more of a **conciliarist**—one who says that the chief authority of the Church is the counsel of bishops and not the pope. So the hierarchy of the Church he sees is emerging from below—and is not imposed from above. Möhler also has what could be called an organic ecclesiology—the Church as a living, **corporate personality**. Authentic Christianity is lived out not as solitary individuals but in the midst of the evolving community of the Church and its developing consciousness. Just as an individual's consciousness develops over time, so on a larger scale does the consciousness of the Christian tradition develop.

Möhler sees the **Holy Spirit** as at work in the larger developing Christian community. One of his earlier works prior to *Symbolism* is called *The Unity of the Church*, published in 1825. In that, he spells out his view of the Holy Spirit and of the Church. And the Spirit is the Spirit of the Church within the body of believers. So the formation of the Church should happen from the inside out. As the spirit of a person should leave the body of a person, so the Spirit of the Church leaves the body of the Church.

Later in *Symbolism*, Möhler focuses on the Church as **Eucharistic presence**. The Eucharist becomes his master metaphor for talking about the Church. The visible Church is an extension of Christ's body, continually becoming that through the Eucharist. Through the Eucharist, the tradition, and the Spirit, the Church is the objective form of Christianity. The Church is the actual living presence of Christ in the world, through which he does his saving work.

Sources and Further Reading

Dupré, Louis. *The Quest of the Absolute: Birth and Decline of European Romanticism*. Notre Dame, IN: University of Notre Dame Press, 2013.

Hinze, Bradford E. 'Roman Catholic Theology: Tübingen'. In *The Blackwell Companion to Nineteenth-Century Theology*, edited by David Fergusson, 187–213. Chichester: Wiley-Blackwell, 2010.

Livingston, James C. *Modern Christian Thought: Volume 1, The Enlightenment and the Nineteenth Century*. 2nd edn. Minneapolis, MN: Fortress Press, 2006.

Vidler, Alec R. *The Church in an Age of Revolution*. Rev. edn. New York: Penguin, 1990.

Welch, Claude. *Protestant Thought in the Nineteenth Century. Vol. 1, 1799–1870*. New Haven, CT: Yale University Press, 1972.

10

Ritschlianism

10.1 'Classical Liberal Theology'

Ritschlianism, or what has been called Classical Liberal Protestant Theology, dominates German theology from the closing decades of the nineteenth century through to the First World War. In the United States, it is the dominant theological form in the academy in the first thirty years of the twentieth century. 'Liberal theology', in the twentieth century, usually refers to this period, these theologians, and/or their heritage. They often preferred to refer to themselves, however, as 'New Protestantism' or 'Modern Theology'.

Their detractors come to refer to Ritschlianism as *Kulturprotestantismus*, 'Culture Protestantism'. This comes from the Ritschlians' emphasis on how Christianity should be about the business of improving society with Christian values. They think of German culture as a Christian culture. With the coming of the First World War such a close identification of Christianity with particular forms of German culture came under sharp criticism, however.

One of the easiest ways to approach the common conceptual elements of the Ritschlians as a group is to see the kinds of things they are **against**. They are put off by theological **speculation**—especially in the form of Hegelian theology, it seems—and by theology that uses too many philosophical categories. They are also against **dogmatism**—specifically confessional Protestantism. They are against individualistic **enthusiasm**—which you see in Pietism and would often include within 'enthusiasm' any theology that is overly emotional, such as that of Schleiermacher. One can see some echoes of Enlightenment 'rational religion' in these concerns.

To consider their positive emphases, one can see that, like Schleiermacher, the Ritschlians think that theology should be based on **experience**—on living faith. So even though they may not like everything about Schleiermacher, he is definitely in their background. They also commonly display the influence of both **Neo-Kantian** thought and **historical** criticism.

Ritschlianism is strongly influenced by **Neo-Kantian** thought. Neo-Kantianism wanted to save theology by appealing to a relatively private realm apart from the public and so minimizing public claims to truth. In the late nineteenth century, there is an increasingly dominant positivism or empiricism: the only domain that is valid is what can be talked about scientifically. Along with that was a metaphysical agnosticism—that we cannot know anything beyond what can be scientifically verified. During this period, Hegelian Idealism was in decline. The Neo-Kantians are going to respond by returning to Kant. Key for the Ritschlians is the return to practical reason as the locus of religion. For such an approach, scientific positivism is not a threat to religion because it is in a different domain. Neo-Kantianism emphasizes such a division between the scientific domain and the human domain.

Also during this period, critical **historical** scholarship was on the rise. Especially influential is the historical–critical study of the Bible. The Ritschlians are going to vary in critical severity when it comes to Scripture: Herrmann is more conservative, Ritschl and Harnack are in the middle and Troeltsch is more critical. One significant characteristic of the Ritschlian or 'Classical Liberal' emphasis upon historical–critical biblical scholarship, however, is that it is joined with their Neo-Kantian emphasis upon the ethical as the locus of religion. They drew on Semler's idea that when we are looking back to find what is the essence of Christianity, what we find is the ethical–religious kernel of the teachings of Jesus. The religion of Jesus is ethical and universally humanitarian. The Ritschlians' focus on the religiousness of Jesus touches on the historical core of Christianity which is also its most properly religious domain.

10.2 Ritschl

Albrecht Ritschl (1822–89) was among the strongest and broadest influences of Protestant theology in the last quarter of the nineteenth century. Ritschl sought to present a persuasive modern theology—a theology that made sense to the people of the time and was believable for the modern

German person. The son of a Lutheran pastor, he was educated in **Mediation Theology**—and studied under Rothe and F. C. Baur. He also took part in the Prussian **Union Church**, in opposition to the Lutheran Confessionalists. Influenced by the Protestant theology at **Tübingen**—especially Baur and his more historical orientation—he ends up teaching at Bonn and then at Göttingen for the bulk of his career.

Ritschl does not end up being satisfied by Mediation Theology. And he thinks that Baur's metaphysical and speculative commitments distort his historical work. Ritschl also had issues with Pietism; he saw it as a monastic withdrawal from the world and overly mystical. As such, it is not properly Protestant. This was also his main problem with Schleiermacher's theology as well—he believes that it is too mystical and inward. Ritschl thinks that theology should have more of a regard for society at large.

Much of the work that Ritschl did was as a Church historian. His area of specialization was Luther and the Reformation, so when he turned to doing his own constructive work he framed it as Neo-Protestant. He thought that the best theology should recover the true Protestant impulse. He was a supporter of the Prussian Union Church—if there is a Christian identity then it should be a broadly Protestant identity, instead of a Calvinist or Lutheran one.

Ritschl, indeed, saw his own theology as continuing the work of the Reformation. He thought that even the Reformers were too caught up in certain older, antiquated forms—and that Protestantism needed to even more radically return to the message of the New Testament. This is what would actually meet the needs of the Modern world.

Ritschl's systematic theology is entitled *The Christian Doctrine of Justification and Reconciliation*. Published between 1870 and 1874 in three volumes, it is probably more correct to say that this work *contains* a systematic theology. The first volume is a history of doctrines of justification and reconciliation in the Middle Ages. The second volume is how these doctrines are treated in the New Testament. The third is Ritschl's own constructive formulation of these doctrines. It is this third volume that becomes popular and leads to the founding of the Ritschlian school of theology.

10.2.1 Against Metaphysics

Key to understanding Ritschl's theology is his opposition to metaphysics. He believed that religion needed to have a secure, independent basis such that Christianity would be effectively insulated from conflicts with natural science, philosophy and historical criticism.

When it comes to philosophy, Ritschl thought that Christianity should not be dependent upon some kind of philosophical foundation. He is against what he considered to be speculative rationalism—especially the Hegelian idea that theology should be subordinated to philosophy. He violently reacts to Hegelian speculative transformation of theology, seeing instead the Christian religion as opposed to speculation. Ritschl can be seen as advocating a Kantian modesty as opposed to a Hegelian speculative immodesty.

Ritschl is against what he called the infection of Christianity by metaphysics. It was not just Hegelianism that he had a problem with, but it was the **Hellenization** of Christianity. He saw this speculative temptation as being a problem for theology not only in the nineteenth century but also early on in Christian history. He argues that metaphysics has been corrupting theology since the time of the apostles. Often his opposition to metaphysics coordinates with his opposition to Catholicism. (Though this might be a chicken-or-egg situation.)

Ritschl thinks rather that God is known through revelation in a **personal** manner. God is only known in his action towards us. So Ritschl is opposed to natural theology. Theology only has to do with the revelation of God in Christ in Scripture as mediated by the Church. So there is always going to be an experiential element of personal trust. He also did not care for the creedal statements of the Church because there was too much philosophical baggage.

Metaphysics—in Ritschl's rather constricted understanding of it—is a general theory of things. Ritschl counters that people are not things and so not within the domain of metaphysics. He believed that metaphysics confused the two distinct realms of nature and of spirit. Metaphysics has to do with nature; religion has to do with spirit. (God too is a person, not a thing.) From his perspective, metaphysics cannot distinguish between nature and persons. It only has to do with things and cannot speak to the personal. Religion has to do with the domain of value while metaphysics is the realm of facts that cannot tell one anything about their worth.

10.2.2 Value Judgements

Key to Ritschl's understanding is his emphasis on value judgements. He, here, is inspired by the Neo-Kantian philosopher **Rudolf Hermann Lotze (1817–81)**, who was actually a colleague of Ritschl's at Göttingen. The key distinction that Lotze makes is between causal judgements and judgements of value. There are judgements that have to do with the causal relations within the system of nature—with regard to facts about how things are related to each other—and judgements that have to do with worth. The former are objective judgements, but the latter are value judgements. Value judgements are the higher, more significant of the two for human beings. The spiritual and moral have to do with this domain.

Judgments of fact	Judgments of value
science and philosophy	religion
objects as known	objects' practical worth
disinterested	evaluating relative to human goals
natural	spiritual

On the side of facts, you have disciplines like science and philosophy, which consider objects as they are known. One is to be disinterested and objective when it comes to facts. On the value side of things, however, is where one considers the practical worth of something—how something is evaluated relative to human goals or to your purposes in particular. This is the domain of religion and the spiritual.

In the background here is the threat of the empirical sciences with regard to freedom. The more science aspires to a total explanation of things in terms of the laws of physics, the less and less it seems that human freedom makes sense in a scientific perspective. It seems like everything can be determined relative to prior causes. Thinkers like Lotze and Ritschl wanted to stake out a domain that was distinct from that—where human freedom and value have meaning and are not an illusion that is merely a function of known scientific objects in motion. We want to keep hold of something distinct about humanity and human freedom.

Religious knowledge has to do with value judgements as natural science has to do with understanding the mechanical regularity of causes and effects. So, for a value judgement, what is of worth for you is what is central. That is what makes something of value. It has to do with your personal involvement. This, then, is the domain of morality and religion and what is most important for human beings.

Thus, religion has to do with freedom—in fact they say that the religious side of things has to do with our freedom from life's natural conditions. One way that discusses this has to do with our lordship over nature. We are somehow independent of nature. Nature is a causal nexus—a system of deterministic, fatalistic causes and effects. We are free from that. The religious has to do with our distinction from and lordship over that.

So religion, in the Neo-Kantian perspective, is about practical reason. It has to do with the distinctively human—with human persons, our values and our relation to other human persons. Also in the background is the perceived failure of natural theology. Ritschl would say that God can only be known in his special revelation. God is known to us in his worth or his value for us—ultimately as revealed in Christ. So, while both Ritschl and Schleiermacher focus on religious experience, Ritschl has a different understanding of that experience. He thinks that Schleiermacher's understanding is too subjectivistic, because it has to do with feeling, while the better understanding of the religious experience is the ethical one.

10.2.3 The Jesus of History

Ritschl would say that historical fact is appropriated through the value judgement of faith. This is particularly true in Christianity with the historical fact of Jesus. The only access we have to Him is through the value judgements of the Early Church. We do not have bare data but a value-laden interpretation. He would say that you cannot get behind the value judgements of the Church to get to something like the objective fact of Jesus. However, Ritschl does not reject fact when it comes to Jesus—he is still interested in getting as close as possible to the historical person of Jesus. (There is some equivocity here.)

The starting point of theology for Ritschl is the historical revelation of Jesus. This is the core of the historical reality of the Gospel and of the New Testament. It is because of this that theology is not merely subjective or mystical. Its object is the historical reality of Jesus, the origin of Christianity. The essence of Christianity is something that can be discovered historically. As an historian, Ritschl thought that theology should be based on historical investigation—of the origins of Christianity and Christ's historical life. Ultimately, he thought that the Scriptures provided a dependable testimony to who Jesus was.

However, faith in Christ is still a value judgement. It is not merely an inference from history; it is historical facts become revelation. Faith is always a personal encounter with Christ within the domain of value judgements.

Ritschl recasts the original Christological doctrines in terms of the person of Christ and His work. He is not all that interested in the supernatural but rather in understanding the divinity of Christ in relation to who he was as a person. Ritschl denies the validity of traditional Christological doctrines—about two natures and things like that—because he thought they were too abstract and too beholden to metaphysical categories. He thinks that he is following Luther's lead in this—that Christ is always Christ for us. The only way we have to talk about Christ is to talk about his personal impact upon us.

Christ's vocation for Ritschl is to establish a universal ethical fellowship. The main point of Jesus's preaching is the realization of the Kingdom of God, which is a universal ethical fellowship.

When Ritschl talks about the work of Christ, he talks about his obedience and faithfulness. So Christ is the perfect revelation of God as love, and because of this Jesus has the value of the divine for us. This is what he means to us. Christ's divinity then has to do with his relation to us, not about some metaphysical juju going on out there. Faith is a value judgement; it is not a theoretical statement in regard to his nature(s). The deity of Christ is ultimately a value judgement of Christ as being God for us. As Ritschl writes, 'Because He does for us what only God can do, He has the worth of God for us.'

10.2.4 Justification and Reconciliation

Ritschl also focuses on Christ as the Redeemer. In Christ's work as God's instrument of redemption, Christ brings about the forgiveness of sin—and this is primarily presented as re-establishing our communion with God.

'an ellipse with two foci'	
gift—what God does	task—what we do
religious	ethical
justification	reconciliation
individual	Kingdom

Ultimately, for Ritschl, Christ's work is twofold; it is a work of justification and reconciliation. Ritschl describes the religious life as 'an ellipse with two foci'. As a circle is defined by a centre, an ellipse is defined relative to two central points. In the Christian life, the first focus is that of gift. In some places, he says that this is the religious side. It has to do with justification—with what God does. The other side is the Christian task. The Christian life is not just a gift, and it is not just ethical duty. It is both grace and work, or both gift and task. The task has to do with the moral or the ethical as working towards bringing about the Kingdom. This is our ethical vocation—living a life of love to bring about a loving community. The ethical side of things is reconciliation. He says that reconciliation is the evidence of justification—or that reconciliation expresses justification. This is what we do.

The key is that justification makes reconciliation possible. Starting with God's initiative, God reveals himself to us. In Ritschl's broader philosophical perspective, in justification we are freed from nature's necessity. We are given freedom (justification), and we act out of that freedom (reconciliation). Other ways of talking about this ellipse are that on one hand you have the individual's justification, and on the other the individual's communal work of ushering in the Kingdom.

Justification is the gift side of things. It has to do with the forgiveness that is the end of our separation from God. Ritschl would say that the real punishment that we are being saved from is our feeling of guilt and estrangement. In forgiveness our separation from God is removed, and justification is our experience that God is thus delivering us. We are being brought back into a personal relationship with God. So instead of a purely objective accounting or substitutionary atonement, justification here focuses on experience. He is re-emphasizing the personal—our relationship with God. We are now in a loving fellowship with God. It is not that God's regard for us changed, or that we were objects of wrath and now God has mercy on us because of Christ. Rather, our separation from God was ended and now we are in a loving relation with Him. Ritschl would say that this justification only happens through Christ.

Reconciliation is the task. It has to do with re-establishing a relation. Normally, this would be thought of as a reconciliation between the person and God through the work of Christ. For Ritschl, however, it has to do with the realizing of the Kingdom of God. Reconciliation is more horizontal, whereas justification is vertical. So this is more about realizing the community. This realizing of the Kingdom of God happens through the Church. It is this realization of the Kingdom of God that Ritschl saw as central to the historical Jesus's teaching.

10.2.5 The Kingdom of God

In considering Ritschl's thought of Christianity as 'an ellipse with two foci', it is probably the case that the Kingdom predominates. The ultimate focus among the two foci is the Kingdom, the ethical side of things. This is the moral component of Christianity—the Kingdom of God is a social ideal to be realized in love for God and neighbour.

Ritschl's understanding of what he thought Jesus meant by the Kingdom of God was primarily ethical and not eschatological. God's purpose for the world—in good modern form—is not beyond the world but is rather to produce a moral community of free individuals united by brotherly love. This sounds like the Modern Moral Order of the Enlightenment's Providential Deism. This also resonates with Kant's idea of a kingdom of ends—seeing each person as an end in themselves and not manipulating them for some other end.

So how should we live our Christian freedom in the midst of the world? The answer to this question has to do with vocation. Vocation is the way that one serves the Kingdom of God in one's everyday circumstances. It is the particular way that the love of God and the love of the neighbour are brought together in a person's life. For Ritschl this seemed to mean that one was a good Christian by being a good German citizen—indeed a good citizen of the world in that he thought that the Kingdom of God should be about developing relationships among Christian nations.

It is with these kinds of ideas that Ritschl and his followers are charged with *Kulturprotestantismus*—'culture Protestantism'. Ultimately there is no real contrast between the Church and the world. The task of the Church seems to be the same as the task of the world. This is another reason that Ritschl's critical of Pietism, because Pietism is other-worldly. It has to do with a withdrawal from society. He is also very critical of eschatology, because it would in many ways put the current order of things under judgement.

10.3 Harnack

Adolf von Harnack (1851–1930) is the most well known of the Ritschlians. In our time, it is not unusual to find someone who knows about Harnack but not Ritschl. Harnack's father was a Pietist Lutheran professor of theology. Harnack himself becomes a professor of Church history at the University of Berlin and comes to be known as the pre-eminent Church historian of his age. In his own day, he had an international reputation, and was the personal advisor to the German Kaiser and helped the Kaiser write the declaration of war to the German people in what would be the First World War. He had a very close tie to the established order in Germany and emphasized a union between Christianity and national life or German culture.

He is probably best known for a series of extemporaneous lectures that he gives between 1899 and 1900. A transcript of these lectures is published in 1900 under the German title *Das Wesen des Christentums*—literally 'The Essence of Christianity'. In 1901, it is published in English as *What Is Christianity?* This is easily the most famous of the Ritschlians' works and one of the most popular theological works in the modern era.

In these lectures Harnack brings forward a metaphor (though not original to him) that would get a lot of play in Ritschlianism and in Liberal Protestantism: the distinction between the kernel and the husk when it comes to Christianity. The kernel has to do with what is essential in Christianity; it is what has permanent value. The husk is the part that is accidental; it is what you can get rid of. It is necessary, therefore, to distinguish between the indigestible shell or husk and the tasty and beneficial meat of the kernel.

The kernel of Christianity for Harnack was the message and teaching of Jesus. This is known through historical–critical examination of the Gospels. When it comes to what is really important with regard to Jesus, it is his teaching, not his story nor his identity, that is fundamental. It is not the person or nature of Christ or the work of Christ. The essence is his teaching.

The husks, the accidental bits, were the things that did not really fit with the modern age—things like miracles or apocalypticism. The Gospel, for Harnack, is directed at essential human nature, which he thinks does not change over time. Yet, there are particular cultural forms that change through history. This understanding is from his career as an historian—thinking about what kind of continuity there is in the midst of that which comes to be and passes away over time.

Figure 10.1 Harnack.

'Adolf Harnack' by User Tagishsimon on en.wikipedia—Project Gutenberg eText 13635, http://www.gutenberg.net/
dirs/1/3/6/3/13635/13635-h/13635-h.htm. Licensed under Public Domain via Wikimedia Commons.

kernel	husk
essential	accidental
Jesus's message	miracles, apocalypticism

He identifies what the kernel is with the primitive Gospel—as opposed to what he would call dogmatic Christianity.

Like Ritschl—and other Ritschlians—Harnack is set against Greek speculation. He thinks that one of the principle culprits in the barnaclization of the pristine hull of Christianity is its being associated with Greek thought—its Hellenization. In this, he thinks Christianity was drawn away from its essence—which is inner and moral. Harnack's programme against Hellenization is played out in his *History of Dogma* (1886–90)—a large multi-volume work. Harnack thinks that in trying to get rid of these later accretions of Hellenized doctrine that he—along with Ritschl—seeks to complete the Reformation. He wanted to purify the New Testament doctrines and get back to the original Gospel. Luther sought to present the Gospel free from the husk of ecclesiastical and authoritarian dogma, but Harnack wanted to go further. He did not want to stop at ridding the Gospel of its Medieval Papist accretions, but to go on to the Patristic Greek additions as well.

In this sense, Harnack follows the Neo-Kantian anti-metaphysical impulse of the Ritschlians. He also does so in seeing the heart of Christianity as being primarily ethical. He thinks that Christianity has become unpalatable when it is brought into the domain of trans-ethical metaphysical beliefs. When these became of defining concern for the Christian faith (say, in the Nicene Creed), this was a distortion of the Christian faith. The Gospel is not invested in philosophy or science of any kind. It has to do, rather, with the human spirit.

Harnack ends up becoming very popular. He scratches the itch that a lot of people had in Germany and elsewhere. Many people in the late nineteenth century were uncomfortable with some of the classic statements of Christian belief. And so, Harnack goes to the extent, later in his life, of saying that Christians need to update the creeds—removing all the metaphysical language … and the virgin birth as well, while we're at it—which he believed was a later mythical addition. He also suggests that only the books of the New Testament should be canonical.

Harnack would describe the essence of Christianity as the Gospel of Jesus Christ—not the Gospel about Jesus. It is his message, his good news that is the normative essence of Christianity. This is what is permanently valid. The essence of Christianity then is the religion of Jesus, not a religion about Jesus. What then is Jesus's distinctive teaching? After historical-critical sifting, what does Harnack think Jesus really taught? There are three points in Harnack's understanding of Jesus's teaching.

The essence of Christianity

'the kingdom of God and its coming'

'God the Father and the infinite value of the human soul'

'the higher righteousness and the commandment of love'

First is the '**kingdom of God and its coming**'. What Harnack means by this is that the Kingdom is the rule of God in people's hearts. God will rule in the hearts of people—this is the coming Kingdom. If Jesus is an apocalyptic teacher, it is not about the end of the world—it is about the coming of the Kingdom into the hearts of people. God will reign in our hearts.

Second is '**God the Father and the infinite value of the human soul**'. Here, the key to Jesus's teaching is that God is the Father. The Gospel of the Son is not about the Son—it has to do with the Father. God is our Father and because of that all humans should be seen as having an infinite value—God loves all humans. This is a movement against any kind of particularism. Jesus' message about God is a universal one. This is reminiscent of Lessing's *Nathan the Wise*: God the Father does not pick favourites but loves everyone the same.

The third aspect of the Gospel of Jesus Christ is what Harnack calls '**the higher righteousness and the commandment of love**'. The higher righteousness implies that there is a lower righteousness. The higher righteousness is beyond merely following a law or a moral code that is about external actions but has rather to do with our hearts. You are righteousness if you love your neighbour. It is not just your externally following certain rules but having the right disposition of heart—that you act out of a foundation of love towards the other.

You can see all three of these elements as interrelated. The coming of the Kingdom into people's hearts is something inward. It has to do with taking into account that God should be seen as our Father, and our Father loves us and all people. A transformation of the heart is what is sought—actually loving God and your neighbour. Sometimes Harnack is summarized in terms of the Fatherhood of God and the brotherhood of man.

That said, Harnack is not going to present a purely inward Christianity. He thought, like most of the Ritschlians, that this should cash out into a particular orientation and way of living. He, like Ritschl, will talk in terms of one's worldly vocation. He would say that one of the mistakes that Christians have made in the past—in the Middle Ages and in Pietism—is to see living out the Gospel as meaning an ascetic withdraw from the world. Harnack thought this was fundamentally wrong. Rather, to live out the Kingdom and your love for your fellow person has to do with your worldly vocation in the midst of the world and culture. This entails social concern—you should be concerned for the poor in your midst. This is part of how the commandment of love and seeing the infinite value of the human soul should cash out in the world. Because of that value—that value being very Kantian—we should be concerned even for the least of these.

10.4 Herrmann

Johann Wilhelm Herrmann (1846–1922) is distinguished as the most important systematic theologian of the Ritschlians. Though he is not as well known as Harnack or Ritschl, Herrmann is perhaps more significant in terms of his influence for twentieth-century theology due to his students Karl Barth and Rudolf Bultmann. Like several of the figures we have talked about, Herrmann's father was a Lutheran minister. While studying at Halle with Thulock, he meets Ritschl. He becomes a professor of theology at Marburg, and has Barth and Bultmann among his students.

10.4.1 Pietism vs. Intellectualism

Herrmann's thought reflects a Pietist heritage, not unlike what we saw in Schleiermacher. Like the Pietists and like Schleiermacher, Hermann sees a personal experience of Christ at the core of Christianity. Barth probably gets his appreciation for Schleiermacher from Herrmann. In that personal experience of faith, we have an immediate and lived certainty.

Herrmann was the first theologian to openly ally with Ritschl. As a Ritschlian, Herrmann had the same kind of opposition to metaphysics—the use of philosophical ideas in theology. He believed that, like Kant or Schleiermacher, religion had a domain of its own. Reflecting what he thought were Luther's sentiments, he asserted that Christian faith did not have anything to do with *welterkennen*, with the knowledge of the world. Faith is something otherwise than worldly knowledge and speaks prophetically against the wisdom of the world. The wisdom of the world is here taken to include philosophical ideas in general, so he resonated with the Neo-Kantian rejection of metaphysics. Herrmann also was opposed to confessional orthodoxy. But the primary beef he had with Calvinist or Lutheran orthodoxy was that it was overly intellectualized; there was too much of an emphasis on Christianity as being about intellectually affirming the right things.

Faith for Herrmann—true faith as he would call it—was not mere intellectual acceptance or affirmation of creedal points. He thought it is very dangerous to identify faith with simply believing in doctrine or lining yourself up with the right confessional standards. You were missing the point of Christianity, of actually being a Christian. True faith, then, had to do with *Erlibnis*—personal lived experience. So faith was intensely personal for him. He would say that it is not being dependent upon the wisdom of the world, but it is self-authenticating. And so it does not need a defence. In fact, trying to defend the Christian faith is betraying it. It is putting itself under the judge of a pagan lord. You should not expect Christianity to match up with the wisdom of the age—it is at odds with it. But it does not need a defence anyway because it has an inner certainty.

Herrmann talked about this experience of faith as an experience of liberation. The fundamental experience of Christianity was the experience of redemption through Christ—that we are somehow liberated through the work of Christ. This experience of freedom through liberation through faith is the cornerstone. So where do we get this experience of liberation? Herrmann would say that we get it when we encounter Jesus.

10.4.2 History and Jesus

What Herrmann meant by an encounter with Jesus is that we have an encounter with what he called the 'historical fact of Jesus'. He called the particular fact that we encounter 'the inner life of Jesus'. Through historical examination, we somehow come into contact with the inner life of Jesus. Our encounter with the inner life of Jesus is where we have the transforming, liberating experience of faith. So he would say faith is not based on doctrines or on Scripture, ultimately—because both of these things can be called into question historically. They are at best probable and therefore cannot serve for a basis for faith—which is a certainty. Historical investigation then cannot be a sufficient ground for faith. So if you want to base your faith on the Bible, you are really basing your faith on the historical study that justifies the Bible—which can never be more than probable.

Herrmann makes a strict distinction between science and faith. He wished to see religious faith as independent from scientific knowledge and free from the criticism of science. Behind this is a distinction Herrmann makes between **nature** and **history**. Nature is the domain of science—things we can know with demonstrative science. History is the domain of what we experience and those things in which we have faith. It is also the domain of freedom. This is something that is distinctive about Herrmann—that history is a domain that lacks conclusive proof. In this domain, you are free to decide to trust or not.

Nature	History
science	experience
necessity	freedom
demonstrable knowledge	inner life

Religion has to do with the historical because it has to do with *Erlibnis*—with lived encounter. Again, you can see the growing division in the German academy between the natural and the human sciences. As sciences like physics became more and more ascendant, they were realizing that other things that had been seen as sciences or fields of inquiry could not measure up to that. The human sciences—having to do with the study of human things like history or literature—were being viewed as the lesser sisters.

Religion had to do with that *Erlibnis*. Fundamentally, it had to do with personal trust. It was on the more 'human' side of things that one encounters persons and trusts them; it is where we have ethics and religion. In this Herrmann sees himself as following Luther by freeing Christian theology from worldly justification. In fact in his main book, *The Communion of the Christian with God*, the subtitle is 'described on the basis of Luther's statements'. Over and against science and metaphysics, Herrmann thinks Christian theology has to do with the domain of freedom—with everything that gives human life purpose and meaning.

The certainty that Herrmann is looking for was not certainty about any particular fact per se but about one's personal experience in the encounter of an historical fact. This encountered fact is Jesus' inner life. The certainty of faith comes from one's personal experience and one's encounter with the historical fact of Jesus' inner life. The inner life of Jesus is experienced as an absolute—as something that is not merely probable on the basis of the historical reconstructions. In order to attempt to head off potential (or indeed actual) confusion, Herrmann distinguishes between different kinds of history. He distinguishes between *historische* and *geschichtliche*. The first, *historische*, has to do with the merely probable results of historical criticism. The second kind of history, *geschichtliche*, is where Herrmann places the inner life of Christ as it is appropriated by faith. The second is history that has to do with faith. Herrmann was criticized for not being totally consistent here—as we will see in his public debate with Martin Kähler.

historische	mere probable results of historical criticism
geschichtliche	absolute inner life of Christ as appropriated by faith

10.4.3 *The Communion of the Christian with God*

Herrmann's central work is entitled *The Communion of the Christian with God* (1895). In this work his emphasis is on faith as a personal experience of God in Christ—a personal encounter with the inner life of Christ. Not unlike Schleiermacher, Herrmann asserts that when you are encountering Jesus' inner life, you are encountering his communion with God. What is distinctive about Jesus is that he is in unique and constant communion with God. So when you encounter the inner life of Jesus, through him you are in communion with God.

We are in a personal communion or relationship with God through Christ, and this is the central presentation of the faith. However, Herrmann shies away from any kind of identification with a mystical perspective. He thinks that you can get to the inner life of Jesus through history. He really wants to call the inner life of Jesus a historical fact.

Herrmann talks about Scripture, saying that the Word of God is mediated through Scripture. Again, he is talking about an encounter. Scripture is not in-and-of-itself the Word of God; the Word of God is an event where God speaks to you through the mediation of Scripture. It is as if in Scripture another dimension opens up. Through a text or a book, a personal dimension opens up for a Christian—the historically dependent text of Scripture opens up onto an encounter that is an absolute truth. There is absolute truth and certainty that is revealed to us there. This comes as a kind of gift.

Not unlike Schleiermacher, the deity of Christ then has to do with the quality of the encounter that we have with Him. Instead of using the metaphysical language of the classical confessions, Herrmann says that there is something about the quality of the encounter that makes us say that Christ is divine—mostly because it is through the mediating of Christ that we are brought into full communion with God. Christ is the meeting point between the divine and human because it is in Christ that we are brought into communion with God. We are brought into communion with God through Christ's inner life in which he is in full communion with God.

10.5 Kähler

Martin Kähler (1835–1912) is not a Ritschlian and was in many ways critical of the Ritschlian project. Kähler is a kind of forerunner of twentieth-century Dialectical Theology. A professor of New Testament at Halle, he studied under Rothe and Tholuck. He was very much a product of the Pietist Awakening. He ends up being quite critical of Mediation Theology and its attempt to reconcile faith with historical criticism. Kähler thought that we should not base our faith on waiting for the deliverances of historical criticism. He famously (if not originally) makes a strong distinction between two kinds of history: *Historie* and *Geschichte*.

Historie	scientific, critical history
Geschichte	history shaped by confession

The first, *Historie*, is that which has to do with scientific or critical history. Kähler asserts that if you are going to approach the Gospels this way—if you are going to try and find the Jesus of history—that this is going to be a blind alley. The project of historical–critical reconstruction of the 'Jesus of History', as somehow distinct from the 'Christ of Faith' as found in Scripture, is a fantasy.

The second, *Geschichte*, is history shaped by confession. It is a subjective history, a faith history. This is a history that starts with confession—in particular with the confession of Jesus as Lord. A presuppositionless history—a history assuming nothing—will yield little. The history that can actually mean something has presuppositions and prejudices. This is not bad history, but a proper kind of history—especially when it comes to what is important to us and most especially when it comes to Jesus. Kähler would say that if you are looking for the real Jesus, he is to be found not apart from (or somehow digging beneath or behind) the faith of his disciples but precisely in the faith of His disciples. The real Jesus is not a Jesus apart from interpretation but is accessed through the correct interpretation of faith. The real Jesus is to be found in the faith of His disciples—namely in the apostolic preaching of the resurrected Lord. This is what we have in the New Testament, and this is our access to Jesus.

Kähler viewed the search for the historical Jesus as a blind alley. You ended up with either very little and/or something that was perpetually contested. Kähler wants to say that Christian faith does not rest on historical criticism, but rather the apostolic proclamation itself is a sufficient basis for Christian faith. Here we are in a place where we can understand the title of his well-known book: *Der sogenannte historische Jesus und der geschichtliche, biblische Christus—The So-Called Historical Jesus and the Historic Biblical Christ* (1892).

There is a public argument between Kähler and Herrmann about the relationship between Jesus and history. Herrmann seems to think that *Historie* can provide some scientific neutral basis for Christian faith. Kähler basically comes to the conclusion that the presuppositionless, scientific *Historie* is ultimately a myth. So for Herrmann, the ground for faith is the earthly Jesus. For Kähler, the ground of faith is the risen Christ as presented in the New Testament.

10.6 Troeltsch

Ernst Troeltsch (1865–1923) is classified differently by different people. He was a late student of Ritschl and started his career as a professor of systematic theology at Heidelberg—but for the remainder of his career he switched over to the University of Berlin where he was chair of philosophy.

Troeltsch, in many ways—definitely on the Protestant side of things—stands at the end of nineteenth century Protestant thought and looks forward to certain twentieth-century problems. He brought up problems that would end up sticking with us in the twentieth century. He was also a central figure in what comes to be called the History of Religions School, which initially was closely related to the Ritschlians. The History of Religions School was interested in looking at the Old and New Testaments as being related to the cultures in which they originate. In particular, they looked at other religions in other cultures in the context of the Old Testament and the New Testament, in order to consider Scriptural religion comparatively. Troeltsch contributes to the birth of comparative religious studies and the project of studying different religions from a neutral (non-confessional) perspective.

Unlike Ritschl, Troeltsch would say that the key event in Modern history is the Enlightenment, not the Reformation. In his more constructive thought, he argues that the Enlightenment has changed the way we think in the modern world. The most significant change that happened is that we now have what he calls a historical consciousness—we are now aware of how things develop in history. It is from the perspective of such an historical consciousness that Troeltsch addresses Christianity; he thought that Christianity should be treated like any other historical religion. In this he was very different from Ritschl, Herrmann and Harnack.

Troeltsch presented three principles that guide our historical consciousness. **First** was **the principle of criticism**—by which he meant that all tradition was to be critically scrutinized. One does not take anything for granted as truth but looks at everything equally critically. The **second** principle was what he called **the principle of analogy**. What makes critical scrutiny of the past possible for him is our present knowledge of things. We are always talking about the past in analogy to our present experience. In order to investigate the past, you have to assume that past events are like present events. So from this perspective, he is going to say that since you do not experience miraculous theophanies today, you should not expect events in the past to be any different.

The **third** principle was what he called **the principle of correlation**. If we are going to explain events, we have to see that events are deeply interrelated. Events have meaning in relation to each other. Here he is primarily talking about cause and effect: to understand an event we have to understand its causes and its effects. Everything happens for a reason.

In Troeltsch's mind, these principles of historical consciousness undercut any kind of **dogmatism**—by which he meant no knowable event in history can be singled out as absolute. All of the events in history are relative in these same kinds of ways. So from that perspective, what is the absoluteness of Christianity?

Troeltsch's best-known work is entitled *The Absoluteness of Christianity and the History of Religions* (1902). By 'absoluteness', he means what is normative or what stays the same over time. In particular, he is investigating the question of how and whether one can say that one tradition is normative. How does one tradition tell us what we should believe? How does something come to have absolute and unchanging value in history, which seems to be a process of becoming? He is asking the question of how a religion can be valid, and he will come to the conclusion—at least at one point in his life—that Christianity has a superiority; but at best it is a relative superiority. One of the ways Troeltsch comes at this is with his notion of a '**religious *a priori***'. Not unlike approaches that we have seen thus far, he thought that religion of itself has a kind of formal necessity—that there is a distinct domain that is 'religious' and is autonomous and self-sufficient. The 'religious *a priori*'—something that is apart from our empirical experience—cannot be reduced to other domains. As such, it is an essential part of human life; there is an essential category of the human that is the religious that, presumably, does not change over time in history. However, he would say that the religious domain is purely formal—it does not have any inherent content. That is as close as Troeltsch got to absoluteness: the 'religious' that is absolute—but what exactly that is gets filled-in in different ways throughout history.

Eventually, Troeltsch will stop using the language of the 'religious *a priori*' because it is not terribly consistent with the rest of his thought. The closest he gets to a real normativeness to Christianity has to do with its goal. We can see this in the different editions to the *Absoluteness of Christianity*. In the first edition, he will refer to Christianity as the highest religious truth, but ten years later in the second edition he shifts it to a more consistent kind of relativism. He presents his final position—shortly before he dies—in a 1923 lecture called 'The Place of Christianity among the World Religions'. In this lecture Troeltsch brings to the fore the question of pluralism stating that the historical individuality of the world religions is 'not easily reconcilable' with any claim to supreme validity. Therefore, Christianity cannot claim absolute validity. At best, it can only claim validity for those who were raised with it. With this Troeltsch touches on a twentieth-century awareness of real religious pluralism, and not having a way to judge different claimants to absoluteness.

Another particular contribution of Troeltsch was his presentation of different social 'types' of churches in his work *The Social Teaching of the Christian Churches* (1912). Looking over the history of Christianity, he sees that there were three ideal types of ways of being a Christian in relation to society. The **first** type is what he calls the **sect**. That is characterized by withdrawal from the world—it cordons itself off from the corrupting influences of the world. The **second** is called the **church** type. The church social type is characterized by an engagement with the world. This ends up being a more institutional form of being the Church and is more closely related to culture. The **third** is what he calls the **mystic** type. Where the sect withdrawals itself as a group from the world, the mystic type withdrawals inwardly. It is more of an individual spirituality.

Troeltsch's Social Typology	
sect	withdrawal from the world
church	engagement with world
mystic	inward, individual spirituality

Troeltsch describes all of these different types as being present in modern Protestantism in Europe. However—and this was part of the point of his book—he believes that none of them are suited to living in the industrialized world. After the Industrial Revolution, none of these really address the central concerns of society. In the end, he thinks that a Christian way to live in the modern world is lacking; the previous ways of being Christian do not make sense in the modern world. The Church no longer gives us the cultural unity or ethical guidance that it once did because the world has changed, and there has not been a concomitant change in the Christian way of life that meets the needs of a modern industrialized society.

10.7 Schweitzer

Albert Schweitzer (1875–1965) is a figure of great renown. He is a Nobel Prize winner, acknowledged for working for world peace, particularly working towards the abolition of nuclear arms. He is also well known in Europe as an organist and as one of the great performers of Bach's organ works. A pastor in Germany (at Alsace) and for a time a lecturer at the University of Strassburg, later in his life he becomes a medical doctor and goes to Africa in 1913 to serve there for the rest of his life as a medical missionary. He is commonly looked upon as a model humanitarian.

For our purposes here, we will largely restrict ourselves to the contributions he made to historical Jesus studies with his book *The Quest of the Historical Jesus* (1906). Much of his book is a review of other historically reconstructed 'lives of Jesus' that had been published/attempted over the course of the nineteenth century. His own view is that (from the best that we can tell from historical study) Jesus is an eschatological prophet who proclaimed the imminent end of the world. When he says the Kingdom of God is at hand, he means the new order after the end of the world is going to happen soon and somehow thinks that his death will expedite the end of the world. Schweitzer depicts the historical person of Jesus with the graphic image of one who throws himself upon the wheel of the world that then crushes him. He sees Jesus as something of a tragic hero.

Schweitzer opposed the Ritschlians' views of Jesus—especially the views focused on his moral teaching—because he says you cannot separate Jesus' moral teaching from the historical heart of his teaching which was this eschatological message. Schweitzer was saying: 'If you want to get back to the historical Jesus then this is the Jesus you will get.' The main point of Jesus' teaching was that the world was going to end, and it did not end.

Figure 10.2 Schweitzer.

'Albert Schweitzer, Etching by Arthur William Heintzelman' by The Library of Congress Prints & Photographs Online
Catalog; http://www.loc.gov/rr/print/catalog.html. Licensed under Public Domain via Wikimedia Commons.

So, what then is Jesus' significance apart from his unbelievable eschatology? Beginning with
Paul, the predicted 'end' comes to be reinterpreted as the new Kingdom that begins with Christ—
the end was not the actual end of the world but a beginning of a new way of being in community.
And so this coming Kingdom became a way of talking about this era as being extended into the
future. In this new sense then the Kingdom did come.

In conjunction with this reinterpretation, Schweitzer will talk in terms of the Holy Spirit.
One cannot have a religion focused on the tragic historical Jesus alone. One must speak of the
Holy Spirit bringing Christ to life in our lived experience. In this way, we can take up the Jesus of
history—the tragic figure—and transform him into part of a meaningfully religion. The Kingdom
that we experience and should believe in is not the Kingdom that Jesus preached, but is the lived
nearness of God.

Schweitzer's positive view of what Christianity is to become is summed up in his phrase
'reverence for life'. There was a side to Schweitzer that held a tragic, even pessimistic view—that
Jesus was wrong and was crushed under the wheel of history and that good people should not
expect anything different. Schweitzer looks back at the natural world and human history and
appreciates how someone could say that there is no purpose—there is just this crushing wheel that
stands in opposition to the ethical Christian God. The task of life, then, is the heroic affirmation
of life in the face of the seeming meaninglessness of life—that we would affirm Christ's life in
us even against the seemingly meaningless crushing of Christ in his death. Schweitzer's positive

counterpoint has to do with the mystical presence of Christ. Christ is alive with and in us in the Holy Spirit, inspiring us to love and affirm goodness in the world. Schweitzer would say that we should live out of a will to love. This should be our response to the tragic order of the world, and in this we have communion with God.

Sources and Further Reading

Axt-Piscalar, Christine. 'Liberal Theology in Germany'. In *The Blackwell Companion to Nineteenth-Century Theology*, edited by David Fergusson, 468–85. Chichester: Wiley-Blackwell, 2010.

Dorrien, Gary. *Kantian Reason and Hegelian Spirit: The Idealistic Logic of Modern Theology*. Oxford: Wiley-Blackwell, 2012.

Livingston, James C. *Modern Christian Thought: Volume 1, The Enlightenment and the Nineteenth Century*. 2nd edn. Minneapolis, MN: Fortress Press, 2006.

Stout, Jeffrey. *The Flight from Authority: Religion, Morality, and the Quest for Autonomy*. Notre Dame, IN: University of Notre Dame Press, 1981.

Vidler, Alec R. *The Church in an Age of Revolution*. Rev. edn. New York: Penguin, 1990.

Welch, Claude. *Protestant Thought in the Nineteenth Century. Vol. 1, 1799–1870*. New Haven, CT: Yale University Press, 1972.

Welch, Claude. *Protestant Thought in the Nineteenth Century. Vol. 2, 1870–1914*. New Haven, CT: Yale University Press, 1985.

Wilson, John E. *Introduction to Modern Theology: Trajectories in the German Tradition*. Louisville, KY: Westminster John Knox, 2007.

11

Late-Nineteenth-Century Catholic Theology

11.1 Pius IX and Ultramontanism

In the background of the development of official Roman Catholic theology in the late nineteenth century was the political situation of Italy, which did not become a unified nation-state until 1861. Before then, it was made up of many different independent states, often at war with each other, one of them being the 'Papal States'. During this period, many other countries in Europe were becoming more centralized nation-states. (Germany does so in 1871.) On the way to unifying Italy, Victor Emmanuel II (who is eventually proclaimed the first modern king of Italy) captured the Papal States in 1859. The annexation of the Papal States marked, to a significant degree, the end of the pope's temporal power. The pope was no longer a leader of a state.

During this period the Catholic Church's response to modernity was fundamentally defensive in posture. It saw itself as being under attack; it was literally under military attack. There was a posture of circling the wagons in this period of Catholicism. A common term used in relation to this period is **ultramontanism**. This has to do with an emphasis on the centralized authority of the pope and is often set in opposition to **conciliarism**. While conciliarism was holding that the ultimate authority in the Church resided in the council of bishops, ultramontanism was holding that the central authority of the Church was the pope.

Ultramontanism was moving directly against one of the central impulses of the modern age— an impulse towards autonomy, individual liberty and democracy. Instead of going that direction, the Roman Catholic Church was going in the opposite direction: focusing on one person as the supreme authority in the Church.

Figure 11.1 Pius IX.

Courtesy of the Library of Congress. (No known restrictions on publication.)

Pope Pius IX—often called 'Pio Nono'—was pope from 1848 to 1878. Pius IX, reigning in the midst of this tumultuous period for the Catholic Church, was a charismatic and beloved figure. There was something of a cult of personality around him. He became popular for his resisting of the new secular authorities in Italy. With Pius IX, there was a heightened veneration of not just him as a personality, but of the office of the pope itself. It was with this very popular pope that there arose the Cult of the Holy Father—a special veneration for the position of the pope in modern Catholicism. Pius IX stood in opposition to many of the main cultural currents of the Europe of his day whether they were political liberalism or any other kind of 'worldly' posture. The pope's ecclesial power grew as his temporal power diminished. As the pope's power as a head of state nearly disappears, his position as the head of the Church was amplified.

A significant example of the defensive postures of the Church in this period is what is called the **Syllabus of Errors**—a list of all of the things that good Catholics should avoid, published in 1864. This list of around eighty 'modern' errors takes a stance of stark opposition to all modern progress in the Church or in the State. In order to do so, it takes many previous papal statements (having to do with addressing of local problems or particular issues) out of context and makes them into general or universal condemnations. The Syllabus used extreme language and condemned rather broad categories, such as rationalism, socialism, communism, naturalism, freemasonry, the separation of Church and State, the free press, freedom of religion and so on. Many at the time and thereafter come to consider the *Syllabus of Errors* a sloppy affair. Even Pius IX later admitted that it was 'raw meat needing to be cooked'. Most Catholics at the time (including the bishops) did not know what to do with it. How can one take seriously such strident opposition of modern society in the midst of modern society? It was also troubling to many political leaders. They openly questioned what place Catholics could have in modern democracies. Abraham Lincoln, the president of the United States during the Civil War, was among these openly wary leaders.

Another example of the ecclesial strength and centrality of the Papacy at this time is that in 1854 Pius IX more or less one-sidedly proclaimed the dogma of the Immaculate Conception of Mary— that Mary the mother of Jesus was conceived and born free of Original Sin. What is implicit here was that the pope on his own had the authority to define Catholic teaching.

11.2 Vatican I

The most significant of the Catholic Church's responses to the modern world in the nineteenth century was the First Vatican Council. Vatican I (as it is called) met in 1869 and 1870. Vatican I was the first general council of the Church (the Roman Catholic Church) since the Council of Trent (1545–63) three centuries earlier. There were two constitutions that were voted on and approved in Vatican I. The first, *De Filius*, has to do with faith and reason. The second, which we will dwell on here, is called *Pastor Aeternus*. The constitution *Pastor Aeternus* proclaimed the doctrine of **papal infallibility**. It was here in the late nineteenth century that papal infallibility became the official teaching of the Roman Catholic Church in response to the whittling away of the authority of the pope in other areas.

So what does the infallibility of the Pope mean? *Pastor Aeternus* states:

[When the pope] speaks *ex cathedra*, that is, when, in the exercise of his office as shepherd and teacher of all Christians, in virtue of his supreme apostolic authority, he defines a doctrine concerning faith or morals to be held by the whole Church, he possesses, by the divine assistance promised to him in blessed Peter, that infallibility which the divine Redeemer willed his Church to enjoy in defining doctrine concerning faith or morals and that therefore such definitions of the Roman pontiff are of themselves and not from the consent of the Church irreformable.

This was not a blanket infallibility for papal proclamation then. It is only when he is speaking *ex cathedra* ('from the throne') in the exercise of his office as the shepherd in virtue of his supreme apostolic authority. But not only that, it is only when he is defining a doctrine concerning faith and morals to be held by the whole Church—making a universal proclamation about things that everyone is supposed to believe. The upshot is that papal infallibility only applies when the pope is speaking in the case of these rare official pronouncements. In 1871, shortly after the First Vatican Council, a bishop, John Fessler, gave an interpretation of the teaching on papal infallibility, which Pius IX himself endorsed. Fessler gives a number of qualifications for what counted as speaking *ex cathedra* such that it only applied when the pope was making an official, definitive announcement about something essential to the faith. In the end, very few papal announcements met these criteria. For example, the Syllabus of Errors does not pass. So, while Vatican I affirmed papal infallibility, it was almost immediately scaled back and moderated.

11.3 Neo-Scholasticism

In the mid-nineteenth century there was a revival of the thought of Thomas Aquinas in Europe. Thomas is revived as a bulwark, a resistance, to the modern Nova of the nineteenth century. Going back to Thomas was a way of standing strong against the onslaught of erroneous views, whether they were secular rationalism, German Idealism or anti-rational fideism. Catholic leaders desired an objective definition for the Christian faith—which they thought they found in Thomas Aquinas. Indeed, the thought of Thomas Aquinas gains official sanction. Pope Leo XIII, who was the successor to Pius IX, put forth in the papal encyclical, *Aeterni Patris* (1879), that the theology of Thomas is, in fact, normative for Catholic teaching. With this there was a call to study his work—or at the very least that his thought be presented and taught to more people. So Thomas's philosophical perspective is presented as what is called the *philosophia perennis* or the perennial philosophy—a philosophical perspective that is ever-true. Now this was a rare event in Catholicism; the Church had never before directly promoted any one particular school of theology as the official perspective. This was the first time the Church identified a school of thought within Catholic thought as getting

Figure 11.2 Leo XIII.

the gold star as the best representation of Catholic thought. Again a strong model was needed to serve as a bulwark against the errors of modernity.

The view promulgated by *Aeterni Patris* is an approach often called **Neo-Thomism** or **Neo-Scholasticism**. One of the things that happened was that there were several important centres of Neo-Scholastic study that are founded to support such a programme, such as the Pontifical Academy of St. Thomas Aquinas in Rome and the Institute of Philosophy at the Catholic University of Leuven. A new critical edition of all of Thomas's writings had been commissioned—which was presently not yet complete. (He wrote something like 2,000 pages a year—an astounding amount.) The critical edition of his writings is called the 'Leonine Edition'.

Neo-Thomism, beyond Thomas, developed its own intellectual ethos that was not necessarily connected with him. One of the things that characterized Neo-Thomism was that it was opposed to the kind of historicism that you would see in the Catholic Tübingen School. There was a real tension between theologians such as Newman and the Tübingen School as looking at the development of Christian doctrine in history and the Neo-Thomists.

One of the things that happened as a result of making Thomas's thought the official teaching of the Church was that such attention was given to the *letter* of Thomas that some would argue that it kept the Neo-Thomists from really getting the *spirit* of Thomas's works. One of the expressions of this is what has come to be called 'manualist theology'. Given the mass of Thomas's writings (his *Summa Theologiae* alone being several thousand pages long), one could not expect a widespread programme of thorough and thoughtful engagement with the primary sources when it came to teaching students. It was necessary to summarize and digest Thomas's teaching. So for the broader teaching of the Church, the students were not as much reading Thomas as they were reading these digested, ordered manuals that were to have presented Thomas's ideas—in which he is presented largely a-historically. A figure often associated with manualist theology is a theologian named **Réginald Garrigou-Lagrange (1877–1964)**—who defended New-Thomism into the twentieth century when there was reaction against Neo-Thomism and Neo-Scholasticism. (We will return to Garrigou-Lagrange in Chapter 15.)

What are some of the ideas that are ingredient in Neo-Scholasticism? First, the Neo-Scholastics did not see any contradiction or any dissonance between **faith and reason**. This was due to a highly rational accounting for the content of the Christian faith. Second—when it came to **grace and nature**—they made a fundamental distinction between the order of grace and the order of nature. They adopted an earlier idea of a *natura pura*—a pure nature. This is nature that is separate from the order of grace. Here they read Thomas as saying that humans have a natural end to their lives which is distinct from their supernatural end which is enabled through grace. There is a distinct natural order that has its own imminent end or purpose. Grace is then a super-added order that is different than nature and operates extrinsically to it.

11.4 Catholic Modernism

The term 'Catholic Modernism' originated as a term of derision and warning. A 'Modernist' in this context was one who departed from tradition more than someone else would like. Certain Roman

Catholic thinkers, largely French scholars, between 1890 and 1907, are lumped into this category. In 1907, there was an official condemnation of such 'Modernism' by the pope at the time.

Catholic Modernism has never been a single programme nor does it possess a party line but if there is any general mood or emphasis present among these thinkers it is that there is an incompatibility between some traditional Catholic beliefs and modern scholarship. Therefore, some of these traditional Catholic beliefs need to be reinterpreted. Foremost in what they meant by 'modern scholarship' is the challenge of historical awareness and of historical criticism of the Bible. Also—beyond historical criticism—they are raising the question whether there are not better, more appropriate philosophical frameworks than the kind of Aristotelian framework that is set forward in Neo-Scholasticism. Is there a better philosophy than Aristotle?

Leo XIII—though he was the pope who made Thomism the privileged teaching of the Church— tried to encourage the younger scholars to engage with modernity. Many different Catholic thinkers take up this challenge and come to be associated with Catholic Modernism, including the Englishman George Tyrrell (1861–1909) and the Italian Ernesto Buonaiuti (1881–1946). Likely the best-known representative is **Alfred Loisy (1857–1940)**. A French priest and a professor at the Catholic University of Paris, he was also a Hebrew and Assyrian specialist. While he taught and wrote from the perspective of modern historical and biblical criticism, he also sought to find a synthesis between confessional Catholicism and a modern historical–critical perspective. One of the things that he became known for was his public argument with Harnack (who we should recall was German and Protestant-to-the-point-of-being-anti-Catholic). He felt that Harnack, though a celebrated church historian, was insufficiently historical in his approach to theology. Harnack's approach for Loisy was a historical insofar as he wanted to dump traditional Christology and return to the 'original' essence of Jesus' teaching; Loisy saw this as presuming that one can leap outside of history and then leap back in to the prior point of one's choosing. We are always in the midst of the development of the Church; as nineteenth-century Christians we do not have the option of being first-century Christians. One cannot simply discount the development of Christianity between Christ and us.

Another significant idea that Loisy put forward was a distinction between what he called the **historical sense** of a text and the **traditional sense** of a text. The traditional sense is that which has to do with faith. As a confessing Catholic, he believes that there is a validity to holding onto the traditional sense of the way biblical texts have been understood through the tradition of the Church. One can hold onto this as the traditional sense while still investigating the historical sense of the text—which is often different than the traditional one. The traditional sense of the text is simply the way the text has come to be read in the history of the Church. But the historical sense is what we are investigating as historical–critical scholars.

Against Harnack, Loisy held out a proper place for tradition—you do not just get rid of it as something that has been added on, but the truth is to be found in the whole. One needs both the historical sense and the traditional or faithful sense. So in the second, 'traditional' sense Loisy follows Newman and his *Essay on the Development of Doctrine* in seeing how Christian self-understanding has developed over time.

In 1893, Pope Leo XIII published an encyclical entitled *Providentissimus Deus*, which declared Scripture as inspired in all of its parts and free from error. This was taken to be an official pronouncement against higher criticism and a serious challenge to scholars like Loisy. In 1903, five of his books were put on the Index of Forbidden Books—an official list of books that Catholics are not allowed to read. And in 1908, Loisy was formally excommunicated. However, in 1909 he became a professor at the Collège de France, a highly prestigious public institution in which there is only one professor in the nation for a given topic at a given time who gives public lectures on their given topic. So Loisy is excommunicated in 1908, but then is immediately celebrated as one of the pre-eminent French Bible scholars of his time in the broader culture. One can see the desperation and dissonance between the official work of the Catholic Church and the broader scholarly community—even the broader theological community.

In 1907, Pope Pius X in the encyclical *Pascendi Dominici Gregis* officially condemned 'modernism'. Then in 1910, the Roman Catholic clergy is required to take what is called the 'anti-modernist oath' or 'oath against modernism'. To be a Roman Catholic priest, you had to take an oath against modernism. After Pius X died in 1914, this kind of anti-modernist regime was relaxed considerably and people were allowed to publish on modern biblical criticism. (The tumultuous story of Catholic theology in the twentieth century continues in Chapter 15.)

Sources and Further Reading

Del Colle, Ralph. 'Neo-Scholasticism'. In *The Blackwell Companion to Nineteenth-Century Theology*, edited by David Fergusson, 375–94. Chichester: Wiley-Blackwell, 2010.

Livingston, James C. *Modern Christian Thought: Volume 1, The Enlightenment and the Nineteenth Century*. 2nd edn. Minneapolis, MN: Fortress Press, 2006.

Loughlin, Gerard. 'Catholic Modernism'. In *The Blackwell Companion to Nineteenth-Century Theology*, edited by David Fergusson, 486–508. Chichester: Wiley-Blackwell, 2010.

Vidler, Alec R. *The Church in an Age of Revolution*. Rev. edn. New York: Penguin, 1990.

Part III

Twentieth-Century Crisis and Modernity

12

Kierkegaard and Nietzsche

We begin our discussion of twentieth-century theology in what might be an odd place by talking about two figures from the middle and late nineteenth century: Søren Kierkegaard and Friedrich Nietzsche. Kierkegaard and Nietzsche are often regarded as being prophets, as being men out of time. In fact, they are constantly claimed by whatever is in vogue in twentieth-century or even twenty-first-century thought. In the early twentieth century, they were the first existentialists. In the late twentieth century, they were the first postmodernists. There is obviously something going on with these guys if they can be seen to be foreseeing such significant movements in continental philosophy. They are also prophets in the critical sense—both of them are intensely critical of their own time. They provide a critique that perhaps does not come to fruition until the twentieth century—until we get on this side of the First World War.

Here, we take Kierkegaard and Nietzsche as representing two major trajectories of thought from the twentieth century up until our own day. Both Kierkegaard and Nietzsche represent critiques of modernity that came to fruition in the twentieth century in late modernity or postmodernity at the very least, modernity becoming self-critical.

12.1 Kierkegaard

Throughout his short life, **Søren Aabye Kierkegaard (1813–55)** remained an independent writer who never held an academic position—as far as we can tell he probably never even held what we would think of as a proper job. He really did not have time to do anything else; he was principally occupied as a highly prolific and often experimental author. His writing career largely falls within the years of 1841 to 1851. In that decade he wrote around thirty books, some as long as 500 or 600 pages.

Living in Copenhagen, the capital city of Denmark, he spent his time writing, and taking walks—sleeping occasionally. Mostly, he wrote. His works are often difficult to understand, which is one of the reasons there are so many interpretations of them. He wrote in an intentionally indirect manner—he indeed wrote his doctoral dissertation on irony.

Gary Dorrien asserts that Kierkegaard is 'arguably the greatest religious thinker of the nineteenth century'. And yet, he is almost universally misunderstood by his contemporaries. He wrote so strangely and so much that his Danish contemporaries really did not know what to do with him, and he is largely ignored outside of Denmark until the early twentieth century. He wrote in Danish, which was not a widely known language in the rest of Europe, unlike German or French.

Figure 12.1 Kierkegaard.

'Kierkegaard Olavius' by Christian Olavius Zeuthen (1812–90), http://www.kunst-fuer-alle.de/deutsch/kunst/kuenstler/kunstdruck/christian-olavius-zeuthen/16328/1/112089/kierkegaard-im-cafe—chr–zeuthen/index.htm. Licensed under Public Domain via Wikimedia Commons.

Nevertheless, Kierkegaard comes to have an enormous influence on twentieth-century theology and philosophy. This can be seen in the work of major Protestant theologians of the first part of the twentieth century—figures like Barth, Bultmann and Tillich. But there are also significant philosophers in the twentieth century—like Heidegger, Sartre, Wittgenstein and Derrida—who are influenced by Kierkegaard. (It must be said, Kierkegaard himself likely would have found much of his reception unrecognizable, but that's life—or being dead, as the case may be.)

The son of a poor peasant who became a successful businessman, Kierkegaard was the youngest child of seven, who by the time he reached his early twenties had lost all his siblings save one, and his mother. He studied theology at the University of Copenhagen for ten years—a long time. During the 1830s in Copenhagen, Hegelian Mediation Theology is the reigning theological discourse. Along with this, Kierkegaard also studied significant portions of Schleiermacher's *Glaubenslehre*. After finishing his dissertation he travelled to Berlin for a number of months and heard Schelling's late lectures. However, for most of the time Kierkegaard spends in Berlin—less than a year—he is shut up in a room writing his first book, *Either/Or*. (This ends up being his longest book, and is published in two volumes.)

He was influenced by the major early-nineteenth-century theologians—Schleiermacher, Hegel, Schelling and the Romantic thinkers. He also looked back to figures like Jacobi and Hamann, and their critiques of modern thought and Kantian thought. He latches onto their spirit of questioning a triumphant modernity, and draws on the three major streams of the nineteenth century—Kantian thought, Schleiermacher and Hegel.

12.1.1 Critique of Hegelian Philosophy

Kierkegaard consistently critiqued the dominant Hegelian philosophy and theology in Copenhagen. **First**, Kierkegaard emphasizes the individual over and against the group—whether that group be society at large, the crowd, the public, mass media or the state. During this period, we see these social expressions of humanity becoming powerful and dominant forces in this part of the modern world. But Kierkegaard wants to see the individual as having an irreducible value. Individuals are valuable not because they are expressions of a broader historical spirit, expressions of a certain cultural milieu or inasmuch as they fit in with the values of a particular group, but inasmuch as the individual has an irreducible value in and of themselves. The human individual is indigestible.

Second, he emphasizes the finitude of human reason. Human reason is something that is all too human (as Nietzsche would put it). We do not have a God's-eye-view and are not capable of attaining absolute knowledge. This again is against his picture of Hegel's understanding. He would say from that perspective that a system of existence is impossible. Existence cannot be understood as a comprehensive system—only God can do that, and we are not God.

Third, when it comes to the relationship between religion and philosophy, Kierkegaard sharply parts company with Hegel. Like many Enlightenment thinkers, Hegel sees religion as a simplistic presentation of what could be known more fully in philosophy; Kierkegaard sees it as more than simplified philosophy and holds that this kind of approach, at the very least, violates what religion thinks of itself. Christianity claims to be the highest, deepest truth and not merely the handmaid of philosophy. Theology is not philosophy for dummies. Rather, in Christianity we are given a truth to which philosophy does not have full access. Christianity and Christian theology claim to present or reveal the very truth of human existence and the human situation, not a lesser version of it. Kierkegaard views his task as a thinker as that of clarifying Christian concepts, as giving Christianity its proper due and not reducing Christianity to philosophical ideas.

Fourth, Kierkegaard parts company with Hegel's tacit and explicit understandings of God. Hegel's understanding was such that God's reveals himself in human consciousness itself and ultimately in philosophy. Hegel sees God as immanent and unfolding in the development of human consciousness, whereas Kierkegaard emphasizes that God is truly other and transcendent—such that there is an 'infinite qualitative distinction' between God and humanity. With Kierkegaard you are not going to wonder whether God and humanity are ultimately the same thing.

12.1.2 Transcendence and Paradox

To get at a more fundamental difference between Hegel and Kierkegaard is to see that Hegel seeks mediation into a unified, systematic perspective, while Kierkegaard has a central place for transcendence and paradox. Here, Kierkegaard has an influence or at least a deep resonance well into the twentieth century. For Kierkegaard, thinking about God commonly runs into paradox. The truest way that we can think about that which is beyond our understanding is in a form that recognizes its limitation—and it looks odd. We run into odd ways of talking, because we are not talking about normal everyday things. We are using our normal everyday language of talking about the origin of the world itself. Our language is not made for that, so it is going to look and act strangely.

One of the distinctive phrases that Kierkegaard introduces to describe God's transcendence is to say that there is an 'infinite qualitative difference' between God and humanity. There is a difference between God and humanity—they are not the same thing—and that difference is qualitative, rather than quantitative. It is not as if there is a scale of being or a univocal plane of being and that we are on level thirteen while God is on level two million; this would be a quantitative difference. Kierkegaard is recovering the classical understanding of God, that he is not a super powerful being. He is not us written large. Beings like that are called the gods—like Zeus or Apollo. God is not one of those. God is not a competing force in the world of forces; he is the ground and origin of being himself.

Kierkegaard's objection to the obscuring of the transcendence of God and the paradoxical nature of Christianity is not solely a philosophical matter. He wants to reiterate the radicalness of Christianity to Christians. He lives in a society that sees itself as Christian; to be a Dane was to have a baptismal certificate. Kierkegaard sees this cultural Christianity as a pale imitation at best. He wants to reintroduce Christianity into Christendom. By this, he means he wants to reiterate how radical and what a fundamental difference a basically Christian perspective of the world makes—especially to people living in the modern world. He is not interested in accommodating Christianity to modernity. In *Fear and Trembling*, he describes how the theology of his day 'sits all rouged and powdered in the window and courts [philosophy's] favor, offers its charms to philosophy'. The imagery is that theology has made itself a prostitute trying to attract the customers of modernity. So, with this, he is critical of the theologians of his day who adopt ultimately suspect secular terms as the criteria by which to reinterpret Christianity. Kierkegaard believes they have this backwards. They are forgetting the truth of Christianity in trying to get it to measure up to something else.

Kierkegaard would even attack the practice of defending Christianity. How do you defend the truth in a courtroom of lies—or against false criteria? How do you defend Christianity on modern terms? In this, he is attacking the conservative theologians of his age—the apologists, who try to prove that Christianity is true, using the modern ways of thinking of their time. He argues that they are compromising Christianity just as much as the liberal thinkers who are changing Christianity into a mere puppet for their current values. So, Kierkegaard often writes as something of a prophet, even though his tone is not always prophetic—often it is playful and ironic. Sometimes a joke can get across a prophetic point more effectively than yelling at somebody. His point is not simply to criticize his society, but to declare the truth of paradoxical Christianity and to communicate what it means to be a Christian. When he occasionally summarizes what his thought is all about, he says that he is trying to understand what it means to become and to be a Christian.

12.1.3 The Present Age

In this context of the middle of the nineteenth century, Kierkegaard presents some particularly prescient meditations on what he calls the Present Age. The actual title of the book in which this is discussed is translated into English as *A Literary Review* (1846). (It is also translated as *Two Ages*. Sections of it are often republished and translated as *The Present Age*.) In this work Kierkegaard talks about the public sphere—the sphere of mass culture and mass communication, and the press as an organ of public opinion. While he lives in an age before radio, television or the internet, Kierkegaard is keenly aware of how mass communication in the form of newspapers is transforming what it means to be human in the modern age … and not for the positive.

Kierkegaard sees the press as giving birth to an entity called 'the public'. He refers to it as a 'phantom', something that is not tangible and yet is powerful. One of the things that the public does is that it *levels*. Public opinion is an abstract and 'unreal' entity of what people think—what 'they' say. This being of fashion has come to determine what is good or valuable. Exactly *who* is identifying and giving something value is not given; it is just as if this is what 'everyone' thinks—and that is the perspective from which the press writes. There is this ghostly entity of 'the public' that presents how we are to act and what we are to think. It is similar to peer pressure, but without concrete individuals. The public lives, like parasites, from individuals when they are not being individuals. It is a parasite that lives in our psyches, but we (when we are not 'us') are the ones that give it life.

Kierkegaard has a definite hostility towards the press and journalism. However—and this is a common move that Kierkegaard makes—he does not simply reject and abandon that which he is critiquing. He does not abandon the media of his day, but he addresses the culture through its own medium and style. He uses the style to try to attempt to influence culture in a different direction.

Figure 12.2 Kierkegaard.

'Kierkegaard 20090502-DSCF1495' by Arne List—Own work. Licensed under CC BY-SA 3.0 via Wikimedia Commons.

He often writes in and embraces the *feuilleton* style, a style of this early journalism. The *feuilleton* actually combines many different styles in presenting a certain perspective. Kierkegaard uses this kind of heterogenous style in several of his books. He writes reviews of different aspects of culture (in works like *A Literary Review*), and in doing so seeks to reflect aspects of the culture back to itself. He takes the material from this ephemeral world of popular culture and uses it as a medium to address the age. He is a strange prophet—speaking to the age and critiquing it through its own terms.

Kierkegaard believes that ultimately the cure for the malady of the age—our shallowness, emptiness and nihilism (although he did not use that term)—is that we need to develop our inwardness and our relationship to God. To become an individual before God, you have to break your reigning social conditioning, and break through the illusions of the modern ethos. Almost all of the people he is writing for, by and large, would consider themselves to be Christians. He wants to wake them up to reality of the Christian faith. Ultimately, the essential truth of Christianity is the truth that is revealed and mediated through the person of Christ. He is not just a symbol of humanity, but He is our truth. He is the true human life that is given to us in the midst of our immanent untruth. This is a deeply Christocentric perspective. This does not mean, however, that Kierkegaard is a nice churchman.

12.1.4 Christendom

Kierkegaard critiques what he calls Christendom—specifically the Lutheran Christianity of his day. In Denmark at this time, Lutheran Christianity was the official religion of Denmark; the State Church belonged to a division of the Danish government. Kierkegaard causes a great stir in Copenhagen in the last year of his life because of something referred to as his 'attack on Christendom'. He published many newspaper articles and, finally, founds his own paper, *The Moment* (*Øieblikket* in Danish). He writes ten editions of this paper as a pamphlet with the point of presenting harsh criticism of the official Lutheran Christianity in Denmark, and dies with the last issue on his desk, ready to be published. What he is attacking is not Christianity as such—quite the opposite. He is attacking false religion. He is attacking nominal Christianity and the established order that would redefine Christianity as basically baptizing whatever the given cultural norms happen to be.

Kierkegaard sees his task as one of reintroducing Christianity into Christendom. Thus he thinks himself a prophet or missionary into a culture in which everyone is Christian. At the end of his life, he is critical to a rhetorical extreme (calling ministers cannibals and the like), and really wanting to wake people up in a rather grand style. This bludgeoning style is not indicative of the vast bulk of his writings in which he is positively evangelistic (though in often bizarrely subtle ways), seeking to bring people into a new and better way of looking at things and of living.

12.1.5 Indirect Communication

Kierkegaard has a particular way of writing that he describes in terms of **indirect communication**. A good part of what he writes does not appear under his own name: He used various pseudonyms. During the great part of the first half of his writing career—or the 'first authorship' as it is often called—he wrote as different characters. Imagine, for instance, a book written by Ivan Karamazov. He implicitly represents different perspectives. He writes from different (somewhat idealized) perspectives that people of his time would have adopted to one degree or another.

The point of this—aside from being interesting—was to elicit self-reflection and ultimately personal transformation. His point was not just to pass on information but also to help people change their lives. My telling you that it is a good thing to love your neighbour, and you accepting this as true, is different from you *loving* your neighbour. You cannot take control of another person's mind and make them be good. They would not be a person anymore. How can one person communicate in such a way as to edify or build up another person? Rather than simply pass along information, how do you build someone up? What can a person do with another person that will help make them better?

Through indirect communication, Kierkegaard presents a perspective that is attractive (to some degree) to those who have a similar perspective. As they read a given pseudonymous work, they are not just coming into contact with this literary figure or character—they are also given the opportunity to come into contact with themselves. The reader is given the opportunity to confront him/herself, and also to come to see his/her own way of looking at things through someone else's eyes. Kierkegaard realizes that our defences are usually up when someone is trying to criticize or attack our way of living and thinking—we are often pretty deaf to preaching in that sense. In this is a way of communicating indirectly, so that we let our defences down. There is the 'thou art the man' moment. He is trying to influence people through a highly literary way of communicating.

Kierkegaard's works (and pseudonyms)

Either/Or (1843)	Victor Eremita, 'A'. Johannes the Seducer, Cordelia, 'B' or Judge William, an anonymous Jutland pastor
Two Upbuilding Discourses (1843)	
Fear and Trembling (1843)	Johannes de Silentio
Repetition (1843)	Constantin Constantius, the Young Man
Three Upbuilding Discourses (1843)	
Four Upbuilding Discourses (1843)	
Two Upbuilding Discourses (1844)	
Three Upbuilding Discourses (1844)	
Philosophical Fragments (1844)	Johannes Climacus
The Concept of Anxiety (1844)	Vigilius Haufniensis
Prefaces (1844)	Nicolaus Notabene
Four Upbuilding Discourses (1844)	
Three Discourses on Imagined Occasions (1845)	
Stages on Life's Way (1845)	Victor Eremita, Johannes the Seducer, Constantin Constantius, a Young Man, the Fashion Designer, William Afham, a Married Man, Frater Taciturnus, Quidam, Hilarius Bookbinder
Concluding Unscientific Postscript to Philosophical Fragments (1846)	Johannes Climacus
A Literary Review/Two Ages (1846)	
The Book On Adler (1847, unpublished)	
Upbuilding Discourses in Various Spirits (1847)	
Works of Love (1847)	
Christian Discourses (1848)	
The Crisis and a Crisis in the Life of an Actress (1848)	
The Point of View for My Work as an Author (1848, unpublished)	
The Lily of the Field and the Bird of the Air (1849)	
Two Minor Ethical-Religious Essays (1849)	
The Sickness unto Death (1849)	Anti-Climacus
Three Discourses at the Communion on Fridays (1849)	

Kierkegaard's works (and pseudonyms)

Practice in Christianity (1850)   Anti-Climacus

An Upbuilding Discourse (1850)

Two Discourses at the Communion on Fridays (1851)

For Self-Examination (1851)

Judge For Yourself! (1851, unpublished)

The Moment (1855)

12.1.6 The Existing Individual

The existing individual is at the heart of Kierkegaard's thought. He presents a way of thinking that is both **about** and **for** the existing individual. Because of this, he is often called the 'father of existentialism'. Kierkegaard's 'existentialism' (a term he himself never used) can be seen in his insistence that philosophy should not be stranded in the realm of abstract and general ideas, but should be about our lives. Descriptively, Kierkegaard's thought is about the existing individual. He presents various analyses of the life of the existing individual—of what it means to be a human being. Kierkegaard will come up with an understanding of the nature of the human self or **the structure of the self**. He will think of the human self as a synthesis—a set of relations. So the self for him—as opposed to Descartes—is not just a thinking thing, but is fundamentally dynamic. It is not a static thing at all; it is a set of relations within the self, relations to others and relations to God. The relations constitute the self.

Kierkegaard also talks about **the sickness of the self**: not just what the self is but of how things go wrong with that which we are. While he describes the disorder of the self in terms of **anxiety** or **despair**, he, ultimately, talks about it theologically in terms of **sin**. The principal works in which he discusses both the nature of the self and the sickness of the self are *The Concept of Anxiety* (1844) and *The Sickness unto Death* (1849). He talks about the structure of the self, how the self is distorted and sick, but he also examines the remedies of the self—ultimately, in faith and grace one can have healing through Christ.

When Kierkegaard is thinking about the self, he is not just looking for a definition—he is examining how there are different ways for the self to be. He discusses different ways of living in terms of different **existence-spheres**—different perspectives on life or ways of living. These are different ways of relating. If the self is a set of relations, here are the different ways the relations can be configured. So, this is a philosophy about the human, existing individual. It is describing it, its sicknesses and its maladies.

But it is also a philosophy **for** the existing individual. What Kierkegaard is trying to put forward is something that is not just diagnostic, but that is also therapeutic and upbuilding. He wants to help the existing individual to become what they should be, which is, ultimately, a responsible self before God. For Kierkegaard, this means to choose a *truer* life—to live as that which we are, and not to live a life of illusion.

12.1.7 The Existence-Spheres

existence-sphere	organizing centre	social exemplar
The Aesthetic	self, pleasure	the seducer
The Ethical	the other, the group, ideals	the married person
The Religious	God	the celibate

There are three different stages or spheres of existence for Kierkegaard: that said, maybe there are two, maybe six—there are different ways of counting. In some places, Kierkegaard identifies the Aesthetic and the Ethico-Religious as the two basic views of life. He also divides 'Religious' into Religiousness A and Religiousness B, and then he develops different spheres between the aesthetic, the ethical and the religious. The most consistent accounting is to say that there are three: the Aesthetic, the Ethical and the Religious.

These ideas are set forth primarily in four different works. *Either/Or*'s two volumes represent the aesthetic and ethical perspectives, respectively. *Fear and Trembling* is written from the perspective of the ethical sphere person, but addresses the religious, focusing on the case of the *Akedah*, Abraham's binding of Isaac on Mount Moriah. What do you do with 'the father of the faith', whose most supreme act of fidelity to God is being willing to do something that certainly looks to be unethical? *Stages on Life's Way* is like *Either/Or* with multiple sections by different 'authors' writing from different perspectives. The last significant work for seeing Kierkegaard flesh out the relationships between the existence-spheres is the non-pseudonymous *Works of Love*. This looks at the ethical from the perspective of the religious. Whereas *Fear and Trembling* shows a stark difference between the ethical and the religious, *Works of Love* presents the ethical—our relation to the other—and love in relation to the religious, we will see how deeply interrelated and unified the ethical and religious are.

The first of the existence-spheres is the **aesthetic** sphere. The aesthetic way of life is centred on the self and the self's desires and pleasures. It is primarily seeking self-fulfilment. What becomes evident is that this way of living—a way of life that is primarily focused on self-fulfilment—is not fulfilling. A life centred on the self is not fulfilling to the self—in fact, as he would say, there is no self there to fulfil. You are just a series of sensations from moment to moment. That is all that appears as valuable—relative degrees of pleasure. The aesthetic way of life—simply trying to follow your desires—ultimately ends in failure. It is ultimately destructive of the self. We see this in volume one of *Either/Or*. The aesthetes therein who are trying to think through an aesthetic life are quickly moved to seeing how life is deeply empty, meaningless, and torturous. This kind of life is also ultimately destructive of other people. People are just functions of your own desire. The symbol or social exemplar of the aesthetic perspective is the seducer. The infamous last part of *Either/Or* volume one is called 'The Seducer's Diary'. This is a symbol of the aesthetic sphere where the other simply exists as something that is there for the pleasure of the self. There is no 'other' for the aesthete, and they will just use and abuse the other person inasmuch as it is pleasurable.

The second existence-sphere is the **ethical**. This is a way of looking at life that is centred on the group or an ideal. This is not just what is good for me, but what is good for society, the other, or just what is good in an ideal sense. One of the key aspects of the ethical is going to be commitment. Part of your defining of yourself is not just yourself—you define yourself in relation to an ideal, to another person or to other people. The ethical self is fundamentally responsible to something beyond the self. Kierkegaard uses marriage as symbolic of the ethical—as exemplifying commitment and responsibility. If you live as an aesthete in marriage, you are not going to have a happy marriage—or you are not going to have a marriage at all. A marriage is the symbol of a human relationship in which you are committed to that other person—that defines the relationship. You are responsible and responsive to another. But, ultimately, Kierkegaard observes—we see this in *Works of Love*—that the ethical is all too readily torn down into the aesthetic. We can easily use the ethical or ethical ways of thinking and manipulate them by our selfish desires. We can use ethical talk or selfless talk as a mask for our self-interest. In the end, though, the ethical cannot be grounded in itself. It is insufficient for what it is trying to do—just as the aesthetic is insufficient for what it is trying to do.

One should begin to notice here a kind of immanent progression from a lower sphere to a higher sphere in that the criterion or the desired end of the lower sphere cannot ultimately be met within the lower sphere and can open to that which is beyond it. Kierkegaard would argue that the ethical pushes beyond itself towards something, and it is in this context that he will talk about what he calls the **teleological suspension of the ethical**. 'Teleological suspension' is a good translation for Hegel's *Aufhebung*. It has to do with being oriented towards an end and a purpose, but that end or purpose is beyond the current sphere, so there is a 'suspension' involved. Suspension, here, should be seen in two different senses. It is a suspension in the sense of being put out of play (like being suspended from school or from playing a sport or being in suspended animation) but also in the sense of being held in place (as with a suspension bridge). This is something that is at once put out of play and held in being—two seemingly opposite ideas.

This is a key to what can be identified in Kierkegaard as the structure of the relation between the higher and the lower. (This can be seen clearly in his fascination with Matthew 6.) From the perspective of the lower, the higher seems impossible. It seems you have to choose one or the other. Either you have the lower and the higher is impossible, or you have to totally abandon the lower in order to get the higher. No man can serve two masters. This is the negative part. However, we also see the other side of 'suspension' later, when Jesus says to seek first the Kingdom of God, and all of these things will be added to you. The higher is not the destruction of the lower, but it is the only way the lower can be there at all in truth. The lower is preserved in the higher. It is suspended from it. So we see the either/or and the both/and. Only from the higher perspective can you see how the lower is reconstituted and fulfilled from its *telos*. It is teleologically suspended. Its fulfilment is beyond it. It is not immanent to it.

From the aesthetic perspective, either you are going to live a life centred on your pleasure, or you will live an ethical life—you have to choose between the two. You cannot live an ethical life while just doing whatever seems pleasurable at the moment. However, from the ethical perspective you will then come to see that the ethical perspective is the truly pleasurable, self-fulfilled perspective. The aesthetic cannot live up to the aesthetic sphere's own criterion the way that the ethical can—

and likewise the ethical cannot live on its own unless it is suspended from the religious. Ultimately, the religious is what is needed to keep the ethical from being degraded and manipulated into the aesthetic again. We need to find our ultimate self-fulfilment and security that keeps us from trying to manipulate security and meaning out of others.

The final existence sphere is that of the **religious**. The religious sphere has to do with centring one's life not on the self, the other, or an ideal, but on God. Your relationship with God is the absolute that founds and suspends the rest of your life. The rest of your life is held in being by your relation to God. You can ultimately only have a self—what you are looking for with the aesthetic view—in your relation to God. You can ultimately only love the other when you first have your relationship with God. That is the only way you will be secure enough to not need to manipulate other people.

Kierkegaard distinguishes between different kinds of religiousness: **Religiousness A** and **Religiousness B. Religiousness A** is general religiousness. The core of it is trying to relate to the absolute (God) absolutely. This is not the same thing as having a Theistic worldview. It is not just an intellectual stance—it is an existential stance. The religious is not just believing that there is an absolute, but having the absolute—God—be the absolute in your life. That is different. He would say that that is the difference between the Christian and the demon. The demon has a proper worldview—knowing that God is God—but does not make God the first thing in its life. He talks about this in abstract terms as relating absolutely to the absolute and relating relatively to the relative. However, the more you seek to do this the more you become aware of your failure. The more you try to relate to God absolutely—to make Him God of your life—the more you realize that you are failing to do this. The greater your religious consciousness is, the greater your guilt is. That is the end-result of Religiousness A, guilt-consciousness. This is the highest awareness that religiousness can get us—our total failure. That is the highest realization that we can have.

This sets the stage for what Kierkegaard calls **Religiousness B** or paradoxical-religiousness. Christianity, for Kierkegaard, is not just another version of religion. With Christianity you have something fundamentally different arising. This is primarily to do with how the religious relation is transformed in the light of Christ. What is central here with Religiousness B is Christology.

12.1.8 Christology

Perhaps different from many of the thinkers in the nineteenth century, Kierkegaard is deeply orthodox in his approach to Christology. He begins with a fundamental affirmation that the historical person of Jesus of Nazareth is God incarnate. What does that mean? He says that this Christology is central to Christianity, but Christians have all too often become deaf to the extraordinary nature of this claim.

Kierkegaard will talk about the Incarnation in terms of the **absolute paradox**. This absolute paradox can be taken in three different senses. **First**, Jesus is absolute paradox in that in Jesus you have the unity of the divine and the human generally. Between the divine and the human is an infinite qualitative distinction; they are fundamentally different from each other and yet they are united in Christ. The **second** sense of the absolute paradox is that God existed as a particular human being in history. Hegelians might have agreed with the first sense of the paradox in saying that humanity and divinity are united together, but Kierkegaard means that the individual Jesus of Nazareth in particular was fully and uniquely God. Kierkegaard is clarifying the Christian confession that he thought was being muddied. The **third** sense is that our eternal destiny as existing individuals is contingent upon our relation to this person in history. We traditionally say that our eternal salvation is contingent not upon our relation to something outside of history or some idea but ultimately upon our relation to this other human being who was God in history. These ideas come to the fore in *Philosophical Fragments* (1844) and *Concluding Unscientific Postscript to* Philosophical Fragments (1846).

What Kierkegaard is bringing up is that the Jesus of History is the Christ of Faith. In the background, D. F. Strauss is causing quite a stir in Denmark with his recently published *Life of Jesus Critically Examined*, and Kierkegaard is familiar with his ideas. The Ritschlians go on to focus on the Jesus of History over and against the Christ of Faith. The Christ of Faith is made up of later beliefs that are added onto the Jesus of History, and they want to get back to the Historical Jesus. However, in the twentieth century, we will see Bultmannians focusing on the Christ of Faith as what is really important and not as much the Jesus of History. Kierkegaard is affirming that the Jesus of History is the Christ of Faith and that, as such, Jesus is either the object of faith or the sign of offense. We should not be surprised when people find this unbelievable, because the claim is truly extraordinary. For those who are not Christians, Christianity (particularly these claims about an odd Jew 2,000 years ago) is rightly taken as something that is offensive to the understanding. Kierkegaard is not trying to get Christianity to measure up to some kind of external secular discourse.

Finally, Christ is not just the only absolute paradox, but is also the **Truth in Existence**. He is the revelation of the true human life. Jesus is the criterion for human existence. Not only is he that, but he gives us that true human life and is in this sense the **Gift** and the **Saviour** who gives us the gift of life. Christ is the **Teacher** who imparts that life to us and gives us something that we lack. Christ is also the **Prototype**, the model of our human existence. So, Christ is the answer to the problem of human existence and to the question of how should we then live. Kierkegaard's is a profoundly Christological theology. We will see echoes of this when we get to the twentieth century when we have a reawakening of Christologically oriented theologies.

12.2 Nietzsche

The son of a Lutheran preacher, Prussian-born **Friedrich Nietzsche (1844–1900)** penned most of his books between 1872 and 1888. In his latter years Nietzsche began to slide into insanity. Nietzsche is supremely interested in enhancing life, in affirming life to the degree of going beyond its present forms. He sees that life entails a going under—that lesser forms of life have to die for greater forms to live—including those forms within oneself. You have die to parts of yourself to become greater and for your life to become transformed. He sees Spinoza as a kind of precursor to this. Even though he makes derogatory comments about Spinoza as a philosopher trying to overly

Figure 12.3 Nietzsche.

'Nietzsche187a' by F. Hartmann—Photography by F. Hartmann in Basel. Public domain. Scan processed by Anton (2005). Licensed under Public Domain via Wikimedia Commons.

mathematize reality, he still feels that Spinoza is a kindred figure—especially in being an outsider in his time. But Nietzsche also resonates with Spinoza's emphasis on immanence. He focuses on the immanent life—the life in which we are caught up.

Nietzsche is going to be another prophetic figure. He is going to prefigure some particular strains of twentieth-century atheism. He writes in his famous passage from *The Gay Science* of the madman in the market, declaring that God is dead, and that we have killed him. At the end of that speech, the madman says, 'I have come too soon.' He comments that 'God is already dead', but 'it has not reached you yet'.

12.2.1 The Chaotic Universe and the Affirmation of Life

Chaos is the heart of what the universe is for Nietzsche—at least from our limited human perspectives. We project our orderly anthropomorphisms upon the universe. We project values of order, organization, form and beauty upon it. But, there is no law—in a human sense—to the universe. There is simply the chaos of a meaningless necessity. There simply is what is. It does not make sense. The only sense we find in the universe is what we project upon it. The universe does not imitate humanity, but the values that we see in the world are values that we create—and he does not think that this is a bad thing. Rather, what humans should do is own up to our creating of value. The good, order, beauty and wisdom that exist in the world are things that we create. We should own our being creators of value—at least the great among us who actually do so. Nietzsche's philosophy is fundamentally a philosophy of the affirmation of life. In order to really understand Nietzsche's thought, this is key. The heart of Nietzsche's thought is a **yea-saying**. We should affirm and say 'yes' to life—the life that we actually have. That is what *The Gay Science*, the joyful wisdom, is: the affirmation of this world in which we live. He will write in *Thus Spoke Zarathustra* that we should be 'faithful to the earth'. Do not deny this world. Do not call it evil. Say yes to it. Affirm the world in which you live.

Out of this affirmative core, Nietzsche violently opposes any life-denying or 'nay-saying' impulses. The nay-sayers—those who deny life and prefer another world of the 'spirit' to this world—are maligners of life. They call life evil in the name of another world—'the Apart, the Beyond, the Outside, or the Above'. Nietzsche directs our attention to how this dualism between this world and another world (which functions to primarily demean our world) has arisen in human history. He says that people like Plato are big proponents of this world-denying vision. He says that the most dangerous of errors is Plato's invention of pure spirit and the good in itself. He is opposed to what he calls the 'world-slanderers', because he believes that this is the only world there is. If one is going to put all of one's value in a world that is not this world—that is not the world that you actually live in—then one is sacrificing real good to an illusion.

Nietzsche is opposed to the renouncer, who seems to soar beyond this world and its desires. He does not like these religious types—like the ascetic who is willing to die to this world in the name of the world of spirit. He thinks that that is what all religion is, what he calls a 'slow suicide'. It is all about denying life and trying to get everyone to believe that they are sick so that they can find a cure in another world. He calls this an immense ingratitude for the goodness of the world.

Nietzsche finds Christianity to be a prime culprit here. He sees the priests and ministers of Christianity as 'preachers of death'. They celebrate death, sacrifice and self-mutilation. He names Christianity 'Platonism for the masses'. Christianity has made the world a worse place. He writes in *The Gay Science*, 'The Christian decision to find the world ugly and bad has made the world ugly and bad.' It is not that the world is ugly and bad, but the effects of hating the world have made hateful things appear in the world. Instead of this terrible hatred of life, we should affirm life. All of this critique of Christianity—primarily in Nietzsche's social milieu—is in the name of an affirmation of life.

It is in the context of the affirmation of life that we should understand Nietzsche's presentation of an *amor fati*—a love of fate. He says that we should embrace the way things are—not as a lesser

---

Major works of Nietzsche

The Birth of Tragedy (1872)

The Untimely Meditations (1873–6)

Human, All Too Human (1878)

Daybreak (1881)

The Gay Science (1882, 1887)

Thus Spoke Zarathustra (1883–5)

Beyond Good and Evil (1886)

On the Genealogy of Morals (1887)

Major works of Nietzsche

The Case of Wagner (1888)

Twilight of the Idols (1888)

The Antichrist (1888)

Ecce Homo (1888)

Nietzsche contra Wagner (1888)

---

situation or a pale shadow of spiritual reality. Nietzsche preached a doctrine of **eternal return** or 'the eternal return of the same'. This is that we should wish that whatever happens should happen again and again forever. The essential meaning of the eternal return is that our affirmation of life is not to be qualified in any way. We are not looking for something better that is coming; there is not something better around the corner. It is an affirmation of the way things are, and to will that things be eternally the same.

Thus is understood Nietzsche's idea of the **will to power**. The will to power is the will to life. He would say that the will to power is the essence of life. A living thing wants to act, to discharge its strength. This would be taken on the individual level, but he also sees that this is what the larger natural world is. It is a world of dynamism. It is not static, but a continual moving, evolving, and surviving—it is an urge toward life. Life as such is always appropriating. That is what life does. It is metabolism. You are always taking in another life in order to survive yourself. Life is always overpowering other lives. It is always imposing its form on others and exploiting other life forms. That is its continual moving-forward; that is the progress of life. Such life is a continual transformation. Nietzsche says that you might think that this appropriation is bad or violent because you think of things as staying the same—but that is not the case. Things are constantly changing, and this is just the way that things change. To think otherwise is to celebrate death or dead things. Living things constantly change, and they constantly change by metabolizing other living things. Life is this transformation—reappropriating and reinterpreting what came before. The form that life has is always a fluid form. It is a rising out of this drive of life.

12.2.2 Slave Morality

It is from this perspective on what life and reality are like that Nietzsche presents his criticism on what he calls slave morality. He writes about this in his *On the Genealogy of Morals* (1887). Nietzsche has been described by Paul Ricoeur as being a 'master of suspicion'. He critiques Enlightenment morality by describing where such morals come from.

Nietzsche says that morality begins with a **master morality**. The master morality is simply that those who have power create value. This happens on the biological level—whoever does the eating imposes the form—and it happens on a social level—whoever has the power imposes the form. The powerful and creative are good. That is what 'the good' is: what has been created by those with the power to do so.

Figure 12.4 Nietzsche.
Courtesy of the Library of Congress. (No known restrictions on publication.)

However, what would happen if those who were oppressed began to moralize? What if they came up with a morality of their own? Nietzsche says that this would be a morality of *ressentiment*. (He uses the French term.) Instead of having a master morality—a morality that comes from the masters and celebrates their values of having power and creating value—a **slave morality** would be a morality based on resenting masters. This kind of morality, for Nietzsche, is an inversion of nature; it is a celebration of weakness. The slaves make their station in life into the ideal. The slaves make weakness 'good' and the attributes of the strong to be 'evil'. He says that the value-judgements of good and evil in the origins of morality in Western society have been inverted.

12.2.3 The Transvaluation of All Values

Nietzsche sees in the Christian Europe of his day humanity's wilful degeneration and celebration of what is life-negating. It is with this in view that he wants to return to a proper life-affirming way of looking at things. In *Thus Spoke Zarathustra*, he presents what he calls the **three metamorphoses** of this retransformation. The first metamorphosis is the **camel**, a beast of burden, and his depiction of the renouncer. The camel is the one that would see life as a burden and would renounce it for another life. Then there is what we would see Nietzsche as in his more critical moments: the **lion**, the strong beast—the destroyer—that tears up the status quo. But this is not the highest ideal for Nietzsche because that is still just a negation. The lion is a negation of a negation, being a negation of a life-denying order. The highest metamorphosis is the **child** who does not see wrong or the distortion but is innocent. The child can say 'the sacred yes'. They can affirm the world as it is.

Instead of just wanting to destroy Western culture, he wants to see the replacement of traditional religion and morality with what he calls the 'transvaluation of all values'. There should be a revolution in our understanding of value to put the will to power as the true basis of value—not any celebration of weakness or another world but of the way life really is. This manifests itself for Nietzsche in a celebration of what he calls the power of great souls. He admires great creators— artists, usually. (Here is Nietzsche in a Romantic mode.) The celebration and love of life has to do with our recreating and reappropriating what came before. He would say that the artists are on the cutting edge of this by rejecting what came before and taking it up and making it into something else. This is what all life does. The best human representation of this life is to take up and transform the values that have come before.

Nietzsche would see in creativity the fullest kind of yea-saying—not just a saying 'yes' to the world but being a part of the 'yes' that the world is. He would say that we should look to those who take up the love of life with no restrictions and that we are not capable of this now. He definitely does not think that he is capable of this because there is too much of the lion in him, but he sees the child as something to come. There needs to be a destruction first; the death of these old values has to come to pass before there can be a rebirth. Those that would have that pure affirmation of their way of life Nietzsche calls the *Übermenchen*—the 'over men'. This is a new kind of humanity that has become free from the life-denying values of the past.

12.2.4 Nihilism

Truth for Nietzsche—as a harbinger of a kind of postmodernism—is a social construct. Truth is something that humans have made. All truth is relative or it is only our projections upon the world. There is no truth in and of itself. When we look at the world we are only putting human values there that we then find. He however does not hold this consistently insofar as he is talking about the way the world and life really are.

Nihilism for Nietzsche is his diagnosis for the modern self in modern society. Nietzsche is not a nihilist. He criticizes modern society as being nihilistic and empty because it is lying to itself. It is in denial. The emptiness of life is part of this nay-saying; there is no active value in life. He would even say that the particular character of modern nihilism is that we do not even believe in God anymore. We do not believe in Christianity—this Platonism for the masses—we do not even have that value system anymore. So when he says that God is dead, he is saying that we are still acting as if these Christian values still have meaning—but ultimately we do not even really believe in them. Traditional beliefs and values are dead on the inside. People are just going through the motions.

While Nietzsche believes that Christianity is a slave morality that celebrated weakness, he thinks that is better than having no values at all. What he means by the death of God is that the false values and slave morality have died and nothing has come to replace them. We are in that in-between time. The camel is dead, and we are in the time of the lion, but we have yet to behold the child. The current state of Western society for Nietzsche is one of nihilism; we have yet to experience the transvaluation of values.

12.3 Malaise: Living after the Death of God

We recall that Charles Taylor gives three senses of secularity, and what we are talking about here with Nietzsche and the death of God is **Secularity 2**—an actual decline in practice and belief. People do not believe in God anymore and do not act like they believe in God anymore. This death of God manifests itself as a lack of meaning. While this is operative in a more covert manner in the nineteenth century, with atheism becoming a live option in Western society, the twentieth century is where you start to see the gears slipping and stripping. Belief is certainly no longer axiomatic, no longer natural. More and more people are not believing or practising any sort of religion traditionally understood.

Even in contemporary unbelief, there are still often reference points for God. When people talk about themselves as secular, that is largely a negative descriptor: it is as if the secular in the twentieth century is haunted by the ghost of God. This exclusive humanism defines itself in relation to earlier modes of belief. This is reminiscent of the nihilism of which Nietzsche spoke. It does not have its own way of talking. Those that do not believe in God can only speak of themselves in negative terms of those who did believe in God. This is coming out of the nineteenth century and into the twentieth century.

We also see coming out of the nineteenth century with Nietzsche, and as a consistent undercurrent into the twentieth century, an understanding of what William Desmond calls the 'dark origin'. What is most fundamental in the world or in reality is **inhuman**. It is wild and does not operate by the canons of rationality. This is the underside of scientific rationality—the world is ultimately something our reason can explain to us with a 1:1 correspondence—and the suspicion that ultimately reality is something that does not play by our rules at all. This can be seen in philosophers such as Nietzsche and Schopenhauer, but it is also seen in the writings of people such as **H. P. Lovecraft** in his 'weird tales'. Lovecraft writes about all of these what we would want to call supernatural things, but he is very explicitly an atheist. He does not believe in the supernatural. He says that these horrifying characters and these insanity-inducing things that happen are a way of talking about the universe that is ultimately inhuman. He does not believe in the supernatural, but he does believe in the universe as being inhuman. We want to act like it is a nice human place, but it is ultimately not hospitable to human values.

In the twentieth century, this wild and inhuman cosmos without will also seep into the wild and inhuman or pre-human world within us. **Sigmund Freud** will talk about how our persona is rooted in something that is irrational or amoral. The primacy of the 'dark origin'—the irrational, amoral, violent forces—runs below the surface in the nineteenth century and will start to come to surface in the twentieth century. It is an anti-humanism or at least an anti-anthropocentrism.

12.4 Trajectories

We conclude our presentation of Kierkegaard and Nietzsche by considering how we can think about them as representing important trajectories for the philosophical and theological thought to come after them. Often, Kierkegaard and Nietzsche are paired together as foundational figures for Continental thought in the twentieth century. This likely began with Karl Jaspers, a philosopher in the twentieth century who helped to popularize Kierkegaard in Germany.

As a rough heuristic, we can see a couple of different trajectories in the twentieth century that we can identify with Kierkegaard and Nietzsche as a starting place to see where things end up going.

There is a Kierkegaardian trajectory—which ironically passes through some who reject Kierkegaard and not through some of those who claim him. These are theologies that more or less reject an accommodating posture towards modernity. Kierkegaard critiqued and rejected classical liberalism before it was born; he provided an approach that funded the demise of classical liberalism before it even existed. Kierkegaard represents an approach that is fundamentally **confessional**. If one is to be a Christian theologian, one needs to take the claims of Christianity more seriously than the desire to measure up to the canons of secular rationality. A confessional trajectory begins with the Christian confession. This would include Barth and a lot of dialectical theology and all to the more recent postliberal and postsecular theologies. Here, Kierkegaard anticipated something of a postmodern critique of secular modern reason. What we are going to see with so-called postmodernity in one sense is that what modernity called 'reason' is actually just one particular story that has a history. It has no foundational legitimacy over and against the claims of faith. This is what François Lyotard talks about when he talks about incredulity towards meta-narratives. A meta-narrative is a story that claims to legitimize itself by neutral reason. The postmodern view will say that 'reason' is always the reasoning of particular humans in history.

This will level the playing field at the very least. From such a 'Kierkegaardian' postmodern perspective, there is no reason to say that the discourses of secular reason are superior or to be the criteria for the discourse of faith. Ultimately, the secular started with some kind of covert or anti-religious confession and faith and is not superior or 'enlightened' in any fundamental sense. Kierkegaard anticipated such a critique of imperial reason and gave a fully theological version of postmodernity. Such a 'Kierkegaardian' postmodernity says that religious faith is as foundational as any other fundamental claim to reality. This is one trajectory, which is kind of a return to the foundation of Christian confession through theology.

Such a confessional trajectory is manifest in the twentieth century in more or less independent Catholic, Protestant and Orthodox forms. *Nouvelle théologie*, Balthasar, and some postsecular theologians are Catholic theologies that are starting from a fundamentally confessional perspective. Perhaps Rahner fits here as well as some of the liberation theologies. In the Protestant vein you have Barth, Fundamentalist and Evangelical branches of theology, and the so-called postliberal and post-secular theologies. Bultmann is sometimes in this category, as are some liberation theologies. All of the main Eastern Orthodox theological directions in the twentieth century are arguably confessional—Neo-Patristic theology definitely so.

The trajectory on the other end of the spectrum or continuum is the Nietzschean one. Here we see an **atheism**, and what Taylor will talk about as **Secularity 1**. This is the public discourse becoming more and more Godless and religion-free. This is atheism as a dominant public discourse. We are not going to see a whole lot of this in modern Christian theology; it is self-consciously anti-theological.

In our heuristic schema, we can see a continuum of different degrees of relation opening up between a purely confessional perspective and an anti-confessional perspective that would see God-talk as unnecessary at the very least and perhaps harmful. For the story of modern Christian theology in the twentieth century there is a highly significant trajectory between the Kierkegaardian Confessional and the Nietzschean atheistic trajectories that continues, to one degree or another, in the tradition of the Classical Liberal Theology of the nineteenth century. This can be seen as a **secular** trajectory within modern theology.

Confessional theologies	Catholic	Nouvelle théologie	Ch. 15
		Balthasar	Ch. 18
		Rahner?	Ch. 18
		Liberation theologies?	Ch. 19
		Postsecular theology	Ch. 21
	Protestant	Barth	Ch. 13
		Bultmann?	Ch. 14
		Evangelicalism and fundamentalism	Ch. 17
		Liberation theologies?	Ch. 19
		Postliberal theology	Ch. 21
		Postsecular theology	Ch. 21
	Orthodox	Neo-Patristic synthesis	Ch. 16
		Russian Religious Renaissance/Sophiology?	Ch. 16
Secular Theologies		Classical Liberal Theology	Ch. 10
		Russian Religious Renaissance/Sophiology?	Ch. 16
		Bultmann?	Ch. 14
		Tillich	Ch. 14
		Rahner?	Ch. 18
		Liberation theologies?	Ch. 19
		Revisionist and secular theologies	Ch. 20

Secular atheism

Secular theologies are liberal theologies. You are starting with the secular discourse and then reforming theology on the basis of that. Bultmann and Tillich in some parts can be seen to fit in this kind of approach. Sometimes Rahner and liberation theologies do as well. Many figures of the Russian Religious Renaissance and the Sophiologists in particular were framed as following such a trajectory by most orthodox theologians for the better part of the century. The revisionist and secular theologies take this secular approach self-consciously.

Sources and Further Reading

Buckley, Michael. *At the Origins of Modern Atheism*. New Haven, CT: Yale University Press, 1987.

Dorrien, Gary. *Kantian Reason and Hegelian Spirit: The Idealistic Logic of Modern Theology*. Oxford: Wiley-Blackwell, 2012.

Pattison, George. *Kierkegaard and the Theology of the Nineteenth Century: The Paradox and the 'Point of Contact'*. Cambridge: Cambridge University Press, 2012.

Pyper, Hugh. 'Kierkegaard, Søren'. In *The Oxford Companion to Christian Thought*, edited by Adrian Hastings, Alistair Mason, and Hugh Pyper, 368–70. Oxford: Oxford University Press, 2000.

Simpson, Christopher Ben. *The Truth Is the Way: Kierkegaard's Theologia Viatorum*. London: SCM Press, 2010.

Taylor, Charles. *A Secular Age*. Cambridge, MA: Belknap Press of Harvard University Press, 2007.

13

Barth

Chapter Outline

13.1 Theology of the Word of God

Paul Tillich writes that the nineteenth century ended on 1 August 1914, the beginning of the First World War, the Great War. With the outbreak of war in 1914, we see the end of the optimistic mood of the twentieth century. The world that breaks apart, or at least comes into question, with this war is seen to be supported by the reigning theologies of the day—namely Ritschlianism or Classical Liberal Protestant Theology. There is great disillusionment with the previous decades' sources of hope. It is in this tumultuous context that theology sees a radical reorientation.

Karl Barth (1886–1968) comes to be central to Protestant theology from the 1920s to the 1960s. He is easily the most important theologian of the twentieth century—perhaps the most important theologian since Schleiermacher. The influence of his thought towers above twentieth-century theology in something like the way the thought of Kant, Hegel and Schleiermacher influenced theology in the nineteenth century. Like these figures, Barth's work is not always clearly understood and responded to accordingly. Part of this had to do with his principal work, the *Church Dogmatics*. It is a truly massive work (thirty-one volumes in its current English translation—fourteen thick volumes in its older), written over almost thirty years, and even then it was left incomplete. He planned five 'volumes' and got through most of the fourth. Few people climb the Mt. Everest of the *Church Dogmatics* to the summit. Because readers read selectively (and usually from the earlier parts), they only half-understand what he is getting at and usually do not get around to a fuller view of his more mature and developed thought. Nevertheless, even such a piecemeal appropriation has had such an influence to serve as a watershed for a significant part of the twentieth century. Even for those who are going to disagree with him—and he sets himself up for violent disagreement—he often sets the starting point for the discussion. If you were going to do Protestant theology in the twentieth century—at least up until the 1960s—you had to be in dialogue with Karl Barth. He is the looming figure who one cannot responsibly ignore.

Born in Basel, Switzerland, Barth was inspired to study theology by his confirmation classes as a child. He eventually studied under the likes of Adolf von Harnack and Wilhelm Hermann, two of the central figures of Classical Liberal Protestant Theology. While Harnack was the more popular of the two, Hermann is the one who Barth is more impressed with, not just as a thinker, but as a model of the theological vocation. Herrmann emphasized that theology must be done within a framework of faith.

After his years in the university, he became a pastor, serving for ten years (1911–21) in the town of Safenwil, in northern Switzerland, where he was engaged in the task of preaching from week to week. He found himself hard pressed to find what to say week after week to common people in the midst of economic hardship. He ended up getting involved in a form of Socialist activism there. Along the way he abandoned the liberal theology of his education. It was thin soup for the day-to-day difficulties of life. With the outbreak of the First World War, while he was in the midst of his pastorate at Safenwil, Barth's transformation was spurred on. Most of Barth's former teachers—including Harnack and Hermann—supported Kaiser Wilhelm's war declaration. Barth concluded from this that the liberal theology of his day was bankrupt and hopelessly compromised.

Figure 13.1 Barth.

'Karl Barth Briefmarke' by Unknown—*Briefmarke aus eigener Sammlung, selbst gescannt.* Licensed under Public Domain via Wikimedia Commons.

In response to these crises, Barth sought to return to the confession of faith—in a very Protestant manner—by rediscovering the Bible. He wants to re-engage with what he calls the 'strange new world within the Bible'. You can hear echoes of Kierkegaard in reintroducing the strangeness, not of some new version of Christianity, but of classic Christianity—that genuine Christianity in the midst of modernity is a radical option. Barth studied Scripture, especially the letters of Paul. He began an intensive study of the Epistle to the Romans in 1916, and ends up in 1919 publishing a book that is his commentary on Romans, *Der Römerbrief* (*The Epistle to the Romans*). He later completely rewrites it, and republishes it in 1922. The *Römerbrief* served as a manifesto for a new theological movement that broke away from Classical Liberal Theology.

In 1921, Barth was appointed the honorary professor of Reformed Theology at Göttingen. His time teaching here was a period of intense learning for him, of studying classical Christian thinkers like Augustine, but also the classics of Protestant thought—Luther, Calvin and later Reformed writers.

13.1.1 Dialectical Theology

The movement that Barth played a key part in beginning has many names. Probably the name used most at that time is **dialectical theology**. It is also called **theology of crisis**, using the Greek term *krisis*, which has the same kind of overtones and meanings as the English word, but there are others as well (as we will see below). This new movement is also called the **theology of the Word of God**—the *Wort-Gottes-Theologie*. Later it comes to be called **Neo-Orthodoxy**. Followers never use this term themselves, but others argue that they have brought orthodoxy back up to date. It is a new appropriation of orthodoxy.

Early on, there arose a loose alliance of theologians, led by Barth, including figures like Bultmann, Brunner and Gogarten. Paul Tillich sympathized with dialectical theology early on, although he is a bit different, as we will see. The closest to a formal organ of presentation for dialectical theology was the journal *Zwischen den Zeiten* (*Between the Times*), founded in 1922, and lasting until 1933—although the group of dialectical theologians started to part ways towards the end of the 1920s. It did not last a very long time as a unified group as there were very significant differences between the various thinkers involved. Nevertheless, this group attracted a younger generation of students and theologians, much to the consternation of the older generation, as represented by Harnack, for example—a very public figure who very publicly disliked dialectical theology.

To attempt to characterize it more generally, dialectical theology focuses on **revelation** as the starting point for faith, and with that a strong emphasis is placed on Scripture. It also has a definite **historical consciousness**. Aware that theology is being done in the circumstances of this particular time and place, they saw themselves as being at a turning point from one way of doing things towards another, and between those times—hence the title of the journal. Dialectical theology, in Germany especially, often seeks to be **ecumenical** in the sense of including both Lutheran and Calvinist thinkers. The ecumenism is not reaching out to Roman Catholics or the Eastern Orthodox.

Dialectical theology draws variously on **Kierkegaard**. Specifically, it draws from the grounding of theology in **revelation**, and such a grounding places theology in tension with the established order. You should not expect God's revelation to confirm your suspicions and prejudices. It is a **surprising, uncanny and often paradoxical** word from the outside—it is an in-breaking. The group also shared Kierkegaard's emphasis on the **transcendence of God**. God is not humanity writ large. God is other—or, as they would say, 'wholly other'. Dialectical theology focuses on this wholly otherness of God. Dialectical theologians saw German culture as getting way too chummy with God. They thus take up Kierkegaard's talk about the infinite qualitative difference or distinction between God and the world or between God and humanity. They also emphasized the way in which God is present to us in a **hidden** way. God is revealed in Jesus, but indirectly, paradoxically. God's highest revelation of Himself is in the human person of Jesus of Nazareth; people can be offended at this message and reject it. Here and elsewhere God's revealed-ness is always paired with his concealed-ness, his hiddenness.

There is a defining emphasis in dialectical theology on **crisis**. This should be taken in multiple senses. Part of what they mean by 'crisis' is that this theology is being done in the middle of a world war—in the midst of a crisis of European culture. The latter shows itself to be empty on the inside, and things are falling apart. The theologians associated with dialectical theology (and the journal *Zwischen den Zeiten*) saw themselves as living between two times—one age that is dying and a new age that is coming. The crisis had an eschatological tone. In the midst of this state, they are prophetic—seeing the Word of God as pronouncing judgement (in Greek: *krisis*) upon the world and upon European culture. It is this 'critical' element of crisis that fuels the dialectical theologians' constructive energies. Barth's crisis of not being able to find something to constructively preach about every Sunday drives him to the critical Word of God to find a new way of living in the world.

In dialectical theology, there is generally a negative view towards **Schleiermacher**, the father of Classical Liberal Theology. Specifically, dialectical theologians are critical of Schleiermacher inasmuch as he presents natural humanity as having a strong point of contact with God. In the feeling of absolute dependence, everyone has an inherent connection to God in their natural human consciousness. Dialectical theologians see no room in this schema for sin or for grace. They view Schleiermacher as departing from the historic Christian faith. Schleiermacher's theology does not take into account the radical degree to which humans have fallen. So they are against placing humanity and human religiosity at the centre of theology. They view this as the principal error of nineteenth-century theology. Barth himself has a more nuanced perspective on Schleiermacher.

To return to Barth: He taught at Göttingen as the honorary professor of Reformed Theology there in the early 1920s. From 1925 to 1930, he taught New Testament and Dogmatics at Münster. Part of why dialectical theologians began to fray as a group was that Barth was developing quite a bit as a theologian from his time at Göttingen and his time in Münster. Between the publication of the second edition of the *Der Römerbrief*, in 1922, to the publication of the first part volume of his *Church Dogmatics*, in 1932, he went in a different direction to others in the group. He taught at Münster until 1930, and then at Bonn from 1930 to 1935, when he was dismissed because of the rise of the National Socialist Party (Nazis). In the early 1930s, as the Nazis were in the process of taking over in Germany, Barth was vocal in his criticism of them. The university let him go, and he returned to Basel, Switzerland, where he remained for the rest of his life. However, before he left Bonn, he became a leader in what is called the **Confessing Church** (*Bekennende Kirche*) in Germany. This was made up of a group of Christians who protested against the support that the 'German Christians' (*Deutsche Christen*) had for Nazism and Hitler. The official Protestant churches in Germany—at the very least out of fear—approved of Hitler's seizing of power in 1933. The Confessing Church objected to the German Evangelical churches being hijacked by the Nazi party. The Confessing Church was never more than a significant minority in Germany, but Barth played a major role in it. This was happening while he was writing the early parts of the *Church Dogmatics*, and one can sense a defiant tonality reflected there. On 31 May 1934, Barth was key in writing the **Barmen Declaration**, a public declaration of the Confessing Church against the Nazi party, and protesting against the German Evangelical Church's complicity with the Nazis.

Barth taught in Basel from 1935 until his retirement in 1962. After his retirement, he largely laid the *Church Dogmatics* aside unfinished. He originally planned to write five volumes, and actually only wrote four, without quite finishing the fourth. Interestingly, at Basel (while he is writing most of the *Church Dogmatics*), he developed a long-term, close friendship with one of the other great theologians of the twentieth century, Hans Urs von Balthasar. Barth is Protestant; his confessional trajectory, his return to the confession of the Christian Church is a return to the Reformation. In the early volumes of the *Church Dogmatics*, he positions his thought as against both Liberal Protestantism, on the one hand, and Roman Catholicism, on the other. And yet, he befriends Balthasar, who—in the estimation of many—is the greatest Catholic theologian of the century. D. Stephen Long gives a delightful account of this fascinating friendship in his book, *Saving Karl Barth* (2014).

13.1.2 Reading Barth

If one is used to reading really systematic and structured writing—like much German theology and philosophy—Barth can be kind of a headache. He does not use linear styles of argument. John Webster, one of the eminent Barth scholars, refers to Barth's way of writing as musical—using theme and exposition or theme and variation. He introduces something, he introduces another thing, then he returns to the first, and varies, and extends it. His style is not dense: he takes his sweet time to get around to what he is saying. Reading Barth requires patience. Even his shorter major work, *The Epistle to the Romans* (the *Römerbrief*), is some 570 pages of small print in the popular English translation. If you wish to read Barth, and yet are impatient for an author to get to the point, there is a lot of annoyance in store for you. Barth's argument is ultimately cumulative. One has to take the argument as a whole. If he could give his point in a sentence, he probably would have—but obviously he did not feel like he could, seeing as how he used some 8,000 pages in the *Church Dogmatics* to get out what he had to say.

Another aspect of his style (especially early on) that is exhilarating for some and totally off-putting for others is his assertiveness. Tillich describes Barth's style as a 'demonic absolutism'. Barth will tell you the way things are, and does not pull punches—especially in the *Römerbrief*. The *Römerbrief* is a manifesto, a sledgehammer to the forehead. He is not out to make friends. He is critical of vast swathes of modern thought and culture. He is not taking modern thought for granted—he is criticizing and saying that it is fundamentally off-base from the standpoint of the Word of God. He is representing a voice from on high, and it sounds like he is representing a voice from on high. There is an authority to his presentation, which can be a very powerful experience. It can also sound like 570 pages of someone constantly yelling at you … which can be a bit exhausting.

The reason that Barth is so strident is that he sees theology as being marginalized and corrupted. This is a serious situation. Theology has been marginalized, and it has given up its authoritative voice. It has compromised itself and become corrupted. It has become an echo of cultural fashions, a puppet for the *Zeitgeist*. (One can hear definite echoes of Kierkegaard's attack on Christendom here.) This urgency comes to be moderated over time such that there is a definite difference of tone between the *Römerbrief* and the *Church Dogmatics*.

13.1.3 Barth and Schleiermacher

Barth's relationship with Schleiermacher is more complicated than the kind of caricatures that were sometimes bandied about among the dialectical theologians. Schleiermacher is, in many ways, Barth's dialogue partner throughout his work. He regards Schleiermacher as 'The Modern Protestant Theologian', such that one simply cannot responsibly do theology without being in dialogue with Schleiermacher. One cannot argue against a position without knowing the best representative of that position, and the best representative of the dominant tradition of nineteenth-century theology for Barth is Schleiermacher. Barth thinks that no later figure in this tradition really improved on Schleiermacher; he is the real genius of modern theology, as fundamentally misguided as it may be. Barth then has an enormous degree of respect for Schleiermacher, and does not like it when the other dialectical theologians dismiss him. This is a person that you need to deeply respect, even if you are going to disagree with him—which Barth certainly does.

Beyond this respect, there are real commonalities between Schleiermacher's and Barth's thought. Both of them thought that one must begin from the standpoint of a living faith. Theology is not an abstract exercise; it is not objective in the sense of having nothing to do with one's subjective existence and engagement in life. It is necessary that theology be done in the context of the believing life of the Church. That is as clear as day in Schleiermacher's *Glaubenslehre,* and this is why Barth calls his dogmatics the *Church Dogmatics.* Theology for both men arises from the reflection, activity and devotion of the Church. For both, theology is done in the midst and in the service of the community of the historical and living body of the Church.

Barth also shares with Schleiermacher a deeply Christocentric focus. Jesus Christ is the organizing centre of both their theologies—although Barth is critical of Schleiermacher for not letting Christ be central enough. Barth, when he is reading Schleiermacher on Christ, is concerned that Christ might disappear into a more general human religiousness. Christ might at the end of the day be just an elevated way of talking about humanity and certain human emotions and feelings. Nevertheless, Barth always treats Schleiermacher as someone to be taken seriously and treated humbly.

13.2 *Der Römerbrief*

As mentioned previously, Barth began studying the book of Romans intensively in 1916. In 1919, he publishes *Der Römerbrief,* but then—between late 1920 and mid-1921—he completely rewrites it. This is not a light rewriting. He produces what is ultimately a different book, and publishes it in 1922. It is this second edition of 1922 that proves to be tremendously influential.

13.2.1 A Manifesto

Barth's *Der Römerbrief* is a close reading and a commentary on Paul's Epistle to the Romans. However, it is presented as an urgent and pressing matter for hearers in the present age. It is laid out like a commentary, but it is not your normal commentary. What Barth is about is for the reader to have an encounter with the strange and authoritative world within the text of Scripture. It could be seen better perhaps as an extended paraphrase of Romans. Barth is re-presenting the message of Romans to the twentieth century. This is not merely a scholarly enterprise for him. What we have within Romans is revelation, God speaking through the text. Revelation is taking place, and this partially accounts for the strangeness of the text. It is not just another human reflection on the human situation. It is a human document—and for Barth that means a potentially fallible document. The Word of God is speaking to us in the word of man. Here again is the dialectic between revealing and concealing. There is always a concealing or 'hiddenness' involved in revelation because revelation always comes to us through human words.

And so Barth wants to read the text of Romans as one who has to preach it and proclaim the Word of God. There is a sense of urgency and an authoritative and prophetic gravity to the style. It is a passionate work to say the very least. Hanging over the *Der Römerbrief* is an eschatology such that in revelation there is a sense in which our world is coming to an end. The Word of God is a word of judgement upon us—upon our whole world and our whole way of doing things. It is the end of the world. It is the laying of judgement upon humanity—that is what the Word of God is.

13.2.2 Against Liberalism

Part of the manifesto-nature of *Der Römerbrief* is its opposition to liberalism—to what Barth would refer to as the 'generation of 1914'. With this phrase he is indicting his theological teachers who supported Kaiser Wilhelm II's war plans. As mentioned previously, Classical Liberal Theology—Ritschlianism—dominated the theological scene in Germany through the latter part of the nineteenth century up until the First World War. It was the Barthians and other dialectical theologians who began to refer to Liberalism as culture-Protestantism—as a theology that exists to support the established order.

Barth was intensely critical of Liberalism, to say the least. He believes that in this Liberalism, our relation to God is something that is given in humanity and human culture. In humanity and human culture, God is immanently present to us without revelation or grace. He argues that when they are talking about God they are ultimately not talking about God at all. It is just an exalted way of talking about the creature. God has been forgotten in Christian theology.

What Barth is doing in the *Römerbrief* is publicly and dramatically ridding himself of his prior theological education—but perhaps not as much as he thinks he is. If you read Herrmann— which can be a challenge because it is hard to find Herrmann in print anymore—there are many similarities with Barth. Barth may have been overplaying his parting company. (One imagines him upending a table and knocking over a coat rack while storming out of the party, but then hanging around in the yard in front of the house.) There is no small amount of rhetorical hyperbole and flourish in Karl Barth.

Barth is not just critical. He is not just about dismantling the theology that came before him. He is also constructive in the *Römerbrief*. What we are hearing is the Word of God. God has something to say to us, and from the Word of God—and our faith in revelation—we then can build from the ground up.

13.2.3 Dialectic

The theology presented in *Der Römerbrief* is called 'dialectical'. Coming out of the nineteenth century, one can certainly be excused for thinking of Hegel or at least things Hegel-like with this term. To hazard a perhaps-overly-involved explanation: the way Barth uses the word 'dialectical' here matches up most with the way Kierkegaard uses it. In Hegel's understanding of things (see 7.1.2), you have the three stages: the thesis, antithesis, and the synthesis or the immediate, the dialectical and the speculative. The first moment is one of immediate simple unity. The second moment, 'antithesis', is what Hegel calls the dialectical. This is where you have positions that stand in opposition to each other. Then the third moment is the speculative and is where that which is in opposition is brought back into complex unity. Kierkegaard critiques Hegel by saying he is insufficiently dialectical. He does not pay attention to that second moment enough, he just passes by real difference. He obscures it. This is one of Kierkegaard's biggest philosophical critiques of Hegel. This is the (Hegelian by way of Kierkegaard) sense of 'dialectical' that is intended in Barth and the dialectical theologians: a sense of difference, of contrast and of tension. 'Dialectical' is meant in the context of divine transcendence. When we encounter the Word of God, we are encountering something that is other, different and transcendent. It is not just a regurgitation and re-presentation of the human spirit. We are not meeting ourselves in our projected other but something that is truly different and stands in opposition to us. The infinite qualitative difference between God and humanity prevents the possibility of removing the contrast and tension and reducing Christianity to a placid, systematic unity. In *Der Römerbrief* then, if God's relation to the world is presented, it is in terms of negation. God is not the world or in the world but rather the boundary of the world. God is the other of the world. In this Barth is drawing quite a bit on Kierkegaard. He writes, 'If I have a system, it is limited to a recognition to what Kierkegaard called the infinite qualitative distinction between time and eternity.' That is the core insight: there is a difference between God, the world and us.

While Barth is writing the second edition of *Der Römerbrief*, he is reading Kierkegaard devotionally. He is largely dependent upon the latter Kierkegaard—specifically *Practicing Christianity*, and also *The Moment* writings. He is not reading the playful ironic Kierkegaard, but the Kierkegaard as a passionate preacher of not-watered-down Christianity. It is around the time of the First World War that there is an explosion of interest in Kierkegaard. This revived interest comes along with this new dialectical theology, so he becomes associated with that. He is also associated with existentialist philosophy, as we shall see in the next chapter (Chapter 14). Barth draws on Nietzsche as well, presenting several large block quotes of his in *Der Römerbrief*. He believes that Nietzsche was getting at something, stating how things are fundamentally empty, and coming to an end.

When human beings encounter God in the work and Word of God, the encounter is always two-sided. Because we are part of the world that is in opposition to God, God's Word is always a Word of judgement, a negative towards us. But, interestingly, grace is not distinct from judgement for Barth. They always come together as two sides of the same coin. Grace always entails judgement. It is a confrontation and condemnation of our world. Grace does not remove the judgement. God's Word to us is a word of both grace and judgement. The cross is a judgement upon our world and the work of its redemption. That is one of the strong insights that you get from *Der Römerbrief*—that coincidence of judgement and grace.

This dialectical tension is the reality of God over and against the reality of the world. In God's reconciliatory work through Christ upon the cross, it is not as if God and the world are now on good terms. If we are passing from the world to God, we must go fully under judgement. We are negated in some sense. We die to the world and to our selves.

13.2.4 Krisis

This dialectical aspect of his theology goes hand in hand with Barth's theology being one of **crisis**. Crisis (from the Greek *Krisis*) here, as mentioned, carries with it the sense of judgement, of judgement upon the world. The theology of crisis is as mentioned previously where one sees the coincidence of grace and judgement. The gospel, the good news is a *krisis*, and this judgement is an instrument of our deliverance.

The crisis in *Der Römerbrief* is always paradoxical. God's judgement coincides with God's mercy. God's mercy is evident in judgement; it is because of mercy that God communicates his judgement to us and relativizes our world. He comes to us and opens another way to us, but another way that entails our dying. We only have life through death, and life under the judgement of God is the life of grace. Here, Barth is deeply Reformed. God's relation to us is not founded on our achievements. There is nothing in us as humans or in the world that provides for God's relation to us. God's relation to us is a purely gratuitous gift, and that is why it looks so strange. It is as if there is no point of contact between our life and the life of God that is coming to us seemingly through a wall of death.

Grace—as Barth will say—is asymmetrical. It is an event and an encounter of something that happens to us, and so in a theology of crisis our relationship to God is a negative one. God provides us with something that we do not have. The equation is never equalled and we are never brought up and made equal to God. We are brought over to God's side. We are moving into a life under the judgement of God. God's negative relation to the world is always going to be such that God is 'not the world' and 'not us'. The Gospel is a truth that challenges our other truths; it is not going to appeal to other human truths for its validity. It is going to put them all under judgement, and our encounter with the Word of the God will re-orientate our whole way of looking at things. In the encounter of revelation, God is active and we are passive. We are transformed in this paradoxical gift of grace.

13.3 *Church Dogmatics* I. The Doctrine of the Word of God

The *Church Dogmatics* is a massive work of theology. It is usually organized into thirteen 'part-volumes', commonly designated by Roman numerals (the volume), followed by an Arabic numeral (the part of the volume). For instance, the second 'part' of the first 'volume' is designated I.2 or I/2 or I, 2. (The older English edition has one large physical book for each part-volume, while the newer edition divides each of the part-volumes into more manageable physical books.) The *Church Dogmatics* comprises around six million words, which in the latest edition is around 8,600 pages.

It used to be the vogue to make a stark division between the early Barth and the later Barth—the Barth of *Römerbrief* and the Barth of *Dogmatics*. For this view, there is a significant turn in Barth from the crisis or dialectical mode to a different, analogical mode. However, the more recent consensus is that of continuity and development. Barth does not have a 'turn' or a profound change of mind. There is rather continuity between his works, though there is definite development or maturing. There is indeed significant development within the *Church Dogmatics*. It does not have a static perspective throughout. The first volume is written in the midst of the rise of the Nazi party in Germany, and it reflects that. In later volumes, there is a greater degree of moderation and complexity. The later work moderates the pitch of some of the earlier rhetoric, and perhaps amplifies some of the things that were implicit in the earlier works. The volumes get progressively longer.

The central theme of the *Church Dogmatics* is God's relation to us in Jesus. God is not the object of the human search, but we are the object of God's grace. God establishes a relationship with us in Christ. This is consciously in opposition to the theologies of the nineteenth century. The nineteenth century for Barth largely focused on religious experience (Schleiermacher) or moral experience (Kant). However, theology is not merely about morality or experience but is rather about God's relationship to us in Jesus Christ. Interestingly, Barth comes to be critical of Kierkegaard because he will see Kierkegaard as providing too much of a point of contact between humanity and God— that even in the negative moments of humanity (in our despair) as pointing to our need for God was too much for Barth.

A work worth mentioning is one that Barth writes in 1931, entitled *Anselm: Fides Quarens Intellectum*. This small work on Anselm is published right before he begins to publish the *Church Dogmatics*. Many have taken this little book as representing something of the mode of the coming *Church Dogmatics*, and it certainly has a different tonality than *Der Römerbrief*. The latter is a strident manifesto, while the Anselm book is not confrontational, but rather a reflection within the faith. So with this we see a transition to a different mode, a more meditative and patient mode of exposition. With this book on Anselm, we do not have the crisis that we would see in *Der Römerbrief*, but rather a faith seeking understanding—the translation of the title. This is not about coming to faith, but rather trying to understand and patiently think through, in and after faith. We are trying to understand what it is that we believe, beginning with that belief. This is a mode written from within the Church and also written for the edification of the Church. This is not a confrontation with German culture at large, but is written to the people of God from the people of God. This is not apologetic, even in perhaps the odd sense that *Der Römerbrief* was. It is not about the possibility of Christian belief, but it is starting within it.

Here we have an emphasis on some key ideas that will stay with us in the *Church Dogmatics*: Barth's '**actualism**' and '**particularism**'. Barth is focusing in the *Church Dogmatics* on events, on things that are contingent and not on eternal truths—on states of affairs that have come about. Specifically, what he is talking about is what God has actually done for us in Christ. This is not about possibility or potentiality, but a reality—a particular, historical reality that has a particular character to it. He is not talking about the actuality of the structure of human existence, but about a particular event that has happened. In many ways, the *Church Dogmatics* is a vast exposition of the Christ-event. Barth emphasizes God's sovereign act, that God has done something particular in Christ.

For Barth, this is theology done in an otherwise-than-modern mode. It is not starting from some other discourse or philosophical understanding of the nature of human existence and then going on to thinking about what God has to be like. He is not seeking to secure the foundation for theology from outside of theology. He refers to this as a **dogmatics** which has to do with theology's work as within the Church. Dogmatics operates relative to the proclamation of the Church; it is about the Church's self-examination. It is the way that—with God's revelation as the norm—the Church evaluates itself. Dogmatics is a discursive repetition of what faith affirms about God. It is repeating revelation, but it is trying to bring the Church into line with that revelation—to hear it in the midst of the Church.

The *Church Dogmatics* has four major divisions or volumes: I, II, III and IV. Barth intended to write five, but he stopped in the midst of the fourth. The first volume is a two-part volume on the Word of God. The second volume is a two-part volume on God. The third volume is a four-part volume on Creation, and the fourth volume is a five-part volume on Reconciliation. The fifth part was to be on Redemption, with an emphasis on pneumatology and eschatology. (As a way of trying to keep all of this massive work together as a big structure, the back of every volume of the new edition of the *Church Dogmatics* has an outline of the entire work.)

Volume I is entitled *The Doctrine of the Word of God* and there are two parts to it. The first part was published in 1932 and the second part was published in 1937. Below, we focus on the material from I.1.

13.3.1 Dogmatic Prolegomena

This first volume is described as dogmatic prolegomena. Like other systematic theologies, you begin with thinking about how to proceed. A systematic theology begins by talking about a method, and this discussion is normally called prolegomena. Barth's are 'dogmatic prolegomena'. It is significant that the first volume of the *Church Dogmatics* begins with the Word of God. This is the starting place. Commonly prolegomena have to do with the various norms and sources that you use in presenting your theology, and Barth presents the centrality of revelation—in particular the self-revelation of the Triune God. The key here is God's self-communication. This is the heart of the first volume, and this beginning is a miraculous and revolutionary beginning. It begins with God's initiative and is rooted in faith.

Dogmatic prolegomena are not the same as apologetic prolegomena. Barth is not wanting to establish the Christian truth-claims by some other more widely accepted criteria. He is not wanting to argue the non-Christian into Christianity by using the non-Christian's terms, or by assuming that there is some point of contact between Christian revelation and other human discourse. He would say that the only point of contact is revelation, and this revelation is the starting point for theological reflection.

13.3.2 The Word of God

The centre of Volume I is the Word of God. What is the Word of God for Barth? The Word of God is an act, an event and an encounter. It is something that is done—specifically, something that God does. It is God's activity. It is also something that happens, that comes about. It is not like a natural theology. The act that we are talking about is not something that we can think about in a

Deistic sense. Rather, it is an event that is happening. It is not just happening 2,000 years ago, but is happening in the present—and in that sense, it is an encounter. We are encountering God. God is revealing himself to us. So the event is an active self-revelation from God to us.

Barth will say that the Word of God is ultimately one event that has three different forms expanding out as concentric circles (see diagram). The centre that the other forms share is the act of revelation itself. This is the pure, divine speech-act: God's act towards us. One of the keys is that this is an act. Implied is that God is acting freely. Barth will emphasize the freedom of God. This is not something that was required of God by creation or humanity, and so it is ultimately going to be mysterious. It is irreducible to any particular master-able form. This is a sovereign, free act of God. Ultimately, that act of self-revelation is **Jesus Christ**. Jesus Christ is God's revelation. Jesus is the Word that is God revealing Himself to us. Jesus is God's self-revelation. That is the centre. That is—in the purest sense—what revelation and the Word of God is: God's sovereign act of self-revelation in Jesus Christ.

The second form of revelation is Scripture, and the way Barth talks about it is **Scripture's witness or attestation to revelation**. Barth describes the witness of Scripture as both prophetic and apostolic: prophetic in the Old Testament and apostolic in the New Testament. This is the act of revelation *as witnessed and attested to in human speech*. It is God's Word written. So the written Word of God—Scripture as a witness—is a field of divine activity. It is an attestation to revelation. The one act of revelation is operative through it. Barth is not wanting to make a strict distinction such that Scripture is just a secondary account of the Word of God, as something otherwise than the Word of God. It is a form of the event of revelation, but it is not identical with the act of revelation itself. It is a collection of human texts that is also the bearer of revelation. That is why he talks about it in terms of attestation or witness. A witness sets that to which he witnesses before us. When you witness, you tell what you saw; you bring that which is not present and make it present. The witness carries past revelation into the present and the future. Barth will talk about Scripture as something like a site where the event of revelation occurs.

The third form of the Word of God is **the preaching, proclamation or testimony of the Church**, which is also—like the second form—human speech but is of a different order than Scripture. This is actualizing the event of the Word in the present. Somehow the event of revelation witnessed to in Scripture is proclaimed in the Church. It is heard through the act of proclamation in the Church. Jesus is the one Word of God and the sovereign act of God's self-revelation. This is witnessed to in Scripture such that it can be present to us. Then God's Word is made present to us through the proclamation of the Church. This is not just humans saying things about God. Barth's way of trying to talk about this is by distinguishing the human acts and the divine act while not cutting them off from each other. This is not a liberal identification of the kernel of divine revelation and the human husk. We only have access to the Word of God through Scripture and the proclamation of the Church; in looking at concentric circles, we only approach the centre through the periphery. Barth writes that the work of dogmatics is the self-criticism of the proclamation of the Church—trying to listen to Scripture and to help what we say and do in relation to God to be in accord with what God says and does in Jesus Christ. So Barth would say that we encounter the event of the Word of God in Scripture and the proclamation of the Church. The first is only approachable through the second and the third.

Some more conservative Christians (see Chapter 16) have taken Barth in different ways. Some might think that he has a low view of Scripture because he does not simply identify revelation or the Word of God with Scripture. Scripture is a witness to revelation and revelation is present in the witness of Scripture—but there is not a simple, one-to-one correspondence. Another way of looking at Barth is to say that he has a very high view of preaching. Preaching is in a continuum such that we do not just hear the Word of God in Scripture, but also hear the Word of God proclaimed. There is a miracle that happens in preaching for Barth. In the activity of the Church, the Word of God is bringing about an encounter with God. There is an actual encounter with God that is going on in proclamation in the Church. However, our encounter with revelation is always by way of human words. It is always going to be indirect, so you can see the dialectical part there. We will never get away from the human aspect. It is always going to have the human mediation of the Word of God, but that does not cancel out the Word of God. This is the way the Word of God comes to us.

13.3.3 The Self-Revelation of the Triune God

Interestingly, in the first part of Volume I, Barth goes very quickly from the Word of God to the doctrine of the Trinity. He thinks that in order to properly talk about the Word of God we have to talk about the Triune God. The fact that Barth—so early on in his *Church Dogmatics*—brings in the doctrine of the Trinity is going to be very significant for twentieth-century theology. The doctrine of the Trinity is going to have a huge revival in the twentieth century. You would not have thought this was going to happen if you are looking at nineteenth-century theology. With Schleiermacher, the Trinity is a postscript to his *Glaubenslehre*. The Trinity has very little place in the Ritschlians. Protestant theologians at least seem to be embarrassed by it. Barth puts it right at the centre of everything, and it ends up being a central preoccupation for much of twentieth-century theology.

Barth talks about the Trinity within his discussion of the doctrine of the Word of God. The God that is revealed in the Word is a Triune God. Barth reflects on the Trinity from the standpoint of revelation—or alternatively meditates on revelation from the standpoint of the Trinity. He would say that in the act and event of revelation that is the Word of God, God is at once the revealer, what is revealed, and identical with the effect of revelation. To put this briefly, revelation is a gift of the presence of the Triune God; it is not just information. God is not just revealing information about himself, but is revealing himself to us. God is present in his Word. And for this to be the case, not only is God the origin but he is also the act of revelation—this is the Son—and the reception of that revelation with the Spirit.

Barth will write about Christ as what he calls the objective aspect/reality of revelation. In the incarnation, the Word becomes human, and the specific, objective, actual act of God's revelation is in the person of Jesus Christ. This is what God has actually done: God has actually become incarnate and fully human in Christ. That is the objective reality or the objective aspect of revelation.

The Holy Spirit is the subjective aspect/reality of revelation. God—in the Holy Spirit—is active in our reception of work of revelation. We are made free, enlightened and illumined in what the

Holy Spirit does in us in the act of revelation. It is in the Holy Spirit—as the active reality of revelation in us—that the Church comes into being. It is not that the Church somehow pre-exists the Spirit, but there is always already the enlivening activity and presence of God as the Spirit in our relation to God.

Barth makes some significant steps towards talking about the unity and distinction within the Trinity. God is the **one** subject of revelation. God is the revealer, the revealed and the reveal-ee—united to and enabling the one receiving revelation. God is present through the whole thing; otherwise, it would not be a self-revelation. Rather than it being God revealed, it would be something about God being revealed. God has to be present through the whole thing for it to be the real Word of God, the revelation of God, the gift of the presence of God. The unity Barth talks about—being the subject of God—is the same God. For the **distinction** he talks about, he does not use the term 'persons' as much. When he uses it he often puts it in scare quotes. He thinks that for modern people talk of three persons sounds a bit too much as Tritheism. But in the act of revelation the main point is that there is one subject. This is not like the way we normally get communicated to. In revelation the Speaker is in the Word and in us when He communicates. God communicates Himself, not just information. If we think that there are three different 'persons', we might miss the notion that the revealer is present in his revelation and so within us. Barth will use the term 'modes of being' when it comes to what Christians traditionally call the Divine Persons. Any time you change the classical designations there is going to be controversy, but Barth is trying to find good ways of communicating.

This is all from I.1. Before Barth wrote I.2 he published a small work entitled *Nein! Antwort an Emil Brunner* [*No! An Answer to Emil Brunner*] (1934). Emil Brunner is another dialectical theologian. Brunner possesses a more positive view of the possibility of natural theology, and this is Barth's probably overly harsh response. It is written in the midst of the Nazis' rise to power. He sees theology's complicity in the human powers as being echoed in making theology to be dependent upon natural human reason. For theology to have its prophetic function, the sinful human world cannot have any prior say.

13.4 *Church Dogmatics* II. The Doctrine of God

13.4.1 The Reality of God

Volume II has two parts. II.1 is published in 1939, and II.2 in 1942. The first part is entitled 'The Reality of God'. This is written in Nazi Germany, and the emphasis here is on the doctrine of God—primarily how God is God-for-us. He is not getting that far away from revelation here. If you are going to talk about God, you have to talk about God in his relation to us—in his gracious self-determination.

Barth would argue that God's reality is something that we cannot demonstrate on our own or from nature. The reality of God is only actually known through his self-revelation and presentation. We only know God from God. You cannot start with anything but God and get to God. Only God is the basis of God's own presentation. There is an emphasis here on God's freedom. God's free act of revelation is a gift and a self-bestowal. Scripture is the Word of God because God is present in it. If God is not present, God is not revealed. Revelation is not revelation of helpful tips about relating to God, but is the revelation of God Himself in a way that is otherwise than we are ever revealed to each other.

The reality of God is central to Christian dogmatics. You do not start with a general ontology or with general metaphysics. You do not start with being as such, but you start with God in his reality—and that is as an act directed towards us. The reality of God is not some neutral category of being—the reality of God is always God as in his act of love towards us as a free giving of himself. When Barth is talking about the reality of God, he is not talking about bare metaphysics or ontology but about how the reality of God for us is inseparable from God's act of love. God's loving self-giving can never be separated from the reality of God for us.

Barth talks about what he calls 'the objectivity of God'. One does not start with the possibility of God. One begins with the reality of God, how God has shown up in revelation and is objectively present in it—as opposed to the subjectivity of some God-experience. He distinguishes between what he calls the primary objectivity and the secondary objectivity of God. The primary objectivity of God is that God is immediate to himself. That is God's simple reality that is fully evident only to God. What we have access to is God's secondary objectivity. This is God's mediated objectivity to us. The point, however, is that, ultimately, it is the same objectivity. In the secondary objectivity, we are participating in God's self-knowledge to a limited degree. Thus, secondary objectivity *is* only in relation to the primary objectivity. Our knowledge of God is in participation with God's knowledge of himself. Again, this is not knowledge of certain information, but knowledge of God. Our knowledge of God is always secondary, 'clothed' as Barth writes. It is in relation to this primary objectivity but is not the same. It is mediated; there is always a hiddenness. This is not some kind of justification for our knowledge, but talks about how the knowledge of God at all is possible.

For Barth, Christ is fundamental to our knowledge of God. If we want to know God, we do not know him from anthropology or any other locus of natural theology—we know him in Christ. In 1956, Barth gives a lecture titled 'The Humanity of God', in which he focuses on the fact that we cannot understand God apart from Jesus. Ultimately, God only speaks to us in the humanity of Christ and through the mediation of his humanity. We have no un-mediated, no non-human relation to God, but God is truly present to us in Christ's humanity—and so, in a sense, in our own humanity. Some scholars see such talk about the humanity of God as being in tension with the sense of crisis in the earlier dialectical theology.

13.4.2 Election

Published in 1942, II.2 is about Barth's doctrine of election. This sounds very Reformed indeed. Election has to do with God's freely given covenant, and it is connected with this talk about the reality of God. God is always for us. In his doctrine of election, Barth is not thinking about some kind of abstract concept of an omnipotent will. God's freedom here is not a pure voluntarism. It is not a naked freedom or God's naked sovereignty, but is always centred in the particularity of Jesus as the divine act of love. God's election is God's act of freedom in God's act of revelation and love in Jesus. We only know the freedom of God in the name of Jesus.

In the two natures of Jesus, Barth redefines the doctrine of election in a way that more traditional Calvinists would not find terribly recognizable. The doctrine of election focuses on the incarnation, and in the incarnation you have a dual-election—God's self-election and the election of humanity. God is choosing himself and putting himself forward, while also choosing humanity in this act of self-revelation. First is the divine self-election. The reality of God is that God elects to be gracious to us in Christ; this is God's sovereign election, God's choice. Second, God's election is the election of humanity. In Christ, God chooses—elects—humanity. And this is different than the previous Reformed doctrine of election, which does not necessarily have anything to do with Jesus—election is just that God chooses to save some for his inscrutable reasons. But the election of humanity happens in Jesus. Humanity is elect in Christ's sharing in our humanity. In Christ, humanity is elected—chosen. So God is the actor in electing to become incarnate and electing us into this relationship, in choosing humanity to participate in God's glory. Christ is both the electing God and the elected humanity. Again, it is not that He is a middle-point between God and humanity. He is the relationship and presence of God with humanity—which is a radically different understanding of election.

13.5 *Church Dogmatics* III. The Doctrine of Creation

13.5.1 The Work of Creation

Volume III of the *Church Dogmatics* is on the doctrine of creation. The first part is published in 1945, the second in 1948, the third in 1950 and the fourth part in 1951. III.1 is entitled 'The Work of Creation'. Recall that Barth is not a fan of natural theology. Part of Barth's distinctive take on creation is that it is something that cannot be known from that which is created alone; it has to be revealed. For Barth one cannot get from creation to God, even to God's work of creation. There is no neat paired division of labour for Barth between natural theology (regarding God's work in creation) and revealed theology (regarding God's work in redemption). In fact, for him to talk about creation is to talk about Christ. Creation is known through revelation, and ultimately through Christ.

Not only is the knowledge of the Creator a matter of faith, Barth thinks that the knowledge of the creature is ultimately a matter of faith as well. The reality of creatures is derived from knowledge of God's revelation, and our knowledge of God as the Creator comes ultimately from our knowledge of Jesus Christ. Creation only has meaning from Jesus Christ.

Creation itself is teleological, and that *telos* (end or purpose) can only be understood relative to God's purpose as revealed in Christ. Everything has its beginning, centre and end in Christ. This is a radical Christocentrism. Ultimately, the point of creation is that it has a destiny for fellowship with God in Christ. Barth describes this in relation to **covenant** and **creation**. Creation is 'the external basis of covenant' in that covenant is the purpose or meaning of creation—it is the *telos* of creation. Conversely, covenant is 'the internal basis of creation'. Covenant—relation to God in Christ—is the fulfilment of creation's essential nature.

What Barth is giving us in his doctrine of creation is not a bare cosmology or a natural theology, but is an understanding of the universe that is fundamentally tied up with its fulfilment in Christ. People could read the earlier Barth and say that what he is saying sounds Gnostic—that God breaks into the world and destroys it with judgement/grace. But here in the *Church Dogmatics* the centre of the order of the world is grace.

13.5.2 The Creature

The second part, III.2, is on 'the creature' by which Barth means humanity. Here again, he emphasizes the priority of Christology. We do not know what humans are and then come to know what the humanity of Christ means, but we come to know what humanity is on the basis of Christ. Christ is ontologically and epistemologically prior to our humanity. We know what humanity is through Christ, because Christ is the true human. This is a theological anthropology 'from above'.

Again, the doctrine of creation is based on the doctrine of revelation; and Jesus is at the centre. Jesus defines humanity such that to be human is to be with God. The human is revealed in the person of Christ. The human is derived from God and yet with God, and this is with the doctrine of election. To be properly human is to be elect. That is the fulfilment of humanity.

Barth wants to understand humanity at the heart of creation from the standpoint of redemption and of Christ. Human nature—not just creation itself, which is teleologically ordered towards the covenant—is teleologically ordered towards God. In all of creation, the human has a central place—because in the human, creation is in communion with God.

Here Barth begins—finally—to talk about sin. He talks about sin as the 'impossible possibility'. In sin we go against our very nature. This is very much like Kierkegaard's 'untruth'. We are being untrue not to God but to our very selves and what we are as human beings. We are betraying our inner-most reality—which is to be in relation to God.

In this context, Barth comes back around to his doctrine of the Word and says to be human is ultimately to be in this relationship and to be addressed by the Word. The Word of God is all about God being in relation to us. Jesus, then, is the sum of God's address to the cosmos, and Jesus is what God has to say to us—himself. He does not have a special message for us, or some interesting things to say; he gives himself to us in order to be in relation to us. Ultimately, all of creation is called into this relation, but it is only in humanity that creation is united to God in Christ. The proper human activity is this dialectic of gratitude and giving forth. Human activity is a response to the call of God.

13.5.3 The Creator and His Creature and the Command of God the Creator

The third part, III.3, is titled 'The Creator and His Creature'. In this, Barth deals with the doctrine of providence. Providence is the unfolding of covenant, of the relation to God, over time. Covenant history is the history of the created being, so in this we see his doctrine of creation as a doctrine of ongoing creation. This is something that is unfolding. As the covenant and creation are tied up with one another, that implies that creation is ongoing.

On the other side of this union between creation and covenant is evil as resistance to God's rule. Here the impossible possibility of sin yields an understanding of sin or evil as privation. Ultimately, it is an orientation towards nothingness and sin is not a privation of a certain created order, but is a privation of grace. Sin is not merely a refusal of a certain created law, but it is a refusal of grace itself. So, you see a fusing between what are often seen as distinct categories of the natural and the supernatural or the created and grace.

Finally, III.4 is on the command of God the Creator. When Barth gets to the end of a given volume of his *Church Dogmatics*, he shifts to an explicit discussion of what would be thought ethics. In this part-volume, he depicts how command and freedom are counterparts to each other. He describes the nature of created freedom as being tied up with responsibility. Our task in life is to respond to the initiative of God's call. To do so is to embody true human freedom—which is freedom before God.

13.6 *Church Dogmatics* IV. The Doctrine of Reconciliation

Volume IV is the last, longest and unfinished volume of the *Church Dogmatics*. The heart of the Gospel for Barth is God reconciling all things to himself in Christ (Col. 1:20). The way he organizes the doctrine of reconciliation is around different portraits of Christ as God incarnate and as the agent of reconciliation.

In this fourth volume Barth talks more at length about sin. He pairs reconciliation with sin, saying that ultimately sin cannot be understood in a natural light but can only be understood in opposition to grace. Sin is only really visible in the light of reconciliation. And so sin is not constitutive of humanity for Barth. He presents his understanding of original sin as a bit different than a traditional Augustinian understanding of sin. Original sin is not hereditary or a kind of fated situation with all of humanity. Sin is not a contagion moving through the human race, but has to do with the voluntary life of every human being. It has to do with the sin of us all.

Barth also addresses covenant in this volume. He presents it here as an ordered mutuality between humanity and God. (This certainly seems to be some distance from the harsher prophetic tone of *Der Römerbrief.*) It is a relationship between humanity and God in Christ, but it is rooted in

God himself, in God's loving nature. Again you see him focusing on God's freedom and sovereignty, but what that means here is that God does not will to be God without us. God wills to be what he is towards us. The covenant is rooted within the reality of God—it is not something that God happens to do. Reconciliation and salvation arise from the immanent being of God. It is not something that is secondary to his reality.

13.6.1 Jesus Christ, the Lord as Servant

The first part, IV.1, is entitled 'Jesus Christ, the Lord as Servant'. Going through the three parts of Volume IV, Barth obviously laid this out ahead of time very systematically. In the first part, he deals with Christ's deity as being tied to his obedience, exile and humiliation. As we saw before, in Christ we have the humanity of God. Christ reveals God not as somehow separate and uninvolved in our humanity, but as deeply involved in it. He reveals our humanity in the things that we would think to be least divine: in Christ's obedience. Christ's humility is the best revelation of Christ's deity.

Barth associates this with Christ's priestly office. He goes through the traditional offices of prophet, priest and king in the different parts of volume IV. In all three parts, Barth makes paradoxical points. In the first part, Christ reveals the majesty of God in his humility. God's sovereignty is made most manifest in its self-emptying. Divinity is not best revealed as a height but as lowly.

In relation to Christ in this office in this way, this exposes particularly in us the sin of pride. Christ's deity as manifest in his humility exposes our disordered pride. In relation to Christ in this manner, the Holy Spirit functions to gather us into a new community around the self-emptying God in Christ. We relate to him here especially in faith. Throughout volume IV there are set forth many interrelated ways that we are being reconciled to God through Christ—through faith, hope and love; through the Spirit's gathering us, building us up and sending us; and through the different offices of Christ.

	Particular office	Work of the Spirit	Particular sin exposed	Theological virtue
IV.1 The Lord as servant	Priestly	Gathering	Pride	Faith
IV.2 The servant as Lord	Kingly	Upbuilding	Sloth	Hope
IV.3 The true witness	Prophetic	Sending	Falsehood	Love

13.6.2 Jesus Christ, the Servant as Lord

Whereas part one deals with how Christ's deity is tied to his obedience or is manifest in his obedience and humiliation, part two presents how Christ—through humanity—is exalted. He manifests his humanity in his exaltation. This is his kingly office, and refers to where in Christ we have the true man. He is the royal man, the king, the head of humanity.

The corresponding sin to this understanding of the reconciling work of Christ is the sin of sloth. This is our not living up to the high calling of humanity as presented by Christ. This is our failure to live up to what we are as human beings. The Holy Spirit here works in conjunction with Christ by upbuilding or quickening us into that true humanity. When we relate to Christ in this way, we are relating in hope towards our becoming truly human.

13.6.3 Jesus Christ, the True Witness

The final part, IV.4, speaks to Christ's prophetic office. Here, Barth is talking about Christ's 'self-declaration'—his communicating of his life to us. Here Christ is depicted as the Light of Life that shines forth and communicates itself. The Mediator shines forth in his glory. In this section, Barth also talks about Christ as victor and as the one who affects the reconciliation of us through communicating his life.

The opposition to be overcome here is the sin of falsehood and condemnation. We are not being true to the truth of Jesus. In this, Barth is speaking about how, in communicating his life, we are called into the life of Jesus. He speaks of vocation quite a bit here. We are called, as Jesus is, the true witness and the one that communicates. He is the Word that communicates God Himself, and we are called heralds of Christ to continue this communication. The corresponding theological virtue is that of love. We are called to call others into Christ's life. We are called to be a part of Christ's self-declaration. We are called to hear, trust, and obey God's call to us in Christ.

Again, here at the end the *Church Dogmatics* (as it stands) Barth ends up coming back to the doctrine of the Word of God as at the beginning. The revelation of God is present in our declaration and proclamation of the Word of God. Here the Spirit functions in sending those who are called.

The last bit of the fourth volume is a fragment on the Christian life—specifically, on Baptism—that is published much later, in 1967, after it becomes apparent that Barth is not going to write anymore of the *Church Dogmatics*. He originally intended to write a fifth volume on the doctrine of redemption, but that did not come about.

Sources and Further Reading

Hall, Douglas John. '"The Great War" and the Theologians'. In *The Twentieth Century: A Theological Overview*, edited by Gregory Baum, 3–13. Maryknoll, NY: Orbis, 1999.

Hardy, Daniel W. 'Karl Barth'. In *The Modern Theologians: Introduction to Christian Theology since 1918*, 3rd edn., edited by David F. Ford with Rachel Muers, 21–42. Oxford: Blackwell, 2005.

Hegstad, Harald. 'Karl Barth'. In *Key Theological Thinkers: From Modern to Postmodern*, edited by Staale Johannes Kristiansen and Svein Rise, 65–76. Aldershot: Ashgate, 2013.

Long, D. Stephen. *Saving Karl Barth: Hans Urs von Balthasar's Preoccupation*. Minneapolis: Fortress, 2014.

Thiselton, Anthony C. 'Biblical Interpretation'. In *The Modern Theologians: Introduction to Christian Theology since 1918*, edited by David F. Ford with Rachel Muers, 287–304, 3rd edn. Oxford: Blackwell, 2005.

Webster, John. *Barth*. London: Continuum, 2000.

Willmer, Haddon. 'Barmen Declaration'. In *The Oxford Companion to Christian Thought*, edited by Adrian Hastings, Alistair Mason and Hugh Pyper, 62–63. Oxford: Oxford University Press, 2000.

14

Bultmann and Tillich

Chapter Outline

14.1 Existentialism

14.1.1 Kierkegaard and Nietzsche

Existentialist philosophy came to the fore in the 1920s and 1930s, in Germany and France, drawing considerably on both Kierkegaard and Nietzsche. It is a form of philosophy that focuses on the concreteness and thickness of individual human existence, not some abstract ideal. It begins (presumably) from description—from observing human being 'in action'—drawing from **phenomenology**. Going beyond phenomenology as such a description of the 'goings on' of consciousness, existentialism is also **prescriptive**, there is a strong ethical side—perhaps an oddly ethical side—to existentialism. Beyond describing the way human existence is, existentialism also sets forth what constitutes an **authentic** existence. One can be a human in the wrong way.

In the more prominent visions of existentialist philosophy, an authentic existence is usually one that operates in the absence of traditional moral and religious values. It operates within the postulatory finitism of Secularity 2. There is not any kind of transcendent source or grounding of value—be that moral or religious. This side is the Nietzschean frame of atheistic existentialism. One of the ways this is present in Existentialism is the denial of the human essence. One of Sartre's classic statements of existentialism is that 'existence precedes essence'; so there is no given *telos* (purpose or end) to humanity that we then either fulfil or do not. The task is for us to bravely face this our groundless nature. We have to own up to the fact that we are the ones who are creating our values.

14.1.2 Heidegger

Of particular interest for the story of modern theology in the twentieth century is the work of **Martin Heidegger (1889–1976)**. Heidegger's best-known and probably most influential work is *Being and Time* (*Sein und Zeit*), published in 1927. (Indeed, Heidegger's *Being and Time* and Wittgenstein's *Philosophical Investigations* are generally seen as the two most important works of philosophy in the twentieth century.)

Heidegger himself takes significant inspiration from the Romantics. He, like the Romantics, was looking for a way of reconnecting the constituents of the Classical Synthesis—seeing how the separation between human consciousness and the world and the divine was something that was to be overcome.

Central to Heidegger, specifically to what he has to say in *Being and Time*, is the question of being—*Sein*. Heidegger says that being is our most fundamental idea or category when it comes to thinking about the world, and yet we have not even gotten to the point of asking the question of what we mean by it. Heidegger wants to reawaken the question of being. He says that we have forgotten or have fallen asleep to this most basic of questions because we have merely taken over certain definitions and understandings of being from Plato and Aristotle. He wants to answer the question of being in a novel way: by way of an **existential phenomenology**. The best way to answer the question of what being is is to look within—our closest viewpoint on being as such is the being that we are. Being is best viewed, not as an exterior object, but rather from within. Heidegger wants to begin with the structure of human existence. The term he uses for this human existence is *Dasein*. (There is no handy English translation so this is usually just left in the German.) He wants to investigate *Sein* from the vantage point of *Dasein*. As he examines the structure of human existence, he finds it to be *In-der-Welt-sein*—being-in-the-world. Instead of the traditional modern opposition between the subject and the object, we are always on a more fundamental level of our consciousness in relation to the world. We are always already connected to the world, and this is usually below the level of our usual conscious thought. Our most basic relation to the world is not in our focal awareness regarding objects, but in the background of our practical being-in-the-world and coping with the world. We live in a background framework of meaning in relation to the world that we do not often think about. Our practices tell us more about our fundamental human being and about the world than the things we think about more consciously.

Heidegger finds that this being-in-the-world has a fundamentally temporal structure. Temporality is the fundamental structure of human being or *Dasein*. All of our thinking and acting happens within the frame of the always interrelated *ekstases* (being outside of oneself) of time: the past, the present and the future. We always have a past or as Heidegger calls it a **thrownness**. We do not create our situation; we find ourselves 'thrown' there.

For the present Heidegger uses the term **fallenness**. What he means here is that we are too often caught up in our everyday activities and are not aware of the deeper realities of our human existence. There is a shallowness to our common everyday way of thinking. He talks about this in terms of fallenness, and the echo here is Kierkegaard's understanding of the crowd when talking about the present age. We simply take on what people say about things; we become a function of a they-self. We do not take responsibility for our lives, but go with the flow.

Finally, we are always oriented towards the future. For this Heidegger uses the term **understanding**. That is our moving towards, projecting ourselves into the future. Our future-oriented is always co-determined by our thrownness and our fallenness. Ultimately, he says that these three things together—this temporality—can be characterized as *Sorge* or **care**. At the most foundational level of what humanity is is care or concern. There is a directedness or vector to human life. For Heidegger however this vector, this arc of human life, is always coming out of oblivion (thrown into a meaningless situation beyond our remembering) and where it is going is death that awaits our finite existence. Part of the fallenness of everyday life is that we do not think about that; we do not own up to the necessity of our own death. Part of authentic being is going to be courageously owning up to our finitude and death that Heidegger calls **being-towards-death**. We come into being in a particular historical place, we take responsibility for our lives and courageously face up to our finitude.

Another key idea in *Being and Time* is that of **anxiety** or *Angst*. One of the things that draws us beyond our everydayness and draws us into an awareness of our real, finite situation is the experience of anxiety. (There is a significant degree of demonstrable and yet unacknowledged dependence upon Kierkegaard's *The Concept of Anxiety* [1844].) It is the anxiety of being free, of having choice, but being finite, having only certain options regarding which one has no control. For Heidegger, for all of the determining 'givens' of our finite situation, one thing that is certainly not given is a set of rules to tell us what to do with our freedom. It is between such finite necessity and non-teleological possibility that we experience anxiety. The heart of Division Two of *Being and Time* is Heidegger's search for an authentic human existence. An authentic existence is ultimately taking up your given concrete situation as your own.

Both Rudolf Bultmann and Paul Tillich have theologies that draw heavily on existentialist philosophy and especially on the philosophy of Heidegger. Both of them saw existentialism as a great boon for the revivification of theology in the twentieth century. They see existentialism and Heidegger as helping modern people rediscover a properly Christian understanding of human existence.

14.2 Bultmann

Rudolf Bultmann (1884–1976) is considered to be the greatest New Testament scholar in the twentieth century. Even those who really disagree with him give him a place of honour as remaking the landscape of New Testament studies. He became especially influential in theology in the 1950s and 1960s. After the Second World War, Bultmann's theology came to be seen as a major alternative to that of Barth. Part of the difference between the two comes from their respective Protestant backgrounds: Barth is Reformed, while Bultmann is Lutheran.

Bultmann's father was a Lutheran pastor. He studied at many different places: Tübingen, Berlin and Marburg, with such Ritschlian luminaries as Harnack and Herrmann. He was a fellow student at times with Karl Barth. He also studied with such eminent biblical scholars as Johannes Weiss—a New Testament scholar—and Herman Gunkel, an Old Testament scholar. Gunkel introduces him to form criticism, of which Bultmann becomes the foremost proponent in using with the New Testament. Also from Gunkel—and the Ritschlians as well—he gets a neo-Kantian perspective. They emphasize the stark distinction between facts (what happened) and values (what matters), and Bultmann takes on this disjunction to some degree.

Bultmann taught the New Testament at Marburg for most of his career, from 1921 to around 1951. He was not just an academic, but also an involved churchman—being, after 1936, the chairman of the Marburg Lutheran committee. It was while he was at Marburg that he struck up a friendship with Heidegger, who taught at Marburg from 1923 to 1928, and publishes *Being and Time* in 1927. Heidegger was involved in Bultmann's seminar on Pauline ethics—almost immediately after Heidegger arrived at Marburg. Bultmann regularly attended Heidegger's lectures. They met together one-on-one regularly and read through the Gospel of John. They even held a joint seminar on Luther's commentary on Galatians.

Part of what is going on in Heidegger is that there is a *laicized* Christianity—a Christianity stripped of dogma. In his talk of fallenness and authenticity, Heidegger is trying to find a way of having something like Protestant Christian ethics without the Protestant Christian theology. It is a faux-Pauline way of looking at things. Though Bultmann recognizes that the kind of existentialist philosophy that Heidegger is putting forward is a secular version of Christianity, he does not think that this is necessarily a bad thing. He believes that Christianity needs to move into the modern world and that existentialist philosophy can provide a ground for a common language between our world and the world of the New Testament. He thinks that Heidegger's understanding of human existence can help theologians navigate the question of how to be Christians in the modern age.

Heidegger and Bultmann also shared an interest in Kierkegaard. For Bultmann, Kierkegaard and Nietzsche are two of the real decisive figures for modern theology. There are many references to Kierkegaard in Bultmann's corpus—such that Kierkegaard scholars can refer to Bultmann's corpus as being 'soaked' in Kierkegaard. Even if one thinks Kierkegaard is being severely misread, there is no doubt that there is a definite dependence whether it be Christology, eschatology or ethics.

14.2.1 Biblical Studies

Bultmann made a significant mark on the historical–critical approach to the Bible in the twentieth century. In particular, he presented groundbreaking work on **form criticism** as applied to the Gospels. Form criticism here has to do with trying to see the developing tradition that lays behind the written text as we have it. Earlier oral content is modified through different layers of tradition, and one can identify different layers—earlier and later—by certain forms of expression (hence, 'form' criticism). By analysing different linguistic forms one can develop a periodization of the development of tradition. For instance, the earlier veins in the tradition will have more Semiticisms or Aramaic. That is a form that identifies a period in tradition. Form criticism usually assumes that the earlier traditions are going to be the most historically accurate.

In 1921, Bultmann publishes *The History of the Synoptic Tradition*. He incorporates in this with form criticism, the approach of the History of Religions School (*Religionsgeschichtliche Schule*) where the New Testament is seen as a syncretistic document—drawing eclectically on elements of the different religions and philosophies in its cultural milieu. Not only is there the early Jewish tradition but the New Testament writers also brought in ideas from many different extra-Scriptural influences—like Hellenistic philosophy, mystery religions and Gnosticism.

Bultmann applies a radical historical–critical lens to the historical Jesus. His conclusion— going along with Albert Schweitzer—is that there is little that is historical in the Gospels. In the late nineteenth century, Schweitzer pronounces the quest for the historical Jesus to be largely a failure. Bultmann will say that what we have in the Gospel traditions principally has to do with *Sitz im Leben*—the lived situation of the communities that produced the Gospels. These are the situations that we see in the Gospels; they show less what Jesus said and did than the situation of the communities in which these traditions arose. When it comes to historical fact, the Gospels primarily tell us about the life of the early Christian community and very little about Jesus. The best

Figure 14.1 Bultmann.

that we can say about Jesus, in Bultmann's view, is that Jesus existed and proclaimed the Kingdom of God.

One might well ask at this point, 'Why then does Bultmann care about theology?' Key here is to recall Bultmann's maintaining of the neo-Kantian distinction (of his Ritschlian teachers) between fact and value. There is what happened and what matters. When it comes to Jesus, the heart of the Christian faith, we cannot say much about what happened. But this is not what ultimately matters.

14.2.2 Jesus, History and Faith

Bultmann makes a strong distinction between the Jesus of history that we can know through historical–critical methods—which ends up being very little—and the Christ of faith. He would say that if we are looking for the Jesus of history the New Testament does not provide us with the materials for us to get there. What it does give us is the Christ of faith. It gives us Christ as proclaimed, the **kerygma**, the Christ preached.

While Bultmann certainly valued historical–critical methods, he also said that they were inadequate for Christian faith. The results of historical criticism are not going to give one what is important for Christian faith. One cannot use history to get to the things that Christianity believes. As opposed to the Ritschlian theology, Bultmann advocates a focus on the Christ of faith. Ritschlian theology wanted to return to the historical preaching of Jesus in order to get rid of the husk of the later proclamation of the Church and get back to the kernel—again the preaching of Jesus. Bultmann is going to go a different direction. Instead of focusing on the preaching of Jesus, he sees the heart of Christianity as the Christ that is preached by the early church: the Kerygmatic Christ.

Bultmann makes a neo-Kantian distinction between fact and value, with value as the domain of experience and that which is more important for human life. What really happened is not as important as our experience and the meaning of that experience for us. **History** has to do with sifting out different contingent facts, but **faith** has to do with our values. The New Testament is not as much about presenting the raw materials for knowing things about history as it is about proclaiming something of great existential import.

When it comes to the message of the New Testament, history tells us all that we need to know from it. This is what Bultmann calls 'the that'—*das Dass*—of Jesus. That Jesus was, that he is not imaginary is something history can tell us that. But beyond this, biblical faith is not the same as history. Biblical faith is not just concerned with 'the that' of Jesus, but is concerned with *das Was*—'the what' of Jesus, or the meaning of Jesus. Biblical faith for Bultmann presupposes the 'that' of Jesus—the fact that he lived, preached the Kingdom and died upon the cross. But that is not all. The message, 'the what' is the meaning of 'the that'.

Bultmann here (like Barth) displays no small degree of dependence upon Herrmann, who focuses on the significance of experience and the living community. He thinks that the things believed about the Christ who is proclaimed in the New Testament are identical to the historical Jesus. One however cannot verify this historically. Herrmann, too, thinks that the quest for the historical Jesus is basically misguided. If you are looking to historical-critical methods to give you what is most important in Christianity, you are barking up the wrong tree.

If 'historical' here is taken in the sense of being historically proven, then the historical Jesus is not relevant to Christian faith. But here Bultmann again makes the distinction between *historie* (historical) and *geschichte* (historic). *Historie* has to do with our knowledge of what actually happened; there is always going to be uncertainty here. *Historie* by its very nature can never be fully known and is always going to be revisable based on further information. For Bultmann, this can never be the basis for the certainty of faith. Faith has a certainty that does not belong to historical inquiry. *Geschichte* has to do with the existential significance of Jesus. Bultmann says that for this faith does not need to know anything about Jesus beyond that he lived and died.

As a dialectical theologian, we can see Bultmann's proximity to Barth here. Faith has to do with an encounter with the Word of God. It is an existential encounter. As such, it is not something that we have control over; it is not something that we can justify. We are on the receiving end of it. The Word of God and the works of God can only be known with eyes of faith and not through our own works. For Bultmann (here creatively appropriating his Lutheran heritage), 'works' here includes the 'work' of historical and empirical confirmation. *Historie* is in the domain of 'works' and not of 'faith'.

As a dialectical theologian, Bultmann sees God's activity as being hidden and/or paradoxical. It is never the kind of thing that sees the light of day in our normal examinations of history. The 'what' of what Christians believe is that God has acted decisively for us in Jesus Christ. To be an existing person—Bultmann here drawing on Heidegger—means that you have to take ownership of what you are as a person and live authentically. He thinks that Christianity provides an idea for this kind of authentic life. What it provides is a new life through Christ. The kerygma, the Gospel, for Bultmann is that there is a new life that is available to us through faith in Christ.

14.2.3 Demythologization

Perhaps Bultmann's most lasting contribution to modern theology is his project of demythologization. This idea became quite influential beyond New Testament circles and outside of Germany around the end of his career. At this time, Bultmann begins to be internationally known in theological circles and not just in biblical studies. He introduces this concept in an essay entitled 'New Testament and Mythology: The Problem of Eliminating the Mythological Elements from the Proclamation of the New Testament' (1941).

Bultmann holds that the modern scientific worldview contradicts a mythological understanding of the world and that we as modern scientific people have to give up on a mythological understanding of God and of God's activity in the world. By mythological he means a pre-scientific understanding of the world—for instance, the belief that the universe is three-tiered, with the earth in the middle, heaven above and hell below. He would put the miraculous and various supernatural interventions—where there are divine beings moving around and doing magical things—in the same category. He would say that such a mythological worldview was held by the ancient biblical authors. The New Testament authors specifically wrote within the context of Jewish Apocalypticism and Greek Gnosticism. Modern people cannot take this world literally. Bultmann's aim here is not to debunk or denigrate the Bible. His purpose is rather apologetic—to present

Christianity as believable for modern people. Like his classically liberal teachers, he thought that the modern believer needs to distinguish between mythology and history. Likewise, he thought that in order to get to what is important in Christianity you have to sift out what is the essence from the dross. While this sounds like the Ritschlians, Bultmann effects a certain reversal. What they see as the most valuable thing—the history—is not what he sees as the most valuable thing. Bultmann says that what matters is not the history but the mythology. To be precise, what matters is the *meaning* of the mythology. This is important to understand, because when Bultmann talks about demythologization he is not talking about cutting mythology out of Christianity. He sees mythology as where the real value is, but it needs to be interpreted properly. If one, as a modern person, simply attempts to take biblical imagery at face value we are missing the meaning of it. We then only miss the point of what these pre-modern people were trying to communicate with this mythological language. We have short-circuited a proper interpretation of the Bible.

Demythologization says that you can believe in the Christian message—the kerygma—without accepting the pre-scientific, mythological worldview. The key here is to understand what myth in Bultmann's understanding does. Myth speaks about the divine and about human existence. He says that myth expresses the otherworldly in terms of this world. As such, it is not to be taken literally. It is fundamentally figurative language. It is using pictures from this world to talk about something that is other than this world. Biblical mythology also concerns our place in the world. It is a picture of our place in the world. It is not just about God, but it is about human existence.

Bultmann thinks that the picture of human existence that is presented in the New Testament, the meaning of the mythology, is in fact at odds with the way many modern people would think about themselves. In the world of the Bible, the origin and meaning of the world is beyond the world. The world is dominated by hostile powers and we are ultimately not in control of our lives. We need to be delivered by that which is beyond our power and ability. As you can see, part of what Bultmann is doing here is that he is taking what he calls the mythology of the New Testament and is interpreting it existentially rather than objectively. This tells us about our human being in the world. Demythologization wants to keep a biblical understanding of human existence without literally accepting the prescientific imagery.

To demythologize is in a significant sense to de-objectify. It is to interpret Scripture anthropologically instead of cosmologically. It is not primarily telling us as much about the way things are as about the way human existence is. It is telling us about the human situation. (It ultimately ends up looking not un-similar, shall we say, to Heidegger's understanding of human existence in *Being and Time*.)

Bultmann does not want us to extract and reject myth but to properly interpret biblical myth as talking about human existence. He even sees demythologizing as beginning in the New Testament itself—particularly in the way the New Testament reinterprets the Old Testament. The later writers take earlier statements as referring to a deeper reality. Even within the New Testament, Paul's earlier letters have a more literal eschatology in which there is going to be a literal end of the world right around the corner. In John, however, writing later, there is a reinterpreting of this literal eschatology as being realized in the person of Jesus.

Through this process of demythologization, we are given the heart of the biblical message—which for Bultmann has to do with human existence and an encounter with God. It is about our situation and what God is doing for us. The heart of the Gospel is about believing in Jesus Christ, which is one's existential transition from an inauthentic existence to an authentic existence.

God, for Bultmann the dialectical theologian, is seen as wholly other. As wholly other, one cannot think of God objectively because God is not another object in the world. God's activity is not a worldly event. Ultimately, only faith can see the things of God because they are of a different order from our normal way of looking at the world. Faith then will see all things as dependent upon God. Bultmann would say that faith entails a belief in providence, that all things are dependent upon this radically transcendent God. At the end of the day, he denies that the resurrection is an empirical fact; it is not something that we can know historically, as an object of *Historie*. What the resurrection is is a symbolic way of talking about the significance of the cross. The cross brings about a salvation that is a new life—dying to the false security of the world and aligning ourselves to the life of God.

14.3 Tillich

Paul Johannes Tillich (1886–1965) is the most celebrated theologian in the United States after the Second World War. He probably has had an influence beyond Protestant theology that is broader than Barth's. There are non-theological and non-religious people who are interested in Tillich. He is seen as providing an understanding of religion for non-religious people. In many ways, Tillich represents a renewal of a liberal understanding of religion—an understanding of religion (looking back to Schleiermacher) presented to its 'cultured despisers'.

In his work as a theologian, he is trying to make Christianity make sense to someone who might be a religious sceptic. Like Bultmann, he is the son of a conservative German Lutheran minister. He studied theology and philosophy in Berlin, Tübingen and Halle, and ended up being awarded his doctorate in philosophy in 1910 after which he did his licentiate in theology at Halle in 1912. Both times, he wrote on Schelling. Tillich had an abiding interest in nineteenth-century German Idealism.

A significant turning-point for Tillich came during his time serving as a chaplain in the First World War. In the devastation of the war, he felt like he was experiencing something like the end of world; he had several emotional breakdowns. During this time, he read Nietzsche (which is apparently not unusual for German soldiers) in the woods in France. Nietzsche significantly influences Tillich's way of thinking. He also read Kierkegaard, although Nietzsche is probably more influential to his thought. When it came to Kierkegaard, he was primarily interested, like Heidegger, in his psychology. Tillich's relationship with Kierkegaard can best be described as both heir and saboteur. He ends up taking some of Kierkegaard's ideas but is opposed to other ideas—such as Kierkegaard's emphasis on the 'otherness' of God.

After the war, Tillich taught in Berlin from 1919 to 1924. There, he gets involved in *avant-garde* politics and the Bohemian art scene. He ended up teaching in several places in Germany—Marburg, Dresden, Leipzig and Frankfurt. While he was at Marburg, he becomes influenced by Heidegger.

Figure 14.2 Tillich.

'Bust of Paul Johannes Tillich (daylight)' by Richard Keeling—Own work. Licensed under GFDL via Wikimedia Commons.

During his career in Germany, Tillich worked towards what he called 'a theology of culture'. This phrase comes from a lecture that he gave in 1919 called 'On the Idea of a Theology of Culture'. In this, he examines the boundary between religion and secular culture and tries to find a constructive relation between them. In order to do so, he presents a way of thinking about religion as what he calls the **depth dimension** in all cultural life. Religion is not a separate dimension alongside others like art, politics, ethics, family life, etc. Religion is rather the depth dimension of all of those things. It is not its own domain, but rather the unconditional element in all human culture.

It is in relation to this depth dimension that Tillich presents religion as related to one's **ultimate concern**. The 'concern' here is Heidegger's word for 'care'—*Sorge*. It is our orientation in everything towards something that is ultimate or beyond that which is finite. Tillich would say that to focus one's ultimate concern on something that is finite is idolatry. In this important lecture he also introduces the concept of **theonomy** as in distinction from both autonomy and heteronomy. One of the defining elements of modernity is an emphasis on autonomy (self-rule) over against any kind of heteronomy (being ruled by another). Tillich would say that beyond both of those there is the theonomous dimension in that God is not another that is in charge of you but is rather the depth dimension of your reality as well as others.

In 1933, Tillich publishes a book, *The Socialist Decision*. He was involved with some socialist groups in Germany, and in this book he attacks the Nazi Party. Consequently, he is suspended from his position and, seeing the writing on the wall, fled Germany. He ends up as a professor at

Union Theological Seminary in New York City, where he stayed for around twenty years, until his retirement in 1955.

While he was at Union, Tillich published and became well known in the United States for a collection of sermons entitled *The Shaking of the Foundations* (1948). In 1951, he published the first book in his three-volume work, *Systematic Theology*. Tillich came to be the most widely known American theologian, and arguably something of an intellectual superstar. In 1955, after retiring from Union, he moved to Harvard to teach. There, he prided himself on not attending any religious services—he did not like being required to go to chapel while teaching at a seminary. He regularly spoke during this period to large audiences (for large fees) across the country, and in 1959 he even made the cover of *TIME* magazine. In 1962, Tillich moved to the University of Chicago. He died in 1965. Tillich's most significant work for the history of modern theology is his *Systematic Theology* published in three volumes in 1951, 1957 and 1963.

14.3.1 Method of Correlation

Before getting into some of the specifics of Tillich's *Systematic Theology*, we will address his theological method. He calls his theological method a **method of correlation**. He says that the task of the theologian is to address the modern human being's existential situation but also to attend to a community and its tradition and symbols. Theology is about correlating these two elements. This method is a correlation of that which is outside of Christianity—common, human experience in the modern world—and that which is inside of Christianity—its tradition and its symbols. Theology should be mediating between those two sides not violating or getting rid of either one. It is mediating between Christianity as a living tradition that has an historical reality and contemporary culture.

The method of correlation as mediating between:	
existential situation	Christian symbols
contemporary culture	historical reality
addressing this situation	dependent upon this
from outside of Christianity	from inside of Christianity
'form'	'content'
asking questions	providing answers

Ultimately Tillich would see religion and culture forming parts of a larger whole. He is not a dialectical theologian in the sense of seeing Christianity and contemporary culture to be some kind of fundamental opposition. One of the ways he tries to bring the two together is that he says that culture asks certain questions and provides the 'form' of thought, whereas religion provides the answers and the 'content' of thought.

Theology for Tillich is showing how the Christian symbols provide answers for the big human questions in modern culture. There are pressing and seemingly unanswerable questions in contemporary culture, and Christian theology shows how the Christian symbols provide answers for these questions. Key here is Tillich's understanding of the nature of **religious symbols**. Religious symbols always point beyond the realities that they express. Religious symbols are about God, but God is ultimately unconditioned and is, thus, beyond finite, historical symbols. So all ways of talking about God are symbolic for Tillich. The one non-symbolic way of talking about God is in terms of 'being itself'; being itself—or perhaps the ground of being—is not symbolic when it comes to talking about God. (One can hear the resonances with German Idealism and Heidegger.)

The method of correlation as correlating existential situations and the Christian symbols is to be differentiated from other popular theological methods. Tillich is opposed to what he calls a **supernaturalistic** method, insomuch as it does not give proper attention to the situation—to the lived questions of modern humanity. He is also opposed to a **naturalistic or humanistic** method, which does not properly attend to the need to go beyond our given human situation. It does not see that what we have in the human situation are questions and not answers. It fails to see that our situation points us beyond our situation.

14.3.2 I. Reason and Revelation

There are three volumes and five parts to Tillich's magnum opus, *Systematic Theology*. The 'volumes' are the separate books that were published over time. The 'parts' are the real structure of the work. In each of the parts one can see the correlated 'question' and 'answer'. Volume 1 is published in 1951, and contains the first two of the five parts. Part I is titled 'Reason and Revelation'; Part II is 'Being and God'. Volume 2 is published in 1957, and constitutes Part III, which is entitled 'Existence and the Christ'. Volume 3 is published in 1963 and contains the two final parts: Part IV is 'Life and Spirit', and Part V is 'History and the Kingdom of God'.

Tillich's *Systematic Theology*

Volume 1 (1951)

I. Reason and Revelation

II. Being and God

Volume 2 (1957)

III. Existence and the Christ

Volume 3 (1963)

IV. Life and the Spirit

V. History and the Kingdom of God

Part I of Tillich's *Systematic Theology* is entitled 'Reason and Revelation'. The question that is at issue in this part is that of **scepticism**. The question is: how can we know with certainty any important truth? We want to have knowledge when it comes to important things in life. Unfortunately, 'Reason and Revelation' is one of the more abstract and technical parts of the *Systematic Theology*—and it is the first one. Its philosophical nature tends to throw readers off—because it is talking about the structure of knowledge.

Tillich presents the answer to this question in terms of the Christian symbol of the **Logos**. Again, the question is a contemporary existential situation while the answer is a Christian symbol. Tillich writes that, looking at our nature as knowers, our reason is finite and always entailing conflicting oppositions and polarities—whether that is a polarity between the formal and emotional, the static and the dynamic, the absolute and the relative, autonomy and heteronomy, and so on. All of these dualities, tensions and polarities inhere in our finitude. That is what finitude means for Tillich. There is a relativity and tension that keeps us from certainty. We think in the midst of a structure that qualifies all our thinking, but what revelation gives us is a truth that unifies all of these polarities.

For the Christian, it is ultimately in Jesus as the Logos that all of these polarities are unified. What Tillich is presenting here is that revelation discloses our ultimate concerns, specifically in Jesus as mediating the ground of meaning and life. In Jesus as the Logos, there is a unity that overcomes the polarities.

14.3.3 II. Being and God

The second part is entitled 'Being and God'. The question here that arises from our situation is that of our **finitude**. The question is, how can we withstand the destructive forces that threaten to disintegrate our lives? Our lives are finite and are threatened. How does one withstand existential threat?

The answer to this existential question is the symbol of **God as Creator**. The answer to our finitude is to see that our nature is that of creatures. Our lives are threatened by meaninglessness, guilt and death—or as Tillich summarizes it, we are threatened with non-being. What resists this threat is the power of being, and God as the Creator is where the power of being comes from. So, with the symbol of God the Creator gives us the power to resist threats. God the Creator through our ultimate concern has given us the power to cope with our finitude. God the Creator as the power of being that is active and sustains us in the midst of threat. We are sustained in being by God; it is in this part that Tillich explicitly deals with God as 'the ground of being' or as 'being itself'. God is not any finite being or even the supreme being. God the Creator is rather 'the God above God'—by which Tillich means not any kind of finite thing but the very power of being itself. God is that which makes anything to be and which holds things in being.

It is from this perspective that Tillich says that being itself is the only non-symbolic way to talk about God. All personal attributes about God are symbolic ways of talking. And so, the answer to our finitude is faith in God as being itself. This gives us the courage to be in the face of our finitude.

14.3.4 III. Existence and the Christ

The third part, making up the second volume of the *Systematic Theology*, is 'Existence and the Christ'. The question here is our **estrangement** or **alienation**. We find ourselves alienated from ourselves and from our neighbours. We are cut off. The answer to this, as Tillich says, is **Jesus as the Christ**. Here it is Jesus 'functioning as' the Christ, the Reconciler, as the one healing the alienation. 'As the' is talking about a function. Here, Tillich is primarily interested in the symbol of Christ as bringing together healing contradictions or estrangements.

The issue here is that of existential disruption. Tillich talks about this in existentialist terms. As finite beings, we are threatened by non-being. We are—as existing—estranged from our essence. There is a polarity and a lack of coincidence between our essence and our existence. This disruption is symbolized for him by sin and the Fall. Sin and the Fall are a symbolic way of talking about how our estrangement from our essential nature is at once the result of our freedom and of destiny—of something out of our control. There is an aspect of personal responsibility, but also our existence is estranged from our essence simply because we are human beings. For him, the Fall symbolizes humanity's primordial transition from essence to existence. He does not see the Fall as an actual event in time but rather as a symbolic way of talking about the structure of human existence.

Sin has to do with this estrangement or turning away in contradiction to our essence whereas salvation is bringing about a wholeness. What we have in Christ as the answer to this question of estrangement is what Tillich calls the '**new being**'. Jesus as the Christ is the power of new being. He is the new Adam. He manifests essential human nature in the midst of estrangement. This overcomes the gap between essence and existence, so the symbol of crucifixion presents how the new unification is present even in the midst of profound estrangement. The new essential human being can *be* in the presence of profound estrangement. Salvation then is participating in our estrangement in Christ coming together in that work.

The divinity of Christ for Tillich is that he is the one who has fully actualized our essential nature. In this context, our essential nature is a unity with God. Jesus as the Christ makes this essential non-estranged humanity present and so mediates this new being with us.

Tillich's version of Christian theology is a bit of a mouthful. One must appreciate that he is trying to present Christian theology to those to whom traditional Christian symbols are no longer meaningful. He is reinterpreting the Christian symbols that they might make sense to someone who is more at home with philosophical ways of talking—specifically with existentialist philosophy.

For Tillich, we cannot have access to Jesus apart from his reception as the Christ. That is what we have in the Gospels. They only present Jesus as the Christ. It is this transformative reception of Jesus as the Christ that is what matters for faith. Here Tillich is similar to Bultmann.

14.3.5 IV. Life and the Spirit

In Part IV, 'Life and the Spirit', the 'question' is that of life's ambiguity, ambivalence and lack of authenticity. With the method of correlation, this question is going to provide the form, the language in which the symbols are going to be translated. The question determines the form of the answer, and it often looks as if the Christian symbols are getting reinvested with new content—perhaps some kind of Heideggerian existentialism in Christian dress.

The question in Part IV is the ambiguity of life. Posed as: 'How can our lives be authentic when our morality, religious practices, and cultural self-expressions are so ambiguous?', the answer to this is: 'Spirit'. The symbol 'Spirit' has to do with the meaning of the ambiguity of existence. What Tillich is pointing to here is how human life ends up being regulated by meanings and ideas. He delineates this in many different areas of culture.

Spirit has to do with our self-integration—our moral life. We have a drive to be morally integrated and towards an unambiguous morality. There is also an aesthetic or cultural side to Spirit which is a drive towards creating meaningful artefacts. Our drive towards self-transcendence is what Tillich here identifies particularly as our religious life. So in our moral life, our cultural life and our religious life we are driven towards something unambiguous. The answer to this search is what he calls Spiritual Presence and the Kingdom of God. Instead of the traditional understanding of the 'Holy Spirit', Tillich here talks about 'Spirit' or Spiritual Presence.

Whereas Spiritual Presence is that which answers these questions synchronically, the Kingdom of God is a way of answering these questions more diachronically. This unambiguous life is something that is unfolding over time towards greater self-integration, self-creation and self-transcendence. In this context this fuller life is a social one. Ultimately, this is a life grounded in love. The resolution of the ambiguous relation between autonomy and heteronomy has to have a spontaneity coming from yourself but also is responsive to the other. Theonomy is the power of the Spiritual Presence that is beyond the self and the other and is guiding one towards such a life of love. Much of this material on the Kingdom of God is laid out in Part V.

14.3.6 V. History and the Kingdom of God

The final part is 'History and the Kingdom of God'. The question here is, does history have a meaning? Is there a point to history? The answer to that is to be found for Tillich in the symbol of the Kingdom of God. The question is how there can be anything of permanent value within the flow of history, and the answer to this—the Kingdom of God for him—is that there is an inner aim to history. That inner aim is the elevation to the eternal. History is orientated towards the participation of finite life in the divine in eternal life. This is Tillich's take on eschatology; the finite is brought within the divine at the end. There is an ultimate peace in unity that is not to be found in history but is that to which history is orientated.

Sources and Further Reading

Barrett, Lee C. 'Paul Tillich: An Ambivalent Appropriation'. In *Kierkegaard Research: Sources, Reception and Resources, Volume 10: Kierkegaard's Influence on Theology, Tome 1: German Protestant Theology*, edited by Jon Stewart, 335–76. Aldershot: Ashgate, 2012.

Christoffersen, Svein Aage. 'Rudolf Bultmann'. In *Key Theological Thinkers: From Modern to Postmodern*, edited by Staale Johannes Kristiansen and Svein Rise, 77–87. Aldershot: Ashgate, 2013.

Dorrien, Gary. *Kantian Reason and Hegelian Spirit: The Idealistic Logic of Modern Theology*. Oxford: Wiley-Blackwell, 2012.

Dupré, Louis. *The Quest of the Absolute: Birth and Decline of European Romanticism*. Notre Dame, IN: University of Notre Dame Press, 2013.

Hall, Douglas John. '"The Great War" and the Theologians'. In *The Twentieth Century: A Theological Overview*, edited by Gregory Baum, 3–13. Maryknoll, NY: Orbis, 1999.

Kelsey, David H. 'Paul Tillich'. In *The Modern Theologians: Introduction to Christian Theology since 1918*, edited by David F. Ford with Rachel Muers, 62–75, 3rd edn. Oxford: Blackwell, 2005.

Livingston, James C., and Francis Schüssler Fiorenza. *Modern Christian Thought: Volume 2, The Twentieth Century*. 2nd edn. Minneapolis, MN: Fortress Press, 2006.

Scharlemann, Robert P. 'Tillich, Paul Johannes'. In *The Oxford Companion to Christian Thought*, edited by Adrian Hastings, Alistair Mason, and Hugh Pyper, 706–07. Oxford: Oxford University Press, 2000.

Schultz, Heiko. 'Rudolf Bultmann: Faith, Love, and Self-Understanding'. In *Kierkegaard Research: Sources, Reception and Resources, Vol. 10: Kierkegaard's Influence on Theology, Tome 1: German Protestant Theology*, edited by Jon Stewart, 105–44. Aldershot: Ashgate, 2012.

Thiselton, Anthony C. 'Biblical Interpretation'. In *The Modern Theologians: Introduction to Christian Theology since 1918*, edited by David F. Ford with Rachel Muers, 287–304, 3rd edn. Oxford: Blackwell, 2005.

Thorbjørnsen, Svein Olaf. 'Paul Tillich'. In *Key Theological Thinkers: From Modern to Postmodern*, edited by Staale Johannes Kristiansen and Svein Rise, 101–11. Aldershot: Ashgate, 2013.

15

Early-Twentieth-Century Catholic Theology

15.1 Nineteenth-Century Trajectories

In the preceding chapters, we have presented Protestant theology in the earlier part of the twentieth century: Barth, Bultmann and Tillich. In this chapter we will shift to a different story of Christian theology. To understand the situation of Catholic theology in the early twentieth century, one must look at different trajectories coming out of the nineteenth century. The first trajectory is particularly inspired by the Enlightenment though it would posture itself in opposition to the Enlightenment; this is a more rationalistic and yet 'anti-modern' perspective. It is especially invested in the rational defence of the truth of Christianity. It is an **anti-modern Enlightenment** perspective in the sense of using the tools of modernity against secular modernity and to defend the Christian faith—emphasizing ahistorical reason and objectivity. This was represented by Neo-Scholasticism. Neo-Scholasticism was the officially sanctioned perspective of the Church and grounded in Vatican I and several Papal pronouncements (see Chapter 11). The centres of Neo-Scholasticism were the Angelicum in Rome and the Catholic University of Leuven in Belgium.

The major representative of Neo-Scholasticism in the early twentieth century is **Réginald Garrigou-Lagrange (1877–1964)**, a professor at the Angelicum. He is an exemplar of what is sometimes called 'Strict Observance Thomism'. He is greatly admired by Neo-Scholastics and Thomists of this stripe and often demonized by those who are not.

The other major trajectory coming out of the nineteenth century is a more **Romantic** perspective. Romanticism focused on history and the unique and individual character of that which develops through history. As such they focused on the manner in which tradition develops over time. They focused on development and the 'positive' nature of human products in history. This was originally centred on the Tübingen School of Catholic theology but also John Henry Newman (see Chapter 9).

15.2 Neo-Scholasticism

When we get to the beginning of the twentieth century, the work of thirteenth-century theologian Thomas Aquinas is enshrined in Catholic higher education as the official teaching of the Catholic Church. But in order to do this—to make the teaching of Thomas Aquinas the official teaching of the Church—Thomas has to be digested and presented simply and institutionally, in a way that takes Thomas's extraordinarily subtle and complex thought and simplifies it so that it can be the basis for Catholic religious education—from catechism to seminary.

Neo-Scholastic theology seeks to take Thomas's theology and produce out of it a timeless, unified theology—a return to scholastic theology. In fact, the real emphasis here is going to be on philosophy—on certain proper philosophical categories. In Thomas, they seek to find a **perennial philosophy**—which is primarily the philosophy of Aristotle. The emphasis often ends up being Aristotelian logic and sets of moral rules. Neo-Scholasticism presents this pure system of Catholic thought. It turns out that if one wants to find out what is the simple, eternal truth in Thomas, reading Thomas is going to complicate that. In fact, they often referred to Thomas's sixteenth-century commentators' digestion and representation of Thomas. Suarez is an important commentator for them, in this regard.

It is ironic that this Thomism entails a certain lack of attention to the particularities of Thomas himself, and is mostly going to be a name for the enshrining of the later understandings and interpretations of the Thomistic tradition. So when people are going to break away in Catholic theology from Neo-Scholasticism—from Thomism and Thomists—the dissent often comes from different interpretations of Thomas himself. It is not people saying that Thomas is wrong but that the dominant interpreters of Thomas are reading Thomas wrongly.

Neo-Scholasticism can perhaps better be understood in terms of that to which it is opposed. Neo-Scholastics usually summarize this under the heading of 'Modernism'. In 1910, there is imposed an 'anti-modernist oath', by which clergy are required to take a formal oath against 'modernism'. Thomas Aquinas, in Neo-Scholasticism, is often turned into a cudgel towards the end of stopping the encroachment of modern thought. Whoever does not sign on to a few very technical terms could be censored, fired from their position or even excommunicated.

Another distinctive difference has to do with the relationship between grace and nature. The Neo-Scholastic perspective presents Thomas in such a way that grace and nature are two distinct orders. The natural order has its own distinct integrity, such that there is such a thing as a natural human perfection or end to which grace is super-added towards a supernatural end. The differing perspective that comes up here has to do with integrating grace and nature specifically through the human desire for God—which is a more Augustinian perspective.

15.3 *Nouvelle théologie*

There are two key terms used to depict the impulses for the development of Catholic theology in the twentieth century. Perhaps the best way to talk about what is going to happen in the early twentieth century in Catholic theology is as a movement of ***ressourcement***—a 'returning to the sources'. To place this within the broader sweep of twentieth century Catholic theology, *ressourcement* is going to be paired with ***aggiornamento***—a 'bringing up to date'. *Aggiornamento* is going to be the theme of the Second Vatican Council in the 1960s—bringing the faith up to date.

There are two generations of *ressourcement* theologians. The first generation is all Frenchmen. It includes Chenu, Bouillard and de Lubac—all examined in this chapter. The second generation includes the two pre-eminent Catholic theologians of the later part of the twentieth century (who both wrote in German): Karl Rahner and Hans Urs von Balthasar. The first generation is usually referred to as the *nouvelle théologie*. While there are certainly other important movements in Catholic theology in this period, *nouvelle théologie* is arguably the most significant for the remainder of the twentieth century.

Catholic *Ressourcement*	
1st generation	Chenu, Bouillard, de Lubac (Ch. 15)
2nd generation	Rahner, Balthasar (Ch. 18)

Nouvelle théologie is the name of a Catholic theological movement that happened from the 1930s through the 1950s, among some Dominican and Jesuit theologians in France. The 1930s emerged as a decade of crisis in the world. It was the period of the Great Depression in the Americas, and also the rise of various totalitarian regimes in Europe. Pius XI was pope for most of this decade, and he believed that the cause of a lot of these modern problems was the abandoning of scholasticism.

In France, this was a golden age for Catholic intellectuals—not just theologians, but other Catholic thinkers—who set the tone for this generation. There was an expanding of imaginative theological horizons. We see this in the literature of Charles Péguy and Paul Claudel, both Catholic poets. (The term *ressourcement* is coined by Péguy.) In philosophy, there are such figures as Maurice Blondel, Étienne Gilson and Gabriel Marcel. There are many French Catholic thinkers who were on the cutting edge of literature and philosophy. This encourages some Catholic theologians to think outside of the proverbial box of Neo-Scholasticism. In theology, we see significant figures such as Teilhard de Chardin, Marie-Dominique Chenu, Yves Congar and Henri de Lubac. It is during the 1930s that Catholic theology ends its isolation, and a new openness to Catholic theology is born in the midst of great acrimony and personal suffering brought about by varying degrees of persecution.

The name *nouvelle théologie* is somewhat ironic. Literally it means 'new theology', but the central thrust of many of the theologians associated with the movement is *ressourcement*—that is, returning to the sources of the Christian faith. The so-called 'new theology' is driven by recovering lost tradition—going beyond what it sees as Neo-Scholasticism's frozen-in-time caricature of Aquinas to the richer historical Aquinas and to the treasure house of other neglected patristic and medieval thinkers. This happens in the midst of a Romantic historical consciousness—a revival of interest in history and how things have developed over time.

In general terms, early-twentieth-century Catholic theology has been called a 'tale of two Thomisms'. With this shift, there is an eventual dethroning of Neo-Scholasticism. By the time we get to the 1960s, the widespread Neo-Thomist curriculum coming out of the nineteenth century in Catholic schools has evaporated. From the 1930s to the 1960s, *nouvelle théologie* goes from being censured and rejected by Rome (as presenting an alternate theological vision that is in tension with Vatican I and even the Counsel of Trent), to becoming a major, if not dominant voice in the Church in Vatican II (see Chapter 18). Large parts of what becomes the official position of the Church come out of *nouvelle théologie*.

Based on the theology in France in the 1930s through the 1950s (largely after two World Wars), it has two centres of intellectual activity. The first is the Dominican centre of study, Le Saulchoir, which has two geographical locations, first in Belgium and then in Paris. In addition to the Dominicans of Le Saulchoir, there are the Jesuits of Lyon-Fourvière in Lyon. *Nouvelle théologie* is not a formal programme that is inspired by any one thinker, or even by one particular group.

Centres of *nouvelle théologie* in France in the 1930s–50s	
Le Saulchoir	Dominican
Lyon-Fourvière	Jesuit

The name *nouvelle théologie* arises as a pejorative term, as often seems to happen. The thinkers associated with *nouvelle théologie* rejected the term. Henri du Lubac—probably the main figure of *nouvelle théologie*—says that he detests the name because he is interested not in something new but in being faithful to tradition. (It would probably be better for us to use the term *ressourcement* for these thinkers. Certainly, it is closer to what they are doing and what they think of themselves. However, the term may be too general and *nouvelle théologie* is usually associated with these people, so we will stick with it to avoid confusion.)

This term originates with Pietro Parente, an Italian who would later become the secretary to the Holy Office. In 1942, he wrote in *L'Osservatore Romano,* an official Church journal, an article critical about what he called '*nouvelle théologie*'. What he means here is broadly 'modern' theology—this new-fangled theology that the kids are into these days.

Before looking at the main theologians, we will first hazard some generalizations of *nouvelle théologie*. We will talk about four common characteristics (as presented by Mettepenningen). **First** is the **French** language. It was written in French by people in southern Belgium and France. What is significant is that it was not written in Latin: it was not written in the official Church language but in the vernacular. In the background of the French language is the Modernist controversy;

the figures condemned by the Catholic Church as 'modernist' were by and large Frenchmen (see Chapter 11). So when the officials in the Church heard about there being things written in French that were challenging Neo-Scholasticism, their mind went right back to the recently denounced troublemakers—the Catholic modernists. This is one of the reasons Rome was suspicious of it: it sounded like a revival of Catholic modernism.

Second is an emphasis on **history** in theology. A properly Christian theology should be incarnational and see the truth of the Christian faith tied up with history. So they critiqued timeless, abstract systems of thought. They wanted to attend to the ways things actually happen, and see the doctrine of the incarnation itself as justifying this procedure.

Third is that it has a **positive** approach—meaning that it returns to the particulars. These theologians sought to return to the particular sources of theology: the particularities of Scripture, and also the tradition of the Church fathers. This is more of an inductive approach. This approach involves a lot of reading and research. They dig to find what the original sources actually say, then try to generalize on the basis of this, reflecting the more general concern for *ressourcement*.

Fourth, and finally, they are, in general, all **critical of Neo-Scholasticism**, and of what comes to be considered as the 'manual' tradition—of a theology that has been crystallized into manuals and handbooks that simplistically present Christian theology and ethics.

Mettepenningen also presents what he calls **four phases** of the development of *nouvelle théologie*. The **first** is what he calls the **Thomistic Ressourcement**, from 1935 to 1942. This centres on the Dominicans at Le Saulchoir. The two central figures here are Congar and Chenu. They are critical of Neo-Scholasticism and call for a reformation of theology. Theology needs a broader framework than what Neo-Scholasticism provides. They advocate a return to history and, by doing so, a return to the historical Thomas—reading Thomas in his thirteenth-century context.

The **second** phase is a more general **Theological Ressourcement** that Mettepenningen dates from 1942 to 1950. Here there is a more extensive return to the sources of the faith—not just to the context of Thomas, but to the Church Fathers. This is done by the Jesuits at Lyon-Fourvière, and they publish various works by theologians like Bouillard and Daniélou that are critical of Neo-Scholasticism and draw heavily on the Church Fathers. This leads up to probably the most significant work of *nouvelle théologie* at the time, Henri de Lubac's *Surnaturel* (completed in 1941, and published in 1946). Significantly, the Jesuits at Lyon-Fourvière establish what will be an influential series of volumes entitled *Sources Chrétiennes* (the Christian Sources), starting in 1942 and ongoing to today. (As of 2015, there are over 500 volumes.) It publishes the original texts of the Church Fathers along with French translations. They have made the writings of the Church Fathers widely available as a resource. The series is influential not just in France, but throughout the Christian world. It provides the material ground for a Patristic revival throughout theology.

It is in this period that the term *nouvelle théologie* as a pejorative comes to be attached to the movement. Pope Pius XII, in 1946 (spurred on by influential Neo-Scholastic spokesmen), addresses the leadership of the Jesuit and the Dominican orders, counselling them on the dangers of 'nova theologia' and encouraging them to return to Thomism. He does not use specific names, but the leader of the orders takes the hint. Also in 1946 (and this is usually what is cited as the origin of the term), Réginald Garrigou-Lagrange publishes an article entitled '*La nouvelle théologie où va-t-elle?*', or 'Where is the New Theology Leading Us?' The implicit answer is 'no place good'. This is the first time that the name is publically associated with these thinkers. Garrigou-Lagrange leads the opposition to *nouvelle théologie*, and in his article he portrays it as a reborn modernism that needs to be suppressed. This leads to Pope XII, in 1950, to put forward a papal encyclical called *Humani Generis*, which condemns—though without mentioning any theologians by name—certain new errors. Even though it does not mention *nouvelle théologie*, it is clearly addressing it by referring to new errors associated with the study centres at Le Saulchoir and Lyon-Fourvière. Because of the papal concerns (or rather tacit papal condemnation), there ends up being inquiries within the Jesuit and Dominican orders. This shuts things down; many of these thinkers are no longer allowed to publish. They are removed from their homes and end up travelling around from place to place.

The **third** phase is one of **Internationalization**. These ideas do not stay in France. People like Edward Schillebeeckx in the Netherlands, Rahner in Germany, Balthasar in Switzerland and Bernard Lonergan in Canada are influenced by them.

The **fourth** and final phase is *nouvelle théologie*'s **Assimilation** into Vatican II. Many of these previously censored theologians are made official advisors, and end up having an enormous influence on Vatican II. Some of them write significant parts of the documents. Neo-Scholasticism is effectively deposed as the sole official position of the Church. Bizarrely, the negative connotations of *nouvelle théologie* are transformed into positive connotations. Congar, Daniélou, de Lubac and Balthasar are all eventually made cardinals. Perhaps ironically, they were homeless for a time, but then move on to take up central roles in the most important event in Catholic theology in the twentieth century.

15.3.1 Chenu

Marie-Dominique Chenu (1895–1990) is regarded today as one of the most significant forerunners of Vatican II. He was also one of the initial figures in *nouvelle théologie*. An intensely productive scholar with a bibliography of some 1,396 works, he studied at the Angelicum in Rome—the centre for Neo-Scholastic study—and did his dissertation under Garrigou-Lagrange, who was quite impressed and wanted him to stay at the Angelicum as his assistant. Chenu, however, wanted to return to the Dominican study house from which he came: Le Saulchoir.

Chenu became the rector at Le Saulchoir from 1932 to 1942. During this time, it was located in Belgium in exile due to the anticlerical laws in France in the early twentieth century. However, the study centre was eventually allowed to return to France, in 1938. At Le Saulchoir the focus of interest was historical investigations into medieval theology—especially that of Thomas. The general ethos of thought there moved in a very different direction to both that of Chenu's teacher, Garrigou-Lagrange, and Neo-Scholasticism of the time. Scholars here were focused on studying medieval theology in its context. For example, the first course that Chenu taught when he returned was on Thomas's patristic sources. He also taught specifically on Thomas's use of earlier theologians like Augustine or Pseudo-Dionysius.

In 1937, Chenu put out a work entitled *Une école de théologie: Le Saulchoir*, which means 'A School of Theology: Le Saulchoir'. This work, which was intended to be circulated privately, is a manifesto for what the study centre is all about; it presents the vision of Le Saulchoir and its methodology. In retrospect, the methodology of this school ends up representing many of the central ideas of *nouvelle théologie*. One of the key postures that was advocated is a **methodological pluralism**—in the sense of simply being open to using different methods. They did not have a 'one-size-fits-all approach', but rather were open to appropriating new and various methods where and when they showed promise. Characteristic of *Le Saulchoir*'s vision is also a reading of **Thomas** as primarily a theologian. They see theology as Thomas's primary project, as opposed to having a distinct philosophical prolegomenon that then shifts into theology. Following on from this example, Chenu sees the work of **theology as always properly operative within the life of faith**. Theology ought not be an abstract or cerebral intellectual enterprise, but is rather something happening in the midst of a believing and worshipping community. Progress in theology is not merely intellectual progress, but it is related to one's spiritual life. The approach presented by Chenu is critical of Neo-Scholasticism and the so-called 'handbook' or 'manualist' approach in which there is a given, closed system that is passed on and designates which conclusions are acceptable from future research. Finally, the methodology of Le Saulchoir focuses on **positive** theology. It looks at the on-the-ground, real variety of faith expressions in history—expecting that Christian truth is found incarnate in the real particularities of history.

Chenu's manifesto became popular within the Dominican order. The other Dominicans read and copy it, and it ends up having a surprisingly broad reception without actually having a publisher. One of the effects of this is that it is seen as bringing Neo-Scholasticism into discredit within the Dominican order. This is an embarrassing situation inasmuch as the Dominican order is the order of Saint Thomas and is thus supposed to be on the vanguard of defending Neo-Scholasticism.

In 1938, Chenu is summoned to Rome and is reprimanded by the leaders of the Dominican order—headed up by his former teacher, Garrigou-Lagrange. They demand that the distribution of the book is stopped. The approach put forward in the little book is classified as 'modernism', and its historical approach to Thomas is seen as leading towards relativism. In 1942, this book is added to the Index of Prohibited Books, meaning that it cannot be published by Catholic publishing houses and certainly is not a book that should be read by good Catholics. Chenu was removed from his posts at Le Saulchoir as rector and as professor. He eventually taught elsewhere in Paris.

An especially influential area of Chenu's contribution to Catholic theology is in the domain of **ecclesiology**. Briefly, Chenu believes that there needs to be a much fuller integration of the laity into the life of the Church and so resists the strong clergy–laity division within the Catholic Church. One of the ways this manifests itself is that he thinks that the priesthood should be opened to daily life. In France, at this time, there was a group of what are called the 'worker-priests'—ordained priests who took jobs with common labourers in order to minister to them. In part of the 1950, encyclical *Humani Generis* is aimed at Chenu and Congar because of their support for the worker-priests. The Vatican is nervous about the rumours of possible Marxist and Communist connections with the worker-priest movement. Because of this controversy, Chenu ends up being expelled from Paris altogether by his superiors in the Dominican order in 1954. However, he returns to serve as an advisor to a bishop at Vatican II.

15.3.2 Congar

It is arguable that **Yves Marie-Joseph Congar (1904–94)** has influenced the Church more than any other twentieth-century theologian—largely because of his influence on Vatican II. A Dominican from Belgium, he studied at Le Saulchoir with Chenu as his advisor. There, he discovered the historical dimension of theology. He eventually became a professor at Le Saulchoir, while Chenu was the rector. This is largely when Le Saulchoir was located in Belgium.

During the Second World War, Congar saw combat against Nazi Germany, and was a prisoner of war for five years. He, like Chenu, is very prolific: He penned thirty books and some 1,600 articles. His driving passion is ecumenism, the unity of the Church. Symbolic of this is the manner in which he prepared for ordination as a priest: He spent time studying Thomas's commentary on John 17. John 17 became a scriptural touchstone for his ecumenical vision.

Among Congar's beliefs are that, as a precondition for ecumenism, the Church needs to reform. In fact, the Church needs to change its way of thinking about itself as having business as usual broken up by occasional punctiliar reforms. Rather, the Church should always be reforming. He believes that it should see itself as constantly in a process of reformation. This idea, however, made many Catholics uneasy. Congar sees such reform and ecumenism as a precondition for evangelism. The Church has to be unified for its message to be heard by an unbelieving culture. The divisions of the Church have seriously harmed the work of the Gospel in the world.

By the 1930s, Congar emerges as one of France's leading theologians. His focus is on ecclesiology. One of the big contributions to his work is his thinking of the Church along the model of a *communio*. He—like Chenu—emphasizes the role of the laity and the need for a stronger relation between the clergy and the laity. The work of the Church should be something that is deeply interconnected with everyday life. Congar argues that the reason behind the rampant secularization in Europe—in France in particular—is that the Church, itself tragically divided, has also fostered a division between faith, on the one hand, and the rest of life, on the other. Understandably, those who are not especially religious perceive that religion has nothing to say about the rest of life. Part of the problem, as Congar sees it here, is the overly hierarchical image of the Church. He thinks that this came about from overreaction in the Counter-Reformation. In the Catholic Church's response to the Protestant Reformation, it crystallizes into an overly authoritarian and hierarchical structure. This, in turn, contributes to a culture of unbelief, because unbelief will come about when the Church is divided. Congar lays the blame for the loss of Western culture at the feet of the Catholic Church for having hardened its division over and against the Reformation.

One of Congar's most influential books is entitled *The True and False Reform in the Church* (1950). Recognizing that this talk of reform would make Catholics uneasy (and think of Protestantism), he writes about true and false reform. True reform is reform without schism. As such, he sees the Protestant Reformation as false reform. Splitting the Church is not good reform. This book influenced Pope John XXIII and contributed to his vision for the second Vatican council.

Congar also—coming out of Le Saulchoir and broadly out of *nouvelle théologie*—perceives one of the best ways to bring about this reform is through retrieval or *ressourcement*. Part of the problem is that the defence of the tradition often ends up being a defence of relatively recent tradition. *Ressourcement* theologians want to expand the awareness of tradition in terms of the deep tradition as a resource for reform. Congar points back to the Church's own, but often neglected resources for reform.

In 1954, both Congar and Chenu support the worker-priests and are then removed from their teaching positions at Le Saulchoir by the Dominican order. Congar had published a supportive article on the worker-priest movement in 1953. This is one of the reasons that he is singled out and removed from his position. In fact, in 1954 he is not allowed to teach in any Dominican centre of study. Some theorize that the worker-priest issue is likely something of an easy excuse to deal with Congar who is making people uneasy with his talk about ecumenism.

Congar ends up moving around from place to place, living in Jerusalem and Cambridge for a time. He is eventually allowed to return to France. His homeless status affected him quite a bit on a psychological level—rejected by the family of his order, humiliated and lonely. In many ways, he was a broken man in this period—he describes himself as someone killed but still alive. It is very poignant to think of someone who spent his life working towards the unity of the Church, only to find himself ostracized by the Church.

Nevertheless, Congar and his ideas come to play an important role in Vatican II. In fact, Congar was one of the first theologians to be asked to draft some of the texts. He helped to write around half of the documents of Vatican II, and it is largely his understanding of the Church as *communio* that became a dominant picture in the documents. Many refer to Vatican II as 'Congar's Council'. In addition to his work on ecclesiology, Congar also published an influential three-volume work on the Holy Spirit in 1979 and 1980. In 1994, when he was ninety years old, he was made a cardinal.

15.3.3 Bouillard

The second 'phase' of *nouvelle théologie* is associated with the Jesuits of Lyon-Fourvière. **Henri Bouillard (1908–81)** of the Jesuit order studied at Fourvière in Lyon. He completed his PhD at the Gregorian, the Jesuit University in Rome—and then returned to Lyon-Fourvière to teach theology in 1941.

Bouillard's first influential work is *Conversion et grâce chez s. Thomas d'Aquin: Étude historique— Conversion and Grace in Saint Thomas Aquinas: Historical Study*, published in 1944. This work sets a bit of the trajectory for the Fourvière Jesuits' approach to Thomas Aquinas. Central to it is his critique of the Neo-Scholastic approach to reading Thomas. He emphasizes the necessity of understanding Thomas's historical background and situation. Bouillard sees the manual tradition as misrepresenting Thomas by reading him out of context and putting things into the text that are not there.

For Boulliard, a central disagreement with the Neo-Scholastics is over the nature of theology, which for him is not an immutable science, or a completed system, but rather a continual practice. Theology is not a collection of timeless answers to timeless questions—there are new questions and new answers need to be formulated all the time. Part of this is a Romantic impulse of realizing on a philosophical level that we have no access to truth apart from language and other historical forms. All of our human thinking is thoroughly linguistic and historical, so we should not feel surprised when we find that theology is that way as well. To the ears of many, this sounded like 'modernism'—when you start paying too much attention to historical relativity it is a slippery slope to relativism.

Bouillard argues in this work that Thomas's understanding of grace does not allow a strict division between the natural and the supernatural. The division between the natural order and the supernatural order is at the centre of the Neo-Scholastic understanding of Thomas Aquinas. Bouillard asserts that this is indeed not Thomas's understanding of grace. He states that if you look at other thinkers, this gulf was something that was created after Thomas, and then read back onto Thomas through the commentaries of the sixteenth century. There ends up being a significant controversy that is related to Bouillard and Henri de Lubac, and they are made to leave Lyon-Fourvière in 1950 and are forbidden to publish (see 15.3.5).

Bouillard was also a fairly prolific writer. Significantly, he wrote a two-volume work on Karl Barth in 1957. In this extended appreciation and dialogue with Barth, he sees him as a significant dialogue partner for Catholic theology and goes to some length dealing with and addressing the real points of contention between Barth and Catholicism. In 1967, an abbreviated version of Bouillard's work on Barth is published as *The Knowledge of God*.

15.3.4 Daniélou

Jesuit **Jean Daniélou (1905–74)** was deeply interested in the Church Fathers. After studying at Lyon-Fourvière for a time, he received doctorates from the Institut Catholique Paris, and the Sorbonne. His main area of study was Gregory of Nyssa. He is significant because he was one of the founders of the *Sources Chrétiennes* series with Henri de Lubac. In fact, the first volume of *Sources Chrétiennes* was edited by Daniélou on Gregory of Nyssa's *Life of Moses*. Daniélou also became a *Peritus*—an official expert—at Vatican II.

One of Daniélou's appraisals of the situation of Catholic theology in the earlier part of the twentieth century is relative to its relation to Catholic modernism. He believes that Catholic modernism has the right questions and worthwhile concerns, but that it ends up faltering in its answers to them. The more serious problem is that when modernism is officially rejected by the Catholic Church, the questions are made suspect. Daniélou challenges this 'throwing the baby out with the bathwater' approach of making the questions illegitimate when certain answers to the questions have been judged illegitimate.

One of the issues that Catholic modernism raises is with overly rationalistic theology. The common answer to that in modernism is agnosticism. Daniélou thought that the better direction to go is to see how the rationalistic perspective is to realize that this is a recent development in Church history. (One can see the emphasis on history here.) This kind of understanding is not broadly representative of the tradition of the Church. The rationalism of the recent tradition (Neo-Scholasticism) is an aberration, and this could only be seen by studying the longer tradition through *ressourcement*.

The other issue that modernism has is the manner in which theology is overly isolated from other disciplines. The theology at issue makes itself immune from criticism by removing itself from secular discourses. The modernist answer to this problem is, however to largely adopt the given canons of secular reason, including the most extreme conclusions of historical criticism. Daniélou perceives that the better approach is for there to be a dialogue with contemporary disciplines in theology. Theology should neither accept what other disciplines have to say wholesale nor reject them wholesale. This reflects the old Augustinian approach of spoiling the 'Egyptians'. There are things of value in the 'worldly' disciplines, but one must be discerning in approaching them.

15.3.5 de Lubac

Henri de Lubac (1896–1991) is probably the most significant of the *nouvelle* theologians. From Lyon, he joined the Lyon province of the Jesuits when—not unlike what was going on with Le Saulchoir—the French Jesuits were not allowed to operate within France and was located in England at that time. So, he spent some time in England. He was conscripted into the French military in 1914 during the First World War, and was in Flanders in 1916, witnessing some of the especially horrific action of the war. He received a head wound there, the effects of which would give him problems for the rest of his life. He ended up returning to England after 1918. As he was in preparation there, his superiors (who were not terribly impressed with him) did not think that teaching was in his future. He had no formal education beyond his Jesuit formation and was largely left to his own devices.

De Lubac ends up developing formidable resources for his future work through his own self-teaching. He reads most of Thomas Aquinas on his own (inspired by Etienne Gilson's book on Thomas). He also begins working his way through the Church Fathers systematically. De Lubac begins taking notes from the Church Fathers and ends up compiling masses and masses of research material which he uses in many of his later books. In many of his works, he is working out the insights of the research very early on in his studies. When one reads his work, this is evident in his style of writing—he uses a lot of quotations to let the tradition speak for itself.

When the Jesuits were allowed to return to France in 1926, one of the main study centres was in Lyon on the Fourvière hill—hence 'Lyon-Fourvière'. De Lubac spent a lot of time at Lyon-Fourvière, developing a friendship with fellow Jesuit Pierre Teilhard de Chardin who became quite controversial and influential outside of Catholicism as an advocate for human evolution. De Lubac taught at the theology faculty in Lyon and eventually ended up teaching in Lyon-Fourvière, along with Bouillard and Daniélou. In 1942, he was one of the co-founders of the *Sources Chrétiennes* series. He is quite critical of Neo-Scholasticism based on his long and deep study of the Church Fathers. He thinks that this is key to the recovery of the depth of the Christian tradition. One of the insights that came out of the recovery of the Christian tradition is that Neo-Scholasticism's strict division between grace and nature simply does not represent the broad tradition of the Church.

De Lubac was a member of the French Resistance during the German occupation of France in the Second World War. He was vocal (and also publishes in secret) about how National Socialism is incompatible with Christianity, especially when it came to anti-Semitism. One of his close friends and fellow Jesuit Yves de Montcheuil was caught and executed by the Gestapo.

Select works of Henri de Lubac

Catholicisme (1938, expanded edition 1947)

Corpus Mysticum (1944)

The Drama of Atheist Humanism (1944)

Le Súrnaturel: Études historiques (1946)

Exégèse médiévale (1959–65)

De Lubac writes several influential books. In his simply titled *Catholicisme* (1938; exp. edn 1947) he presents a Christian holism—a Christian view of the unity of creation and history, of the person and society, and of individual and community. Things that seem to be opposed to each other are united in Catholicism—trading on the resonance of the word 'Catholicism' as meaning universal or holding together. That is key to what Christianity is—the holding-together of the world in harmony. One of Christianity's operative ideas is that of universal community. The community of Christ in some sense embraces all. Here, he puts forward something that will come up again and again in his work—his embracing of paradoxical tension. Catholic Christianity is a series of paradoxes. The ramifications of this picture oppose, for de Lubac, any fortress mentality in Catholicism. It should be embracing and interacting with the world. Many thinkers regard *Catholicisme* as the key book to twentieth-century Catholicism—they include Congar, Balthasar, Pope John Paul II and Pope Benedict XVI.

Another important book by de Lubac is his *Corpus Mysticum* (1944). The title refers to the mystical body of Christ. It is an historical study about how the notion of the mystical body of Christ fundamentally changed over time. The mystical body of Christ in modern Catholicism is used to refer to the Church. In the patristic and medieval periods, however, the mystical body of Christ refers specifically to the Eucharist. This is an historical study of how this significant change happened.

In 1944, de Lubac also publishes a book entitled *The Drama of Atheist Humanism*. Here, he works through such figures as Marx, Comte, Feuerbach and Nietzsche, presenting an understanding of them. He shows how atheist humanism abandons part of the paradoxical harmony of humanity. In absolutizing humanity, it is actually harmful to humanity and will eventually lead to the destruction of humanity. He concludes that atheistic humanism at the end of the day is an anti-humanism.

Two years later, he publishes his landmark *Le Súrnaturel: Études historiques*. This book causes him trouble until his retirement. There in the title is 'historical studies'. It is an ad hoc work, and an editing together of a series of articles that is not terribly systematic. There is not yet a full English translation of it. Later in his life, largely because of the controversy that arose around it, he takes sections out of it and revises and expands them into two other books: *Augustinianism and Modern Theology* (1965) and *The Mystery of the Supernatural* (1967). These books expand upon some of the central ideas of *Le Súrnaturel*.

Key to de Lubac's work on the supernatural is his criticism of the Neo-Scholastic division between the natural and the supernatural. The way he approaches this critique is through historical studies of the whole notion of the supernatural—of how different understandings arose in particular historical contexts. And so he is not presenting his ideas as an innovation but as representing the more original, authentic tradition.

First, de Lubac addresses this issue in *Le Súrnaturel* through, in particular, the reception over time of Augustine's teaching on grace. (He also looks beyond Augustine to the other Church Fathers.) In de Lubac's understanding, Cajetan and Suárez, early modern Catholic thinkers, are the principal proponents of a two-tier understanding of grace and nature or, as de Lubac calls it, an 'extrinsicist' view of grace—that grace is purely external to the natural order. With Cajetan and Suárez in the sixteenth century, there is a creation of the distinction of grace on one hand and 'pure nature' on the other. What is assumed here is that nature is a closed system that is not inherently related to grace. So what grace does is make us something that we innately are not. It is a transformation of, and indeed a fundamental going-against, nature.

One of the fundamental elements that is forgotten in such an understanding, but is present in the Church Fathers and Augustine and Thomas, is that within the natural there is an innate desire for the supernatural—that for humans there is an innate desire for communion with God. A communion of grace—the beatific vision—is the end for which humans were created and which all humans desire. That is the fulfilment of humanity, and the desire for it is innate to humanity, but natural humanity cannot have a natural fulfilment of that desire. There is a natural desire for the supernatural, and that means that nature (here human nature) is not a closed system. Rather, de Lubac observes that nature and grace in the broader Catholic tradition are deeply related. The ordinary and the natural are always oriented beyond themselves and towards elevation. The Image of God in the Christian tradition is closely tied to desire, and the desire for God is revelatory of the very goal of human nature. Our orientation towards deification is the deepest part of our humanity and is not something extrinsic to us. He goes back to the Church Fathers to point out that this is the original both Greek and Latin understanding of salvation.

De Lubac brings to attention that to see God and nature as two separate orders is to make God something like the world. This is not to understand the fundamental distinction. If you misunderstand the transcendence of God, you will make the immanence of God impossible. So God is not another being that is in a different space but is transcendent. He is not a being, but is the origin of being itself or simply 'being itself'. He cannot be set in opposition to beings in a zero-sum game.

De Lubac advocates reading Thomas as following the Church Fathers on this issue such that there is a natural desire for the supernatural in Thomas's understanding of things. There is no true destiny for humans apart from the work of Christ. Now, there are texts in Thomas that seem to go to the contrary, but he explains that these are thought experiments. Thomas will talk about pure nature, but it is as a thought experiment, a conceptual abstracting of nature from a relation to grace that it never actually obtains in reality.

As mentioned, this book causes considerably controversy since *Le Súrnaturel* directly challenges one of the key understandings in Neo-Scholasticism. This division is part of what they think Thomism is. De Lubac does not help things, because in *Le Súrnaturel* there are many fairly lightly veiled insults towards the Neo-Scholastics. He is not trying to avoid a fight.

De Lubac is seen to be the leader of *nouvelle théologie*. With the publication of *Humani Generis*, de Lubac is ordered to leave Lyon in 1950 and is forbidden to teach or publish for around a decade. His books are removed from Jesuit libraries and are withdrawn from sale. *Humani Generis* effectively marks the end of his academic career. Because of this, he really never is able to present a systematic, constructive position of his own. His thought is largely gleaned from his commentaries on and his presentations of the thoughts of others.

De Lubac continues to write nevertheless. He contributes to the rehabilitation of Origen as a significant orthodox theologian. He writes several books on Buddhism. He also completes four books on Teilhard de Chardin. (Some of this is at the request of his Jesuit superiors: Teilhard comes under quite a bit of criticism for his advocacy of evolution, and de Lubac writes several books to defend him.)

Despite *humani generis*, de Lubac becomes a *peritus* at Vatican II. Along with Congar, he is one of the first to be asked by Pope John XXIII to draft some of the major texts. Ratzinger—one of the key figures in Vatican II, who eventually becomes Pope Benedict XVI—says that Vatican II moved in the direction of de Lubac's thought.

After Vatican II, de Lubac is considered to be a conservative theologian. In 1972 he helps to found the journal *Communio*, a conservative theological journal, along with Ratzinger and Balthasar. After his retirement, he spends a lot of his time working on and publishing a multi-volume work on medieval exegesis, *Exégèse medieval*. This work is about the manner of reading certain higher or spiritual senses of Scripture that are latent within the literal and how this kind of reading developed as the proper way of approaching Scripture as Scripture. De Lubac sees the interrelation between nature and grace as being connected to the interrelation between the literal meaning and spiritual reading of the text.

Sources and Further Reading

Consemius, Victor. 'The Condemnation of Modernism and the Survival of Catholic Theology'. In *The Twentieth Century: A Theological Overview*, edited by Gregory Baum, 14–26. Maryknoll, NY: Orbis, 1999.

Flynn, Gabriel. 'Introduction: The Twentieth-Century Renaissance in Catholic Theology'. In *Ressourcement: A Movement for Renewal in Twentieth-Century Catholic Theology*, edited by Gabriel Flynn and Paul D. Murray, 1–19. Oxford: Oxford University Press, 2012.

Flynn, Gabriel. 'Yves Congar'. In *Key Theological Thinkers: From Modern to Postmodern*, edited by Staale Johannes Kristiansen and Svein Rise, 213–24. Aldershot: Ashgate, 2013.

Kerr, Fergus. 'Henri de Lubac'. In *Key Theological Thinkers: From Modern to Postmodern*, edited by Staale Johannes Kristiansen and Svein Rise, 202–12. Aldershot: Ashgate, 2013.

Kerr, Fergus. *Twentieth-Century Catholic Theologians*. Oxford: Blackwell, 2007.

Komonchak, Joseph A. 'Returning from Exile: Catholic Theology in the 1930s'. In *The Twentieth Century: A Theological Overview*, edited by Gregory Baum, 35–48. Maryknoll, NY: Orbis, 1999.

Livingston, James C., and Francis Schüssler Fiorenza. *Modern Christian Thought: Volume 2, The Twentieth Century*. 2nd edn. Minneapolis, MN: Fortress Press, 2006.

Mettepenningen, Jürgen. *Nouvelle Théologie—New Theology: Inheritor of Modernism, Precursor of Vatican II*. London: T&T Clark, 2010.

Milbank, John. 'Henri de Lubac'. In *The Modern Theologians: Introduction to Christian Theology since 1918*, edited by David F. Ford with Rachel Muers, 76–91, 3rd edn. Oxford: Blackwell, 2005.

Rowland, Tracey. 'Catholic Theology in the Twentieth Century'. In *Key Theological Thinkers: From Modern to Postmodern*, edited by Staale Johannes Kristiansen and Svein Rise, 37–52. Aldershot: Ashgate, 2013.

Schreiter, Robert J. 'The Impact of Vatican II'. In *The Twentieth Century: A Theological Overview*, edited by Gregory Baum, 158–72. Maryknoll, NY: Orbis, 1999.

16

Twentieth-Century Eastern Orthodox Theology

Chapter Outline

16.1 The Russian Religious Renaissance and Exile

At the beginning of the twentieth century, Eastern Orthodox theology was largely unknown in the Western world. Nevertheless, as we have seen, Eastern Orthodoxy had its own formative engagements with modernity in the nineteenth century. The Orthodox theologians that would come to be known in the West in the early twentieth century were a fruit of the rich intellectual movement called the 'Russian Religious Renaissance'.

The Russian Religious Renaissance of late nineteenth and early twentieth centuries originated among Russian intelligentsia as an elite philosophical and literary enterprise. Around the turn of the century, the institution of the Russian Orthodox Church suffered from poor religious education. Many intellectuals lost their faith as young men. Many took up the Marxist banner of liberation only to become disillusioned with its reductionism, materialism, determinism, positivism and collectivism. They were 'early adopters' of Marxism who soured on it before the coming revolution.

In the face of such disillusionment with the nihilistic fruits of Western modernity, the Russian Religious Renaissance was a religious quest and a sense of Christian truth impinging on human life as a whole. As such, this bloom of religious sensibility found its guides in figures such as eminent nineteenth-century Russian luminaries Fyodor Dostoevsky, Leo Tolstoy and Vladimir Solovyov. It held forth the ideal of *sobornost*—a free unity of persons—that was equally opposed to 'Western' individualism and incipient Marxist authoritarianism.

This **first generation** of the Russian Religious Renaissance—including such figures as Nicholas Berdyaev, Pavel Florensky (16.2) and Sergius Bulgakov (16.3)—signalled and inspired a sea of change for many intellectuals in Moscow and St Petersburg. (There is some overlap with the literary Russian symbolists.) Most of these thinkers of the first generation—born in the 1870s–80s and beginning their careers in Russia—lost their faith for a time before returning to the Church. Building upon nineteenth-century Western ideas, they thought about Christianity through an active, creative engagement with modern culture. Many contributed to the influential volume, *The Problems of Idealism* (1902).

An extreme corner of the Russian Religious Renaissance consisted of a 'new religious consciousness' looking for a coming 'new Christianity' to supplant 'historical Christianity'. This new consciousness was something of a new age apocalyptic movement with the expectation of new revelations. This trajectory helped to paint the Renaissance to outsiders (and successors) as potentially dangerous.

In the end, the elite cultural renewal of Christian consciousness that was the Russian Religious Renaissance could not stand against the brutal and brutish populist flood of the Bolshevik Revolution. Many of these thinkers were arrested and deported. Thus, the Western world's ignorance of Eastern Orthodox theology would change drastically with the Russian Revolution and the creation of the USSR. With the Bolshevik Revolution of 1917 more than a million people left Russia. Many of those who were not banished by Lenin were imprisoned and killed by Stalin. Pavel Florensky, for example, was spared from expulsion from Russia in 1922–3 only to be arrested years later on false charges under Stalin, sent to Siberia and ordered to be executed by a secret tribunal. In 1922–3 many of the leading intellectual lights of Russia were fired from their academic posts, especially religious philosophers, and were expelled from Russia—most leaving in 1923 on what came to be called the 'philosophy steamer'. Because of these events, early-twentieth-century Orthodox theology is mainly the product of a diaspora—of Russians outside of Russia—often Russian émigrés in Paris and some who then moved on to the United States.

The **second generation** of the Russian Religious Renaissance—born in the 1890s–1900s and active in the mid-1920s–30s—left Russia as young people. Unlike the first generation, the second generation—including figures like Georges Florovsky (16.4) and Vladimir Lossky (16.5)—was more of a conservative defence of Orthodoxy against modernizing tendencies. Rebelling in a sense against previous generation's 'modernism', these figures acted more as gate-keepers. While this second generation would come to be entitled 'Neo-Patristic', both generations of the Russian Religious Renaissance entailed a rediscovering of the Church Fathers—though they would have different understandings of how to appropriate/follow the foundational work of the fathers. Orthodox theology for much of the remainder of the twentieth century was strongly shaped by the second generation.

From its roots in the nineteenth century towards an increasing crystallization in the Russian Religious Renaissance in the early twentieth century, modern Eastern Orthodox theology consistently identified itself vis-a-vis its understanding of the West. The 'East' and 'West' are often presented in monolithic terms—with the 'West' being individualistic, rational/positivistic, anthropocentric, egalitarian and legalistic while the 'East' is seen as communitarian, intuitive/mystical, theocentric, hierarchical and personal. It seems, especially with Russian émigrés in Paris, that when the Orthodox referred to Western or more specifically Roman Catholic theology they were usually thinking of the then-ascendant Neo-Thomism/Neo-Scholasticism.

| 'West' | individualistic | rational/positivistic | anthropocentric | egalitarian | legalistic |
| 'East' | communitarian | intuitive/mystical | theocentric | hierarchical | personal |

16.2 Pavel Florensky

Pavel Florensky (1882–1937) was a Renaissance man: a philosopher, a theologian, a man of letters, a scientist and a priest. A prolific author, Florensky was not expelled from Russia in the 1920s because of his usefulness as a scientist. Nevertheless, he continued to wear the cassock and cross while he lectured.

His magnum opus (a revision of his master's thesis) is *The Pillar and Ground of the Truth* (1914)—a grand and strange work ostensibly on the nature of reason. Its critical edge is a rejection of the reductionistic materialism of the reigning scientism—the 'knowledge of physics'. In chapters presented as a series of letters to a friend, Florensky expounds on paradox (or 'antimony'). Presenting Church Fathers as holding together contradictions in theology, Florensky held the paradoxes of the Christian faith—supremely the Trinity—as the highest and most fundamental truths. The attaining of this truth is presented as work of ascesis, a work of the spiritual life—a transformation. Philosophy, theology and spiritual discipline are joined such that our desire for truth is fulfilled in the experience of the Triune God. Also, in this work Florensky included a chapter on Sophia displaying his dependence upon, and creative (and more theologically oriented) appropriation of, Solovyov's sophiology. Florensky and Bulgakov became friends and shared such a creative taking-up of Solovyov's ideas.

In his later work, Florensky contributes to a modern Orthodox theology of the icon. Otherwise than the seemingly 'realistic' ego-centric linear perspective that Florensky sees as a product of the Renaissance in the West, icons work with a reverse perspective. Whereas in modern linear perspective the Western rational ego would lay claim to mastery of the world of that which is depicted, with an icon the movement reverses: another world is disclosed and the subject is drawn in. Thus the icon traverses the boundary between heaven and earth, the spiritual and the physical. In 1933, Florensky was arrested. After years in a prison camp, he was executed (likely in 1937) by the Bolsheviks to be buried in a mass grave with tens of thousands of other victims.

16.3 Sergius Bulgakov

Florensky's friend, Sergius Bulgakov (1871–1944), was a Marxist professor at Moscow University when he began to make his way back to Christianity. Under the influence of Dostoevsky and Solovyov, he came to see the emptiness of Marxism and its materialism. He was eventually ordained to the priesthood and worked for ecclesial reform in Russia. Bulgakov was fired from his post at the University of Moscow in 1918 and was one of the religious philosophers deported from Russia in 1922–3. Bulgakov became one of the earliest and most well-established theologians among the Russians newly-arrived to Paris in the 1920s. He was one of the co-founders of St Sergius Orthodox Theological Institute in 1925 and was (along with Florovsky—who was invited to participate by Bulgakov) intimately involved in the ecumenical Fellowship of St Alban and St Sergius. (His involvement in the ecumenical enterprise was manifest in his ill-fated proposal of an 'Episcopally Blessed Intercommunion' between the Anglicans and the Orthodox.) In the 1930s, in part due to Vladimir Lossky and Georges Florovsky's vocal opposition, his teaching on Sophia was condemned by the Moscow Patriarchate and the allied Church in Exile (which became the Russian Orthodox Church Outside Russia [ROCOR])—both jurisdictions to which he did not belong. He continued to be supported by his Metropolitan in Paris, the Exarch Evlogy (who had left the jurisdiction of the [in his mind, compromised] Moscow Patriarchate to serve under the Patriarchate of Constantinople). In 1944, Sergius Bulgakov died of throat cancer.

Bulgakov, perhaps characteristically for a thinker of the first generation of the Russian Religious Renaissance, occupies something of a middle ground between his nineteenth-century predecessor, Solovyov and patristic emphasis of the second generation of the Russian Religious Renaissance. While he can be seen to follow and to develop Solovyov's thought, Bulgakov possessed a more expansive knowledge of the Church Fathers and the theological tradition more generally. Yet Bulgakov read the Fathers otherwise than seeking a single 'mind of the fathers' (as characterized by the 'Neo-Patristic Synthesis'). Bulgakov carried on a reflective dialogue with patristic theology—which he viewed as itself a complex and unfolding dialogue. For example, *The Lamb of God* begins with a more appreciative chapter on the heretic Apollonaris and goes on to give a more critical reading of the more orthodox Cyril of Alexandria. Like Solovyov, Bulgakov also sought a constructive engagement with the theological and philosophical currents of the West. Here he saw that using the Fathers as one's sole resource would leave the contemporary theologian with the task of addressing many issues that they did not. Bulgakov's constructive spirit was manifest in his view of how—as the Church Fathers utilized Greek philosophy to think through the faith in their day—the theologian today could differently represent and express dogma using ideas from the varying philosophies of the day.

Bulgakov's magnum opus, written later in his life, is his great trilogy: *On Godmanhood* or *On Divine Humanity* (here reminiscent of Solovyov's famous lectures). This trilogy consists of a work on Christology (*The Lamb of God* [1933]), a work on Pneumatology (*The Comforter* [1936]), and a work on Ecclesiology and Eschatology (*The Bride of the Lamb* [1945, published posthumously]). The broad vision presented is that of the Son and the Spirit revealing the Father to humanity and drawing us into communion (like the two hands of the Father in Irenaeus's picture). The result is the Church as the Bride of the Lamb filled with the Spirit being drawn to the Father through the Son and the Spirit. A central and deeply informing site for this communion and drawing-together is the Eucharistic liturgy—the meeting of heaven and earth.

A key way of thinking of the relation between God and humanity (indeed creatures generally) for Bulgakov was to be found in his controversial understanding of Sophia. Sophia, the creative wisdom of God, for Bulgakov is a 'between' (in some ways comparable to the Western discussion of 'analogy'). Sophia is at once uncreated wisdom—the creation-ward face of God, that in God is oriented towards creation, the humanity of God—and created wisdom—the God-ward face of creation, that in creation is oriented towards God. Sophia names this 'between' of Divine Humanity or Godmanhood. Bulgakov's Sophiology was viewed, as we will see, by many as compromising a proper sense of divine transcendence—of the fundamental difference or distinction between the Creator and the creation. In fact, Sophiology declined after Bulgakov's death (in 1944)—though it would have something of a revival in the later part of the twentieth century.

16.4 Georges Florovsky and the Neo-Patristic Synthesis

Archpriest Georges Florovsky (1893–1979) was likely the most well-known and arguably the most influential Eastern Orthodox theologian of the twentieth century. Florovsky was born in what is presently southern Ukraine to an academic family. (His father Vasily Florovsky held various teaching and administrative positions.) After his education, Georges taught briefly in Odessa before leaving Russia in 1920 for Sofia in Bulgaria and then Prague before ending up in Paris in 1926 to teach at the St Sergius Orthodox Theological Institute. After spending the Second World War in Yugoslavia, Florovsky moved to the United States in 1948 to serve as professor and then dean (from 1950) of St Vladimir's Orthodox Theological Seminary in New York (1948–55). He would later teach at Harvard (1956–64) and Princeton (1964–72).

As a sickly and bookish young man, Florovsky was inspired by the Russian Religious Renaissance (and related) thinkers such as Solovyov, Berdyaev, Florensky and Bulgakov. He was deeply influenced by Florensky's *The Pillar and Ground of the Truth*. ('Florensky' and 'Florovsky' can be easy to mix up.) While in Prague (before he moved to Paris in 1926), Bulgakov was his confessor. Yet Florovsky came to be troubled by the mystical and Sophiological sides of the Russian Religious Renaissance. Turning against Sophiology and more exclusively towards the Fathers, Florovsky came to have a dominant and polemical voice in the second generation of the Russian Religious Renaissance. For instance, while he wrote about Solovyov throughout his career, he shifted from a positive regard for Solovyov to renouncing him in the 1920s—forming his own perspective in contradistinction to Solovyov. Such a fundamentally polemical edge would indeed extend throughout his career—a partisan orthodoxy-as-opposed-to-heterodoxy stance that cast a long shadow in twentieth-century orthodox theology. (In fact, it seems Florovsky had a lifelong pattern of growing hostile towards and breaking with whatever intellectual community he was part of.)

Throughout his career, Florovsky wrote historical works—largely on the Church Fathers and Church History—intent on making contemporary theological points/interventions. His magnum opus is *Ways of Russian Theology* (1937). The critical side of this work focused on what Florovsky termed as the **pseudomorphosis** of modern Russian theology. The 'pseudomorphosis'—transforming-into-something-false—of modern Russian theology for Florovsky consisted of its 'Babylonian captivity' to external thought forms be it with the Slavophils, Solovyov or twentieth-century Sophiology. As part of his broader rejection of much of the Russian Religious Renaissance, Florovsky viewed Solovyov's dabbling in Gnosticism, Kabbalah and non-Christian mysticism with deep suspicion. This distortion was due, for Florovsky, to Russia's lack of access to the Fathers and contagion from Latin Western ideas. This was aggravated in the nineteenth century by German Idealism—a twisted root that needed to be removed if Russian theology were to return to health. Sophiology in Bulgakov and Solovyov before him was guilty of replacing Christ with Sophia under the spell of foreign philosophies and so exemplified Russian theology's Western captivity. Because of its corrupting influence, Florovsky set 'theology' over against 'philosophy' set over against the 'theology'—here meaning hewing close to the language of the Church Fathers (see below on the 'Neo-Patristic Synthesis').

The positive proposal that Florovsky presents in *Ways of Russian Theology* is that of what would come to be called the **Neo-Patristic Synthesis.** This return to the 'land of the Fathers'—as the proper, faithful way forward for orthodox theology after being freed from 'Western captivity' (seen supremely in the atheist triumph in Russia)—was also styled 'Christian Hellenism'. This struck explicitly against the principally Protestant anti-Hellenism (beginning with Harnack and influential throughout the twentieth century) which rejected the Church Fathers as compromised due to their being infected with the foreign influence of Greek philosophy. The perhaps ironic rejection of recent philosophical theology (such as that of Sophiology) in favour of the classical philosophical theology of 'Christian Hellenism' was justified for Florovsky insofar as Byzantine Christianity was the ancient root of historic Christianity and was not to be abandoned or bypassed through the adoption of later philosophical ideas. The mind of the Church Fathers functioned as an authority to advocate and maintain a unified pan-Orthodox identity (against the background of the Russian émigrés) insistent that the Orthodox Church is the true and undivided Church while all others have departed from it.

Florovsky himself never did more than provide programmatic sketches or basic outlines of such a Neo-Patristic Synthesis. Nevertheless, Florovsky presented several key themes of the Neo-Patristic Synthesis. Indeed, he sometimes simply identified or at least summed up such a synthesis with Chalcedonian Christology. The emphasis on **mystery** and apophasis in the Chalcedonian definition of 451 is present in the negations of misunderstandings framing the mystery of the Incarnation. The focus on the person of Christ (along with the doctrine of the Trinity) also lent to the particular emphasis on **personhood** in Neo-Patristic theology. The Christian affirmation of the centrality of life and activity of Christ entailed an affirmation of the significance of the free actions of persons in history—as opposed to either a timeless philosophical teaching or what Florovsky saw as a kind of evolutionary or teleological determinism in Bulgakov. Finally, Florovsky focused on the doctrine of **creation**—the stark contrast between God and the world as dependent, contingent and gift. It is this contingency of the world as presented in the doctrine of *creatio ex nihilo* that

Florovsky saw as being threatened by Sophiology—insomuch as Sophia seemed to be both created and uncreated.

Under Florovsky's leadership, the Neo-Patristic theology of the critical second generation of the Russian Religious Revolution would come to be the dominant paradigm for Eastern Orthodox theology for most of the twentieth century. As mentioned above, the emphasis on the Church Fathers explicitly associated with the so-called 'Neo-Patristic Synthesis' of this second generation in many ways paralleled and benefitted from the movement of Roman Catholic *ressourcement* happening at roughly the same time in France (though it must be said that the Catholic *ressourcement* theologians—as presenting and reflecting upon the whole wealth of the Church Fathers East and West—had a broader sense of 'the Fathers' and the tradition than either the more dogmatic programmes of Catholic Neo-Scholasticism [as Neo-Thomist] and Orthodox Neo-Patristic theology (as Neo-Palamite after Lossky's influence) would allow.

16.5 Vladimir Lossky

Vladimir Lossky (1903–58) was ten years younger than Florovsky. He came from St Petersburg—by way of Prague (like Florovsky)—to arrive in Paris in 1924. There he studied the Western Middle Ages—the mysticism of Meister Eckhart in particular. Though they shared many ideas, Florovsky and Lossky moved in different circles and did not work together. Unlike Florovsky, Lossky—being of a different age—was more on the periphery of the Russian Religious Renaissance; he was not a part of it before leaving it like Florovsky. Florovsky was closer to Vladimir's father—the philosopher Nicolai Lossky (who helped bring Florovsky to St Vladimir's in the United States after the Second World War). Nevertheless, Florovsky's message found fertile soil in Lossky's thought and work.

Lossky's principal work, *The Mystical Theology of the Eastern Church* (*Essai sur la Théologie Mysterique de l'Église d'Orient*), was based on a course of lectures given in 1941–2. While it was the only book he published during his lifetime, it was the nearest thing there is to a positive presentation of the Neo-Patristic Synthesis. In Lossky's work, the Neo-Patristic Synthesis had a central place for the thought of fourteenth-century theologian St Gregory Palamas and the apophatic theology of Pseudo-Dionysius (though Athanasius, the Cappadocian Fathers [Basil the Great, Gregory Nazianzus, and Gregory of Nyssa] and Maximus the Confessor are significant as well).

Pseudo-Dionysius's apophatic theology sought to approach the mystery of God by way of negation—and saw this as more fundamental than kataphatic or affirmative theology. True knowledge of God is not expressed in language but consists in the experience of God—thus mystical theology cultivates the capacity of withholding from forming concepts of God and so not conforming God to our concepts. An especially useful way of maintaining the mystery of God and guarding personal experience of that which transcends concepts is the embracing of opposites (supremely in the Incarnation, but also in Trinity, creation and redemption) in such a way that one points beyond human understanding (an insight that is actually central for the more Sophianic Florensky). This orientation towards mystical union with God is likewise to be experienced and celebrated in the sacraments.

It is in this context of mystical and apophatic theology that Lossky locates the contribution of Gregory Palamas. Central for Palamas is the distinction between God's unknowable/incommunicable essence (God's *ousia*) and His revealed/communicable energies (*energia*): His transcendent essence and His immanent energies. God's energy was understood in terms of personal expression and action in the world. True knowledge, that is experience, of God as participation in divine energies. After Lossky, Neo-Partistic theology was increasingly Neo-Palamite—drawing on not only patristic sources but medieval Byzantine sources as well.

During the 'Sophia Affair', Lossky publicly opposed Bulgakov. In 1935 Lossky was asked by the Moscow Patriarchate to provide a report on Bulgakov's teaching. His report saw Bulgakov's Sophiology as collapsing the distinction between created and uncreated as deterministic and overly beholden to German Idealism. Bulgakov's Sophiology was found to be heretical by the Holy Synod of the Russian Church largely due to Lossky's report. As a result, Lossky is shunned by the St Sergius Institute; this in turn spurred him on to start the competing Institute of St Denis in 1945.

16.6 Third Generation and Beyond

16.6.1 Alexander Schmemann

What could be called the third generation of the Russian Religious Renaissance were to some degree shaped by Florovsky's Neo-Patristic vision and its antipathy towards Sophiology. (Of the three singular figures in this section, the widely-influential John Meyendorff fits this characterization best.) This third phase would hold a key place in the Orthodox theological discussion from the Second World War to the end of the twentieth century.

Fr Alexander Schmemann (1921–83) came from a Russian family that moved to Paris when he was a child. While he was a student of Bulgakov, for whom he had a high regard—he was wary of Sophiology. Schmemann joined Florovsky in the founding of St Vladimir's Orthodox Seminary in the United States where he taught church history. He succeeded Florovsky as dean of St Vladimir's and would serve there until his death in 1983. Though he joined Florovsky in America at St Vladimir's, he was not closely aligned with the desire for a Neo-Patristic (or Neo-Palamite) synthesis. He saw a general sense of decline after Constantine insofar as the church focused less on communal participation and more on individual mystical experience—especially in monasticism. (He saw Pseudo-Dionysius as being a significant influence in this regard.)

Schmemann is best known for his contributions to liturgical theology. His theology (like that of Bulgakov) is a holistic theological vision grounded in the liturgy—a theology that arises from experience as much as ideas. This approach is presented in his doctoral dissertation from 1959 published as *Introduction to Liturgical Theology* and his popular book, *For the Life of the World* (1963). In accord with the mystical emphasis of Eastern Orthodox theology, Schmemann saw a close tie between theology and worship such that liturgy opens up and reveals a different dimension of life and the world. Eucharist, in particular, reveals the purpose of creation: the presence of the kingdom of God, communion with God and sharing in God's life. It locates the human being's place as receiving all things—the world—and offering them back to God in thanksgiving.

Schmemann contributed to the liturgical movement originating in Paris in the 1940s and 1950s and flowing from Catholic *Ressourcement* through Vatican II (which Schmemann attended as an observer) and onward. Schmemann saw the liturgical movement as an awakening to Orthodox sensibilities and insights beyond the confines of Eastern Orthodoxy. Indeed, Schmemann's work has been influential beyond the Orthodox world in Roman Catholicism and Anglo-Catholicism—especially in the United States.

16.6.2 John Meyendorff

Fr John Meyendorff (1926–92) was born in Paris the son of Russian parents. He was taught at St Vladimir's Orthodox Seminary in the United States and eventually became dean following Fr Alexander Schmemann. Meyendorff's *Byzantine Theology* has been influential in introducing the broader English-speaking world to the Orthodox tradition. Both Meyendorff and Schmemann played key parts in founding the Orthodox Church of America (which is … one of the Orthodox Churches in America … it's complicated).

He would follow Lossky in seeing Neo-Patristic theology as being the Neo-Palamite. He wrote several works on—including a popular introduction to—the work of Gregory Palamas and also made available some of his writings. Meyendorff saw Palamas something like how some Neo-Scholastic Catholic thinkers' saw Thomas: as a theologian of particularly 'modern' relevance—as presenting a kind of religious existentialism in his emphases on participation with the divine energies and holistic mysticism.

Meyendorff spurred a greater interest in Palamas while cementing the Neo-Palamite character of much (though not all) of the Neo-Patristic movement.

16.6.3 Dumitru Stăniloae

Fr Dumitru Stăniloae (1903–93) taught at the Theological Institute in Bucharest, Romania. He was quite prolific—writing hundreds of academic articles and even more journalistic articles of cultural analysis. He laboured over decades to produce an expanded Romanian translation (in 12 volumes) of the Greek *Philokalia* in addition to other translations of the Fathers. His great original work was an extensive, three-volume, dogmatic theology—likely the grandest example of the Neo-Patristic project—his *Orthodox Dogmatic Theology* (1978).

Stăniloae's theology is something of a correction to an orthodox over-emphasis (in reaction to Sophiology) on the transcendence of the Creator. He focuses rather on a 'constant overlap' between heaven and earth such that the Creator is operative through creation, present in the world through symbols and manifest in the experience of the sacraments. By meditating on the presence and action of God in Christ through the Church, Stăniloae sees no discrete division between the natural and the supernatural. The world is a means of divine revelation and communion insomuch as it, the cosmos, has a telos of deification; the 'arc' from creation to consummation encompasses the 'arc' of fall and redemption. Stăniloae's grand dogmatic theology is a pre-eminent example of the reintegration of God, humanity and the world in something like the classical synthesis in a characteristically Orthodox idiom.

16.6.4 Some Recent Orthodox Theology

In the past few several decades, there has been a significant shift in Orthodox theology. More Orthodox theologians are engaged in dialogue across ecclesial boundaries. At the same time other Christians—Catholics and Protestants, perhaps especially Anglicans—have come to embrace the treasures of the Eastern tradition as part of the great common tradition of classical Christian thought. There is a broader recognition of a common Christian identity—East and West. Beginning especially with Schmemann, and more recently with theologians like John Behr and David Bentley Hart, it is evident that Orthodox thinkers in the United Kingdom and United States have had enough of a reflective distance to enable a more robust and fertile (and less caricatur-ish) interaction between East and West. There has been a decided shift in the centre of gravity to the United States. More recent Orthodox theology is less rooted in ethnicity, less the product of the diaspora and more produced by converts.

Substantively, there has been a shift of attention from romantic idealization and assumed consensus of 'the mind of the Fathers' towards seeing the rich tapestry of the Church Fathers in their particularity. This critique or revision of Florovsky's methodology reflects more of Bulgakov's approach who read the Fathers as somewhat less-than-monolithic. For example, his *Lamb of God* begins with an appreciative perspective on the heretic Apollonaris and a more critical reading of Cyril of Alexandria. There has also been a revival of interest in Sophiology beginning in the 1990s. The once recessed voices of Bulgakov and Florensky again came to the fore. Recent theology reflects this kind of engagement—a reflective dialogue with patristic theology with a greater awareness of a need for creative and constructive engagement with more recent ideas.

Sources and Further Reading

Berger, Calinic. 'Dumitru Stăniloae'. In *Key Theological Thinkers: From Modern to Postmodern*, edited by Staale Johannes Kristiansen and Svein Rise, 393–402. Aldershot: Ashgate, 2013.

Gallaher, Brandon. 'Georges Florovsky'. In *Key Theological Thinkers: From Modern to Postmodern*, edited by Staale Johannes Kristiansen and Svein Rise, 353–70. Aldershot: Ashgate, 2013.

Gavrilyuk, Paul L. *Georges Florovsky and the Russian Religious Renaissance*. Oxford: Oxford University Press, 2013.

Gavrilyuk, Paul L. 'Vladimir Lossky's Reception of Georges Florovsky's Neo-Patristic Theology'. In *A Celebration of Living Theology: A Festschrift in Honour of Andrew Louth*, edited by Justin A Mihoc and Leonard Aldea. London: Bloomsbury, 2014.

Hareide, Sigurd. "Alexander Schmemann". Kotiranta, Matti. "Vladimir Lossky". In *Key Theological Thinkers: From Modern to Postmodern*, edited by Staale Johannes Kristiansen and Svein Rise, 403–14. Aldershot: Ashgate, 2013.

Kotiranta, Matti. 'Vladimir Lossky'. In *Key Theological Thinkers: From Modern to Postmodern*, edited by Staale Johannes Kristiansen and Svein Rise, 379–91. Aldershot: Ashgate, 2013.

Louth, Andrew. 'French *Ressourcement* Theology and Orthodoxy: A Living Mutual Relationship?' In Ressourcement: *A Movement for Renewal in Twentieth-Century Catholic Theology*, edited by Gabriel Flynn and Paul D. Murray. Oxford: Oxford University Press, 2012.

Louth, Andrew. *Modern Orthodox Thinkers: From the Philokalia to the Present*. Downers Grove, IL: IVP Academic, 2015.

Papanikolaou, Aristotle. 'Orthodox Theology in the Twentieth Century'. In *Key Theological Thinkers: From Modern to Postmodern*, edited by Staale Johannes Kristiansen and Svein Rise, 53–63. Aldershot: Ashgate, 2013.

17

Conservative Protestants in America

17.1 Fundamentalism

Coming out of the nineteenth century, the shift that is going on in the modern milieu is going to bring about some strong reactions. It is becoming more apparent that the physical universe is a vaster, older place—a place to get lost in. It has an unsettling effect that makes many more traditionally minded people uneasy. One way of thinking of Fundamentalism is as a reaction to this uneasiness and as an attempt to hold on more rigidly to something that is easily available. That often is literal biblical details that you can trust in and that you can hold on to as being totally trustworthy. As there are developing understandings in geology and biology—in terms of cosmic and biological evolution—there is also a greater rigidity in holding to a 'literal understanding' of the first couple of chapters of Genesis. (A more common understanding throughout the history of Christian interpretation is a multi-level way of seeing the meaning of the text in different types and analogies.)

Charles Taylor in *A Secular Age* refers to the '**Age of Mobilization**' as lasting from the nineteenth century to the middle of the twentieth. There is a transition going on here, in which religion, especially in America, is not centred on ecclesial structures. Where there is organization, it is often anti-hierarchical. The organization happens in more of a democratic groundswell and so is best thought of in terms of '**movements**' than established 'churches'. In this period, there is also a greater self-conscious awareness of being one among many movements. There are many different Christian groups in America, and they are very much aware of each other—even if they are defining themselves over against their neighbours. This is all happening in the context of various revivals and the Great Awakenings in America and on the American frontier. Whereas there were once more formalized churches defining people's identities, now particular Christian identities are seen in terms of **denominations**, which have a greater awareness that there are many different and somewhat co-existing Christian groups, regardless of their opinions of each other.

In many ways, Fundamentalism and Evangelicalism will mirror the eighteenth- and nineteenth-century Awakenings (be they Pietist or Revivalist). At the centre of all of these lie Bible study and personal holiness. However, some of the significant forces that come into play in the later nineteenth and the early twentieth centuries in American Christianity are related to a couple of big issues. German higher criticism or historical criticism of the Bible casts doubt on the most literalist understandings of Scripture. Higher criticism presented Scripture, as we have it, as developing over time, with reports of events often reflecting more of the later concerns of the authors or editors than actually presenting a historically accurate record of what is depicted. The second challenge is the emergence of Darwinian evolution—particularly as it is seen as a challenge to a 'literal understanding' of the first chapters of Genesis.

In the period from 1880 to 1920, we have divisions happening within several different denominations in America over biblical criticism. Several denominations are holding heresy trials, usually for professors at their seminaries for accepting these kinds of approaches to Scripture. Often there are divisions, with one group splitting off from a denomination and forming yet another.

A lot of this development in America is centred in Presbyterianism. Conservative Presbyterianism, in particular, has a strong reaction to the historical–critical approach to the Bible. In 1910, there is a meeting of the Presbyterian General Assembly in which they affirm what comes to be called the 'five fundamentals'. These become the common tenets of Fundamentalism (though there are often additions regarding pre-millennial eschatology). It should be noted that most of these positions are rejected by the dominant Ritschlian theologians of the day in Germany.

The 1910 Presbyterian General Assembly's "Five Fundamentals"

Verbal, Plenary Inerrancy of Scripture

The Deity of Jesus

The Virgin Birth of Jesus

Substitutionary Atonement

The Physical Resurrection and Bodily Return of Jesus

The first and foremost is the verbal, plenary inerrancy of Scripture. The latter is without error in all of the parts ('plenary') down to the very words themselves ('verbal'). All of the rest of the 'fundamentals' follow on from this one. These become the five common fundamentals that are defended over and against those who would deny them. These are fundamental theological dogmas that need to be defended against the ascendant theological establishment in Germany.

As previously stated (see 8.4.1), the faculty of Princeton Theological Seminary proves very influential for American Christianity. The inerrantist Presbyterian faculty there produces a series of pamphlets entitled *The Fundamentals* which defend traditional understandings of Scripture. This is another source of where 'Fundamentalism' comes from—it reflects the ideas presented in these pamphlets.

By the mid-1920s, various groups which align themselves with these kinds of pamphlets are trying to block the teaching of evolution in public schools in America. A famous flashpoint here is the Scopes trial of 1925, in which those who are trying to prevent evolution from being taught in schools lose. By the time we get into the middle of the 1920s, the Fundamentalists have failed, by and large, to take control of education and broader Christian bodies. They are usually going to be on the losing end of battles over the control of denominations, seminaries, missionary boards and so on. By the time it gets to this stage, Fundamentalism is largely going to have more of an isolationist mentality—withdrawing from the apostate, worldly 'Christian' groups into the fortresses of the elect.

When it comes to the beliefs of Fundamentalism in America, there are deep roots in nineteenth-century Princeton theology (Presbyterian, Calvinist). A significant figure here is **J. Gresham Machen (1881–1937)**. A Presbyterian and a student of B. B. Warfield at Princeton, he eventually teaches New Testament at Princeton and is regarded as one of the leaders in Fundamentalism. While he is there, Princeton Seminary is reorganized to be more open theologically, and not the exclusively Calvinist seminary that it had been hitherto. After this occurs, Machen leaves Princeton and founds **Westminster Theological Seminary** in 1927. In 1936, he later leads a group of Presbyterians in breaking off from the broader denomination to found another group, the Orthodox Presbyterian Church.

Fundamentalism should be seen as coming into being as one dialectical pole in the so-called **Fundamentalist–Modernist Conflict**. It is an oppositional group which defines itself in opposition to 'modernist' or 'liberal' apostate versions of Christianity. Machen's initial approach is to force the liberals out of the Presbyterian Church. Thus, the Fundamentalist perspective is stridently polemical and, ultimately not apologetic. They are not trying to convince liberals that they are wrong; they are trying to smoke them out and defeat them. They want to take control of the various ecclesial entities or seminaries and kick out the people who believe the 'wrong' things. The Fundamentalists largely fail at this. Instead, they go off and form their own groups.

Another key aspect is that of **eschatology**—specifically **pre-millennial dispensationalism**. This is deeply engrained in American Fundamentalism. **John Nelson Darby (1800–1882)**, a member of the Plymouth Brethren, is a significant pioneer of pre-millennial dispensationalism. The Bible of choice for pre-millennial dispensationalism is the *Scofield Reference Bible*. It is the King James Version of the Bible with extensive notes by Cyrus Scofield, first published in 1909. It is a study Bible that interprets Scripture in the notes through the gloss of the historical–eschatological framework of dispensationalism. It is a popular-selling study Bible, even today.

Dispensationalism holds that there are between three and eight (depending on the group) different 'dispensations' in history—that is, different ways that God has chosen to deal with humanity. In common with most of the versions is a distinction between the Mosaic covenant of the Old Testament, the dispensation of the Church, and the coming eschatological dispensation(s), including some version of the millennium—the thousand-year reign of Christ on Earth.

The people considering themselves Fundamentalists are going to be strongly influenced by this kind of eschatological view, and in this they are going to differ from the earlier Princeton theologians. Another aspect of early-twentieth-century Fundamentalism that differs from nineteenth-century Princeton theology is its strident anti-intellectualism. The academy has shown itself to be apostate, and its primary approach to problems in the Church is separation and schism. There is no posture of apologetic engagement with those with whom it disagrees.

Between the two world wars, American Fundamentalism gets sidelined. Followers lose control of most of the denominations and seminaries, thus losing face in the broader culture. 'Fundamentalism' becomes a pejorative term—followers are the butt of jokes in broader American culture. In the 1930s, they largely withdraw into independent churches and smaller denominations. By the 1940s, there is significant numeric decline in fundamentalist groups—save for some important exceptions, such as the Southern Baptists and the Pentecostals. They also have a definite influence on the Lutheran Church, Missouri Synod.

17.2 Evangelicalism

Evangelicalism, sometimes called Neo-Evangelicalism, is difficult to talk about because it does not have a formal structure. In fact, this lack of formality is characteristic of it. Evangelicalism can be identified as a loose network of personalities and also as a particular kind of culture. Para-church organizations are also influential as the organs of identity for Evangelicalism—often missions organizations.

Evangelicalism is also associated with various organizations like the NAE (the National Association of Evangelicals), or the ETS (the Evangelical Theological Society), but also with smaller para-church organizations like Youth for Christ, Campus Crusade for Christ or Worldvision. Evangelicalism is also associated with certain schools and publications. The more prominent schools include Trinity Evangelical School, Fuller Theological Seminary and Wheaton College; the most important publication is *Christianity Today*.

Here, we briefly present some of the key figures and personalities in Evangelicalism. Intellectual **Carl F. H. Henry (1913–2003)** criticizes the separatism and anti-intellectualism of Fundamentalism. As one of the early and outspoken leaders in Evangelicalism, he helps to frame it as distinct from Fundamentalism. Evangelicalism, for Henry, should be apologetic, making its case to the broader culture and not giving up on it. Henry wants to achieve something similar to Karl Barth at a time when Barth is being recognized as a theological force in America. He wants to present the Gospel as relevant to modern men and women. This is a consciously evangelistic posture.

Another key figure is **Billy Graham (1918–2018)** who begins his evangelistic career in 1949. Both Henry and Graham contribute to the founding of *Christianity Today* as an organ representing the perspective that they want to bring forward. Again, this is an evangelistic posture, reaching out to the broader culture.

Harold Ockenga (1905–85) is the first president of the National Association of Evangelicals and also helps to found Fuller Theological Seminary. Fuller's intentions are to represent no one denomination but rather a broader evangelical coalition and the broader ethos of conservative Christianity in America as oriented towards reaching out to the culture.

John Edward Carnell (1919–67) is one of the foremost figures in Evangelicalism to contribute to apologetics. Instead of trying to root out the liberal heretics, he wants to address their critiques and concerns. He becomes president of Fuller Theological Seminary from 1954 to 1959.

Figure 17.1 Graham.

Courtesy of the Library of Congress. (No known restrictions on publication.)

Another significant figure associated with Evangelicalism is **Francis Schaeffer (1912–84)**. From the 1960s to 1980s, he is a defining personality for many evangelicals. For a time much of his activity is centred on a retreat in Switzerland called L'Abri.

Finally, **C. S. Lewis (1893–1963)**, although himself not an evangelical but beloved by evangelicals, is worthy of mention. Lewis, a British convert to Anglicanism, writes many hugely popular apologetic works, such as *Mere Christianity* (1952). In it, he makes a case for a basic Christianity apart from any particular sectarian boundaries to those outside of Christianity. His writings are highly influential among Evangelicals even today.

Beyond identifiable personalities, there is often no clear delineation marking an 'inside' and 'outside' of Evangelicalism. (Though this has not kept many from regularly taking upon themselves the onerous task of letting people know, they have departed from its amorphous boundaries.) If Evangelicalism is anything in an organizational sense it is a coalition—and a rather loose coalition at that—and this is intentional. Early on, there are many conservative Christians who are sympathetic to Fundamentalism's beliefs but put off by its overly polemical fortress- or separatist-mentality. They think this indeed defeats the mission of Christianity to share the Gospel with the broader culture. They believe that a more acceptable name to talk about themselves and the kind of Christians they are is as 'evangelical'; they wanted to evangelize. There is a sense in which Evangelicalism here is a Fundamentalism that has become self-critical.

Evangelicalism is more than Fundamentalism with a new paintjob however. The evangelicals reject Fundamentalist isolationism from the broader world and from other Christians. In 1942, the National Association of Evangelicals comes about as an attempt to overcome conservative Protestants' separation into many isolated groups. Since they are seen to have much in common, a way towards cooperation is sought. Evangelicalism is broadly an ecumenical movement among conservative Protestants, who have before been little splinter groups who did not want anything to do with anyone else. Evangelicals have a greater sense of a common project.

There have always been several **common concerns among Evangelicals**. They are concerned about the **secularization of the Church**: they worry about the Church losing its way and becoming too close to the culture of the day. They are also anxious about American Christianity becoming too privatized. It is too focused on individual, private life and is not concerned about culture and the broader society. Christianity should be **concerned about society at large**. While they do not want the Church to mould itself after the culture, evangelicals are concerned that Christianity is losing its influence on the broader culture. While it is common today to think of Western society as post-Christian, this turn (towards Secularity 1) starts in America around the time of the Second World War. The evangelical response to this perceived loss of a voice (perhaps in no small part due to the damage done by the Fundamentalists) is to have Christianity reach out and address the broader culture and society. It is out of this sense of outreach that there is widespread revival in post–Second World War America—specifically in the 1950s. (It is because of this revival that the way things happen in the latter part of the 1950s is often still unconsciously held up as the ideal for ecclesial and cultural life for American evangelicals even to this day.)

Evangelicalism was, from the beginning, an intentionally **transdenominational** movement. In fact, there are those who end up being unwilling to consider themselves to be 'evangelical' or who are uneasy about the term because they do not want to lose their distinct denominational identity. The unity of the evangelical coalition does, however, have distinct limits; indeed, it identifies itself in **contradistinction to Liberal Theology**. Usually what is called Neo-Orthodoxy gets lumped in with Liberalism as well. To a lesser degree, evangelicals also define themselves **against Catholicism**. They are self-consciously Protestant.

It is difficult to characterize the central beliefs of Evangelicalism as there are a variety of foci and emphases. It is a loose coalition and not any kind of formal denomination, so generalization can at times be like herding cats. Nevertheless, the following are **five central beliefs** that Molly Worthen sees as coming up consistently, though with various emphases and differing interpretations. **First**, Evangelicals hold to the central and infallible authority of Scripture. This is commonly but far from universally framed in terms of inerrancy. **Second** is Christ's unique saving work. Salvation (usually understood in terms of substitutionary atonement) is uniquely available through Christ. This is a driving motive behind evangelism and missions work.

Third is an emphasis on personal conversion. This focus on a personal and usually highly emotional conversion experience can be seen as coming out of the Pietist Awakenings back even into the eighteenth century and the revivals on the American frontier in the nineteenth century. This is often framed as a particular, punctiliar 'get saved' experience in which one is 'born again'.

A **fourth** emphasis is personal moral transformation or holiness. This is usually framed in forms of temperance—and here primarily temperance in the form of abstaining from alcohol and extramarital sex. Note that these were seen as particularly male vices that threatened stable family life.

Finally, the **fifth** emphasis is an interest in worldwide evangelism. This arises out of points two and three. Because Christ's work is unique—if you are going to be saved you have to be saved by Jesus—and one must be personally converted in order to be saved, there is then an impetus to share Christ's work with those that have not heard.

Common emphases in Evangelicalism

1. The central and infallible authority of Scripture; usually inerrancy

2. Christ's unique saving work; usually substitutionary atonement

3. Personal conversion

4. Personal moral transformation

5. Worldwide evangelism

Molly Worthen, in her book, *Apostles of Reason: The Crisis of Authority in American Evangelicalism*, observes that beyond these central emphases there is a certain tension or anxiety that characterizes Evangelicalism, which is consciously between two worlds or two seats of authority. For evangelicals to address the broader culture apologetically, they have to somehow negotiate the tension between the Bible as the central authority and secular reason as an authority. Unlike fundamentalists, evangelicals are unwilling to just dump secular reasoning. There is tension between the Bible and secular reason such that if one moves too far towards secular reason one comes to be viewed as a threat. Something very common in evangelical churches is that an overeducated—or perhaps 'wrongly' educated—pastor is viewed as dangerous. While they seek to avoid the separatist or polemical defensiveness of Fundamentalism, Evangelicalism cannot entirely leave this behind. Often, evangelicals will—usually in times of stress—default into an anti-intellectualist Fundamentalist posture. When it comes down to it, they will prefer doctrinal purity over relevance or relation to the world. If there is a perceived threat, they will often oppose free inquiry or collaboration with other Christians.

We see in Evangelicalism a carrying forward of the deep modern tension between the Enlightenment and the Pietist Awakenings. Evangelicalism—perhaps drawing from the Princeton theology of the nineteenth century—seeks to use the tools of the Enlightenment to counter the critiques of the Enlightenment and so to defend the faith of the Awakenings.

The reason that tension and a crisis of authority characterizes Evangelicalism is that at the end of the day evangelicals are not open to creative mediations between these two sources of authority. One source of authority is going to bend to the other one. They are not going to be like the Romantics (partially due to lack of historical consciousness). Ultimately, they want to use Scripture as the authority and then to prove that it is right on the terms of secular discourses—which might be a very difficult thing to do. It is a continual tension. And so Evangelicalism—even though it is trying to reach out and address the broader culture—is perpetually locked in conflict. This is not just an external conflict like the fundamentalists, but an internal conflict between wanting to engage with the world but not being able to accept the worldly perspective. They are caught between the two. It is at once a virtue to engage with the world and a temptation of compromising with the world.

A significant event in Evangelicalism is the International Conference on World Evangelism in 1974, held in Lausanne, Switzerland. There were some 2,400 participants from 150 nations, representing some 135 different Protestant denominations. This is a symbolic representation of Evangelicalism as a transdenominational reality. Included in the 'Lausanne Covenant', which was produced at the meeting, is the affirmation of 'the divine inspiration, truthfulness, and authority of both Old and New Testament Scriptures in their entirety, as the only written word of God, without error in all that it affirms, and the only infallible rule of faith and practice'. (Francis Schaeffer is influential in pushing for this language.) Here, we have an indication of the centrality of the notion of **inerrancy**. For many Evangelicals, the inerrancy of Scripture is foundational to the Christian worldview and is, as such, not optional. Scripture as divine revelation has to be perfect because God is perfect—otherwise it would not be the Word of God. Charles Hodge, using the model of the natural sciences, presents the Bible as a divine storehouse of facts. Scripture presents us with inerrant facts upon which we can build a theology that attends to those facts properly. Inerrancy is a way of bolstering the traditional Protestant understanding of *Sola Scriptura*. The ultimate foundation of Christian faith and practice is the Bible, and in order to be that it has to be without error. For the Christian faith to have a solid foundation—the foundation being the Bible—Scripture has to be inerrant.

A significant development in Evangelicalism is the Evangelical Theological Society, established in 1949, largely as an Evangelical alternative to the Society of Biblical Literature (ETS)—even today. Members of the ETS must affirm yearly a doctrinal statement that runs thus: 'The Bible alone, and the Bible in its entirety, is the Word of God written and is therefore inerrant in the autographs.' They would later add a brief statement about the Trinity. The central and defining place of inerrancy is evident; nevertheless, there is a bit of built-in wiggle room in the statement. The Bible is held to be inerrant 'in the autographs', which means the original documents that original authors wrote—which of course we do not have. Even if you cannot make your case for how these particular passages make sense with one another or with what we know about history, you can say that you believe that in the original autographs it makes sense and our problems have to do with later corruptions of the text.

A final significant locator for Evangelicalism is Reformed theology. In America, this is the defining milieu for Evangelicalism—usually Dutch Reformed Theology, which is associated with **presuppositionalism**. Usually in the context of Reformed Christian apologetics, presuppositionalism presents an understanding of philosophy and reason that takes into account original sin. Put simply, it entails that a non-believer cannot properly reason about Christianity because s/he has the wrong presuppositions. One can only have the right assumptions if one's mind has been transformed by the Holy Spirit. This brings in a Calvinist understanding of conversion and salvation into the epistemological apologetic realm. A couple of the significant figures in this area are Abraham Kuyper and Cornelius Van Til, both Dutch thinkers. Van Til immigrated to America and he taught at Princeton. He eventually helped to found Westminster Theological Seminary along with Machen.

Despite its best efforts, evangelical theology has largely not influenced academic theology beyond its own borders. Very often—especially in times of crisis—evangelical theology has a tendency to retreat into a fundamentalist fortress mentality. When tension arises, the concern for a more narrow doctrinal purity consistently wins out over a broader engagement with other Christians, the Christian tradition, and/or the broader culture.

17.3 Pentecostalism

Pentecostalism has much of its origin in the Wesleyan–Holiness tradition. Its roots are in the Methodists. There are revivalistic camp meetings in America focused on the possibility of perfection or striving towards holiness. In the 1880s, several of these Holiness/Methodist groups merge into the Church of the Nazarene. It is the biggest group representing this vein of Wesleyan Methodism. Pentecostal leaders grew from within these Holiness groups.

Beyond the Holiness group heritage, premillennial dispensationalism intertwined with revivalism figures prominently in Pentecostalism's background. There is a sense of the impending end of the world, and that fuels the work of evangelism and revival. In the last days specifically, there is an outpouring of the Holy Spirit. In the final days, with such an outpouring of the Spirit, people are empowered and are sent out by the Spirit to preach the 'full gospel' in the light of the coming end. So, the Pentecostal movement is from the beginning tied up in eschatology, but is always driven by its eschatology towards evangelism and missions. Evangelism is all the more important because the end is nigh.

The two most influential of the founding figures of Pentecostalism are **Charles Fox Parham** and **William J. Seymour. Charles Fox Parham** is a former Methodist preacher from Topeka, Kansas. In 1901, he founds what he calls the 'Apostolic Faith' movement. There are a couple of key aspects to this movement that will prove influential for Pentecostalism at large. The first is the dramatic experience of divine encounter that is **baptism in/with the Spirit**. Another distinctive characteristic is **glossolalia**—speaking in tongues. This becomes a centrepiece of the Pentecostal experience, and is largely why it is called 'Pentecostal'—being named after the events in Acts 2. There, on the day of Pentecost and as a sign of the special outpouring of the Spirit, the gathered

Figure 17.2 Apostolic Faith Mission.

'Apostolic Faith Gospel Mission 1907' by http://ifphc.org/ and http://ifphc.org/. Licensed under Public Domain via Wikimedia Commons.

believers speak in tongues. The real historical event that is the birth of Pentecostalism is the **Azusa Street Revival**, which lasts for three years (1906–09) in Los Angeles. The leader of this revival is an African American preacher named **William J. Seymour (1870–1922)**. The revival is centred on the Apostolic Faith Mission in Los Angeles—an extension of Charles Fox Parham's Apostolic Faith.

Seymour and many other early Pentecostals see speaking in tongues as the supernatural gift of being able to speak other living languages. The Holy Spirit has made the gifted believers able to speak other languages in order to preach the Gospel. Because these are the final days, the Gospel has to be preached to those who have not heard it who speak other languages, so the Spirit has miraculously given people the ability to speak these other languages. Early Pentecostal missionaries are often disillusioned because no one understands them. Eventually, the theology of glossolalia gets adjusted to seeing the gift of ecstatic tongues as the inspiring of an ability to speak in an unknown tongue or a prayer language, and not necessarily in another human language.

In 1914, the Assemblies of God is formed. This will be the most stable group or denomination in Pentecostalism. It is difficult to identify formal organization in Pentecostalism because of its very nature as being ecstatic and charismatic. Pentecostal groups are usually focused around a particular charismatic leader, and often last the tenure of that leader's ministry, thereafter splintering into different groups.

Pentecostalism spreads and grows significantly in the Americas and in Africa. The Assemblies of God becomes a major denomination quickly: by the late 1970s, it has 1.3 million followers. In the latter part of the twentieth century, the expanding edge of Christianity is largely of a Pentecostal Christianity on the periphery of the Western world. This is the fastest growing segment of Christianity. It is hard to get numbers when you are talking about 'two-thirds of the world', but it could be that as many as a third of Christians worldwide are Pentecostal—as many as 600 million and counting.

We will close with some distinctive theological understandings represented in Pentecostalism. First, is the understanding of the '**full Gospel**'. Salvation for Pentecostals is not just about one's standing before God, it is also you being saved in your moral behaviour. Salvation entails a conversion to personal holiness. (One can see the Wesleyan–Holiness background here.) Beyond personal holiness however, the full Gospel also involves—for many Pentecostals—physical well-being or the healing of the body. The Gospel is good news for our bodies as well as our spirits. This will at times turn into a health-and-wealth gospel. Evidence of this 'full Gospel' coming to you is baptism in the Holy Spirit as evidenced by speaking in tongues. The 'full Gospel' is a vision of salvation as being holistic well-being—being delivered from not just sin but from poverty and misfortune. Ultimately, only the Holy Spirit can guarantee true Christianity in its fullness in the person.

There are two classical Pentecostal doctrines centred around the relation between the phenomena of glossolalia and Baptism in the Holy Spirit. These are affirmed early on, and reaffirmed by the Assemblies of God general council in 1991. The first is the doctrine of **subsequence**, and the other is the doctrine of **consequence** or **initial evidence**. The doctrine of **subsequence** has to do with an understanding of baptism in the Holy Spirit. Baptism in the Holy Spirit (or 'Spirit Baptism') is an experience that a believer has subsequent to conversion. It is a special experience that is distinct from receiving of the Holy Spirit upon conversion. One can be 'saved', but not yet baptized with the Holy Spirit. One's 'full salvation' comes to one subsequent to one's conversion. The roots of this subsequent Spirit Baptism are in the Wesleyan–Holiness movement's teaching about a 'second work of grace', in which one is filled with the Holy Spirit in a special kind of way that enables one to live a holy life.

The other distinctive ingredient doctrine is that of **consequence** or **initial evidence**. This specifically has to do with glossolalia or speaking in tongues. Speaking in tongues is the consequence or initial evidence of Spirit Baptism. How do you know that you are baptized in the Spirit and that you have received the 'full Gospel?' You know because you speak in tongues. Glossolalia is the initial evidence of Spirit Baptism. For Pentecostals, this is the normative pattern for becoming a Christian in the fullest sense. Beyond believing or conversion, there is a subsequent special work of the Holy Spirit in Spirit Baptism, and the consequence or initial evidence of Spirit Baptism is speaking in tongues.

Sources and Further Reading

Anderson, Allan. 'Pentecostal and Charismatic Theology'. In *The Modern Theologians: Introduction to Christian Theology since 1918*, edited by David F. Ford with Rachel Muers, 589–607, 3rd edn. Oxford: Blackwell, 2005.

Cox, Harvey. 'The Myth of the Twentieth Century: The Rise and Fall of "Secularization"'. In *The Twentieth Century: A Theological Overview*, edited by Gregory Baum, 135–43. Maryknoll, NY: Orbis, 1999.

Gifford, Paul. 'Fundamentalism'. In *The Oxford Companion to Christian Thought*, edited by Adrian Hastings, Alistair Mason, and Hugh Pyper, 255–57. Oxford: Oxford University Press, 2000.

Gregersen, Niels Henrik. 'Protestant Theology in the Twentieth Century'. In *Key Theological Thinkers: From Modern to Postmodern*, edited by Staale Johannes Kristiansen and Svein Rise, 21–36. Aldershot: Ashgate, 2013.

Johnston, Robert K. 'Evangelicalism'. In *The Oxford Companion to Christian Thought*, edited by Adrian Hastings, Alistair Mason, and Hugh Pyper, 217–20. Oxford: Oxford University Press, 2000.

Livingston, James C., and Francis Schüssler Fiorenza. *Modern Christian Thought: Volume 2, The Twentieth Century*. 2nd edn. Minneapolis, MN: Fortress Press, 2006.

Robeck, Cecil M., Jr. 'Pentecostalism'. In *The Oxford Companion to Christian Thought*, edited by Adrian Hastings, Alistair Mason, and Hugh Pyper, 530–32. Oxford: Oxford University Press, 2000.

Worthen, Molly. *Apostles of Reason: The Crisis of Authority in American Evangelicalism*. Oxford: Oxford University Press, 2014.

Part IV

The Late Modern Supernova

Introduction to Part IV:

Disparate Trajectories and Cross Pressures

The period after the Second World War, the 1960s and onward, can be characterized as a period of unsettledness, anxiety or even alienation. This feeling of unsettledness arose from certain tensions or cross-pressures. A principal tension is between a desire for meaning and unity in the midst of increasing plurality, diversity and fragmentation. When Charles Taylor talks about the spiritual shape of the present age, he refers to it in terms of a great plurality or a 'supernova'. The 'nova' of the mid-nineteenth century—where there is an increasing plurality of different positions—goes 'supernova' after the Second World War.

Secularity 1	retreat of religion from public life	20th century	storey above the ground floor
Secularity 2	decline in belief and practice	19th century	ground floor
Secularity 3	change in conditions of belief	14th(?)–18th centuries	basement/foundation

Before describing this plurality further, let us pause to return briefly to Charles Taylor's different senses of secularity. Secularity 1 is the more commonly understood sense of a retreat of religion from public life; the public spaces are emptied of God. Secularity 2 is an underlying decline of religious belief and religious practice. The most fundamental level is Secularity 3, the change in conditions of belief with the emergence of modernity. Secularity 2 arises in the nineteenth century. In the twentieth century, we see the retreat or disappearance of religion from public life and public discourse. Part of the tension in late modernity in the West is the cross-pressure between such a secularized public discourse (Secularity 1) that far outstrips any actual absence of religious belief (Secularity 2). We talk as if we are no longer religious, but we often are and quite intensely so.

When Taylor talks about Secularity 1, he talks about it in terms of an immanent frame. Our standard public discourse in the West is an immanent one, operating without (explicit) reference to the transcendent. Our framework of understanding privileges the immanent. This does not rule out the possibility of religiousness; the immanent frame can be lived in and thought of as being open to the transcendent. This generates a certain tension or cross-pressure. But many opt for the simpler closed world of the immanent frame stripped of reference to the transcendent.

'closed world structures'

---

science vs. God/religion

narratives of subtraction

narratives of rise of modern moral-political spaces

narratives of rise of the autonomous self

In describing this immanent frame, Taylor refers to different 'closed world structures'—things that people commonly assume about the world in Secularity 1 that bring about this immanent perspective. These are perspectives that are taken as being axiomatic and have an aura of objectivity to them—even if it is indeed nothing but the transient glow of the Zeitgeist. These are some of the 'official stories' of late modernity. The first is that science is in opposition to God and religion. To believe in science is ultimately to be a materialist. It is to be mature and courageous in the face of the cold realities of a universe without God and superstition.

Second, we have narratives of subtraction as an assumed way of looking at things (see Introduction). Narratives of subtraction see looking at the world without reference to God or the transcendent as simply looking at reality as it is, and, as history has developed and progressed, people have become more reasonable and stop believing in God. Modernity is simply the subtraction, the scraping off of the accretions of superstition.

Third, is the dominance of the narratives of modern moral–political spaces, or of how our given way of being today is the superior way of being. The rise of the modern political order is taken to be the product of a kind of necessary progression towards maximal mutual benefit. (Somehow this yielded perhaps the bloodiest century in human history.)

Finally, there are the narratives of the rise of the autonomous self. In the present age, we have come to an adulthood in a self-determined mode of human being free of past prejudices. We are the legislators of our own meanings.

All of these 'closed world structures' insinuate themselves as assumed axioms, as givens. However, as mentioned above, for many people it is not as simple as this. There are those who are atheists, but there are also orthodox believers (and many places in between). For religious believers in late modernity, there is a tension or cross-pressure between seeing the fullness of human life being beyond human life (being orientated towards transcendence with the natural being fulfilled in the supernatural) or seeing the fullness of human life being within human life (the only goal for human life is human flourishing here in the present).

Beyond this experience of tension, late modern religiosity can be characterized in terms of **plurality**. In the modern search for meaning and unity, there ends up being multiple answers to what holds everything together. Peter Berger—one of the most well-known (former) advocates of the secularization thesis—has recently said that the best way to understand modernity is not in terms of the decline of religion but in how secularity has generated a pluralism. This is especially apparent in the latter part of the twentieth century.

Part of the situation that we are in is that how we are to live is to an increasing degree not *given*. There is increasingly no monolithic way of being. Everyone usually has to figure out for themselves what they think about God and religion, what they think about what they want in terms of a family, or what they think about government. These are options, and we tend to know many other people—perhaps friends or even family members—that think very differently about these things. From 'big things' like God, family and society as a whole, to simply what to eat or what to wear, these matters are not given. You have to think about them, and people have very strong opinions on one side or the other. Part of what is happening in the latter part of the twentieth century is that the background practices and beliefs for our lives—that which was once given or assumed—are being dragged into the foreground as things about which we now have to consider and make decisions about them. This is one way of thinking about pluralism: the expanding of the foreground and the shrinking of the background of our practices and belief. Less and less can be taken for granted. We can think of the difference between the diet of someone five hundred years ago and the supermarkets of today. You cannot just grab the first thing you come across. (At our local supermarket that would be flowers. Do not eat the flowers. Then there are the lottery cards. You probably should not eat those either.)

When it comes to religion, something like this is the case as well. (You should probably not eat the first thing you come across in church either, but that is not my point.) It is from this perspective that Taylor says that we are now living a spiritual supernova—a 'galloping pluralism on the spiritual plane'. Taylor refers to this period since 1960 as the Age of Authenticity. We have gone over a tipping point in this big transition from fate to choice—from background givens to foregrounded options. This 'authenticity' has often been presented in terms of trying to find out what it means to 'be yourself' or 'to find yourself'. One's own identity is something that needs to be figured out.

In the progress of modernity, there has been a liberation from assumed institutions. This has ramped up in the West since the 1960s. You can see that in terms of growth of choice and freedom, and in terms of increasing respect for differences. Also, this is often seen in framing more and more of our lives in terms of consumerism, of 'preferences'. What were once givens are now sexual, political and religious preferences.

Berger makes the point that on the flip side of this liberation is uncertainty, anxiety and alienation. We find ourselves in a situation today where there are many different ways of being. When we internalize this external pluralism, our own beliefs are relativized. We cannot take what we believe for granted, because your neighbour believes something else. The fact that there are other people who believe different things internally relativizes our beliefs. It makes it more difficult for us to hold them absolutely, and therefore it makes us uncertain. Pluralism in society leads to a pluralism of the mind. There are now multiple competing voices within ourselves. Pluralism brings about a cognitive dissonance or, as Berger calls it, a cognitive contamination. Pluralism relativizes our own beliefs and undermines our ability to be certain about our beliefs. It puts things under question. Even if you still think that your current beliefs are true, there is an aura of doubt that causes anxiety. What we are looking for is a meaning in life, and if we cannot fully have that answer we are anxious that we might be wrong—taking our life down a dead-end road.

This liberation from assumed ways of being ends up affecting a deracination. We are being torn up by the roots. We no longer have roots or a starting place. We no longer have assumed beliefs and practices, because more and more of those are being brought into the foreground. Things that were our root beliefs that allowed us to negotiate other things are then becoming options that themselves have to be negotiated (and how?).

To deal with this anxiety, Berger talks about two particularly popular options for coping: **fundamentalism** and **relativism**. These are ways of getting rid of the anxiety that comes from uncertainty. With **fundamentalism**—here talking in the broader sense and not necessarily about the particular early-twentieth-century religious movement (see Chapter 17)—there is a promise of certainty and the elimination of doubt. Now, there can be many different kinds of fundamentalism. There are religious fundamentalisms, anti-religious fundamentalisms, political fundamentalisms, aesthetic/artistic/fashion fundamentalisms, etc. What they do is to simply deny that there are any other viable options. They deal with pluralism in a particular domain by demonizing everyone else. You keep the absolute status of your belief in that there are no other reasonable options. The intention here is to restore the taken-for-granted nature of certain beliefs. But this kind of fundamentalism is always going to be fragile and needs to be constantly maintained. This is why fundamentalists have an aggressive stance; they have to keep fighting to keep things at bay because today it is very difficult to escape different views. The principal tactic is some form of isolation. It is a fanatical posture in which other groups are not recognized as anything but enemies.

The other option is that of **relativism**. You see this in some varieties of postmodernism. Instead of trying to get away from relativity, they embrace relativity itself as a kind of superior knowledge. Instead of rejecting the plurality, they reject the search for meaning or unity. As mentioned previously, the anxiety and tension is that we are searching for meaning in the midst of increasing plurality. The fundamentalists want to reject the increasing plurality, while the relativists want to reject the search for meaning. Peter Berger cites Simone Weil, who refers to the hungry comforting themselves with the thought that food does not exist in the first place. One can simply give up on reality and truth. The only virtue is tolerance. The end of such a perspective is a moral nihilism. There simply cannot be a society when its constituents have abandoned the notion of there being a common reality.

18

Later Twentieth-Century Catholic Theology

In the 1960s, Catholic theology in the West goes through a theological renaissance which is largely prepared for by the *nouvelle theologie* movement in France (see Chapter 15). The Catholic theological rebirth of the twentieth century equals Protestant theology in terms of creativity and constructive engagement. For the first time in about four hundred years, Catholic theology is on the leading edge of the Christian theological imagination.

18.1 Vatican II

Vatican II is the most significant event in twentieth-century Roman Catholicism. With the Second Vatican Council, the Neo-Scholasticism that was instated as the official way of thinking for the Catholic Church in Vatican I is overcome.

18.1.1 Precursors

Pius XII (r. 1939–58) gives several papal encyclicals throughout the 1940s that are seen as leading towards what we see at Vatican II. The encyclicals that he gives signal the greater openness towards things like critical biblical scholarship, liturgical reform and the relation to those outside of the Roman Catholic Church. An increasing openness towards these things seemed to be signalled in these encyclicals.

The most significant precursor is *nouvelle theologie*, which paves the way through its project of *ressourcement*. What allows Vatican II to make such radical changes is that people believe that these radical changes are not innovations, but rather come from the history of the Church: They are traditional. You had to have had the *ressourcement* (the increasing awareness of the Church Fathers and medieval theologians) to allow the questioning of the more recent tradition—specifically from the Council of Trent and Vatican I. And so, Vatican II can go slightly against the grain of Trent and Vatican I because it is in line with the broader tradition of the Church, and the *ressourcement* of *nouvelle theologie* helps them to do that. This recovering of the tradition is going to serve for the foundation of the reform of Vatican II.

18.1.2 Pope John XXIII

Born Angelo Giusseppe Roncalli, Pope John XXIII (r. 1958–63) is influenced by *nouvelle theologie* and is especially interested in Yves Congar's understanding of reform. What the Church needs is a reform that does not split the Church, but instead enables it to bring about its mission. When John XXIII begins his time as pope, many expect from him a caretaker administration; he is not expected to change things. However, immediately after becoming pope, he starts planning to have a second Vatican Council and to have some of the exponents of *nouvelle theologie* as experts in it. He becomes pope in 1958, and announces the council in 1959. This is a surprise not only to the broader Church, but to the Papal Curia as well. They are quite taken aback. This is only the second general church council since the Council of Trent, the first being what is now called Vatican I. Both Trent and Vatican I—the hitherto only modern church councils—were held in reaction (or at least response) to a great threat to the Catholic Church: the Protestant Reformation for Trent, and modernism for Vatican I. In contradistinction to these councils, Vatican II is presented from the beginning as a different kind of council. It is not to be a council meant to deal with a problem, or as a response to a threat, but rather it is formed to present a constructive vision of a revivified Church with a positive engagement with the world. At the very least, it promises a more optimistic tone.

Vatican II convenes at the end of 1961, and has four sessions, the final one ending in 1965. While the Curia tries to control the council, the bishops at the council end up demanding their own agenda. It is truly conciliar—a meeting together of the bishops from all over the world who will play a huge part in what comes. It is a much more democratic vision of a council. While John XXIII dies during the council, Paul VI succeeds him and is intent on completing and implementing the council. The council produces sixteen documents.

From the beginning, Vatican II is not intended as an emergency council dealing with a threat. It is framed as a pastoral council. It is about making positive moves towards the Church being better at its work in the world. One of the animating ideas for the Second Vatican Council is *aggiornamento*—which means 'bringing up to date'. This is an active engagement that stands in stark relief to the way things had happened in Vatican I. It is seen by many as a real reversal of policy from the nineteenth century and the earlier part of the twentieth century. However, a characteristic of the Second Vatican Council is that this particular *aggiornamento* is not a celebration of novelty or just following along with the culture. *Aggiornamento* is to be done by way of *ressourcement*. The Church should be renewed—but renewed by way of retrieving the insights of its own tradition. That way, it can renew and bring it up to date—but not in a sense of sloughing off the broader tradition as irrelevant, but rather by being traditional. The great tradition of the Church is seen as the principal resource for bringing things up to date—for renewal in the Church.

Figure 18.1 John XXIII.

'San Giovanni XXIII, opera di Bonaldi Giovanni' by Khristell—Own work. Licensed under CC BY-SA 4.0 via Wikimedia Commons.

18.1.3 Vatican II Documents

We will walk through some of the significant achievements of the Council as represented in its documents. The first document is **Sacrosanctum concilium**, the Constitution on the Sacred Liturgy (1963). This document addresses several different matters. While it looks at liturgical reform, there are certain ecclesiological insights in the background drawing from the vision of the Church as *communio*. The liturgy of the Mass needs to be reformed so that the laity are not just spectators. Thus, the laity will not just watch the 'real Church' happen in the activities of the clergy, but they rather will be participants as well and should be brought in formally as such. This is bringing to the fore, Congar's ecclesiology that focused on fellowship and participation. He used the term *koinonia*—the Church as a common sharing together. Drawing on this, the Mass becomes a site where the Church as *communio* is instituted. The Church continually comes into being as this fellowship—not just with one another but also with God in the Eucharist. The celebration of the Eucharist is to be a concrete enactment of such a *communio* ecclesiology. This entails such things as having the liturgy be done in the vernacular rather than just in Latin. Another significant change is that the presider will face the people. Previously, he would face the Tabernacle in the front of the room—but instead the priest is to turn around, such that the Eucharist was seen as happening in the midst of the congregation. Finally, there is a greater role for lay leaders and Eucharistic ministers. It should be seen that these liturgical reforms are presented not just as fitting the culture of twentieth century better, but as a better representation of the Patristic theology of the Church. *Communio* is a better understanding of the Church than a more priest-centric and hierarchical understanding of the Church. (It should be noted that the priesthood and the hierarchy still play a fundamental role.)

The sixteen documents of Vatican II

Sacrosanctum concilium, Constitution on the Sacred Liturgy, 1963.

Inter Mirifica, Decree On the Means of Social Communication, 1963.

Lumen Gentium, Dogmatic Constitution On the Church, 1964.

Orientalium Ecclesiarum, Decree On the Catholic Churches of the Eastern Rite, 1964.

Unitatis Redintegratio, Decree on Ecumenism, 1964.

Christus Dominus, Decree Concerning the Pastoral Office of Bishops In the Church, 1965.

Perfectae Caritatis, Decree On Renewal of Religious Life, 1965.

Optatam Totius, Decree On Priestly Training, 1965.

Gravissimum Educationis, Declaration On Christian Education, 1965.

Nostra Aetate, Declaration On the Relation Of the Church to Non-Christian Religions, 1965.

Dei Verbum, Dogmatic Constitution On Divine Revelation, 1965.

The sixteen documents of Vatican II

Apostolicam Actuositatem, Decree On the Apostolate of the Laity, 1965.

Dignitatis Humanae, Declaration On Religious Freedom, 1965.

Ad Gentes, Decree On the Mission Activity of the Church, 1965.

Presbyterorum Ordinis, Decree On the Ministry and Life of Priests, 1965.

Gaudium et Spes, Pastoral Constitution On the Church In the Modern World, 1965.

Another significant document is **Lumen Gentium**, the Dogmatic Constitution On the Church. Henri de Lubac helps to write this document. It is considered to be one of the real masterpieces of Vatican II. A long time in preparation, it has many different revisions. First off, it presents in a more formal way a different understanding of the Church as the people of God. It presents a *communio* ecclesiology that we see with Congar—as the gathered communion of believers—as a necessary understanding of the church to be held in tension with the more hierarchical vision of the Church as seen in Vatican I. *Lumen Gentium* also places a strong emphasis on the local church. There is a presentation of ecclesiology such that in each church there is represented the fullness of the Church. The *communio* is not simply those people that are gathered, but is also the communion between one church and the whole Church such that the Church is present in any given gathered community.

There is also discussion in this document of other Christian communities—the relationship between the Roman Catholic Church and other non-Roman Catholic Christians. It sees other Christian communities as having some validity as Christians. This opens up a dialogue with the Eastern Orthodox Church, the Anglican Church, and with Protestant theologians. (There are also Protestant theologians invited to Vatican II as guests and observers.)

Unitatis Redintegratio—the Decree on Ecumenism—explicitly states that it is a scandal that the Church of Christ is divided. (This includes an implicit recognition that there are other Christians.) They are trying to find a way of talking about how there can still be a Roman Catholic Church while the Church as a whole is divided. This document introduces the distinction that says that the Church of Christ 'subsists in' the Roman Catholic Church. It subsists in, but is not identical to, the institution of the Roman Catholic Church. 'Subsists in'—in subsequent commentary—is commonly put in scare quotes because there is a lot of discussion over what exactly 'subsists in' means.

Like *Lumen Gentium*, the emphasis in *Unitatis Redintegratio* is that Protestant churches are not to be seen first and foremost as heretics, but as separated brethren/Christians/communities. Along with this kind of language from Vatican II that laments division of the Church, there is a desire to welcome Eastern Orthodox and Protestant Christians.

Nostra Aetate—the Declaration On the Relation Of the Church to Non-Christian Religions—is primarily about Jewish–Christian relations. This is the first time the Roman Catholic Church formally addressed anti-Semitism and revokes its past formal position of blaming of the Jews as being the people bearing primary guilt for the death of Jesus. What is being introduced here is an

Figure 18.2 Vatican II Rome.

attempt at having a new approach to Judaism. There is also hinted in this document the idea that grace is operative in other religions. Here is where Karl Rahner has some influence.

Dei Verbum—the Dogmatic Constitution On Divine Revelation—is produced in 1965, with Henri de Lubac playing a significant role in it. *Dei Verbum* focuses on the nature of Scripture. Its main point is that Scripture—while divine—is truly human, and as human it is historically conditioned. Scripture therefore should be studied as something that is historical. This is a significant shift. Hitherto, any hint of historical relativity in relation to Scripture smacked of Modernism and was forbidden. The inspiration of scripture is presented not as if God is using the human author as an instrument, but with the human author as a genuine agency—so Scripture is indeed a human document. *Dei Verbum* states that Scripture is without error with regard to matters of salvation as this is ultimately the purpose of Scripture. So when it comes to its purpose Scripture does not fail and is not in error. However, the purpose of Scripture is not to be a treatise on natural science or on political history—so we should not necessarily expect it to be without error when it comes to those things. The Bible is also understood as being read and interpreted by the living community of the Church in an ongoing tradition of understanding. Thus, *Dei Verbum* represents the attempt to find a more robust understanding of Scripture as continually read and understood in relation to the teaching authority of the Church and as guided by the Holy Spirit. One of the emphases here is that Scripture needs to be more easily accessible to all people inasmuch as that is possible.

Dignitatis Humanae—the Declaration On Religious Freedom—simply affirms that religious freedom is a human right. This is something that is explicitly rejected in Vatican I, for 'error has no rights'. Nevertheless, with Vatican II the Catholic Church becomes a significant advocate for religious tolerance all throughout the world.

Ad Gentes—the Decree On the Mission Activity of the Church—again reflects some of Rahner's ideas, that grace is operative and truth is to be found in other religions. When it comes to the missionary activity of the Church, it says that the Church is itself a missionary institution. To understand the Church properly is to understand it as always already involved in mission. The mission of the Church is connected to the missions of the Trinity—specifically the missions of the Son and the Spirit. The mission of the Church is about the coming of the light of the Trinity into humanity.

Finally, *Gaudium et Spes*—the Pastoral Constitution On the Church In the Modern World—focuses on the social dimension of salvation. It ends up being a very significant document for what comes to be called Liberation Theology. It is heavily influenced by Chenu and de Lubac. Part of the mission of the Church is to bring about a more human world, which means that Christians should be concerned about the struggles of the poor and oppressed. The Church should have concern for the material well-being of human beings, and this is rooted in the *Imago Dei*. All human beings as human beings have inherent dignity and so should be treated with basic rights and not oppressed.

18.1.4 After the Council

The Second Vatican Council has a huge impact both within and without the Roman Catholic Church. Within it, the most obvious immediate impact is liturgical reform. Everyday Catholics' experiences of the Mass change considerably. For the first time for some, people begin to understand what is going on in Mass now that it is said in the vernacular. Outside of the Roman Catholic Church, there is a real rise in ecumenical contact between Roman Catholics and other Christian groups. There is a real opening for Roman Catholics and Protestants to talk to each other and to recognize each other as Christians.

Contemporary Catholic theologian Tracy Rowland describes there being three basic groups or theological clusters when you look at the theological landscape after Vatican II. The key issue for understanding all of them is their different accounts of the relationship between faith and reason or nature and grace. These are the differences that all of these groups have. Still, today, you cannot say 'the Catholic view' of faith and reason or grace and nature, because they really disagree with each other. First, **Neo-Scholasticism** is still an influential force. Here is an extrinsically related grace and nature as separate domains.

Second is so-called **Transcendental Thomism**, which basically means Karl Rahner. He is regularly characterized by non-Rahnerians as a naturalizing of the supernatural.

Third are the ***Ressourcement*** theologians. These are the people who are, to put it roughly, supernaturalizing the natural—seeing how the natural is taken up into the supernatural. They end up forming major groups after the council, and these are not the only groups.

Influential groups/theological clusters in and after Vat II	
Neo-Scholasticism	'Neo-Neo-Thomists'
Transcendental Thomism	*Concilium*
Ressourcement Theologians	*Communio*

Not everyone was happy with Vatican II. Many were troubled by it for different reasons. The conservatives were frustrated by the changes of stances and practices and troubled by the loss of past customs—such as the Latin Mass. So there are little splinter groups in Roman Catholicism who reject Vatican II. The progressives, however, become frustrated that it is too conservative. Vatican II could have brought about much greater changes in the way the Church does things in its relation to the world and other groups, but it does not due to ecclesiastical bureaucracy.

The council happens in the early part of the 1960s. In the 1970s, we see a moderating of the progressive mood of the council—something of a move back to the middle. One way of seeing the post-Vatican II landscape is to look at two international journals. The first is established in 1965—the last year of the council—and called *Concilium*. Its animating idea—and this largely represents the Transcendental Thomism group—is to continue the renewal in theology that began with Vatican II. It is to promote the spirit of Vatican II and is founded by Karl Rahner, Schillebeeckx, Hans Küng, Yves Congar, Johann Baptist Metz and also Joseph Ratzinger, who later becomes Pope Benedict XVI. This journal represents the more progressive direction immediately after Vatican II—carrying forward the *aggiornamento* of Roman Catholicism. Another journal is founded in 1972 that represents the moderating posture mentioned above called *Communio*. This is going to represent those who split off from *Concilium* who thought that it was heading in the wrong direction. They have reservations about taking on modern ideas too uncritically, about letting the secular world set the agenda for the Church. *Communio* is founded by Henri de Lubac, Balthasar, Daniélou and Joseph Ratzinger. The founders all became cardinals by the time they die—and one of them becomes pope. In the remainder of this chapter, we will consider a major representative of each of these perspectives: Karl Rahner (from the Transcendental Thomism and *Concilium* side) and Hans Urs von Balthasar (from the *Ressourcement* and *Communio* side). Beyond these two groups, there are still those who hold onto a Neo-Scholastic perspective; Rowland describes them as Neo-Neo-Thomists—those who are still defending Baroque Scholasticism over and against *ressourcement* theology.

18.2 Rahner

Arguably the most significant Catholic theologians in the twentieth century after Vatican II are **Karl Rahner** and **Hans Urs von Balthasar. Karl Rahner (1904–84)** became a Jesuit at the age of eighteen. He studied for his doctorate in philosophy at Freiburg. While he was there, he attended the seminars of Heidegger from 1934 to 1936—and his work shows the influence of Heidegger's thought.

Rahner's first significant work is entitled *Spirit in the World*, published in 1936. This is the dissertation originally written for his doctorate in philosophy, however, the Catholic faculty did not accept it as they thought it was not close enough to their reading of Thomas Aquinas. He ends up getting a doctorate in theology a year later. Rahner taught for a time at Innsbruck, until the outbreak of the Second World War—at which time Innsbruck was closed. He served as a pastor during the war. After the war, he returned to Innsbruck and taught there from 1948 to 1964.

In the 1950s, Rahner's work was considered to be at the margins of what is acceptable and was held in suspicion by many conservative theologians. For a time, he had to submit his writings to a Roman censor before they could be published. Yet in the 1960s, his work comes to be considered in the mainstream of Catholic theology. He is a *peritus* at Vatican II and is regarded as one of the really significant shapers of the Council. After this, he no longer needed a Roman censor, since his work came to represent one of the main streams of Catholic thought after Vatican II. He taught at the University of Munich for a time, and then spent the latter part of his career, from 1966 to 1984, at the University of Münster.

Rahner was quite a prolific author with thousands of publications. He principally wrote essays that were occasional writings—dealing with a given situation or controversy. These occasional essays of his were collected together in his *Schriften zur Theologie*—or *Theological Investigations*—published from 1954 to 1984. This massive work is often compared to Barth's great *Church Dogmatics*, although it is more a huge collection of essays on all manner of topics. He describes himself as a dilettante—interested in many different topics and writing about many different things. In German, this work is comprised of sixteen volumes—in English translation, twenty-three volumes.

Many people look to a later work of Rahner, *Foundations of the Christian Faith: An Introduction to the Idea of Christianity* (1976), as his most systematic. However, Rahner did not consider this to be anything like a condensation of his thought. It is not a summation or synthesis of his thought, but rather is addressing a particular issue—the ultimate reasons for faith.

In Rahner's earlier works, one can see the definite influence of Heidegger. However, it would be inaccurate to call him a Heideggerian. He mostly borrows from Heidegger in an ad hoc manner. He does not take over Heidegger's whole framework, but he uses some of Heidegger's ideas and makes them his own.

Rahner is often described as a **Transcendental Thomist**. The meaning here is that he is synthesizing modern philosophy and the traditional Catholic thought of Thomas. 'Transcendental' here refers to Immanuel Kant. Rahner, at the very least, is more positive about modernity and modern philosophy—wanting to make Christian faith accessible to modern people. He is going to address certain ways that Christianity has come to be seen as less plausible—specifically for more philosophically inclined modern people. He wanted to understand the Christian faith as something that could be not just understood and believed but genuinely experienced by modern people.

18.2.1 The Experience of God

Let us investigate further the sense of 'transcendental' for Rahner. For him being related to God is fundamental to what makes us human. Rahner would say that our experience of God in the world is our most fundamental human experience. Part of this is coming from his early work, *Spirit in the World*. What he means by this is that we are always already related to and experiencing God—whether we know it or not. This experience of God is related to all of our loving and our knowing. Any act of loving or knowing is always already related to God.

When we know things, we always know particular limited objects. Every particular limited object entails another awareness—an awareness of an unlimited and infinite being. Every experience of finite being is always against the background of an awareness of an infinite or unlimited being, and Rahner says that this is God. He describes this with the German term *Vorgriff auf esse*, the 'preapprehension of being'. This is a pre-grasping of God as unlimited, infinite being. In all of our awareness, God is the ultimate framing goal or horizon in which all of our other human doings or relatings are framed. God is that *esse*, and our experience of thought is always reaching out beyond particular objects. There is a dynamism to mind, and a drive that makes knowledge possible. He talks about God as a horizon or background against which we know particular things. What is significant here is that this background cannot be foregrounded. God is fundamentally unfathomable. He is the background against which all things are known. To know something is to know it in the foreground, but you cannot bring the background into the foreground. So God is going to have an ultimate mystery to Him.

Dimensions of experience

Categorical	Foreground	Finite and particular things	Direct knowledge
Transcendental	Background	Infinite	Indirect knowledge

It is in relation to this kind of understanding that Rahner will say that all of our experience has two dimensions: there is the dimension of the **categorical** and the dimension of the **transcendental**. All of our experience always has these two dimensions together. The categorical dimension of our experience has to do with finite and particular things. We can understand them because they fit into categories—here you can see the Kantian aspect. However, there is also the transcendental dimension of experience. All experience is of these particular finite objects, but it is also going beyond particular possible objects of thought and desire. We do not just experience objects, but we experience that which is beyond them—as a background. He says that this is the experience of God, whether we know it or not, as the ultimate, infinite background. He talks about this as 'transcendental'—meaning different things. First, he means it in a more traditionally Kantian sense, that our experience of God is the condition of the possibility of categorical experience. God as being part of our experience is what makes it possible for us to experience anything else. He is the light by which you see things. This other dimension is also 'transcendental' because it is always transcending, going beyond the finite. We can have no pure intuition of this ultimate horizon of being and understanding.

You can see here that there is a strong emphasis on God as mystery. Our knowledge of God is always going to be indirect, because when we have direct knowledge it is knowledge of particular objects. We do not experience God the way that we experience everything else, because God is not another thing—God is the other side of the finite things that we can only experience. He is the other side of our finitude. God is ultimately incomprehensible. He is that which comprehends and the comprehensive horizon by which other things show up. When we are going to talk about this transcendental experience, we always have to use categorical language. So Rahner would say that God is present to all of us always as the persistent mystery that is the background of our existence.

18.2.2 Christ

Rahner thought that the person of Christ is unique and yet should be understood in relation to a broader understanding of humanity's relation to God. The essence of humanity, what makes humans 'human', is our inherent relation to God. The human properly understood is our relation to God; to be human is to be related to God. We are an infinite openness to God. Properly understood, humanity is not a rival to God, but is an openness to God. So when he understands Christ, he understands Christ as being radically human in this sense. Christ is the truly human. He is the one most radically given over, being utterly open to God. Christ's divinity is in his being the most fully human of all.

Anthropology for Rahner is imperfect Christology. Humans have yet to live up to their own humanity. Humanity is only properly understood from the standpoint of Christ; Christ shows us what humanity is. Rahner is sometimes represented as reducing Christianity to something that all humans already are (and so 'naturalizing the supernatural'). But he can also be seen to be defining humanity on the basis of Christ. Christ is the main reference point that makes a true understanding of humanity and true human being possible. Either Rahner is being humanistic and reducing Christianity to philosophical language or he is being radically Christological and redefining humanity itself. However understood, Rahner presents Christology as the criterion for anthropology. Divinity is not something that is in opposition to Christ's humanity, but is the ultimate fulfilment of Christ's humanity. In his *Theological Investigations*, Rahner writes that 'the incarnation of God is … the unique, supreme, case of the total actualization of human reality'. What makes Christ unique is that he is the total actualization of humanity. It is as if openness to God is there potentially in humans across the board, but only in Christ is it actualized.

When Rahner writes about Christ he says that Christ should not merely be seen as a remedy for sin, because this would make sin at the centre of God's activity and Christianity. Ultimately, there is no theological understanding of humanity apart from humanity's fulfilment and actualization in Christ. Rahner focuses on the person of Christ and presents a Christologically shaped picture of humanity.

18.2.3 Grace

For Rahner grace is not a consequence of the work of Christ, but rather the incarnation (and especially in the death and resurrection of Christ) is the peak of God's gracious activity. Grace is God's self-communication; it is His giving of Himself to us. Rahner would say that grace operates on the level of transcendental experience. It is not on the level of the categorical. It is something beyond our normal experience, and it has to do with an alteration of our broader horizon. In our experience, grace is the coming near of God. He would say that it is on the more tacit level that grace is either accepted or rejected. It is not in our focal/foreground awareness that we are dealing with grace, but it has to do with this transcendental/background experience. So, grace is something that we experience, but not in the way that we experience determinate things.

One of the ramifications of this is that grace is something that is offered universally. It is not specially offered to one person and not another, but it is constantly in our experience. Grace constantly informs human spiritual life. So, for Rahner natural humanity is always already graced humanity. The difference between the two is only a theoretical distinction. With this we have a technical Rahnerian term: the '**supernatural existential**'. 'Existential' is a Heideggerian term for a fundamental structure of human experience. The 'supernatural existential' identifies the supernatural as a part of the fundamental or transcendental structure of human existence. Human nature always has the goal of relating to God—whether we are aware of it or not. It is rooted in the structure of human existence itself.

Yet, Rahner would say that this kind of grace can be accepted or rejected. To reject grace would mean something like living in dissonance. He would say that if grace only remained at this tacit level we would never be sure that God was offering himself to us or that we have accepted this grace. In Christ, God's self-gift is explicitly presented to us and we accept it explicitly. This is the highpoint of grace. He even goes so far as to say that Christ is the highpoint—or the point—of creation. God created the world in order to fully give himself to the world. Nature itself is Christological.

Part of the understanding of grace that Rahner has entails his controversial idea of **anonymous Christianity**—that people can be thought of as anonymous Christians. In his understanding of grace, it allows for the fact that we can accept grace without knowing that that is what we are doing. Grace is a part of this movement towards Christ, therefore we can accept Christ as the end of the movement without knowing that that is what we are doing. This is a way for him to talk (for Christians) about the potential salvation of our non-Christian neighbours. It is important to realize that Rahner presents this idea as a way for Christians to think about others. While some object that this disincentivizes the work of missions and evangelism, Rahner replies that this kind of understanding in fact enables missions by assuming the presence of grace as a movement towards God that enables people to hear the Gospel as an answer to their desires. Anonymous grace can be called forth in expression in explicit faith. Again, you cannot have certainty that you are being called or that you have accepted the gift apart from Christ.

18.2.4 Sacraments

Rahner holds a central place for the Catholic sacraments in his thought. He refers to the sacraments as 'real symbols'. What he means by this is that the sacraments symbolize something but also participate in what they symbolize. It is not just a sign for something that is absent, but that in the symbol you are participating in the reality that is symbolized. In the sacraments, the symbols are making real, actual and present what they symbolize. One of the examples that he gives is of a kiss: a kiss does not merely symbolize love as something that is absent, but love is in the kiss and is made present in the kiss.

Rahner presents the Church as the primary sacrament. The traditional seven sacraments of the Roman Catholic Church flow from the primary sacrament of the Church. So, as grace—which is operative in human life—leads to and reaches its peak in Christ, the Church is the primary reality of the presence of grace in Christ and the sacraments are expressions of the Church that came to be discovered later in time. There is a common movement from implicit to explicit presence.

Rahner has been quite influential following Vatican II. His ideas were—and are—often presented in simplified versions in many Catholic seminaries, especially in the 1970s and 1980s. This was the state-of-the-art Catholic theology for a time, and his theology has also ended up being the starting place for many Liberation Theologies.

18.3 Balthasar

Hans Urs von Balthasar (1905–88) is often regarded as the greatest Catholic theologian of the twentieth century. Balthasar and Rahner represent two of the broad streams of Catholic theology after Vatican II—two different styles of doing theology. The difference between them can be framed as relative to the way they view the relationship between theology and the world—or the Church and the world. Rahner represents the *Concilum* direction, while Balthasar represents the *Communio* direction—giving more of a privilege to the tradition. These are not exclusive terms so much as they are points of differing emphasis.

Balthasar was the son of a church architect in Lucerne, Switzerland. He studied German literature and philosophy at various universities—Zurich, Vienna and Berlin—and did his doctoral work on German Idealism. He became a Jesuit in 1929 and studied at a Jesuit school near Munich. He would later describe the philosophy taught there as a 'desert of Neo-Scholasticism'—as 'sawdust Thomism'. However, it was here that he met a figure who would be significant in his development, **Erich Przywara (1889–1972)**. Przywara was influential in the Catholic world in Germany. One of his key contributions was a work entitled *Analogia Entis* ('The Analogy of Being'). Balthasar was influenced by Przywara's understanding of analogy.

Balthasar ended up studying at Lyon-Fourvière for four years with **Henri de Lubac**. He also spent time with Bouillard and Daniélou. Because of this, Balthasar is sometimes treated as part of *nouvelle théologie*. However, his principal and substantial contribution comes in the later part of the twentieth century in his massive *Trilogy*.

Having studied at Lyon-Fourvière, he came to share the *ressourcement* perspective and was intensely interested in the patristic vision of Christianity throughout his life—specifically the manner in which the Church Fathers had a vision of the whole cosmos as related to Christ. It is from this perspective that he is critical of Neo-Scholastic theology. He was also strongly influenced by Henri de Lubac's *Catholicism*, which also presented such a grand, holistic vision of Christianity.

Balthasar never received a theological doctorate—although he did receive his licentiate in theology and philosophy. He also never held an academic post; this gave him a significant amount of freedom and independence. He was ordained and took a position at the University of Basel as a chaplain for Catholic students there. While he was offered a professorship at the Gregorian

University in Rome—probably the most prestigious Catholic university in the world—he chose to stay in Basel. He remained there for eight years, and while there he met **Adrienne von Speyr**—a medical doctor and a Catholic mystic. Balthasar developed a lifelong spiritual friendship with her that significantly influenced his thought and writings.

It is also while at Basel that Balthasar developed a long-term friendship with **Karl Barth**. Barth's demand to take Christian revelation seriously had an ongoing impact on Balthasar's thought. For both men, Christian revelation demands a radical change with God being the primary spontaneous agent. Balthasar also took on from Barth a dramatic perspective—such that theology fundamentally entails interpersonal relations and has a narrative structure. He also shared with Barth a critique of Liberal Protestantism. In fact, Balthasar saw parallels between the kinds of issues Barth had with Liberal Protestantism in some of the post-Vatican II Catholic theologies. The kinds of issues that Barth had with the Ritschlians Balthasar encountered with the *Concilium* crowd. Balthasar wrote a book on Karl Barth—*The Theology of Karl Barth*—in 1951, after Barth had completed the third volume of *The Church Dogmatics*. Thus, Balthasar wrote from the mature perspective of Karl Barth. This work was an extensive engagement with Barth and was framed with a shared interest with Barth for Church unity. There was an ultimate desire to see a unification between Protestants and Catholics. But in order to do this, neither Barth nor Balthasar was willing to overlook the real differences between Catholics and Protestants but instead sought to work through them. If there is going to be a commonality in the Christian communion, it has to be through the common affirmation of a common Christian faith. It is not taking what you believe less seriously, but thinking critically about what you believe in relation to the tradition.

In 1945, Balthasar and von Speyr founded a religious community called the *Johannesgemeinschaft*, the Community of St. John, aimed at lay people. Balthasar left the Jesuits five years later as the Jesuits would not allow him to have this religious community and still remain a member of the Jesuit order. After this, Balthasar dropped off of the ecclesiastical map; there was not really a place for him. He was a Catholic theologian, so he was not someone who Protestants read. He was not a professor, and his formal association within Catholicism was with the small community that he founded. He was relatively isolated in the 1950s, along with his friend Henri de Lubac, and ended up spending most of the rest of his life in Basel leading his community and writing. However, he returned to favour and became quite influential after Vatican II, when he developed a strong reputation as a conservative theologian, helping to found the journal, *Communio*. He was made a cardinal by John Paul II two days before he died.

Balthasar has a large literary output. He wrote some eighty-five books and over 500 articles. One of the earlier works of Balthasar is his *Apokalypse der deutschen Seele*, *The Apocalypse of the German Soul*, a three-volume study of German literature. Balthasar is intensively cosmopolitan—writing about art, literature, culture and music. (One of the common interests between Barth and Balthasar was their love of Mozart.) Balthasar had a vast knowledge of European culture—especially German culture—thus, he writes very broadly about the German intellectual tradition.

Balthasar also wrote—and we see his *ressourcement* perspective manifest here—three important works on what were relatively neglected Eastern Church Fathers. One was on Origen, *Origen: Spirit and Fire: A Thematic Anthology of His Writings* (1938). Here he follows Henri de Lubac in seeking to rehabilitate the figure of Origen as an important and worthwhile source for Christian theology. He also wrote *Cosmic Liturgy: The Universe According to Maximus the Confessor* (1941), and a significant book on Gregory of Nyssa entitled *Presence and Thought: Essay on the Religious Philosophy of Gregory of Nyssa* (1942).

The culmination of Balthasar's work is his magisterial *Trilogy* written between 1961 and 1987 and filling sixteen thick volumes. It is really the only twentieth-century work of theology comparable to Barth's *Church Dogmatics*. It is a grand conversation between modern philosophy and the breadth of the Christian tradition—especially focusing on the Church Fathers and the great medieval thinkers. What we see here, in what really represents the culmination of Balthasar's work as a theologian, is a holding together of the centrality of Christ and all of human thinking and culture. Christ is at the centre and the periphery is everything else in relation to Christ. Henri de Lubac said that Balthasar is 'perhaps the most cultured man of our time', and Balthasar believed that this edifice of Western culture had to be taken up, de-centred and re-centred on Christ. Human culture, for Balthasar, is *Aufhebung* in Christ.

Balthasar uses certain terms repeatedly to talk about this kind of movement: *ab- aus-, und eingerichtet*. He asserts that the lower order is at once *abgerechtet* or broken or trained (taken off where it is wrong), *ausgerichtet* or realigned (putting it into the right direction), and *eingerichtet* or re-established (what the lower is in relation to the higher). The idea is that the order of creation is only properly interpreted in the order of salvation. This is the relationship between the natural and the supernatural in a rough sense.

So, how then are human thought and revelation related to each other? Balthasar, in many places, talks about this relation in terms of analogy, or a relation within difference. There is a dissimilarity: revelation and the world are dissimilar. There is difference and yet there is relation in the midst of that difference. There is similarity, but it never negates the dissimilarity. The *Trilogy* is going to deal with the relation of Christian revelation to different aspects of human thought and being—specifically the three that he organizes the *Trilogy* around: beauty, human action and philosophy.

18.3.1 'Truth Is Symphonic'

The different domains of the human reality hold together in such a way that a common refrain of Balthasar's is that 'truth is symphonic'. In the light of Christ these different domains can be related to one another—not reduced to each other but related to each other in a symphonic manner. So the *Trilogy* is centred around what are called the classical transcendentals—the classical characterizations of being in terms of Unity, Beauty, Goodness and Truth. These transcendental categories of being are universals that transcend particular categories.

However, Balthasar is not an Idealist in only considering 'the Good' or 'the True' in the abstract. For Balthasar, we grasp reality through the senses; we always grasp the transcendentals through the particular and the concrete. We know these ultimate aspects of reality through the particularity of reality as we encounter it concretely. So Balthasar would say that the human subject is always already in relation to these manifestations of being in the way that we live in relation to things in the world. His project is to lay out how our everyday life and experience points to and participates through the transcendentals in God as the origin, ground, and source of being. Never do we encounter generic beings, but rather we encounter beings—and transcendentals are ways of talking about being as such. It is through the transcendentals that we connect the particular beings that we encounter in particular and concrete ways to God at the origin and the unity of these transcendentals.

Balthasar presents a holistic perspective. This is what he is getting at with his expression that 'truth is symphonic': he wants to see how things hold together into a unity. But this is always going to be a difference in harmony. This is not a simple unity where everything just gets reduced to a simple oneness—it is always a complex unity and a difference in harmony. In revelation the Triune God is always going to communicate to human beings in the midst of created plurality. That is the way that revelation has to come to us and the way that God communicates to us. The work of theology is then following that back to God—back to its unity in God.

Balthasar wants to see the transcendentals—the beautiful, the good and the true—as being bridges between God as the ultimate source of being and the finite beings in the world that we experience. The point is that our experience of things in the world will ultimately point us to the dramatic, Triune life of God. Balthasar says that all people have some understanding of these transcendentals without what Christians would regard as revelation. However, while this understanding of the good, the true and the beautiful is only fragmentary, it is a genuine foretaste. Revelation is a fulfilment of our initial understandings of God in the transcendentals of being.

18.3.2 Theological Aesthetics

The title of this first part of Balthasar's *Trilogy* is *Herrlichkeit*—translated into English as *The Glory of the Lord*. The subtitle is *A Theological Aesthetic*. This first and largest part of his *Trilogy* was written in seven hearty volumes and published in the 1960s. Here, Balthasar addresses (among many other things) the place of the senses in our experience of God. Especially in the Incarnation, God is made present to experience. Balthasar wants to talk about the difference the incarnation makes for our understanding of the world and God's relationship to it. The Incarnation should effect a properly Christian understanding of the senses, for in it the manifestation of God is supremely sensual and worldly.

In particular in the *Theological Aesthetics*, Balthasar is writing about **the beautiful**. You can see from the classical transcendentals—the beautiful, the good and the true—generally the themes of the three different parts of the *Trilogy*: first the beautiful, then the good, then the true. In the first part, Balthasar is examining the idea of beauty and how an object of perception is manifest in a particular way. It has a way of presenting itself—or he will say a 'style' of presenting itself. He will write about the beautiful in terms of form and glory. Beauty has to do with the **form** of an object. Form is a contraction of the world, of the totality of being to one degree or another—to greater and lesser intensity—into a particular form. In the beauty of any particular object, you have a coming-together or concentration of the whole world.

Balthasar thinks that beauty as a transcendental has a revealed correlate, and the revealed correlate of the form of beauty is the **glory** of God. In his *Theological Aesthetics*, he writes about how all worldly forms manifest the glory of God—but all of these forms are judged or measured by the central form of Christ as the Word. In Christ as the Word all other forms of beauty are taken up and broken/realigned/reset (*ab- aus-, und eingerichtet*). God is present as Super-Form—beyond all form but approached through the forms of the world; through beauty we have a desire for a form that transcends all of these. Here is a way of talking about the natural desire for the supernatural in an aesthetic mode. This is ultimately to experience the cosmos as a revelation of the love of God. That is the biggest picture of the cosmos. So in the aesthetics, he is trying to help the reader to develop a capacity or a habit of seeing the world as revealing God and fundamentally guided by the form of Christ.

In Balthasar's *Theological Aesthetics*, Christ in the Incarnation is the most direct manifestation of the glory of God. As such, God has a style of manifestation. The way God is manifest in the world tells us things about God. Where do we get to this style of the manifestation of God? Balthasar says that we particularly see it in the Bible as leading up to Christ as the centre of the whole and also in the history of the development of things in the Church thereafter. You have to take into account the particularities of revelation to get a sense for the style of the manifestation of God.

Perhaps in tension with Barth, Christ is not the only point of contact between humanity and God for Balthasar. Christ is however the centre and the height of that contact. The glory of God that is manifest in Christ is a strange glory relative to our common human understandings. The beauty of Christ is paradoxically ultimately revealed in the cross; it is a strange and terrible glory. It is revealed in the cross because in the cross is revealed—in the most fundamental way—who God is, and who God is is a life of love. In God's self is a Triune life of love. In the cross, that freely-given love is most manifest. What God is is most manifest to the world there.

In *The Glory of the Lord,* Balthasar also writes about there being a religious *a priori* and a theological *a priori*. The **religious *a priori*** has to do with ordinary human experience. Our ordinary human experience enables us to see God as a creator through the idea of transcendental beauty. We are able to see hints and traces of the divine in the forms of creation. This of course is something that Barth is going to reject, but here is traditionally what would be seen as a natural theology. Our experience of the world directs us towards God.

The **theological *a priori*** has to do with—instead of beginning with ordinary human experience—beginning with the central revealed doctrines of Christology and the Trinity. These doctrines are things that one cannot know from just looking at the world through our ordinary experience. What is revealed is not just the divine in and through creation but our ultimate end as sharing in the very life of the Trinity through Christ. Revelation (as something that is apart from our common experience) has the end of enabling us to see the Trinity—and to ultimately join in the life of the Trinity—through Jesus and the concrete happening of the Incarnation. This is the place of **grace** for Balthasar. It is the second or gratuitous gift beyond that of creation. Here, he is critical of Rahner, because he thinks that Rahner came too close (in his estimation) of reducing the theological to the religious. He comes too close to reducing grace to something that everyone already has immanently.

Part of Balthasar's presentation of aesthetics is his effort to combat what he sees as a degrading of the aesthetic in the modern world. Beauty or the aesthetic has been degraded insofar as it has been cut off from goodness and truth. Beauty—perhaps more strikingly and obviously than goodness and truth—has been easily accepted as relativistic matter of preference—something merely 'in the eye of the beholder'. It is simply a matter of taste. But Balthasar wants to combat this move towards relativism, which he sees as ultimately rooted in a modern positivism or materialism. If all there is is just stuff then any form is as good as any other form. He wants to see in the form of beauty as manifest in things in the world some relation to a transcendental.

Balthasar is particularly critical here of Protestantism. In Protestantism, there is a lost sense of the sacramental, of our connection to God through concrete, physical reality. Instead, he says that Protestant theology locates the relation to God in an overly-abstract or invisible manner. It does not have a way of talking about relating to God through the visible and the material—and therefore it has contributed to a loss of beauty having any kind of a normative value. Ultimately, with his theological aesthetics, Balthasar is seeking to examine how grace can be perceived in the world.

18.3.3 Theo-Drama

The second part of Balthasar's *Trilogy* is the *Theo-Drama* (*Theodramatik*). The *Theo-Drama* is five volumes and was written largely in the 1970s and early 1980s. Just as *Theological Aesthetic* focuses on the transcendental of the Beautiful, *Theo-Drama* focuses on the transcendental of the Good. It is related to theology in terms of our obedience to the divine Word. There are definite resonances to Barth's work here. The Word is not just to be understood in terms of aesthetic form in the Incarnation—and therefore in other forms of sacramental beauty—but also in the forms of life in the faithful. Balthasar looks to the saints as representing and mediating the form of Christ's life as it relates to the Good. Christ is the prototype or model of the good life. The lives of the saints through history are lesser interpretations in their particular historical contexts of the life of Christ.

The main category or metaphor that Balthasar uses throughout this part is that of **drama**. Drama has to do with agency—with subjects doing things. Actors act and things happen. Things are happening and people are doing things. Just as in the *Theological Aesthetic* he wants to show how all beauty is pointing towards a Christological horizon, in the *Theo-Drama* Balthasar wants to show how all human drama—human ethical and narrative agency—points to a Christological horizon. And as pointing to the Christological horizon, all human drama is therefore broken, realigned and reset (*ab- aus-, und eingerichtet*) in relation to it. In all of these different areas, this relation is his way of recognizing that with Barth Christ is a crisis that puts all of the world and human reality under judgement but not in terms of a simple negation. It is also a taking up and a realigning—and there is some connection between the two orders. The order of Christ is definitely the higher order, but there is relation between the higher and the lower—and Balthasar seeks to characterize that relation. This is where he is parting company with Barth, in seeing a greater relation between our everyday human experience of things and Christian revelation. He was also critical of Rahner as placing Christ and common human experience too much on the same plane.

As the beauty of the world is ultimately through Christ, so Balthasar will refer to human dramas as pointing us to the Trinity as the 'supra-drama'. In *Herrlichkeit* God is presented as super form.

Form leads us towards God, but ultimately the form of God is something that is going to be beyond our normal understanding of forms—in fact, our normal understandings of form through Christ are to be redefined as we come to a new understanding of form and beauty from the one above. So Balthasar will talk about the relation between human activity and the relationship between persons in the Trinity. The Trinity is itself a drama—it is a relation between persons. There is in God's self an eternal I–Thou relation. There is an eternal giving and receiving of love—the traditional term for this is *perichoresis*, referring to a dance. Balthasar represents the Christian understanding of the inner life of the Trinity as one of perichoretic self-donation; it is a giving-forth of love in the divine being between the divine persons. Here, he is talking about the Trinity and God as being fundamentally dynamic—that God is in God's self a drama.

From this perspective, Balthasar talks about the central mystery or the central drama of the Christian faith: the *Triduum*—the three days of Good Friday, Holy Saturday and Easter Sunday. These are the central points of the drama Christ as manifest: Christ's Passion, the descent into Hell, and the Resurrection. Balthasar sees in Christ how human events are related to the inner-relations and life of the Trinity. This is how the divine drama is manifest in the human drama. Primarily what we see is God acting for us. We are taking part in the same drama and story. In the death, burial and resurrection of Christ, we see God acting for us; God is freely acting for our salvation. We see the work of God's initiative on our behalf. Here, God is not being presented as a mere spectator but as an actor in the drama of the human story—indeed, he enters into the sin and suffering of creatures to the fullest extent. He enters into the full loss of humanity. God enters even into God-forsakenness, and end of the work of the Word on Earth is an inarticulate cry of forsakenness. He cries out aloud and then dies.

One of Balthasar's more controversial contributions to theology is his meditation on Holy Saturday. He talks about Hell as a place where God is absent. Ultimately, this is absurd as God is absent from no place, but this has to do with the absurdity of sin. Christ enters even into the depths of alienation from God and the absurdity of the absence of God. God Himself becomes Godforsaken. Holy Saturday for Balthasar is about Christ's total identification with humanity and human sin, death and damnation. He puts things rather strongly, but perhaps properly so.

Another way that Balthasar approaches the dramatic angle of Christian theology is the way in which he sees the Triune God taking part in the drama of the Christian story. He presents the Father as the **author** of the script—which is ultimately a revelation of God's inner life. The script is one of self-giving love that is ultimately God himself. He is the author, and he is also the **actor** in the person of the Son. He is the one who is performing the self-giving love. He is faithfully doing the will of the Father by emptying Himself. Here, he meditates on the patristic understanding of the two wills of Jesus—the human will being in full obedience to the divine will. Finally, the Spirit is the director **guiding** the Son in his performance. The point of the *Triduum* is to draw us onto the stage, to draw us into the dramatic action of God.

The goal in this way of talking about things is to transform our finite freedom in a way that does not absorb or negate our freedom. God even uses our own failures in the drama of human history. God enters into even our God-forsakenness—our sin, death and damnation—to bring us back to himself. Balthasar is trying to come to a richer understanding of the interrelation between human and divine freedom. The relation of finite human freedom to divine freedom is not an overwhelming mechanism that makes us into automatons. Rather, our relationship to God is dramatic. We have real agency and freedom in our relation to God.

Ultimately, Balthasar would say that in Christ divine infinite and human finite freedom are being united. Christ shows us how we can be at once free and obedient. Though these two things seem to be in opposition to one another, Christ dramatically shows us the unity and reconciliation of freedom and obedience.

18.3.4 Theo-Logic

The third part of Balthasar's *Trilogy* is the *Theo-Logic*, which is published from 1985 to 1987. *Theo-Logic* is three volumes long and focuses on the transcendental of the True—the real as being found in knowing or being as it is known. It wants to focus on Jesus as the centre of all being in relation to knowing.

The first volume in the *Theo-Logic* is entitled *The Truth of the World*. What we have in *The Truth of the World* is a philosophical account of truth. This is actually the first part of the *Trilogy* to be published, in 1947. Balthasar later reprints it as the first volume of the *Theo-Logic*. His philosophical account of truth is one of the very first things he works out before he starts this large project. In this volume, Balthasar presents a constructive approach to truth as at once phenomenological and ontological—meaning that truth is something that we have access to through our everyday experience, and that this everyday experience tells us about reality. It has to do with the appearances, but it does not just tell us about that—rather the way that things appear manifests being. There is very generally in Balthasar's account of truth an epistemological optimism (that we can have knowledge) and a realism (that what we are knowing has something to do with the way things really are).

The second volume is entitled *The Truth of God*. Here is where Christ is being presented as the truth of God. Sometimes this part is called the *Christo-Logic*. In Christ, the eternal Logos is revealed in a human being. What difference does the incarnation make when we think about truth? What difference does it make that the eternal Logos became flesh when it comes to our thinking about truth? Here, Balthasar is talking about a theological relationship between the truth of the Trinity and the world through Christ. Through Christ we can see that all personhood has to do with relation—inter-subjectivity—therefore is an echo of the inner-Trinitarian life. Through Christ, there is a uniting of the world to God. There is a reconciling, very generally.

The final volume is *The Spirit of Truth*, in which Balthasar presents a Pneumatology relative to Truth. What the Spirit does in this volume is that he interprets the Son. It is in the Spirit that Christ is known as the Son of the Father. Here, you can see a bit of Barth's Trinitarian Christology early on, where in revelation God is not just passing on information but is present in the Word—and as the incarnate Christ—and as the Spirit interprets that from our end, as it were. The Spirit is the present appropriation of that Word. With this is the ultimately Augustinian idea in both Barth and Balthasar that only a divine person (the Spirit) can expound the truth of the Son of the Father. Only God can reveal God. The Spirit is then the one who will lead the disciples into all Truth. He is the one who leads us into the way of Christ. Implicit in this is an ecclesiology of how the Spirit is manifest in the life of the Church both subjectively (in mystical and charismatic modes) and objectively (in institutional and traditional modes).

Sources and Further Reading

Dorrien, Gary. 'The Golden Years of Welfare Capitalism: The Twilight of the Giants'. In *The Twentieth Century: A Theological Overview*, edited by Gregory Baum, 91–103. Maryknoll, NY: Orbis, 1999.

Kerr, Fergus. *Twentieth-Century Catholic Theologians*. Oxford: Blackwell, 2007.

Kilby, Karen. *Karl Rahner: A Brief Introduction*. New York: Crossroad Publishing, 1997.

Kilby, Karen. 'Karl Rahner'. In *The Modern Theologians: Introduction to Christian Theology since 1918*, edited by David F. Ford with Rachel Muers, 92–105, 3rd edn. Oxford: Blackwell, 2005.

Kristiansen, Staale Johannes. 'Hans Urs von Balthasar'. In *Key Theological Thinkers: From Modern to Postmodern*, edited by Staale Johannes Kristiansen and Svein Rise, 249–65. Aldershot: Ashgate, 2013.

Livingston, James C. and Francis Schüssler Fiorenza. *Modern Christian Thought: Volume 2, The Twentieth Century*. 2nd edn. Minneapolis, MN: Fortress Press, 2006.

Nichols, Aidan. *A Key to Balthasar: Hans Urs von Balthasar on Beauty, Goodness, and Truth*. Grand Rapids, MI: Baker Academic, 2011.

Quash, Ben. 'Hans Urs von Balthasar'. In *The Modern Theologians: Introduction to Christian Theology since 1918*, edited by David F. Ford with Rachel Muers, 106–23, 3rd edn. Oxford: Blackwell, 2005.

Rise, Svein. 'Karl Rahner'. In *Key Theological Thinkers: From Modern to Postmodern*, edited by Staale Johannes Kristiansen and Svein Rise, 225–37. Aldershot: Ashgate, 2013.

Rowland, Tracey. 'Catholic Theology in the Twentieth Century'. In *Key Theological Thinkers: From Modern to Postmodern*, edited by Staale Johannes Kristiansen and Svein Rise, 37–52. Aldershot: Ashgate, 2013.

Schreiter, Robert J. 'The Impact of Vatican II'. In *The Twentieth Century: A Theological Overview*, edited by Gregory Baum, 158–72. Maryknoll, NY: Orbis, 1999.

19

Liberation Theologies

19.1 Political Theology

19.1.1 Germany: Moltmann and Metz

What is called 'Political Theology' developed in Germany, in the 1960s, specifically in West Germany. The two most significant figures are **Jürgen Moltmann** and **Johann Baptist Metz**. In the background of political theology in Germany is the person and work of Karl Marx. Political theology takes as a starting place for theology a moral outrage at the treatment of the poor and the conditions of workers in the modern world. It has built into it a utopian ideal of a just (or at least more just) society or a non-alienated society.

The focus of political theology is the underside of history and society, looking at history from the perspective of the victims of history. Political theologians in Germany—but also in the Americas—are going to use Marxism as a tool for social analysis to yield such perspectives. In Germany in particular, political theology is inspired by the philosophy of **Ernst Bloch (1885–1977)**, whose philosophy, a revised version of Marxism, is characterized as a philosophy of hope. Bloch emphasizes—and blends in with Marx—strong ideas of Jewish–Christian eschatology. He sees that Marxist utopianism ultimately came from biblical roots. Marxist critique is at its root a biblical, prophetic critique of society, and an essential element of this critique is hope. The other side of a biblical critique of present society is the future dimension of hope. Bloch presents a much more positive view of religion when it comes to social transformation—specifically that religion's place in the critique of ideology or the transformation of society is in terms of hope.

In New Testament studies, **Ernst Käsemann (1906–98)**, a student of Bultmann, is a significant influence. After Bultmann, Käsemann effects a revival of eschatology in the study of the New Testament. Bultmann often reads eschatology as something to be reinterpreted into present, existential terms—but Käsemann wants to hold on to a genuinely eschatological dimension in order to be true to the New Testament vision.

Jürgen Moltmann (1928–) is a Reformed theologian, heavily influenced by Karl Barth. Moltmann has written much, but his most significant work in this context is entitled *A Theology of Hope* (1964). In it, he brings together the transformed Marxism of Bloch and the dialectical theology of Barth. Another significant figure is **Johann Baptist Metz (1928–)**, a German Catholic theologian who studied at Innsbrook with Rahner. The two represent the Protestant Barthian stream and the Catholic Rahnerian stream brought to bear to address political situations. Both Moltmann and Metz see the central place of hope in thinking about the transformation of society from a theological perspective. Both are likewise critical of theology as having ignored history. Both of these figures are very consciously post–Second World War theologians. Both are drafted into the German army as teens, and both are captured and imprisoned. They experience being on the losing side of history, so they want to be able to address history and the things that happen in history—and also to address the reality of human suffering. Both feel that such suffering had been insufficiently addressed in theology. Both oppose the individualism of early-twentieth-century theologies as too focused on the individual and their experience, and not enough on the community or the social. They often lay blame here with Existentialism. When they look at Bultmann, Rahner and Barth, they see this earlier generation as too individualistic and so failing to see the properly political dimensions of theology. Theology needs to deal not just with history in general but with concrete history. Both Moltmann and Metz see a social dimension to both sin and the Gospel. Sin is not merely something within the individual, but there are sinful structures of society. Likewise, the Good News is not just about individual transformation but entails social transformation and redemption as well.

19.1.2 America: Reinhold Niebuhr

Reinhold Niebuhr (1892–1971) is often associated with Neo-Orthodoxy although he resists the label. An American theologian, social critic and ethicist—and, up to his time, the most well-known American theologian, Niebuhr believes that Christian theologians have something to say about political and economic issues.

Niebuhr spent a significant period of time as a minister in Detroit where he is sensitized to the exploitation of industrial workers—mainly in the auto industry in America. He serves as a minister, preaching to people who are having a hard time and seeking to negotiate the gap between theology and the socio-economic realities of his parishioners.

Niebuhr's theology is often characterized generally as a **Christian realism**. It is a realism as opposed to the naivety of Ritschlian Classical Liberalism. He falls in line with the other dialectical theologians—the 'Neo-Orthodox' theologians—in being critical of Liberal Protestantism as lacking a sufficient view of sin. They are naïve in that they do not understand the seriousness of sin in the human situation. Therefore, theology urgently needs to address the universality of sin and the way that sin is a pressing concrete and social reality in the life of people.

Niebuhr's main work, entitled *The Nature and Destiny of Man* (Vol. 1, 1941; Vol. 2, 1943), is a Christian anthropology. In it he draws quite a bit on Kierkegaard's theological anthropology—specifically from *The Sickness Unto Death*. The human being is presented as a synthesis that is out of balance. He spends a considerable amount of time trying to understand what sin is—ultimately in terms of rebellion or a selfishness. It is **self-indulgent** in terms of being pleasure seeking or in terms of **self-assertion**, of seeking power. Sin—in the forms of self-indulgence or self-assertion—is rooted in the distorted tension of sinful human being. There is a tension in the human between nature and transcendence, and that tension brings about anxiety or insecurity. Self-assertion and self-indulgence are ways of trying to—and failing to—deal with this anxiety between nature and transcendence. He writes famously in *The Nature and Destiny of Man* that original sin is 'the only empirically verifiable doctrine of the Christian faith'. Yet Liberal Protestantism has ignored it.

19.2 Latin American Liberation Theology

Liberation Theologians will look back on the achievements of such Protestant thinkers as Barth, Bultmann, Tillich and Niebuhr. This forms the reigning establishment in Western theology in the Protestant world. In the mid-1960s, however, there is a big shift, and this is part of the big shift into the supernova that Taylor talks about. These big names begin to lose their voices in the theological discussion. What arises in the place of the dialectical or Neo-Orthodox establishment as dominant in academic theology are plural forms of liberation theologies.

One can talk about these liberation or liberationist theologies as 'particularizing' or 'contextual' theologies. These are different ways of talking about what is being addressed here as a general category. The common thrust here is that they are all realizing that theology is not done with a view from nowhere but is always done from within a particular perspective. There are many different perspectives, and these theologians wish to honour the differences between these perspectives. The context—be it socio-economic, cultural or gendered—from which one does theology matters on a fundamental level.

19.2.1 Latin America

Most of the figures who are the leaders in Latin American liberation theology study initially in Europe but then develop that European theology in a different context in order to address different concerns. The concerns of the communities that they serve are very different to those of relatively affluent Europeans—specifically when it comes to the poverty of Latin America, in that they are in a position of subservience to North America in the Western hemisphere.

The particular situation of Latin American liberation theology is that of poverty and oppression. In the 1960s, in Latin America, there are two different perspectives on the best direction to take to address these concerns: liberation or development. The latter has to do with the way the first world—the capitalist West—has industrialized the third world. This is the reigning perspective in Latin American in the 1950s. But as the 1950s progress, many see Latin America as not so much being developed, as it is exploited—and this becomes more evident in the 1960s. Rather, what they see is a fundamental relationship of dependency between South America and North America. This provides a large advantage to the North, and in the South there is still widespread poverty. Things are not improving in the way that development has been sold. The way forward, then, is not development but liberation—a more radical departure from and/or transformation of oppressive power structures.

Theology in this context is both informed by the suffering of poverty, yet also seeks to address it. Again, the emphasis is placed on the context in which theology is done. A different context for theology is going to make theology have a very different expression because it is going to be driven by different concerns.

19.2.2 Medellín

There are a few particularly significant events that served to give definition to Latin American Liberation Theology. The first is the Second General Conference of the Latin American Episcopal Council (*Consejo Episcopal Latinoamericano*) in Medellín, Columbia in 1968, often shortened to CELAM II. This was a local council gathering together Latin American bishops in Columbia. They wanted to implement some of Vatican II's pastoral reforms. At the same time, they sought to address the particularities of what the mission of the Church should be in Latin America. The theme that comes to the fore is that, in order to make life better for the people they are serving through the Church, the church leaders needed to go beyond the model of development towards that of liberation. There are revolutionary elements to the discourse at CELAM II.

The bishops there denounce the widespread injustice, oppression and exploitation in Latin America, whether it be by the companies and/or governments of North America or by the corrupt governments of Latin America. CELAM II explicitly recognizes that there are structures of society that are sinful. It is because of these sinful structures of society that things like systematic poverty exist. Poverty exists because of sinful structures such that in them humanity's social being is being distorted. Redemption then is not only about reconciling humans to God but also transforming these sinful structures. Not only should the individual life be transformed, but the social life should be transformed as well.

As a way towards this goal of social redemption, there was a call at CELAM II for an emphasis on what were called 'base communities'. This is an emphasis on the laity in the Church. Base communities, sometimes called 'basic Christian communities', are grassroots communities. They concentrate on the laity taking on many roles that were traditionally that of the clergy such that the laity takes an active and not merely passive role in being the Church. It is not an anti-clerical movement but is rather an empowering of the laity.

There are different practices that are encouraged in the Medellín council, such as the reading of Scripture in the context of these lived communities. The laity should read Scripture together, and it is out of this most concrete level—this base level—of the Christian community that they think there is a privileged perspective on Scripture. They can understand Scripture because they are in the context that needs to be addressed. They are living in the situation of poverty and oppression, and so they are in a particular situation that gives them the ability to see what needs to be seen in Scripture. This is also the concrete setting in which their understanding of Scripture should transform the way that they are living. So there is a going back and forth between what they call **praxis**—the practices of the Church—and the reading of Scripture. One begins with praxis, with the situation in which the people are. The base community in that situation reads Scripture. But their reading of Scripture should then bring them to having a different perspective on their situation. There is a hermeneutical circle here. Such theology that arises from the lived situation is going to be a contextual theology. This gives the laity an opportunity to shape the understanding of Scripture.

Another key aspect of what the Medellín conference encourages is **conscientization**—making-conscious or consciousness-raising. One of the things that needs to be addressed is that the poor are not fully aware of their situation. These communities need to be made more aware of what is going on and aware of the possibilities of what they can do to transform their situation—so they can be more active instead of passively receiving. There is a shift of the locus of theology towards these base communities of the Church.

19.2.3 Puebla

The other significant conference for Latin American Liberation Theology is the Puebla conference—the Regional Synod Latin American Bishops at Puebla, sometimes called CELAM III. It was opened by Pope John Paul II. One of the themes that comes to the fore there and becomes widespread in

Latin American Liberation Theology is that of the **preferential option for the poor**. Here, there is a theological recasting of the Marxist siding with the underside of history in saying that God has a preferential option for the poor. These Latin American theologians see in Scripture the manner in which God sides with the poor and the outcast against oppression. From this perspective, addressing the situation of the poor should be a central focus of theology. The poor are, in fact, in a better position to understand Christian theology; they are the primary addressees of God's message of hope. They are in a better position to know God in a sense because they are deprived of everything else. They also have a privileged view of sin. They understand the corruption of the world more keenly because they are its victims. Christianity's preferential option for the poor should seek to take on the preferred perspective of the poor in history and to address the poor and show that they are human subjects that can be active in history.

In Puebla the bishops also take up the theme from German political theology of **eschatology**. They, however, critique Moltmann and Metz as presenting the coming Kingdom of God as excessively other. In their version, it is so different from this world that the Kingdom of God equally condemns all political orders. Such a conception of the Kingdom of God is no help when it comes to trying to transform society in a better direction because all political orders come under judgement. The Latin American bishops want instead to see eschatology or the Kingdom of God as a frame for seeing how the Kingdom is being realized in the present. What does it look like for the Kingdom of God to come? How do we help it usher in the Kingdom?

Emphases in Latin American Liberation Theology

Critique of political and economic idolatry

God as on the side of the poor and oppressed

Christ's suffering in solidarity

Christ as Liberator

Communio understanding of the revitalization of the Church

Kingdom of God entails the transformation of this world

Some of the big themes of Latin American Liberation Theology can be reflected in the emphases of these two regional conferences. First, when it comes to God, Latin American Liberation Theology is going to set forth the possibility of political and economic idolatry. The **understanding of God** can be a way of simply celebrating not God, but the worldly powers that be. As opposed to this, they want to see God as not underwriting the claims of the rich and powerful, but at work in liberating the poor and oppressed. Liberation theologians commonly focus on the biblical narrative of the Exodus. The Exodus is a great example of God siding not with the oppressor, but with the oppressed—and is acting to liberate the oppressed. When it comes to **Christology**, Latin American Liberation Theology focuses on the suffering of Christ as a work of solidarity. This is looking at Christology from the perspective of a suffering people. In the suffering of Christ, he is entering into our suffering and suffers with us. There is a centrality of the cross in the picture of Christ in Latin American Liberation Theology. Jesus is also presented as a liberator; Jesus comes to bring good news to the poor. He is breaking the chains of oppression and leading the poor out of oppression. The Resurrection is to be seen as a sign that God is on the side of the victims. God is on the side of those who suffer. As God raised Christ from the dead, so will God vindicate the victims of history. Finally, there is a particular understanding of **ecclesiology**. Latin American Liberation Theology is largely (but not exclusively) Catholic and often critical of the Church hierarchy. They believe that the revitalization of the Church will come from below and thus focuses on the *communio* model of the Church seen coming from Congar and out of Vatican II. In the Church, the Kingdom of God is coming into the world. The Kingdom of God has to do with liberation in this world and not just in the world to come. In the Church, the Kingdom is impinging on the present world.

19.2.4 Gutiérrez

The one theologian oft cited as the principal founder of Latin American Liberation Theology is the Peruvian **Gustavo Gutiérrez (1928–)**. He studied in Lima for a time, but then travelled to Europe, where he studied at Leuven, Belgium and Lyon, France. Although he is a priest, he ends up being a theological advisor at the Medellín CELAM conference. His most influential work is entitled *A Theology of Liberation* (1971) and is the classic work of Latin American Liberation Theology—in fact, it is largely from this book that 'liberation theology', in general, takes its name.

In it, Gutiérrez presents theology as being contextual. Theology is rooted in and addresses a particular situation, and that swings both ways. Not only should theology be done in the context of the situation of the poor and the oppressed that God wants to address, but also theological reflection that is done in the context of the rich and powerful is affected by that as well. The poor and oppressed should have a hermeneutic of suspicion when it comes to theology that is written from the context of the rich and powerful.

A Theology of Liberation is, among other things, a critique of ideology from within Christian theology. Theology has lent ideological justification to unjust power structures; theology can become a function of oppression itself. In order to counter theology's being co-opted in the name of the established order, Gutiérrez emphasizes liberation as one of the key goals of theology. He calls for the work of theology to be rooted in the struggle of the poor for liberation. In the Latin American context, theology addresses those who hitherto have been presented as non-persons. Theology should emerge out of the experience of the Church community as people struggling with poverty and injustice.

One of the things that Gutiérrez does in *Theology of Liberation* is present a kind of theological method. He says that the proper method for a theology of liberation is a critical reflection on Christian praxis. The key here is that the first moment is praxis. One begins with the lived situation and then reflects critically upon it. This reflection is meant to guide action within the given situation. Theology is not detached from the given situation but arises from it—one begins with a rich awareness of the given situation. This is because all human knowledge is motivated and connected to a given social context whether we are aware of it or not. Theory and practice then should have an ongoing interaction—a going-back-and-forth between the practical, lived situation and reflection on the situation.

Gutiérrez focuses on the political implications of Jesus's life and message. Like many Latin American liberation theologians after him, Gutiérrez emphasizes how Jesus's central message in the Gospels is proclaiming the Kingdom of God. Here, Jesus is in line with the Hebrew prophets in taking the side of the poor. This is the political dimension to the preaching of Jesus.

In *A Theology of Liberation*, Gutiérrez also talks about how sin has to do with the dehumanizing structures of society. There are destructive institutions, and to bring about a change in these theologians need to help raise the consciousness of the population: a *concientización*. People need to be made aware of the structural sin that is the cause of much of their misery.

When it comes to Gutiérrez's ecclesiology, he is influenced by *nouvelle théologie* and Vatican II. The mission of the Church is to incarnate the connection between grace and the world. As such, the Church should retrieve a more proper understanding of the Church itself as a sacrament and a symbol of God's grace.

Gutiérrez's levels of liberation

| historical–political |
| historical–existential |
| soteriological |

Finally, Gutiérrez gives a distinctive understanding of salvation as something that should be seen in the midst of different levels of liberation. He wants to understand salvation in relation to liberation. He presents different levels of liberation as going progressively deeper. The first level is an historical–political level. The historical–political level of liberation has to do with liberation relative to oppressed social classes. This is about improving the lot of the poor in society. However, there is a deeper level of liberation that needs to come about that this first level is dependent upon—and that is what he calls an historical–existential level of liberation. For the poor and oppressed to be liberated and throw off their poverty and oppression, they need to cease to think of themselves as non-persons. They need to become responsible human actors; they need to take an active role in their own destiny. And so to have a transformed self-image, they have to think about themselves differently. But this is also rooted on a more fundamental level, and that is what he calls a soteriological level of liberation. Salvation is ultimately the foundation of liberation, because ultimately it is Christ who leads us to liberation from sin that makes societal liberation possible. It is because of sin that there is a lack of freedom and therefore social injustice. There needs to be a liberation from sin on a deep level to bring about a greater personal freedom and then societal liberation. Gutiérrez is not simply redefining salvation as a certain political project but is wanting to show how the work of Christ is the root and foundation of the coming of Kingdom of God in the transformation of society.

19.2.5 Decline

After the 1980s, there is a general decline in Latin American Liberation Theology. There are four principal reasons for this decline. The **first** is that there is opposition from the Vatican. The Vatican tended to oppose liberation theology largely because there were priests who were getting involved with various Marxist and Communist revolutionaries. **Second**, in 1989 the Berlin Wall falls, symbolizing the retreat of Marxist regimes not only in Eastern Europe but also around the world. This really takes the wind out of the sails of liberation theologians who take inspiration from Marxist utopianism. **Third**, the politics of Latin America becomes relatively more stable in the 1980s. In the 1960s and 1970s, there are many rather nasty military dictatorships in Latin America and almost constant civil war. These die down somewhat in the 1980s, during which the general trend in Latin American countries is the election of Socialist or Social-Democratic presidents. **Fourth**, a significant part of the poor themselves end up giving their preferential option to Pentecostalism rather than politicized Liberation Theology.

19.3 Feminist Theology

Feminist Theology arises from an awareness that Christian theology in the past has been done largely by men and for men, and, thus, has ignored or misrepresented to one degree or another the experience of women. Feminist Theology seeks to remedy this trend by exploring theology from the context of the experience of women.

In 1949, the French philosopher Simone de Beauvoir published the seminal work *The Second Sex*. In it she makes the point that in Western culture men are tacitly and often explicitly presented as 'the first sex', in the sense that the standard for humanity is male humanity with women being 'the second sex' and so judged relative to the norm of male humanity. In 1963, American Betty Friedan publishes her influential work *The Feminine Mystique*. The cultural shifts and anti-authoritarian ethos in the 1960s in America provide fertile ground for feminist critiques of male-centred traditional understandings. Feminist Theology largely develops in this context in 1960s and 1970s in the United States. Much of the Feminist Theology originates within Liberal Protestantism in America, which has a great openness to new ways of approaching theology. Feminist Theology is a theology that intentionally takes the experience of women as a significant source and norm. Like Latin American Liberation Theology, Feminist Theology begins with a particular context or situation—and the particular context of Feminist Theology is women's struggle for liberation. Feminist Theology likewise seeks to contribute to the liberation of women in a patriarchal society.

19.3.1 Feminisms

There are different versions of feminism arising in the twentieth century; we will briefly outline the three most influential. The first is a **'liberal' feminism**. The central idea for liberal feminism is that women are equal to men and so should have equal rights. Women and men share a common human nature, and whatever gender differences there are cultural constructs. Liberal feminism combines a **constructionist** view of gender—that gender roles are just a construct of society—with an **essentialist** view of human nature—men and women share the same common humanity.

'**Radical**' **feminism** says, however, that women are basically different than men. They are biologically different, and this is supremely significant. Feminism should not see how women are the same as men but should celebrate how they are fundamentally different. This is more of an **essentialist** view of gender. Radical feminism places great value on essentially female qualities. Sometimes this is presented as valuing the female qualities as well as valuing particularly male qualities, but usually female qualities are valued over and against particularly male qualities. It is not uncommon for this vision to see womanhood as itself inherently caring, empathetic, peaceful and egalitarian—whereas the male is essentially domineering, hierarchical and warlike. For radical feminists, the opposition between the female and the male is often a zero-sum game.

	Gender	Human Nature
Liberal Feminism	Constructionist	Essentialist
Radical Feminism	Essentialist	Essentialist
Postmodern Feminism	Constructionist	Constructionist

The third prevalent feminism in the twentieth and twenty-first centuries is a '**postmodern**' **feminism**. This version of feminism wants to avoid all generalizations and essentialist conceptions of gender as well as human nature in general. The emphasis here is on difference. Postmodern feminism will agree with liberal feminism to a certain extent by being constructionist. It also views gender as a social construction. However, postmodern feminism will go beyond liberal feminism in presenting human nature itself as a culturally conditioned construction as well. There is no such thing as an essential human nature in which men and women are equal. It wants to emphasize difference. Ultimately, there is no escaping social constructions and getting down to a common, equal nature. This comes out of a post-structuralist context in which the social–linguistic construction is all-pervasive. If you get rid of the social constructions, you will not have anything to talk about. Postmodern feminists emphasize how structures of meaning and categories that are taken to be essential in fact arise from power relations in society. Language is rooted in structural, societal relations. With this, postmodern feminists will see gender as being associated in broader, symbolic structures, divisions or distinctions. They will talk about **gendered binaries.** They would say that in society you commonly have a binary of male and female. In a given society, power and meaning happens through setting up opposed situations, and usually privileging one over the other. Male is typically privileged over female, but there are other associations there. In the male vs. female relation, there is also culture vs. nature (where nature tends to be associated with female and culture with male), spirit vs. matter, reason vs. emotion, mind vs. body, etc. In Western society as it is developed, it has set up these binaries and has privileged the ones that are associated with the male. These are the primary and secondary categories.

Gendered binaries				
Male	Culture	Spirit	Reason	Mind/Soul
Female	Nature	Matter	Emotion	Body

19.3.2 Patriarchy

In order to treat some of the common traits and contributions of Feminist Theology, we will progress through five methodological moments generally speaking. The first moment is acknowledging the oppression of women. This is the initial, negative moment of Feminist Theology. Here is a recognition that in much of traditional Christian theology women are denied full humanity and that the voices of women are largely absent. Traditional theology supports a **patriarchy**—a hierarchy that enforces the male subjugation of women. Many Scriptural texts are used to reinforce the subordination of women. Related to this support of a patriarchal sexist power structure, there is also an **androcentrism** to much of traditional Christian theology. Androcentrism sees the male as the central, normal or 'first' sex, and the female is then an inferior, not fully human, off-standard representation of humanity.

Feminist biblical interpretation sees how androcentrism or patriarchy is present in biblical texts. It will also see how texts of Scripture have been misused over time to justify the subjugation of women. An important work in this regard is Phyllis Trible's *Texts of Terror: Literary-Feminist Readings of Biblical Narratives* (1984). This work specifically addresses texts in the Old Testament in which women are subordinated, excluded and abused. These are texts that are then used to perpetuate such abuse against women. Scripture as a product of patriarchal culture has been used to perpetuate such a patriarchy.

A significant feminist theologian in this domain is **Mary Daly (1928–2010)**, one of the pioneering feminist theologians. Her first major work is entitled *The Church and the Second Sex* (1968). In this work she is representing more of the ideal of liberal feminism in relation to Christian theology. However, afterward she shifts her way of thinking such that in her *Beyond God the Father* (1973) she depicts Christianity as inherently patriarchal and irredeemably sexist. She largely ceases to be a Christian theologian in seeing that in the Christian religion maleness is associated with God to such a degree that it excludes women. If one wants to have a positive view of women, Christianity is going to be nothing but an obstacle. Daly writes that 'if God is male then male is God'. A masculine view of God reinforces a patriarchal society. This is an extreme expression of the critical moment of Feminist Theology.

19.3.3 Particularity

The second significant moment in Feminist Theology (in our heuristic presentation of a general method of sorts) is recognizing the particularity of women's experience. Here, we are on the ground of Liberation Theology more generally in addressing the particular experience of women. Women's experience is different from that of men. As theology is always done out of a particular context and set of concerns so theology done out of the context of women's experience will be different from that of men, animated by different motivating concerns. More generally, there are just differences in the male and female psyche, and we should recognize that particularity.

An important example of this can be seen in an influential early article entitled 'The Human Situation: A Feminine View' (1960), in which Valerie Saiving Goldstein argues that a key point in moving forward and incorporating the experience of women into Christian theology is realizing that women's temptations are not the same as those of men. She makes a distinction between masculine sin and feminine sin. Masculine sin is what is traditionally seen as sin—pride, selfishness, aggressiveness. Feminine sin, however, is more about a failure of agency or a lack of assertion.

19.3.4 Retrieval

The third moment is a moment of retrieval—seeking to retrieve traditions (Christian and sometimes otherwise) in order to inform and fund a more relevant and positive theology for women. When it comes to asking what the sources are for a Feminist Theology one of them is understanding the experience of women, but another source is recovering a memory of other voices within the Christian tradition, Christian history and in Scripture. There are feminist Church historians who look back into the history of the Church in order to find female leaders in the Church in order to bring forward this historical awareness as a resource. Also in this domain you have feminist biblical interpretation that examines Scripture not only to see patriarchal 'texts of terror', but also as having emancipatory potential for women.

German New Testament scholar **Elisabeth Schüssler Fiorenza (1938–)** in *In Memory of Her* (1983) finds in the earliest Jesus movement resources for feminist reform. While it is not necessarily in the final version of the New Testament, there are signs of it in earlier layers of the tradition. You can see this in different ways in Scripture as we have it, such as the way in which women are presented in the Gospels as the true disciples of Jesus in the Passion narratives. Also Jesus's message implies a vision of a discipleship of equals that later tradition had obscured or compromised. Schüssler Fiorenza wants to reconstruct how likely it was in the Early Church that women had greater roles. As a symbol of the kind of retrieval that she is trying to do, the title of the book comes from the story of the woman who anointed Jesus with oil. Mark 14:9 reads that 'wherever the gospel is preached in the whole world, what this woman has done will also be spoken of in memory of her'. And yet we are never told her name. Her name is lost to us, so there is this at once a memory but also a loss of memory. We remember her, but we have forgotten anything about her.

Other scholars look in Scripture and the Christian tradition for feminine imagery of God—such as wisdom imagery in the Old Testament. Also, feminist theologians will draw from outside of the Christian tradition—sometimes from pagan religions or heretical Christian sects or philosophical and political movements—to bring in ideas that can fund a feminist theology. A recurring emphasis here is the prophetic and liberating tradition of Scripture from the Exodus to the prophets to Jesus in which the marginalized are advocated for and vindicated. This moment of retrieval is often presented in conjunction and tension with the first moment such that Feminist Theologies can be seen as reading (retrieved liberative) Scripture against (patriarchal oppressive) Scripture.

19.3.5 Revision

The fourth moment, then, is a moment of revision, of revising traditional Christian doctrines. This goes beyond attending to the particularity of women's experience and finding emancipatory strains in the tradition or in Scripture to doing systematic theology in such a way as to take these things into account. A significant figure in America and probably the best-known feminist theologian in North America is **Rosemary Radford Ruether (1936–)**, who teaches at Garrett-Evangelical Theological Seminary. She is a Roman Catholic theologian who has drawn much inspiration from Latin American liberation theologies. An influential book of hers is entitled *Sexism and God-Talk: toward a Feminist Theology* (1983). In this work, she explicitly utilizes Tillich's method of correlation. As Tillich will talk about the situation which provides the form of theology, Ruether holds that in a Feminist Theology women's experience is the situation that provides the form of theology. Women's experience has a normative function for the way theology is done, to which the traditional doctrines and symbols are then correlated as answers to questions. Other significant feminist systematic theologians are **Elizabeth Johnson (1941–)**—a Roman Catholic theologian and author of *She Who Is: A Mystery of God in Feminist Theological Discourse* (1992)—and **Catherine LaCugna (1952–97)**, author of *God for Us* (1993).

Walking through some of the particular doctrines of systematic theology gives us a fuller view of what feminist systematic theologies look like. **Anthropology** is one of the obvious sites for revision. A feminist systematic theology is going to challenge the understanding of the human as being standardly male. Part of this—with the above list of binaries in mind—is challenging the traditional view that humanity's highest capacity is rationality, such that one is being 'most human' when one is being most rational. Feminist thinkers will say that this is a particularly male approach to humanity. They are wanting to balance this with a feminist emphasis on relationality, emotion and the body. They want to balance reason with emotion, and also to balance preference of spirit with an emphasis on the body—the human as embodied. While there is no shortage of sympathetic material regarding relations, emotions and embodiment in the broad Christian tradition, feminist systematic theologians will give these sites a particular emphasis. Related to such an understanding of humanity is a different approach to sin as mentioned above relative to Saiving Goldstein's work. There may be more characteristically female temptations to sin and male temptations to sin.

When it comes to the doctrine of **God**, different thinkers go in different directions. Ruether argues that a particularly male way of thinking of God is in terms of a dualism—seeing God as separate and distinct from the world. Ruether prefers Tillich's understanding of God as ground of being and being immanent. She is reading transcendence as a dualism, and wants to see God rather as a ground of being and more immanent and in intimate relation. She presents a view that is perhaps closer to a pantheism, emphasizing the immanence of God as a more Feminine emphasis on God. Schüssler Fiorenza wants to draw on the Sophia tradition—the tradition of divine wisdom.

Sallie McFague (1933–) has written on the use of metaphor in theology, and comments that there are many different 'imperialist metaphors' for God that are used in theology. She wants to say that all God-talk is always indirect and metaphorical, and therefore none of the imagery of the tradition is non-figurative. There is then room for more metaphors, and so she thinks that masculine ways of talking about God—say as Father—should be augmented or supplemented with more feminine and maternal imagery, such as talking about God as Mother, Lover or Friend.

Johnson writes in *She Who Is* about expanding the idea of the divine by drawing explicitly on wisdom tradition. She wants to think about the divine using the wisdom tradition of Sophia, but also as a Thomist. She is interested in seeing God as the origin of being and arguing from that perspective that God as Creator and the sustaining origin of being makes 'Mother' an appropriate way of talking about God. She says that in the way that we think about it—at least in many societies—is that the relationship of father is a one-time thing and they often take off. However, mother is more of a sustained and sustaining lifetime relationship. The mother is usually the one who gets stuck with the kids—and that is the relationship that God has with us. It is a continual sustaining. It is not a Deist understanding of kicking things off at the beginning and going out for a smoke never to return, but God's relation to us is a truly nurturing, continual relationship. It is a non-abandoning relationship. Ultimately, she would say that God is incomprehensible—she is a good Thomist in that regard. We do not know what God is. God is the one who is. That is why she entities her book *She Who Is*. We ultimately do not know what God is, so our ways of talking about God are limited—including all of these masculine ways—so we should bring in some other useful and helpful ways of talking. LaCugna presents a picture of the Triune God as social and relational and sees this as a particularly feminine understanding.

There are also different understandings of **Christology**. Ruether asks the question that many other famous theologians have asked: 'Is it possible for a male saviour to save women?' For essentialists, this is more of a problem. If there is a fundamental difference between men and women, how can a male saviour function as a saviour for females as well? In relation to this issue, **Daphne Hampson (1944–)** writes about 'the scandal of particularity'. Jesus as a particular human being is going to be male or female, and he happens to be male. Given this particularity, Hampson says that Christianity cannot escape a position of male dominance. However, Ruether says that Jesus's maleness is not essential to his role in the economy of salvation. There is also an observing here—especially in Catholicism—that it is because of the maleness of Jesus that some Catholic theologians say women cannot be ordained as priests. Jesus's maleness is used as a justification for women being barred from ordination and leadership in the Roman Catholic Church.

Schüssler Fiorenza presents Jesus as a prophet of Wisdom/Sophia. In her New Testament studies, she thinks that what Jesus is doing is presenting a proclamation of the Kingdom of God as being a kingdom of equals. It is an egalitarian Kingdom. More recently, theologians like **Janet Soskice (1951–)** write about how in tradition and Scripture Jesus is associated with various female attributes. For example, an idea of a blood that gives life is something that Soskice says is a particularly female/maternal picture as is the imagery of new birth.

We commonly see in Feminist Theology an aversion to the cross. The cross is seen as making (particularly male) violence central to salvation. Jesus's salvific work is more often tied to the message of Jesus than the sacrifice of Jesus—although certainly not exclusively.

Finally, feminist theologians have a different view of **ecclesiology**. If the hierarchy of the Church that is inherently tied to a male domination does not change, then there needs to be versions of the Church that operate outside of those structures. There needs to be a radically democratic, non-hierarchal ecclesia that flattens the structures of power. Feminist theologians will write of 'women-church' as a different way of doing Church. These are all different examples of the way that different feminist theologians suggest different revisions of Christian systematic theology.

19.3.6 Advocacy

The final moment is one of advocacy. Feminist theologians are focused towards making a better kind of community—on making the world better. Like Latin American Liberation Theology, feminist theology is involved in a societal struggle against injustice. Theologians are accountable to those who are oppressed, so feminist theology should work towards, and encourage, Christ-like compassion for the suffering of others. Such compassion is seen to be a particularly female attribute. Also, Feminist Theology often sees its purposes linked with ecology. The patriarchal structures in Western society can be blamed for much of the degradation of nature, and nature—in the typical binaries—is what is associated with the feminine. Feminist Theology should then entail a different relation to the natural. Instead of being lord over nature, we are to take care of nature. The Feminist Theology's advocacy has to do with promoting the flourishing of the whole of humanity and of non-human nature as well.

19.3.7 On the Margins

The borders of the concerns of feminist theology extend beyond those of the kinds of thinkers discussed thus far—which are largely white middle-class women. These are European or Euro-American women who are claiming to speak for women as a whole and representing 'women's experience'. However, other theologians—non-white non-middle-class women—say what feminist theologians call 'women's experience' actually just means the experience of certain women. Not only is there the oppression of gender that needs to be addressed, but also class and race distinction. There are different veins, trajectories and transformations of Feminist Theology that incorporate and address these distinct domains of experience.

Mujerista **Theology** is a theology from the perspective of Hispanic women. There is also what is called—perhaps confusingly—**Womanist Theology**. Womanist Theology is African American Feminist Theology. Both *Mujerista* and Womanist Theology will have a much stronger emphasis on family and community than many of the feminist theologies previously mentioned which tend to be more focused on individualistic flourishing and freedom, though of course not exclusively so. *Mujerista* and Womanist theologies also have a higher view of the cross, because—like Latin American Liberation Theology—they tend to view the cross as God's identifying with human suffering and oppression.

Thus, there are distinctions not just of gender, but also of race and class—and more recently they are going beyond the concerns of heterosexual women to the domain of what is called **Queer Theology**, which says that all of this theology is still based on a **heteronormativity** in Christianity. As feminist theologies are critical of androcentrism, Queer Theology is critical of heteronormativity in theology. All of these versions of liberation theology are saying that theology always arises out of a particular kind of context or experience and that only doing theology out of the context or experience of a dominant group is not going to speak to the experience and context of non-dominant groups but will rather function to continue to oppress and abuse those given groups. Theology must be done from the contexts of the marginalized to be meaningful to them.

19.4 Black Theology

19.4.1 African American Experience

Black Theology is a theology rooted in and addressing the particularity of African American life and experience. Of the different sets of experiences and sources, these are some aspects that are commonly referred to and drawn from as particularly African American. **First** is the particularity of black religion in the United States. Black religion comes from a background of slavery. The experience of severe oppression is a primordial marker of the African American experience and of African American Christianity. The particularity of African American religion comes out of a crisis. In this sense, it is not unlike the kind of theology that we saw in dialectical theology or Latin American theology—there is a pressing, urgent problem that needs to be addressed. However, the insight here coming out of a slave religion is that God is with his people in their bondage. This colours the way they view Jesus's suffering. When Jesus suffers, he is suffering with them as a people who have suffered—and as Jesus conquers death, he is liberating them.

A **second** distinctive aspect of the earliest of black religion is that this slave religion has an oral heritage of ideas and cultural forms coming from Africa—particularly the West coast of Africa. The slaves did not wipe clean their cultural heritage. In western Africa, in some of the groups there is a belief in an African High God. In the background, there is a pre-Christian monotheism there, along with an honouring of ancestors.

A **third** characteristic is the context of a struggle for full humanity. This is the critical side of African American experience. It is a critical perspective on Christianity from the perspective of African American Christians, seeing that Christianity functions for African Americans in such a way as being tied up in their continual survival and as inherently connected with hope for liberation. A **fourth** and final characteristic is the centrality of the Bible in African American Christianity with a special focus on the Biblical themes of liberation in the Exodus and in the work of Jesus Christ.

Beyond these characteristics (and in especial conjunction with the third), the context of the civil rights movement of the 1960s in the United States is of particular importance for Black theology. The 1960s was generally a time of social unrest in the United States. Here, the most significant figure in the civil rights movement was **Martin Luther King Jr. (1929–68)** who helped mobilize the African American Church's involvement in the civil rights movement and envisioned this social movement as a site of God's work in the world. King saw God as actively at work in the world and in history in the work of the civil rights movement as working towards and bringing about the Kingdom of God.

19.4.2 Cone

James H. Cone (1938–2018) is a significant representative of Black Theology. Cone attended Garrett-Evangelical Theological Seminary (then Garrett Biblical Institute) and Northwestern University. He did his dissertation on Karl Barth, and ended up teaching at Union Theological Seminary. Cone is considered by many to be the father of Black Liberation Theology. An early book of his is entitled *Black Theology and Black Power* (1969)—published within a year of Martin Luther King Jr.'s assassination.

Cone's most influential work is called *A Black Theology of Liberation* (1970). In it he calls for a contextual and prophetic theology for black people in the United States with liberation as an organizing principle. Theology is to be judged by its emancipatory impact: a good theology is one that brings about liberation. The context is black experience and the black struggle for liberation in society. Jesus Christ is understood as the norm for this experience and struggle. Revelation is seen as coming from within the black community—not as a foreign voice but as specifically the black community.

Cone talks about Jesus Christ as the black messiah. For revelation to be truly revelation, it has to speak to the present; it has to speak to the living situation. In Cone's understanding, Christ's present existential identity is that of the Oppressed One. Jesus, then, is 'black' because the messiah is one with the oppressed. He is truly incarnate in the particular kind of suffering and experience that his people are going through. The black God, then, is the God of the oppressed. Cone intentionally reframes the Christian message of the Bible as relating to black liberation. In being revivified by God's message and work of liberation for the African American community, the Black Church can be a sign of hope in a racist world.

19.4.3 Womanist Theology

Womanist Theology largely comes to the fore in the 1980s. This is particularly African American theology that focuses specifically on the perspective and experience of African American women. The term 'womanist' comes from the colloquial 'womanish' as referring to someone who has grown up or is being responsible. It is a theology that wants to celebrate the distinctive gifts of women of colour, and says that African American women have to cope with things that are different from other groups. They have the triple oppression of racism (as addressed by black theology), sexism (as addressed by feminist theology) and classism (as addressed by liberation theology more generally). As black, female and poor, they are in a particularly bad situation. And yet, Christ is to be found in the midst of this oppression. They will emphasize Christ's suffering as God's choosing to have solidarity with poor black women in their suffering. He conquers, and his conquering of sin can be communicated to us in life.

19.5 Postcolonial Theology

After the 1960s, there is a decline in the rest of the world of the two primary colonizing continents: Europe and North America. Postcolonial Theology critically considers the self-image and theology of those colonial powers that also were the primary missionary-sending groups. Beyond this, postcolonial theology broadly represents groups and cultures other than European and North American that are beginning to do theology from their particular cultural perspective. This term is often used to referring to the growth of 'indigenous' Christianity in Asia, Africa and South America. The central insight of Postcolonial Theology is that the culture of the people should not be erased by the Gospel. Often when the Gospel is brought to a place, it is not distinguishable from the Western culture that is introduced along with it. Thus, to be a Christian also means to cease to have significant parts of your own culture in this context. Too often, the Gospel is embedded in a programme of Western colonization—where becoming Christian means to become civilized (whether such 'civilization' was French, American, English, etc.).

In the Catholic context, Vatican II represents a new openness to cultural expressions—in particular with the Mass now being performed in the vernacular. Instead of having the Latin Mass said in India or Japan, the Mass would actually be translated into the language of the people there. Beyond that, however, there is a greater openness to different cultures around the world. Like the Medellín Conference in South America, there are also other councils in other places addressing particular issues relevant to their particular times and places. In 1969, when the **All India Seminar** met in Asia, the primary issue dealt with was the relationship between Christianity and other religions. In Africa in 1974, the **African Synod on Evangelization** met to address the primary issue of the relationship between Christianity and ancestral traditions. To what degree and how should Christianity relate to the various ancestral traditions in Africa? Christianity is there understood in the midst of a world that is alive with the spiritual. So this is a very different kind of theology than that of the missionaries that primarily introduced it to Africa who were more Deistically minded.

In Asia however—the most populous but least Christian continent—there is a greater awareness of other religions. There are many values within Asian religions that are seen as close to the values of the Christian Gospel. They are perhaps closer to the Christian Gospel than many of the Western values that came along with the Gospel. Part of what is going on there in Asia and in Africa is that religion is not seen as something that is distinct from culture. It is difficult if not impossible to talk about an Asian Christianity that does not have any relation to the traditionally Asian religions because religion is so closely tied to the very culture. So, the emphasis—especially in Asia—is how the universality of the Gospel of Christ does not need to seek to erase the particularities of different cultures, but should enrich them.

Sources and Further Reading

Baum, Gregory. 'The Impact of Marxist Ideas on Christian Theology'. In *The Twentieth Century: A Theological Overview*, edited by Gregory Baum, 172–85. Maryknoll, NY: Orbis, 1999.

Chopp, Rebecca, and Ethna Regan. 'Latin American Liberation Theology'. In *The Modern Theologians: Introduction to Christian Theology since 1918*, edited by David F. Ford with Rachel Muers, 469–84, 3rd edn. Oxford: Blackwell, 2005.

Coakley, Sarah. 'Feminist Theology'. In *Modern Christian Thought: Volume 2, The Twentieth Century*, edited by James C. Livingston and Francis Schüssler Fiorenza, 417–42, 2nd edn. Minneapolis, MN: Fortress Press, 2006.

Elizondo, Virgilio. 'Emergence of a World Church and the Irruption of the Poor'. In *The Twentieth Century: A Theological Overview*, edited by Gregory Baum, 104–17. Maryknoll, NY: Orbis, 1999.

Evans, James H., Jr. 'Black Theology in America'. In *Modern Christian Thought: Volume 2, The Twentieth Century*, edited by James C. Livingston and Francis Schüssler Fiorenza, 443–68, 2nd edn. Minneapolis, MN: Fortress Press, 2006.

Hauge, Astri. 'Feminist Theology'. In *Key Theological Thinkers: From Modern to Postmodern*, edited by Staale Johannes Kristiansen and Svein Rise, 593–606. Aldershot: Ashgate, 2013.

Hebblethwaite, Margaret. 'Base Communities'. In *The Oxford Companion to Christian Thought*, edited by Adrian Hastings, Alistair Mason and Hugh Pyper, 67–68. Oxford: Oxford University Press, 2000.

Hopkins, Dwight N. 'Black Theology of Liberation'. In *The Modern Theologians: Introduction to Christian Theology since 1918*, edited by David F. Ford with Rachel Muers, 451–68, 3rd edn. Oxford: Blackwell, 2005.

Jennings, Willie James. 'Black Theology'. In *The Oxford Companion to Christian Thought*, edited by Adrian Hastings, Alistair Mason, and Hugh Pyper, 72–75. Oxford: Oxford University Press, 2000.

Livingston, James C., and Francis Schüssler Fiorenza. *Modern Christian Thought: Volume 2, The Twentieth Century*. 2nd edn. Minneapolis, MN: Fortress Press, 2006.

Muers, Rachel. 'Feminism, Gender, and Theology'. In *The Modern Theologians: Introduction to Christian Theology since 1918*, edited by David F. Ford with Rachel Muers, 431–50, 3rd edn. Oxford: Blackwell, 2005.

Ross, Susan A. 'The Women's Movement and Theology in the Twentieth Century'. In *The Twentieth Century: A Theological Overview*, edited by Gregory Baum, 186–203. Maryknoll, NY: Orbis, 1999.

Stålsett, Sturla J. 'Liberation Theology'. In *Key Theological Thinkers: From Modern to Postmodern*, edited by Staale Johannes Kristiansen and Svein Rise, 617–30. Aldershot: Ashgate, 2013.

20

Revisionist and Secular Theologies

In the period between 1960 and 1980, the dominance of Dialectical Theology waned in mainline seminaries and the academic world. Up to the 1960s, Dialectical Theology—Barth, Bultmann and so on—was something of the status quo. During this time the centre of gravity in the theological discussion shifted from Germany to the United States. Most of the thinkers that will be presented in this chapter and the next are American.

The last two chapters of this text have to do with two general trajectories. While liberation or contextual theology remains a significant voice in theology, we will present two particular kinds of more recent theology in terms of secular and confessional trajectories (the former in the present chapter and the latter in the next).

The secular trajectory has significant resonances with Paul Tillich's theology of correlation. It begins with an understanding of contemporary experience—usually described through philosophical categories—and then revisits or revises the meaning of Christian theology on the basis of this experience. The confessional trajectory of Postliberal and 'Postsecular' Theology follows somewhat in the spirit of Karl Barth—though more ecumenical in scope. This is generally a more traditional, confessional approach with a preference to begin with faith and the Christian confession.

20.1 Revisionist Theology

Revisionist Theology is often associated with the University of Chicago Divinity School—as Postliberal Theology will be associated with Yale Divinity School. The figure who coined the term is David Tracy, who recently retired from the University of Chicago. From the 1960s to the 1980s, the University of Chicago Divinity School was one of the dominant schools for theology in the United States. Paul Tillich ended his career teaching there. It also had a strong connection to philosophical hermeneutics as Paul Ricouer also taught there for a time. There was a strong influence from twentieth-century continental thought.

Revisionist Theology is presented at times as a pendulum swing from Barth and Dialectical Theology back towards a more 'liberal' position—looking back to the nineteenth-century engagement with modern thought in Ritschl and Harnack. They likewise sought to revise Christianity in the light of modernity so as to find a Christianity believable by modern men and women. They both criticized received traditional beliefs in the light of the exigencies of contemporary existence.

There are a few common emphases that are evident in those following a revisionist approach. The **first** is trying to find a way that Christian theology can be seen as claiming to be true. It is trying to find out how—in a contemporary discourse and a contemporary understanding of truth—you can then say that Christianity is true. This is an **apologetic** impulse. While they sought to defend belief like the Deists, revisionist theologians were much more self-aware about revising what they were defending so that it was more defensible.

The **second** emphasis is on the human situation in our particular day and age—which is a situation of **ambivalence**. We are in a troubled situation that is sometimes seen in terms of socio-economic injustice and sometimes in terms of a more generalized anxiety to modern existence. Theology must address these kinds of pressing concerns—the issues and problems of modern human beings.

Third and finally God is seen as needing to be closely related to our experience. Many of these theologies are going to be critical of 'Classical Theism'. (Though a reader should not assume this actually has much to do with classical theism.) When they say 'Classical Theism', they usually mean God as a powerful but distant supernatural agent that occasionally interrupts the natural order.

They wanted an understanding of God that is rather close to our experience, which usually means an understanding of God that is more immanent and even pantheistic.

A general way of talking about these emphases is that they entail a preference for a 'minimalist' theology. This has to do with the third point made, that theology needs to arise from the grounding experiences for what gives God-talk meaning. All of these thinkers were responding to what they considered to be a crisis in God-talk. (You can identify this era when they use phrases like 'God-talk'.) They were trying to find a purchase in our experience that can be correlated with 'God'. However, it ends up being a 'minimalist' theology. It is not as if you start with this experience then move in faith into more of a robust or 'maximalist', traditional Christian theology. Rather, one's understanding of God stays very close to whatever experiential, phenomenological or philosophical starting-point one has to give 'God-talk' meaning.

20.1.1 Tracy

David Tracy (1939–) is a Roman Catholic theologian. He began his career with a brief stint at the Catholic University of America. He left due to his opposition to the Papal encyclical *Humanae Vitae*, which prohibits contraception. He went on to teach at the University of Chicago in 1968.

Much of what Tracy does is considered to be Fundamental Theology, which is giving a philosophical grounding for theology. In his influential work, *Blessed Rage for Order* (1975), Tracy explores the meaning of religious language. He is addressing how religious language is meaningful and specifically the challenge of the Death of God Theologians (see 20.3.3 below) who charged that 'God' is no longer meaningful. A later, significant work of Tracy's is entitled *The Analogical Imagination* (1981) and is about theology and theological method.

Tracy presents a significantly revised version of Tillich's method of correlation. What Tracy proposes is **mutually critical correlation**. With Tillich, philosophy asks the questions and theology then provides the answers. Tracy realizes, however, that in this model philosophy dictates the terms of the discussion ahead of theology. The situation is more complex in that philosophy asks it own questions and gives answers to those questions and theology asks its own questions and gives answers to those questions. There are then two poles: that of the religious tradition and that of the religious dimension of human experience. The correlation has to do with a navigating between these two poles or talking about the relationship between them. In relation to the religious tradition, Tracy saw as fundamental to the project of doing theology one's attending to what he called the **classics**—here being Scripture and major representations of the tradition. The other pole is the universal religious dimension to all human experience (not unlike what we saw with Rahner).

One of the significant contributions of *The Analogical Imagination* is Tracy's understanding of the **three 'publics' of theology**. Theology's task can be seen as addressing three different groups. The first is that of the **academy**. When theology is addressing the academy, it has a particular mode of doing theology that predominates. Fundamental theology is theology that is addressed not to people who share your confession but to reasonable people more broadly. So what is key here is being rational and being honest on the terms of that audience. For theology, this is an external criterion. The theologian is dealing with criteria external to the theological tradition that is different at different times. The fact that there are different canons of rationality is a real point of tension with Postliberal theologians who will argue that this then ceases to be any one recognizable public.

The three publics of theology

The Academy	fundamental theology	external criteria
The Church	systematic theology	internal criteria
Society	practical theology	external criteria

The second public of theology is **the Church**. When theology is addressing the Church, systematic theology predominates. Tracy would say that this is more the kind of theology that we see Karl Barth doing: theology that is addressing the Church and helping the Church to remain loyal to its sources. This is having a critical fidelity to the classics of tradition. He recognizes that the religious classics have a defining and foundational role. The key here is that the Church does do a particular kind of activity in this way that has primarily inner criteria. It has a confessional mode, but that is not its only mode. That is not the only mode of theology or public that it is addressing. It is also addressing those outside of it and needs to know the language of those outside of it.

The final public of theology is that of **Society**. In this, practical theology predominates. This is going to be an external criteria as well, and this is where Tracy is saying that this is in a liberationist mode, where the concern that is being addressed is theology's responsibility for and commitment to the well-being of people in society. For Tracy, the theologian must address these three publics— so bringing together several of the approaches and emphases of theology in the twentieth century.

The big distinction here that Tracy brought back in—largely regarding the first public—is that theology should be a public conversation. Theology should attend to public criteria. Here is where this kind of revisionist theology is a secular theology. Its distinctive horizon over and against other theologies is that it wants to address a secular public sphere which—in the later twentieth century— the public discourse is no longer religious (Secularity 1). In a sense, he is returning to some of the theologies of the Enlightenment. While liberationist or contextual theologies had been addressing those within a particular group in society, Tracy wanted to frame theology at least in part by a broader understanding of the academy and to let theology also be attentive to the good of society.

20.1.2 Kaufmann

Another significant Revisionist theologian who we will mention briefly is **Gordon Kaufman (1925–2011)**, who taught at Harvard Divinity School. Like Tracy, his primary emphasis was that theology needs to be a public endeavour. By this, Kaufmann meant that theology should positively avoid being confessional (or 'positive' in the nineteenth-century sense). Confessional theology is seen as parochial. The main audience for theology is a secular one. The starting place that theology addresses is contemporary experience—which again primarily has to do with insights from the secular world. If religion is going to be a significant source for theology, one must not limit oneself to the insights of any one religious tradition. Theology has to address other religions as well. If you bring in the sources of one religion, you have to bring in the sources of all major religions.

Ultimately, Kaufmann will talk about God very simply as that 'which limits and relativizes the world and all that is in it'. God is the underlying reality of the universe that somehow manifests itself within the universe. God is the ground—the foundation—upon which our normal experience rests. Kaufmann uses very general ways of talking about God that can be acceptable to the maximal number of modern men and women.

20.2 Process Theology

20.2.1 Teilhard

What is called Process Theology was originally based in the University of Chicago, but now is also centred at the Claremont Graduate School in California. The first figure we will deal with is not properly a Process theologian, but is considered by many to be a precursor with many similar insights.

Jesuit **Pierre Teilhard de Chardin (1881–1955)** was something of a polymath: studying philosophy, theology, geology and palaeontology. He received his doctorate in palaeontology from the Sorbonne in Paris, and served as a stretcher-bearer in the First World War. He ended up spending from 1923 to 1946 working in China as a palaeontologist.

After Teilhard (as his name is normally shortened) returned to Paris, he wrote quite a lot. His religious writings, however, were not allowed by the Church to be published until after his death—and then only with a warning included. He lived in New York for the last years of his life—from 1946 to 1955. His most important works are *The Phenomenon of Man*—which is published in the year of his death—and *The Divine Milieu*, published in 1957. These are just two of a flood of his books that came out after his death.

Teilhard offered a speculative vision of a union between science and religion—specifically between evolutionary biology and Christian theology—something like an evolutionary theology. He had a vision of the cosmos as a whole as moving teleologically towards greater complexity. One of the metaphors that he uses about the different layers or levels of the development of the cosmos is as if they were the different concentric 'spheres' of a planet. As a geologist, Teilhard observes the different layers of rock on top of each other—so he talks about the different layers or spheres from matter to life to mind. The first sphere is that of inanimate matter or the **geosphere**. Based upon but not reducible to the geosphere is the **biosphere**—the sphere of biological life. Life is not simply a material mechanism. It is material, but it is not simply reducible to matter. The third sphere is what Teilhard calls the **noosphere**, coming from the Greek word *nous* meaning mind.

What is key here is that when the noosphere emerges, it changes the whole of the reality. It changes (or, from a teleological point of view, reveals) the significance of the cosmos. Creation is developing towards humanity—but the crown of humanity for Teilhard is Jesus Christ. Christ is culmination, the *telos*, the fulfilment of the universe, and in Christ the meaning of the whole is taken up and is transformed. This teleological orientation of history towards Christ—and ultimately towards the consummation of the cosmos in Christ—he designates with the technical term **Omega Point**. Ultimately, the purpose, end and goal of the entire cosmos is intimate, loving communion with God in Christ.

20.2.2 Whitehead

Educated at Cambridge, Englishman **Alfred North Whitehead (1861–1947)** taught Bertrand Russell for a time, and eventually they became colleagues. Russell and Whitehead later collaborated on their *Principia Mathematica*, a significant work in analytic philosophy. Whitehead eventually moved to America to teach at Harvard.

Whitehead spent most of his career as a mathematician, but later in his life he took up a chair in philosophy at Harvard. When he did this he began to construct a metaphysical vision of the nature of reality that took into account relatively recent developments in the natural sciences—namely evolutionary biology and Einsteinian physics. He believed that our understandings of reality as such had yet to take these developments into account. In his time in England, Whitehead was influenced by what are called the British Idealists, or the British Platonists, and there is a definite Platonic flavour to his thought.

Interestingly, a key part of his metaphysics is his understanding of God and the prominent role God plays in his philosophy. His understanding of God develops over time. In his first work on metaphysics, *Science and the Modern World* (1925), his understanding of God was presented more in terms of Spinoza's substance, and he thinks that religion in a modern age needs to drop its outdated mythology. The important aspects of religion are the metaphysical insights within it and not the ethical or the mythological form of these insights. The most important contribution of religion is that it tells us that there is something beyond or behind the normal flux of things that gives the normal flux of things meaning. Reality as we experience it has a ground and a foundation. One of the significant characteristics of Whitehead's philosophy and Process Theology in general is a vision of reality that is fundamentally dynamic. Reality is temporal, constantly in flux, constantly changing. The way the ideal relates to the flux of reality as we experience it—at least as presented in this work—is that it is something that is waiting to be realized. The ideal influences the present as if from the future—drawing becomings towards an ideal.

Whitehead's chief and more mature work is entitled *Process and Reality* (1929). Its key insight is that reality is constituted by process. Reality is irreducibly temporal. Everything in the universe is also ultimately interrelated. He describes the universe as a coming together or a **concrescence**. The universe is fundamentally in process and dynamic; there are no solid billiard-ball-like bits such as would have been found in an older, Newtonian picture of things. The process of the world is also a creative process. It is not just a meaningless churning forth of change, but has a definite teleological aspect to it—and he talks about this in terms of creativity. Every individual thing in the universe is better to be thought of as a becoming or process rather than a static thing.

Figure 20.1 Whitehead.

'Alfred North Whitehead. Photograph. Wellcome V0027330' by http://wellcomeimages.org/indexplus/obf_images/1b/f0/
dcc960cc9b4207bb1d198d9c64a6.jpgGallery: http://wellcomeimages.org/indexplus/image/V0027330.html. Licensed under
CC BY 4.0 via Wikimedia Commons.

dipolar being of things		
physical pole	relevant past	prehension
mental pole	future possibility	potential

As Whitehead describes it, everything in the universe is **dipolar**—a becoming between two poles. There is a physical pole to all things. The physical pole is that which has already come to be; it is the relevant past of a thing. It is what came before. At any given point of a given becoming there is the past part of its story, which is how it has come to be what it is now. This backward-facing aspect of being is called **prehension**—the way in which something contains or 'feels' the previous occasions that brought this occasion to the way it is now. The other pole is what Whitehead calls the mental pole, and that has to do with a thing's future possibility or potential. Everything 'chooses' to actualize certain possibilities and not others. Everything has a physical aspect to it and a mental aspect.

God, like all other entities, is both dependent and changing. God also is dipolar. God, for Whitehead, has two 'natures'. The first nature for God is his **primordial nature**. This is the aspect of God that is eternal. This is the ideal and unchanging pole that is transcendent of the world. Primordial nature provides finite beings in the world with teleological 'initial aim' towards good possibilities—usually presented in terms of novelty and maximal 'enjoyment' (a technical term for Whitehead). God is the ideal lure towards novelty and best possibilities and is, as such, sometimes called the 'Divine Eros' in this regard. This language of 'primordial' can be a bit confusing in that God's 'primordial' nature is not that which is temporally preceding worldly events but that which is always influencing, attracting, luring worldly events with an impulse towards actualizing the best possibilities open to it. God's ideal primordiality is best thought of as something in the future luring beings towards it as an end. God's primordial nature operates on finite occasions'/beings' mental pole.

The other pole is what is called God's **consequent nature**. This is God's physical pole. This is the aspect of God that has prehension and takes in the things that happen in the world. God experiences that which happens in the world and is affected by it—taking it in. As everything is affected by everything else, this is supremely true of God. It is as if God is a repository for everything that happens. Everything that happens adds to God's experience/memory/knowledge. He remembers and is affected by everything that happens in the world, and, thus, changes relative to the process of becoming.

Whitehead and Hartshorne's dipolar God

Primordial Nature	Consequent Nature
abstract essence	concrete actuality
ideal lure	fully actual
influencing the world	influenced by the world
eternal	temporal
absolute	relative
independent	dependent
unchangeable	constantly changing

God and the world in Whitehead's thought are interdependent. The idea here is that Whitehead is wanting to provide for genuine freedom for things in the world. They are not predetermined. God and the world are becoming in relation to each other. God sets the initial direction, the world has freedom in the way that it develops in that direction, and God is then affected by the way things happen and develop. God's relation to the world is one of persuasion. God persuades the world but does not coerce it. God is not a powerful, impassive emperor that holds sway over the world but rather allows the universe freedom in relation to him. At the same time, God is an active and loving force that draws everything in the universe in a good direction.

20.2.3 Hartshorne

Charles Hartshorne (1897–2000) was an American theologian who was deeply influenced by Whitehead's philosophy. Studying at Harvard, he completed in two years, in record time, his MA and his PhD. He was Whitehead's research assistant briefly and ended up teaching at the University of Chicago. Hartshorne helped the University of Chicago become an influential force for Process Theology—aided by figures such as Schubert Ogden (1928–).

Hartshorne's likely most influential work is *The Divine Relativity* (1948). He strives to produce a Christian theology built upon the foundation of Whitehead's metaphysics. What he produces is a form of panentheism in which God and the world are interdependent. For Hartshorne, a God that is temporal, affected by his creation and does not know the future accords with what he sees as the biblical picture of God. Hartshorne gives up on the traditional doctrine of omnipotence. He would rather say that God is the greatest possible power, but what determines what kind of power is possible is the groundwork of Whiteheadian metaphysics. Hartshorne also gives up on the doctrine of impassibility. One of the ramifications of this understanding of God is that God, in God's consequent life, suffers. Not only is God affected by the things that happen, but God truly suffers. Ultimately, he wants to drop such traditional notions of God because having a God that orders everything that happens does not allow for creaturely freedom and also makes God the cause of evil. Part of what is going on here is that he is operating without making the classical distinction between beings and God. If one does not make this distinction and sees God as a being among beings then such traditional attributes cease to make sense.

The Process thought of Whitehead and Hartshorne came to be influential in the 1960s among Protestant theologians in the United States. When Process Theology draws on Process thought it is usually Whitehead-by-way-of-Hartshorne. Whitehead alone is not quite theology, but with Hartshorne he is brought into Christian theological language.

20.2.4 Cobb

John B. Cobb, Jr. (1925–) is the most eminent American Process theologian alive. Born in Japan to Christian missionaries, he was a deeply devout young man. He ended up studying at the University of Chicago with Hartshorne. He taught at the School of Theology Claremont for some thirty years— and it is largely because of Cobb that Claremont came to be the new centre of Process thought. In fact, he (along with David Ray Griffin) was the director of the Center for Process Studies at Claremont.

Cobb was interested in the project of reinterpreting Christian theology relative to Whiteheadian metaphysics. Probably his most significant work is *A Christian Natural Theology* (1965). Here he describes God as, like all other beings, an energy event. He focuses on how God relates to other beings—particularly how he relates to human beings. God primarily relates to us by calling us and offering us different potentialities. That is the force of God's work in the world. Cobb says that this force is ultimately exemplified in the person of Jesus as calling and seeking to persuade people to go in this better direction inasmuch as goodness in a process frame has to do with creativity. Creativity is a life of love and of opening up new perspectives. Cobb talks about Jesus as the divine logos. In Jesus Christ we have an incarnation of the divine logos as a manifestation of the creative transformation that is present in all life.

For Cobb, the primordial pull of God is the divine logos; it is that pull that sets the direction and sets the initial aims of everything. It orients the **telos** of the universe. God in the logos as incarnate in Jesus lures the world towards creative transformation. Yet, in the person of Jesus Christ a particular way of being is brought into history. There is a unique revelation in Jesus of the creative transformation that the logos effects. The persuasion that is operative in all of reality is present in a particularly explicit and intense way in the revelation of Jesus Christ.

This has definite similarities to other ways of thinking previously discussed. Grace is a general operation in the cosmos, and that same operation is revealed or manifest in a particularly intense or vital way in Jesus Christ. This is a way of trying to bring together the particularity of the Christian confession and the validity of a natural theology—a broader understanding of the world.

As a Process theologian, Cobb thinks that what we as humans do matters. Our action changes things. When we make good decisions, it contributes to a larger scheme. This contribution to the world—which, in God's consequent nature, God remembers—this is what he calls **objective immortality**. What we do changes the way things are and is remembered by God. This is his understanding of immortality—not that there is an historical resurrection or that at the end of time we will come back into existence. In fact, he does not believe in an actual, finite end of history. That what we do affects and changes things is our immortality. Because everything affects everything else, that positive change persists beyond our lifetime—just as for any single positive action that we make, where the ramifications persist beyond that action.

20.3 Secular and 'Death of God' Theology

As mentioned previously, for a good chunk of the middle of the twentieth century, Barthian or Dialectical Theology is dominant on the theological scene. Perhaps not surprisingly, Dialectical Theology gives rise to its dialectical opposite. You can see this simply in that if our only point of contact with God is an encounter with the Word of God then if we have not encountered the Word it is perfectly justified for us to be atheists. As a reaction to Barthian Theology, we then have the Death of God Theologies or the 'secular theology' of the 1960s.

Such 'secular' theology does not resist late modernity's closed world structures. Rather it takes up and owns the secular. In fact, many thinkers will see secularization and the secular world as stemming from Christianity as something to be embraced by Christians as the (perhaps unexpected) culmination of Christianity.

20.3.1 Gogarten

Before getting to people who would call themselves Death of God theologians or secular theologians, we can mention a few significant precursors: Gogarten and Bonhoeffer. Both of these figures could have been talked about in earlier chapters (such as 13, 14 or 19), but we will talk about them here.

A contemporary of Barth, **Friedrich Gogarten (1887–1967)** was an early Dialectical theologian. He draws quite a bit on Luther and Kierkegaard. Eventually he will come to embrace Bultmann's demythologization project, and see that what is important in the Christian message is the moral and redemptive existential kerygma, not the objective facts. One of the reasons that other Dialectical theologians are more famous—such as Barth or Bultmann—is that Gogarten was a member of the National Socialist Party (the Nazis), so he tends to be seen as being on the wrong side of history.

In the 1950s and 1960s in Germany, Gogarten is an advocate of a kind of secular theology. He describes it as a 'theology of secularization'. What this means for him is that Christianity should be involved in the world. He sees this as a way of being opposed to modern individualism. Secularization for Gogarten then entails responsibility. The very Christian idea of love of one's neighbour should lead us to be responsible for the world, and this should lead us to a humanism or 'secularism'. Christian love is a love of the world; Christians are concerned for the good of the secular order.

20.3.2 Bonhoeffer

A German Lutheran theologian, **Dietrich Bonhoeffer (1906–45)** taught in Berlin. For a time he was a pastor in some German congregations in London, but he ends up returning to Germany, in 1935, to be part of the Confessing Church. Thus, as Nazism holds sway in Germany, Bonhoeffer does not leave Germany but rather returns to it. He was 29, when he did this, and he ended up directing one of the Confessing Church's illegal seminaries in Finkenwalde. He was associated with a plot to assassinate Hitler. In 1943, Bonhoeffer was arrested by the Gestapo, and was sent to a concentration camp at Flossenburg. The Nazis hung him a month before the end of the war.

During his short life, Bonhoeffer penned many important works, but here we will focus on what he has to say in his last writings. While he was in the concentration camp at Flossenburg, he carried on a correspondence with his friend Eberhard Bethge. Those letters, written between 1943 and 1945, are later published as *The Letters and Papers from Prison* (1951). The question that he puts forward is: 'Who is God for us today?' He reflects on how we live in a 'world come of age'. The modern European world is a world that does not see itself as needing religion. We have come to a time without religion. The concerns of our modern life largely operate totally separated from any motivating concern about personal life after death. We are motivated by concerns in the here and now understood, by Bonhoeffer, as largely without a religious horizon.

Bonhoeffer sought to get to the genuine substance of Christianity without what he saw as mere religiosity—the superfluous religious form. A Christianity that would fit this time of the 'world come of age' is a Christianity that would be in the midst of a contemporary world where religion is in decline. He advocates a Christianity without religion—a 'Religionless Christianity'. Key to such a religionless Christianity is a biblical understanding of God as suffering with humanity. In Christ, God suffers with humanity, and the ramification for this is that the Christian—the Christ-follower—should get involved in making the world a better place and indeed be willing to suffer for the good of the world. (Say, by trying to assassinate Hitler.) Thus Bonhoeffer wants to think of Christianity primarily as a way of living in the world, and Christ should be thought of not as the one who saves us from the world but as rather 'the Man for others'. Christ offers life to others.

Figure 20.2 Bonhoeffer.

'DBP 1964 433 Hitlerattentat Dietrich Bonhoeffer' scanned by NobbiP. Licensed under Public Domain via Wikimedia Commons.

Bonhoeffer suggests seeing Christ as a hidden presence in the world. Christ is at work in the world—even in non-religious people. He will seize the secular opposition to religion as not something to be opposed. Christianity should not be about fighting with the decline of religion but about serving others and making the world a better place. In this service, Christ is at work. He would say that the main issue is not one's personal disposition, but that one takes responsibility in making the world a better place.

20.3.3 American Secular Theology: Altizer and Hamilton

Bonhoeffer and other thinkers who have already been addressed—such as Bultmann and Tillich—have a significant influence on a particular vein of theology in the 1960s, one that wants to radically reimagine Christianity for the modern age and to bring it up to date. One best-selling book that is often related to this movement is by an Anglican bishop named John A. T. Robinson. In *Honest to God* (1963), Robinson draws on theologians like Bonhoeffer, Tillich and Bultmann, and advocates a secular theology for a secular humanity that is free of the outdated aspects of Christianity.

This kind of approach is represented in America by a movement called Death of God Theology (American Secular Theology). What they mean by 'death of God' is akin to when Nietzsche is talking about the death of God in *The Gay Science*—the 'traditional' Christian God is no longer believable. (This would be Taylor's Secularity 2.) For some of them, to talk about the death of God is to say simply that we live in a secular society where thinking about God is no longer a dominant public discourse (Taylor's Secularity 3). However, some of the theologians have a slightly more odd theology—in which God actually dies (though the orthodox understanding of the divine Son's death on the cross gives this thought some precedent). Some significant representatives of Death of God Theology are **Gabriel Vahanian (1927–2012)**, **Thomas J. J. Altizer (1927–2018)**, **Paul Van Buren (1924–98)** and **William Hamilton (1924–2012)**.

After studying at the University of Chicago, and receiving his PhD before Tillich or Tracy taught there, **Thomas J. J. Altizer** ends up teaching English at SUNY Stony Brook. He is commonly considered to be the leading figure in the Death of God movement. One of his best-known works is entitled *The Gospel of Christian Atheism* (1966). The key to understanding Altizer is to know that he is strongly influenced by Hegel. God himself is involved in a dialectical process such that in the incarnation the transcendent otherness is negated. In the incarnation, there is a full *kenosis*: God fully empties himself into Jesus, such that the transcendent God truly dies on the cross. This is a version of Sabellianism, such that in the incarnation the whole Godhead becomes flesh. The key for Altizer here is that in the incarnation, God is no longer an alien transcendence—but in dying on the cross and becoming fully human God enters into the world and becomes absolutely immanent. God is fully present in the world, and this should be experienced as something that is liberating.

William Hamilton came from a Baptist background. He studied at Union Theological Seminary with Reinhold Niebuhr. He also studied with Tillich for a time. His main work is called *The New Essence of Christianity* (1961). Hamilton and Altizer co-authored the influential set of essays titled *Radical Theology and the Death of God* (1966). When talking about the Death of God, Hamilton says that they are talking about less 'the absence of the experience of God, but the experience of the absence of God'. God—in the former understanding of God—is now experienced as absent, so theologians and modern people should begin thinking about Christianity from Jesus and not an absent deity. Hamilton focuses particularly on the historical Jesus as the starting point, and primarily looks at him as a moral exemplar. Christianity is centred around living in the world with Jesus as a moral exemplar—which sounds quite Ritschlian. (As Barth swings away from the nineteenth century, the radical theologians swing back to it.)

20.4 Postmodern Theology

20.4.1 'Postmodern'

The term 'postmodern' is notoriously ambiguous. Usually figures that are labelled as postmodern regularly deny the applicability of the term. To characterize it very generally, postmodernism can be seen as a certain change in a style of thinking or frame of mind that has happened in the last twenty or thirty years of the twentieth century. It can be seen as having often opposing (often simultaneously) relations to 'modernity'. In one sense, the postmodern is beyond or after ('post') the modern. It is going past and perhaps leaving behind some of the goals, assumptions and prejudices of modernity. But there is another sense in which the postmodern is not abandoning the modern but is the logical outcome of modernity and certain modern assumptions taken to their extreme. It is an extreme version of modernity. To see how both of these senses can come together, the postmodern can be thought of as a modernity that has become self-critical. The questioning spirit of modernity has come to question even modernity—the acids of doubt are now being turned upon modern rationality.

There are perhaps some characteristic emphases of the postmodern that can give a bit of a handle on it. There is an emphasis on the **singular** as opposed to the universal. Instead of focusing on what is true at all times, there is a privileging of the particular or the local. Also, there is a focus on **difference** as opposed to sameness. Postmodern thinkers can be thought of as critical of the modern inasmuch as it is imposing universal categories on reality that are violent and distort the particularities in order to make them fit. There is also a privileging of the **plural** over the one. Finally, there is a privileging of relations in a network or plain instead of a hierarchy. There is a **suspicion of power relations**—anything that intends to have authority over anything else.

20.4.2 Derrida

One of the central postmodern philosophers—although he himself was never comfortable with the title—that deeply influenced several postmodern theologians was **Jacques Derrida (1930–2004)**. An Algerian Jew who moved to France as a child, Derrida studied and went on to teach philosophy in Paris. He became the best-known continental philosopher of the 1980s and 1990s—something of a celebrity.

Derrida is critical of 'ontotheology' (a Heideggerian term)—a universalizing and hierarchical approach to the world. Ontotheology is a framework of meaning and control (*logos*) that is supported by both a general/universal understanding of being (*onto*) and an understanding of the highest being in a hierarchy (*theo*). This ontotheological frame of meaning supports a 'logocentrism'— Western thinking's recurring propensity to try to ground our thinking on a notion of presence such that meaning itself is fully present in our ideas or words. Within this logocentrism is a privileging of stability over change, identity over difference and presence over absence—but Derrida would say that change, difference and absence always subvert any desire to maintain identity or claim presence.

For Derrida, meaning is fundamentally fugitive—unstable, not present, mercurial. This is part of what is being pointed out in Derrida's notion of **deconstruction**. Deconstruction for Derrida—and those who followed him—is a tool that is used to attack logocentrism—to show that logocentrism fails to account for the fugitive operations of meaning. Deconstruction uncovers an irreducible ambiguity or ambivalence in texts (written or otherwise) such that the sense of meaning as a fully stable and present entity of sorts is shown to be an illusion. You find that it is an illusion by looking for it. It ends with realizing that our language—meaning and the way we think—is constantly at play, never fully present, always dynamic. Derrida is notoriously difficult to read and understand because it seems like in his writing he is trying to perform the very instability and inherent ambiguity of language that he describes. In Derrida's later work he turns in a decidedly ethical and even religious direction and is profoundly dependent upon and inspired by another French thinker: Emmanuel Levinas.

20.4.3 Levinas

Lithuanian-born **Emmanuel Levinas (1906–95)** became a French citizen in 1930. He studied phenomenology under Edmund Husserl, and later studied the work of Heidegger. A Jew from eastern Europe, many of Levinas's family members died at the hands of the Nazis. The thrust of his thought in the 1950s and 1960s is the fundamental place of ethics in philosophy.

Levinas' key work is entitled *Totality and Infinity* (1961). In *Totality and Infinity*, there is a focus on the face-to-face encounter with the other. 'The other' or otherness or alterity is a huge emphasis in postmodern thought, and this largely comes from Levinas. The other is what we encounter in the other person. However, we should not even go so far as to say the 'other person' because as soon as we begin to characterize the other we start cancelling out their otherness. The other as infinite—outside of finite determination—is made another finite thing in our world. We begin imposing or totalizing the infinity of the other. The opposing posture is to encounter this ultimately unknowable other as an other who puts oneself into question.

With the encounter with the face of the other, we enter into Levinas' discussion of the fundamental place of ethical obligation. Ethical obligation is laid upon us in the encounter with the other. There is an ambiguity here: Is he talking about the human other? the divine Other? It is as if the other comes to us 'as from on high', as he says. The face of the human other has an authority—even an absolute authority—to us. If we do not cancel out its otherness, it imposes an infinite ethical obligation on us. So he will say that the other has an infinity or transcendence or height to it. The other is not our equal, but it comes to us from a height. The primary content of this encounter, that which is called upon us in the face of the other, is 'don't kill me'. The primary obligation is that you shall not kill. The fundamental place in our consciousness of obligation and responsibility to the other is set in opposition to totality—a kind of ontology that wants to cancel out all otherness.

One way that Levinas summarizes his project is talking about 'ethics as first philosophy'. Ethics should be the first philosophy, not a totalizing ontology. It is this emphasis on the other that will make its way into Derrida's later thought.

20.4.4 Taylor

Several theologians have endeavoured to produce postmodern theologies drawing heavily on the work of Derrida and Levinas, among others. **Mark C. Taylor (1945–)**, who studied with Gordon Kaufman at Harvard, is quite influential in the 1980s and 1990s for presenting a theology that incorporated the thought of Derrida—specifically Derrida's early thought. His central work in this regard is called *Erring: A Postmodern A/theology* (1984). In this work, he wants to refigure theology—or 'a/theology', as he calls it. He does not want to privilege one side of the binary of theology or atheism.

In *Erring*, Taylor seeks to refigure theology in the face of the deconstruction of what he sees as the central beliefs of Western culture. Taylor wants to do theology (1) after the **death of God**, (2) in the face of the **disappearance of the self** (for without stable presence there is also a lack of stable identity even to the self), (3) after the **end of history** (for there is no longer any single framework of meaning to understand any kind of purpose or direction to history) and (4) what he calls the **closure of the book** (by which he means there is no stable presence of meaning in texts). What he proposes in the light of these negating things is what he calls a 'deconstructive a/theology'. This radical theology takes up some of the themes of Altizer's Death of God theology. The death of God is a way of not talking about how we can do away with talk about God, but is a site for doing a radical Christology. What Taylor (strongly influenced by Hegel) means by this is that he wants to use some of the traditional Christian language along with Derrida and talk about Jesus as the Word. Jesus is as the Word is writing, the infinite play of meaning. The divine for us is not a transcendent, static eternity, but is this play of presence and absence. That is the most final reality that we can come into contact with the divine. The divine for Taylor is this ceaseless process. It is the process of **erring**: both in the sense of an error and a knight errant.

20.4.5 Caputo

After teaching philosophy at Villanova University, Pennsylvania, for a number of years, and retiring from there, **John D. Caputo (1940–)** teaches in the religion department at Syracuse University for a time. Caputo is one of the major figures in the American reception of Derrida's work in philosophy and theology.

Caputo's project can be summarized using a Derridean logic of the *sans* (the 'without'). He ultimately advocates a religion without metaphysics. To understand what he means, one should first understand his critique of metaphysics and second his understanding of religion. First off, Caputo critiques metaphysics as traditionally conceived and proposes a replacement for it—he does this in, among other places, his work, *Radical Hermeneutics* (1987). He critiques 'metaphysics' as trying to be above the flux and change of actuality in which we are constantly caught up. Metaphysics is a kind of escape to a place other than actuality. Metaphysics also seeks to produce a kind of fixed universality that levels off and violently makes the same particularity, singularity and individuality that we encounter in reality. Metaphysics seeks to impose a totalizing system that would suppress the difference and movement of reality. What we experience in existence is a chaotic flux of difference and change, and metaphysics wants to institute a static unity in place of that.

For Caputo, metaphysics ultimately fails to be faithful to the difficulty of actual life. So in place of metaphysics, he wants to have a **metaphysics without metaphysics**—what he terms a **radical hermeneutics**. In this, Caputo wants to affirm the flux of the world without trying to ground it or found it in any fundamental reality. As he says, he wants to stay with the finite facts on the surface of existence. He wants to do away with any kind of speculation about depths or beyonds. Such a radical hermeneutics is what he calls a **heterology**: a philosophy of difference instead of a philosophy of sameness. It is a philosophy that is sensitive to the other, and as such is both heteronomous and heteromorphous. **Heteronomism** has to do with seeing reality in terms of irreducible singularity. This is the Levinasian aspect; it is an ethical regard for and respect for otherness. If there is any law, it is respect the other. **Heteromorphism** is an emphasis not just on otherness but also on plurality and difference. There are many forms in the changing flux of the world. It is more of the Nietzschean side of Caputo.

What does religion have to do with this? Caputo has quite a bit to say about religion—the two most significant are *Against Ethics* (1993) and *The Prayers and Tears of Jacques Derrida* (1997). Just as he has a critique against metaphysics, he also has a critique against religion—specifically against religion that is complicit with metaphysics. He believes that traditional metaphysical understandings of God and religion elevate the knowledge of God to a false absoluteness. Traditional understandings of God are placed within a more basic framework of universality and sameness. The God of metaphysical religion is the God of the same. Metaphysical religion tends to give a false stability to life and, ultimately, makes light of the radicalness of our finite situation.

What Caputo proposes in place of such traditional understandings of God is a **religion without religion**, by which he means a religion without metaphysical religion. He would say that this is what true religion is. True religion is a passion for the impossible within the very structure of human experience such that there is a religious side to everybody. This follows the same kind of structure as the heterology of his *Radical Hermeneutics*. Religion without religion is heteronomic in that it is about obligation to the other. The human other is structurally identical to the absolute or divine other. Here Caputo is taking up one of the later ideas of Derrida: *tout autre est tout autre*—every other is wholly other. This is the Levinasian side of religion without religion. He wants to keep this ambivalence between God and love. Maybe God is a way of talking about love, or maybe love is a way of talking about God. We cannot know which, and ultimately it does not matter.

Religion without religion is also heteromorphic. This religious obligation to the other is co-constituted with a belief that we cannot get to the ultimate meaning in life. Religion does not exist to pull back the veil and show us reality as it really is. This is a way of short-circuiting our hermeneutical finitude. This is the more Nietzschean side of Caputo's LeviNietzschean religion without religion. That is what Caputo's religion here is. It is trying to hold together these two insights. He frames religion in terms of ethical obligation against the backdrop of the death of the God of metaphysics.

20.4.6 Marion

Jean-Luc Marion (1946–) is a French Catholic philosopher who studied under Derrida. He teaches at the Sorbonne in Paris and at the University of Chicago Divinity School. What we have in Marion—and he is interesting and difficult to classify—is a postmodern philosophical theology that is moving in a confessional trajectory. He is commonly interested in how religious questions are opened up by postmodern philosophy—such that postmodern thought opens philosophy in the direction of theology. His most significant (earlier) work is *God without Being* (1991). In it, Marion works within the conceptual world of Heidegger, Levinas and Derrida, taking on the Heideggerian, Levinasian and Derridian critiques of onto-theology. For Marion, to put it simply, good theology is not onto-theology. Marion's God is best understood in terms of love or the gift. God is not the supreme being but is beyond being. God is the love that is beyond being.

When it comes to the relationship between our ideas about God and God, Marion makes the distinction between an idol and an icon. The idol is the concept that simply reflects its human maker. The idol is the 'visible' in which we attempt to capture God by our understanding in terms of being. This is the domain of being. The icon is the concept which is open to the gift or revelation of the other that gives itself. There is the invisible beyond the frame of being that, in the icon, makes itself present in the visible. The un-representable is becoming present in the presented. Here is a sacramental idea in that somehow our concepts can become the vehicles for the presence of God.

Figure 20.3 Marion.

'JLMarion' by J. L. Marion, http://divinity.uchicago.edu/faculty/marion.shtml and English Wikipedia. Licensed under CC BY 3.0 via Wikimedia Commons.

Sources and Further Reading

Althaus-Reid, Marcella. 'Bonhoeffer, Dietrich'. In *The Oxford Companion to Christian Thought*, edited by Adrian Hastings, Alistair Mason and Hugh Pyper, 78–80. Oxford: Oxford University Press, 2000.

Cobb, John B., Jr., and David Ray Griffin. *Process Theology: An Introductory Exposition*. London: Westminster John Knox, 1976.

Gschwandtner, Christina. *Postmodern Apologetics?: Arguments for God in Contemporary Philosophy*. New York: Fordham University Press, 2012.

Henriksen, Jan-Olav. 'David Tracy'. In *Key Theological Thinkers: From Modern to Postmodern*, edited by Staale Johannes Kristiansen and Svein Rise, 529–36. Aldershot: Ashgate, 2013.

Livingston, James C., and Francis Schüssler Fiorenza. *Modern Christian Thought: Volume 2, The Twentieth Century*. 2nd edn. Minneapolis, MN: Fortress Press, 2006.

Penner, Myron. 'Christianity and the Postmodern Turn: Some Preliminary Considerations'. In *Christianity and the Postmodern Turn: Six Views*, edited by Myron Penner, 13–36. Grand Rapids, MI: Brazos, 2005.

Simpson, Christopher Ben. *Religion, Metaphysics, and the Postmodern: William Desmond and John D. Caputo*. Bloomington: Indiana University Press, 2009.

Ward, Graham. 'Postmodern Theology'. In *The Modern Theologians: Introduction to Christian Theology since 1918*, edited by David F. Ford with Rachel Muers, 332–38, 3rd edn. Oxford: Blackwell, 2005.

Wyller, Trygve. 'Dietrich Bonhoeffer'. In *Key Theological Thinkers: From Modern to Postmodern*, edited by Staale Johannes Kristiansen and Svein Rise, 113–22. Aldershot: Ashgate, 2013.

21

Postliberal and Postsecular Theology

A confessional trajectory in academic theology is not something new in the later part of the twentieth century. A common insight here is that the way forward with theology has to do with retrieval. Barth would focus more on the faith of the Reformers. In Catholic theology, *nouvelle théologie* and later Balthasar are engaged in *ressourcement*—a return to the sources. Whereas the 'radicality' of the Death of God theology is a radical reinterpreting of Christianity, the radicality of confessional theology is a going back to the *radix*, the 'root' of the Christian faith. Whereas the secular trajectory broadly returns to a predominantly Enlightenment perspective, the confessional trajectory seeks to revisit the world that was lost. They are going back and drawing on the pre-modern roots of modernity.

In this final chapter, we will briefly present some more recent thinkers of this vintage in the English-speaking world—North America and Britain. There are four general characteristics that the figures in this chapter share. First, they are all concerned with **creatively retrieving the tradition**. They are all versions of *ressourcement*—with the postsecular theologians consciously drawing on *nouvelle théologie*. In this regard, these thinkers (postliberal and postsecular) are sometimes talked about as 'postcritical'. It is not as if they are naïve or no longer critical, but their relation to the past is not primarily a negative one. An all-too-common twentieth-century posture in theology (and philosophy) is: 'Everyone got it wrong before I came along. You're welcome.' The postliberal and postsecular theologians seek to positively retrieve that which has come before—specifically the pre-modern. Part of what may be even 'postmodern' about such an approach is that it rejects the modern prejudice against the past and for the new and seeks to creatively retrieve previously (in modern theology) neglected resources.

Second, these theologies can also be characterized as **non-foundational**. This is another sense in which these theologies can be regarded as 'postmodern'. These thinkers do not see theology as needing to justify itself before some superior secular discipline. In modernity, we have come to assume that certain secular disciplines are truly authoritative, and that theology is then measured by them, is to be judged by their foreign criteria. (Though, as we have seen earlier in this text, the secular may well be less foreign to theology than it is so thought.) Instead, theology itself is seen as an equally fundamental discipline—if not a more fundamental discipline—than these (supposedly) secular disciplines. There is a basic aspect to theology that does not need a further founding. Theology is as basic a discourse as physics.

Third, these kinds of theologies are particularly **ecumenical**. Though these are primarily Protestant theologies, there is a great deal of attention paid to Catholic and Eastern Orthodox theology. When they are retrieving the pre-modern tradition, they are looking at the great tradition—the common Christian tradition that is common to all. They are concerned about policing the boundaries of a particular confession.

Finally, they all exhibit in one way or another a certain **social concern**—an interest in social issues and politics. Their posture is not one of withdrawal from the world but one of engagement in the pressing issues in society. They seek to provide an alternative holistic vision for modern life rooted in a Christian understanding of the world.

21.1 Postliberal Theology

Postliberalism is not any kind of official designation, but is a loose alliance that orbits around Yale Divinity School and is sometimes referred to as 'The New Yale School'. Postliberal theology in the North American theological academy is often set off against revisionist theology. The revisionists would usually accuse the postliberals of retreating from the challenges of modernity and postmodernity, whereas the postliberals would accuse the revisionists of letting contemporary culture set the agenda for theology to the point where Christians no longer had anything to say. Postliberals are not willing to allow contemporary culture to set the agenda for the interpretation of the Christian faith.

To characterize it generally, postliberal theology focuses on theology's **ecclesial** setting—that it is done within a particular church. There is also a strong emphasis on **narrative**. There is also an emphasis on theology as giving a particular **grammar** of the Christian life. Theology has a regulative function, and this is going to draw from Wittgenstein. However, there is also a sense in which it seems to be descriptive. It is trying to describe the way theology actually functions in communities. By and large postliberal theology is Protestant and to a large degree located in the mainline denominations (like the United Methodist Church) as a kind of response to a situation in which the mainline denominations in America are declining. This is a situation of doing theology self-consciously as a minority.

21.1.1 Precursors

Several theologians who are associated with Dialectical Theology or 'Neo-Orthodoxy' are precursors to postliberal theology. Reinhold Niebuhr sees theology as being critical of culture. His brother H. Richard Niebuhr focuses on Scripture as a narrative and the way that narrative functions within the Christian community. Several of the leading postliberal figures study and write on Barth.

The critical side of Postliberalism is refusing to let a secular description of theology to be determinative. It is focusing on Christian self-description—as opposed to external descriptions— as a criterion for theology. They also often draw on Ludwig Wittgenstein. Instead of the rational foundationalism that we have seen, the philosophy of Wittgenstein focuses on various practices as being foundational in human thought. Communal and linguistic practices are the foundation for human life. Thus, if one wishes to understand Christian beliefs, one cannot do that in isolation from Christian practices.

21.1.2 Frei

From Breslau, Germany, **Hans Frei (1922–88)** immigrated to the United States in 1938. He studied under H. Richard Niebuhr at the Yale Divinity School writing his dissertation there on Barth's doctrine of revelation. He returned to Yale in the mid-1950s and taught there until his death.

Frei is commonly recognized as the originator of the New Yale School. His thought is very close to that of Barth. In a sense, he is attempting to retrieve Barth as a counter to the growing influence of revisionist and secular theologies. Central to Hans Frei's work is the place of narrative and how narrative functions to form identity.

Frei's most influential work is *The Eclipse of Biblical Narrative* (1974). In it, he describes how over the course of modernity the understanding of what scripture is, and how it works has changed from what had been traditionally the case. With the modern focus on punctiliar 'facts', what has been lost is the way in which meaning functions in scripture and how it primarily has to do with narrative. In this regard there has been a 'great reversal'. Instead of seeing Scripture as a grand, meaningful narrative, the Bible has been made into a collection of historical claims and religious ideas. It is a bag of facts and ideas. One then sifts through it to find what facts one thinks are true and ideas one considers to be valid.

For Frei then, biblical interpretation in the eighteenth and nineteenth centuries has eclipsed what he calls a 'realistic reading of Scripture'. It has changed the understanding of meaning by identifying meaning with **reference**. The meaning of the text is largely the historical events behind it—which makes the real meaning of the text something that is only available to experts. The narrative itself is then obscured. Frei wants to focus instead on the meaning of the **narrative**. In this more holistic perspective, the point of scripture is to present a narrative world. Here, he is drawing upon what is called New Criticism. New Criticism is an approach to literature that was in vogue at Yale at the time which focused on looking at the text as a holistic work of art. Frei then approaches scripture in a similar way, suggesting that one must approach it as an aesthetic or narrative whole.

Part of seeing Scripture as a narrative whole is seeing all of the different narratives as interconnected. This was much more common in pre-modern interpretations of scripture. One would see in the Old Testament different figures and types for the New Testament such that the meanings are interrelated. One does not just dig for meaning in a particular bit to see if that is real or not, but one sees the meaning as arising in the whole.

Narrative for Frei is not just a focus on the right way of reading Scripture, but also seeing how stories help us to form our very identity. Our identity is largely narratival—coming from seeing ourselves in the midst of a story. Scripture then should function in our lives as the narrative of a community, the Church, that forms our identity. Our identity is formed in the midst of the shared story of a community, and the shared story of the Christian community is the story of the Bible.

The authority of scripture then has to do with its function in the Christian community. Scripture's function in the Christian community is that Scripture is the foundational narrative that gives us our identity as a community. Doctrines are helpful in that they help us to tell the story better, but they are not the point of the story. The point of the story is for us to live out our identity in relation to that story.

21.1.3 Lindbeck

George Lindbeck (1923–2018) was born to Lutheran missionaries and grew up in China and Korea. He received his PhD from Yale and ended up teaching there from 1951 to 1993. From 1962 to 1965, Lindbeck was an official Lutheran representative observer at Vatican II. This proves a transformative experience for Lindbeck, giving him a strong impetus towards ecumenism.

Lindbeck's seminal work is *The Nature of Doctrine: Religion and Theology in a Postliberal Age* (1984). This little book popularizes the term 'postliberal'. *The Nature of Doctrine* is what Lindbeck thinks are inadequate understandings of what religion and doctrine are. This arises out of his concern for ecumenism and his reflections on what it is that divides Christians. He is thinking about what it would mean to reconcile divided Christian confessions and, thus, the relationship between doctrine and Christian confession.

Lindbeck differentiates his approach to doctrine between two other dominant approaches. The first is what he calls the **cognitive–propositional** approach. In this approach, which Lindbeck identifies as pre-modern, doctrine tells us what is objectively true. Doctrine here operates primarily cognitively like philosophy or science—it gives us true facts. It is grounded on a correspondence theory of truth. Reality 'out there' corresponds and matches up with these ideas.

Another and more recent approach to doctrine is what Lindbeck calls the **experiential-expressive** approach. This is associated with a more 'liberal' approach to doctrine that is primarily rooted in Schleiermacher. Here the primary function of doctrine is that it expresses or symbolizes our inner experiences. They are symbols of our human feelings.

Lindbeck thinks that neither of these is quite right. Certainly, neither is helpful for ecumenism. He finds the cognitive–propositional to be too cognitive—too focused on true and false. If that is the way you are approaching these things, then ecumenism will be undercut by a mutually exclusive logic. One cannot account for the way that doctrine changes over time. Doctrine has developed, so do you say that it was false and it became true?

However, the experiential–expressive approach is too subjective. Lindbeck would say that in this approach, doctrines matter way too little. You are not taking doctrines seriously enough. You have no way of talking about the constancy of doctrine over time. There is only the flux of human experience.

Lindbeck's own approach is what he calls the **cultural–linguistic** approach. What he means here is that dogmas are rules that tell us how we should talk about God and live. Doctrine is a way of reflecting on our communal practices.

He bases many of his ideas from the cultural anthropology of Clifford Geertz. Religions are holistic interpretive schemes for life. They are primarily about our practices and are not just abstract worldviews. They are ways of living. They are more existence-spheres than worldviews. Theology is rooted in our first-order communal beliefs and our communal practices—our forms of life. Doctrines are second-order rules of discourse—just like grammar. The relationship between grammar and a living language is such that grammar comes later and is a second-order description of the way a language works. Doctrines describe the regulatory beliefs that are communally authoritative. They exist to give guidance. The point of doctrine is not doctrine, but guidance towards a certain way of living. Indeed, different individual doctrines will function differently in different Christian communities at different times.

Lindbeck's idea here is that this is a way that Christians from different confessions who might disagree over the particulars of a given doctrine can start to see how those doctrines can be different but function similarly in various communities. For example, a Chalcedonian two natures doctrine is a rule for maintaining the idea that Christ is to be worshipped as the Son of God. We might then be able to agree that Christ is the Son of God, but disagree on the particularities of a two natures doctrine that might serve to alienate Nestorian or Coptic Christians, for instance.

21.1.4 Hauerwas

Stanley Hauerwas (1940–) was awarded his PhD from Yale Divinity School. He studied with H. Richard Niebuhr and Hans Frei. He goes on to teach at Notre Dame for a time, and then at Duke. Hauerwas's principal contribution is in the domain of ethics and can be seen as drawing out ethical and political implications of a postliberal approach to Christian theology. A significant early work of his is *A Community of Character* (1981). Here, Hauerwas argues that in ethics we are not dealing with the abstract universal rules of a rational foundationalism but with particular, concrete communities and the way those communities are formed by narratives. We are always embedded in a moral tradition—particular communities that come before us and form us, and these communities always have their particular stories.

Narrative and community are then formative to our moral identity. Scripture's authority is that it has the practical function of being the story of the Church. It is the founding story of the Church and has ethical implications. For the Christian, what it means to be a good person comes from a community that is formed and founded in the story of Scripture. The vision that guides our character comes from narrative. Christian discipleship—Christian virtue and identity—arises in the midst of the Christian narrative.

There are, however, other narratives. Hauerwas is particularly interested in how the modern liberal story has come to be dominant in the Western world. The modern liberal story is that we are free individuals—free to determine ourselves—and that we have gotten this way through the modern 'subtraction stories'. The modern liberal story is that we have liberated ourselves from the traditional stories and are now 'free' to do as we will. But that is its own particular story, and Hauerwas wants Christians to realize that this (likely) story is not the Christian story. The Church has its task of being a community that is formed by the Christian story and not this other, non-Christian story.

21.2 Postsecular Theology

21.2.1 'Radical Orthodoxy'

What has come to be called Radical Orthodoxy has its origin in England in the 1990s, specifically at Peterhouse in Cambridge. It quickly expanded beyond that. This movement integrates both the Catholic perspective of *nouvelle théologie* and the Protestant perspective of postliberal theology. They have many resonances with the postliberals and the Barthian heritage. Radical Orthodoxy is rooted in these multiple confessional revivals in the twentieth century and intends to be ecumenical.

This 'postsecular' theology is such in that it rejects the secular as being a given authority that can dictate the way theology should be done. Further, it is critical of the idea of the 'secular'. At the very least, postsecular theology seeks out the narrative of how the secular came to be. In this it has a very ambitious, sometimes even audacious frame.

The central figure of the 'theological sensibility' of Radical Orthodoxy is **John Milbank (1952–)**. An early significant book of his is *Theology and Social Theory* (1990, 2nd edn. 2006). Two other significant figures are Catherine Pickstock and Graham Ward. These three theologians edited a collection of essays entitled *Radical Orthodoxy: A New Theology* (1999) that serves as a kind of manifesto for Radical Orthodoxy.

Milbank, himself an Anglican, has used the term 'post-Protestant' to describe the loose programme of Radical Orthodoxy. Radical Orthodoxy advocates an awareness that we need to be open to the full breadth of the Christian tradition—from the Church Fathers to the great medieval theologians, to *nouvelle théologie* and recent Eastern Orthodox thought. The 'orthodoxy' of Radical Orthodoxy is in reference to a general project of *ressourcement*—of returning to the rich pre-modern sources of Christian reflection. The 'radical' bit can be taken in two senses. It is radical in that it seeks to go back to the roots, the *radix*, by being attentive to Christianity's classic expressions. However, it is also radical in terms of its breadth. This kind of postsecular theology argues that if the claims of theology are true then their relevance extends far beyond the ghetto of the academic discipline of theology. They have cosmic ramifications. Christian theology should affect the way we think about all of the rest of life. It should transform every area of life. The breadth of the theological domain affects everything such that there is ultimately no 'secular'.

Figure 21.1 Milbank.

'John Milbank, IEIS conference, The Politics of Virtue, the crisis of liberalism and the post-liberal future-003' by Jwh at Wikipedia Luxembourg. Licensed under CC BY-SA 3.0 lu via Wikimedia Commons.

Like postliberalism, Radical Orthodoxy will refuse to let a secular description of theology be determinative. Postsecular theology, however, tends to have large metaphysical and ontological ambitions—describing God in relation to the whole of reality.

21.2.2 The Myth of the Secular

Postsecular theology can be understood in terms of its drawing attention to the myth of the secular—to be taken in three senses. First is **the myth of secularization**. The claim of secularization—that the world is no longer interested in religion and that as modernity progresses there is going to be a decline in religious faith—is at best a partial perspective. In fact, if you look at the twentieth century, it is an obviously false perspective. There has been a particularly intense growth in religious faith. Secularization is a modern myth. It is a way of justifying a particular way of looking at things, but it does not necessarily describe reality. This is the secularization thesis that sees modernity and religion as in a zero-sum game. Even such central scholars in advocating the secularization thesis, as Peter Berger and Harvey Cox, have come around and said that this thesis is now implausible.

Second is **the myth that the secular is secular**—that there is something that is secular that is not itself always already theological. The secular world has hidden, unspoken beliefs and commitments about the kinds of things theology talks about. The secular is not neutral, but it is its own kind of position or ideology—making what are tantamount to theological claims about the universe and humans. It is an alternative theology. We should not allow another theology to perpetuate the myth of theological neutrality.

The third has to do with **the secular's myths**. The way Milbank presents it is that the founding narrative of secular modernity is that instead of there being as ultimate the loving community of the Trinity in relation to humanity and the world, there is a power struggle. Violence is ontologically basic. There is a flattening out of the world into a set of opposing forces, and the chief arbiter of these forces is going to be the secular state, which will then stand in for God in some sense. Here, Radical Orthodoxy is critical of reductionistic naturalism and says that this particular view of the world is ultimately nihilistic.

21.2.3 Participatory Ontology

The positive view that Radical Orthodoxy presents is what it thinks is a general perspective that is apparent in the Church Fathers and in classical Christianity more broadly. It is a general metaphysical or philosophical description of the Christian worldview which they call a participatory ontology or a metaphysics of participation.

Reflecting a Neoplatonic strain of influence in Christian thought, the idea here is that inasmuch as effects resemble their causes we have a basis for our speaking about God analogically. This is an analogical worldview in which there is an intelligible relation between the world and its continual origin. Created things express something about their Creator. However, this language is analogical—between univocity and equivocity. To speak of God univocally (such that our language drawn from worldly objects applies to God as he is) would be to speak of God as a particularly big and powerful thing in the world. An equivocal understanding would be that our speech about God literally has nothing to do with God. God is totally other to our finite ways of talking—so there is no point in our trying to even talk about God.

An analogical perspective lies in the middle between the univocal and the equivocal. Irish philosopher William Desmond refers to this as a 'metaxological' (*metaxu* meaning 'between') way of talking. For an analogical view the different perfections that we think about that apply to created things do so by virtue of their relation to God. When we use words like 'good', 'wise' or even 'being', we realize that these perfections of being apply primarily to God in a way that we ultimately do not understand and only secondarily to beings. Things *are* inasmuch as they participate in God's gift of being and ultimately in God's being or *esse*.

This is a robust theology of creation—not creation as a particular event that happened at a certain point in time but creation as a continual reality, as God's continual giving of being. Finite being does not exist on its own: it does not subsist independently. The world is suspended from and by God who transcends it; it is a 'suspended middle' between God and nothing.

God, then, is fundamentally, ontologically related to everything. There is no domain that is autonomous from God—not just in our way of thinking about things, but in the very essence and reality of everything that exists. God is inherently related to all things. This is part of the radical extensiveness of such a theological vision. We should be mindful of theology's far-reaching ramifications for every area of life. We should resist any dualisms between the secular and sacred. God is related to absolutely everything, and we should thus seek to understand the world—and our modern world—theologically.

Sources and Further Reading

Cox, Harvey. 'The Myth of the Twentieth Century: The Rise and Fall of "Secularization"'. In *The Twentieth Century: A Theological Overview*, edited by Gregory Baum, 135–43. Maryknoll, NY: Orbis, 1999.

Fodor, James. 'Postliberal Theology'. In *The Modern Theologians: Introduction to Christian Theology since 1918*, edited by David F. Ford with Rachel Muers, 229–48, 3rd edn. Oxford: Blackwell, 2005.

Gregersen, Niels Henrik. 'Protestant Theology in the Twentieth Century'. In *Key Theological Thinkers: From Modern to Postmodern*, edited by Staale Johannes Kristiansen and Svein Rise, 21–36. Aldershot: Ashgate, 2013.

Hardy, Daniel W. 'Karl Barth'. In *The Modern Theologians: Introduction to Christian Theology since 1918*, edited by David F. Ford with Rachel Muers, 21–42, 3rd edn. Oxford: Blackwell, 2005.

Livingston, James C., and Francis Schüssler Fiorenza. *Modern Christian Thought: Volume 2, The Twentieth Century*. 2nd edn. Minneapolis, MN: Fortress Press, 2006.

Oliver, Simon. 'What Is Radical Orthodoxy? Introduction'. In *The Radical Orthodoxy Reader*, edited by John Milbank and Simon Oliver, 3–27. London: Routledge, 2009.

Spjuth, Roland. 'George Lindbeck'. In *Key Theological Thinkers: From Modern to Postmodern*, edited by Staale Johannes Kristiansen and Svein Rise, 499–507. Aldershot: Ashgate, 2013.

Index